THE SEVEN DEADLY SINS

nakaba suzuki presents

28

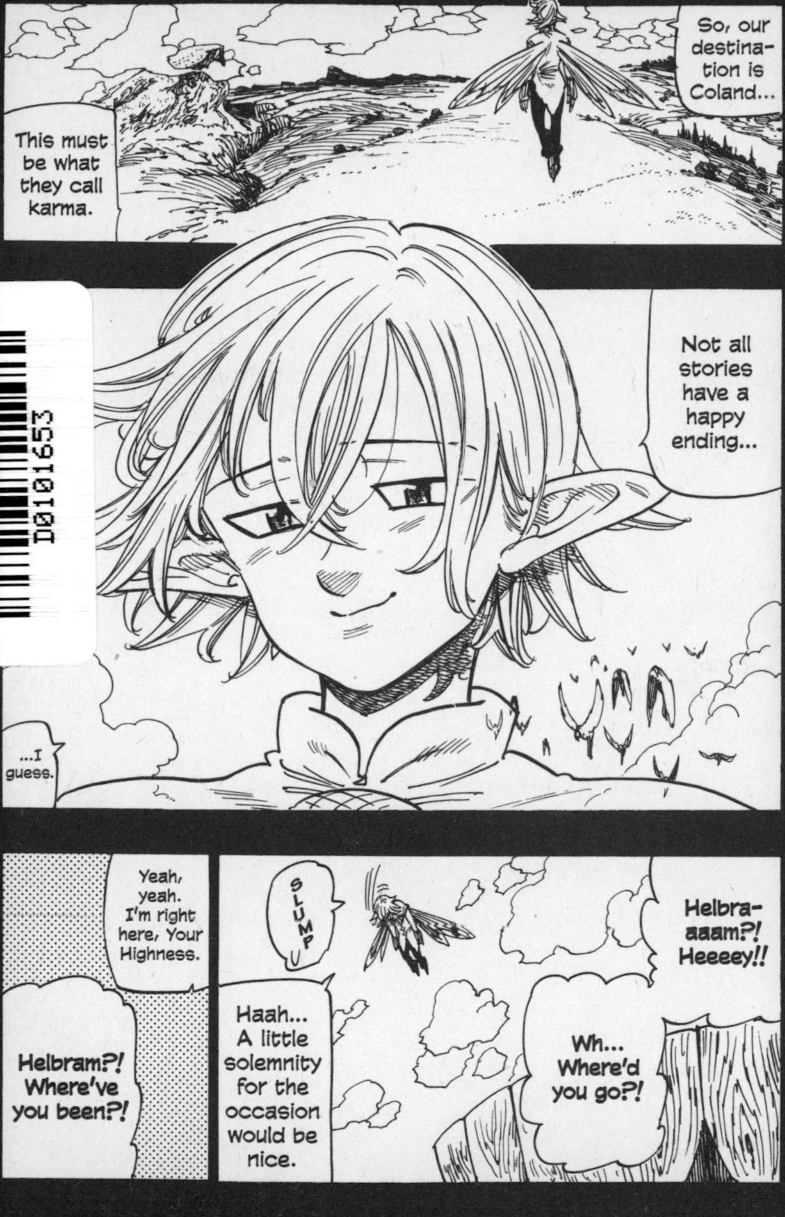

So, our destination is Coland...
This must be what they call karma.
Not all stories have a happy ending...
...I guess.
Helbra-aaam?! Heeeey!!
SLUMP
Wh... Where'd you go?!
Haah... A little solemnity for the occasion would be nice.
Yeah, yeah. I'm right here, Your Highness.
Helbram?! Where've you been?!

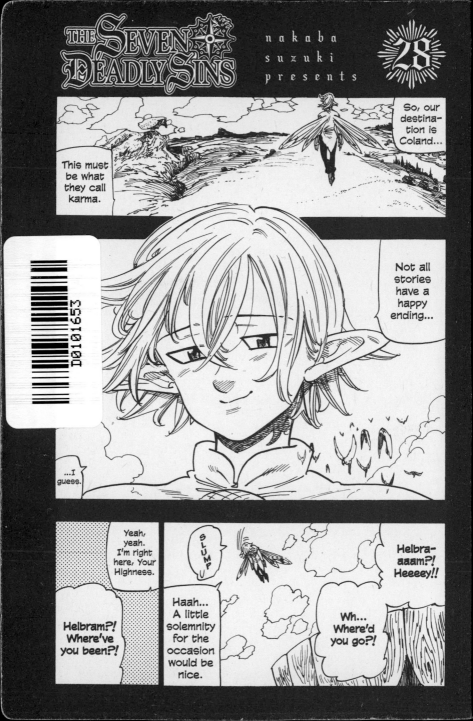

CONTENTS

BOAR HAT

The Seven Deadly Sins

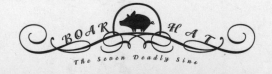

Chapter 223 - The Lovers at a Loss

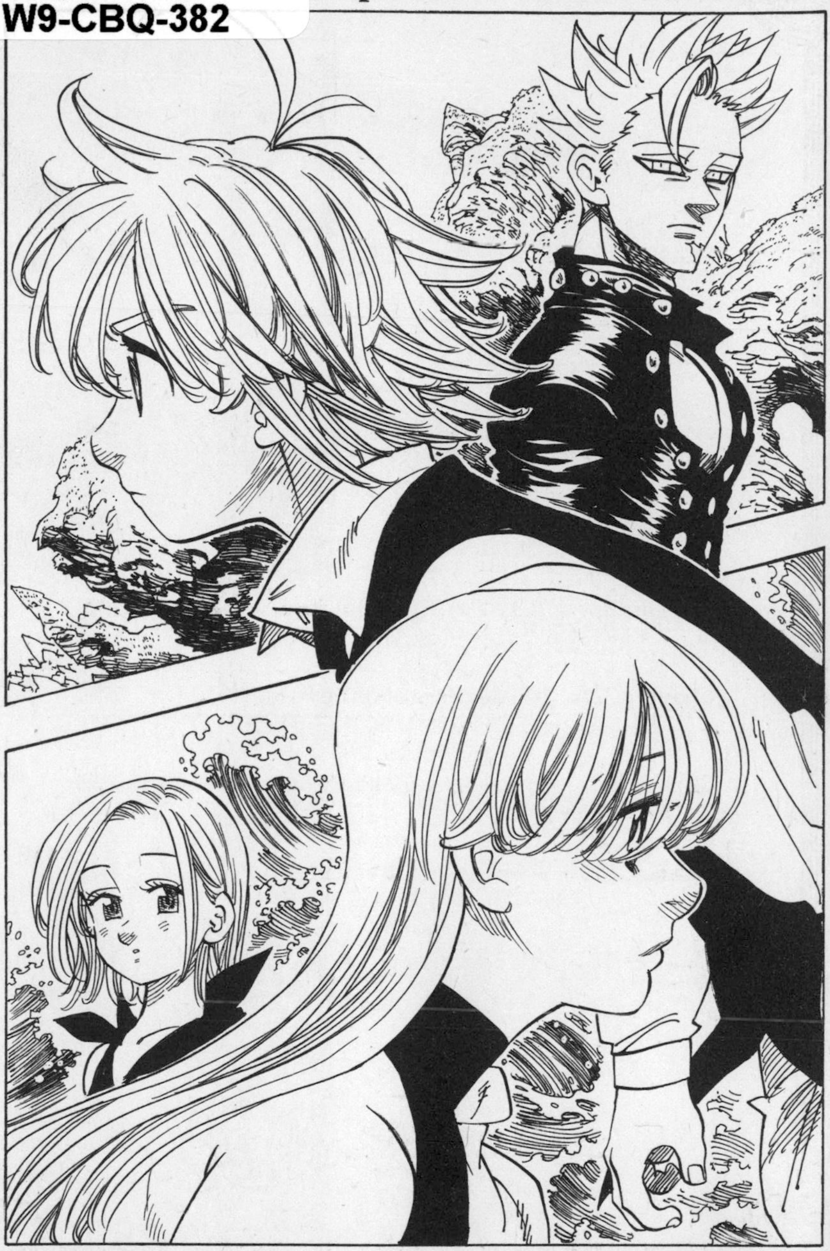

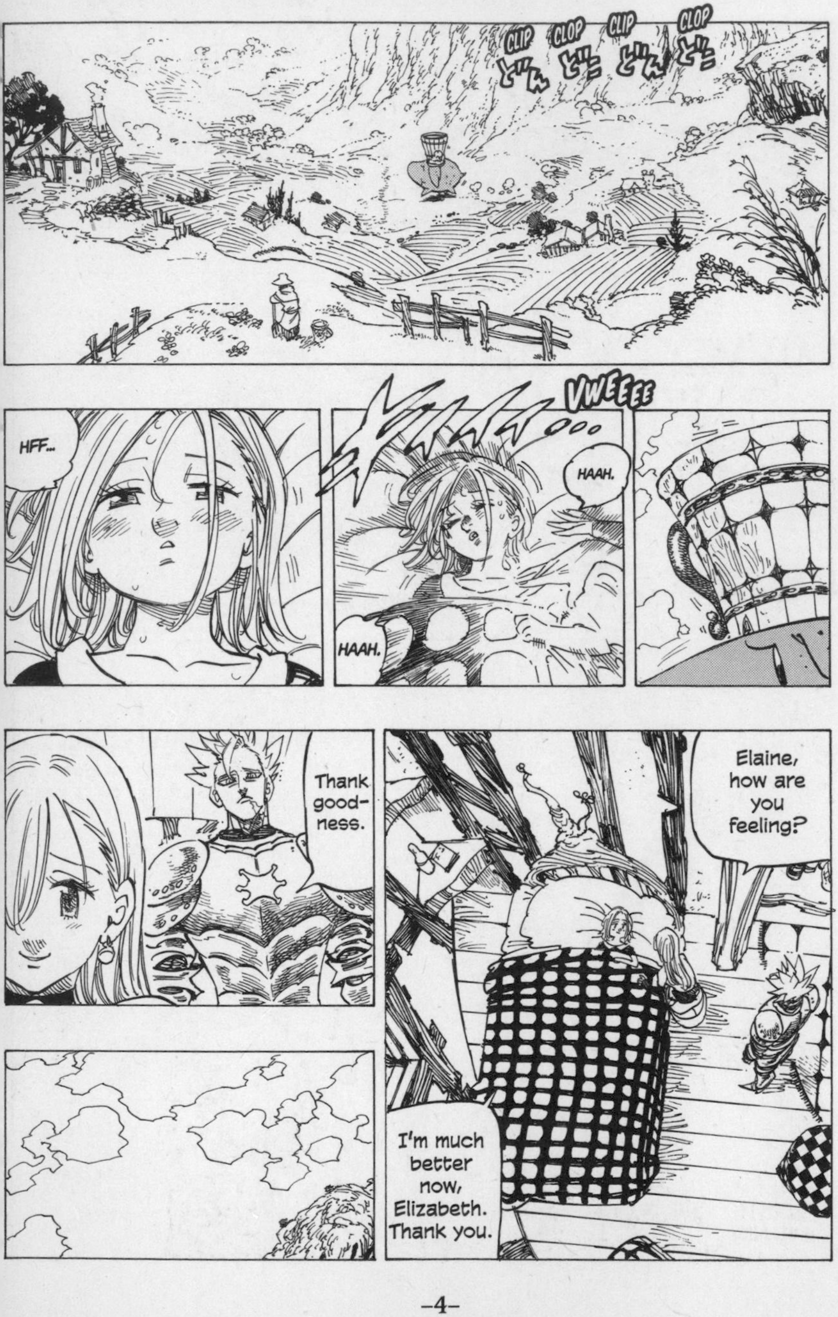
CLIP
CLOP
CLIP
CLOP
VWEEEE
HAAH.
HAAH.
HFF...
Elaine, how are you feeling?
I'm much better now, Elizabeth. Thank you.
Thank goodness.

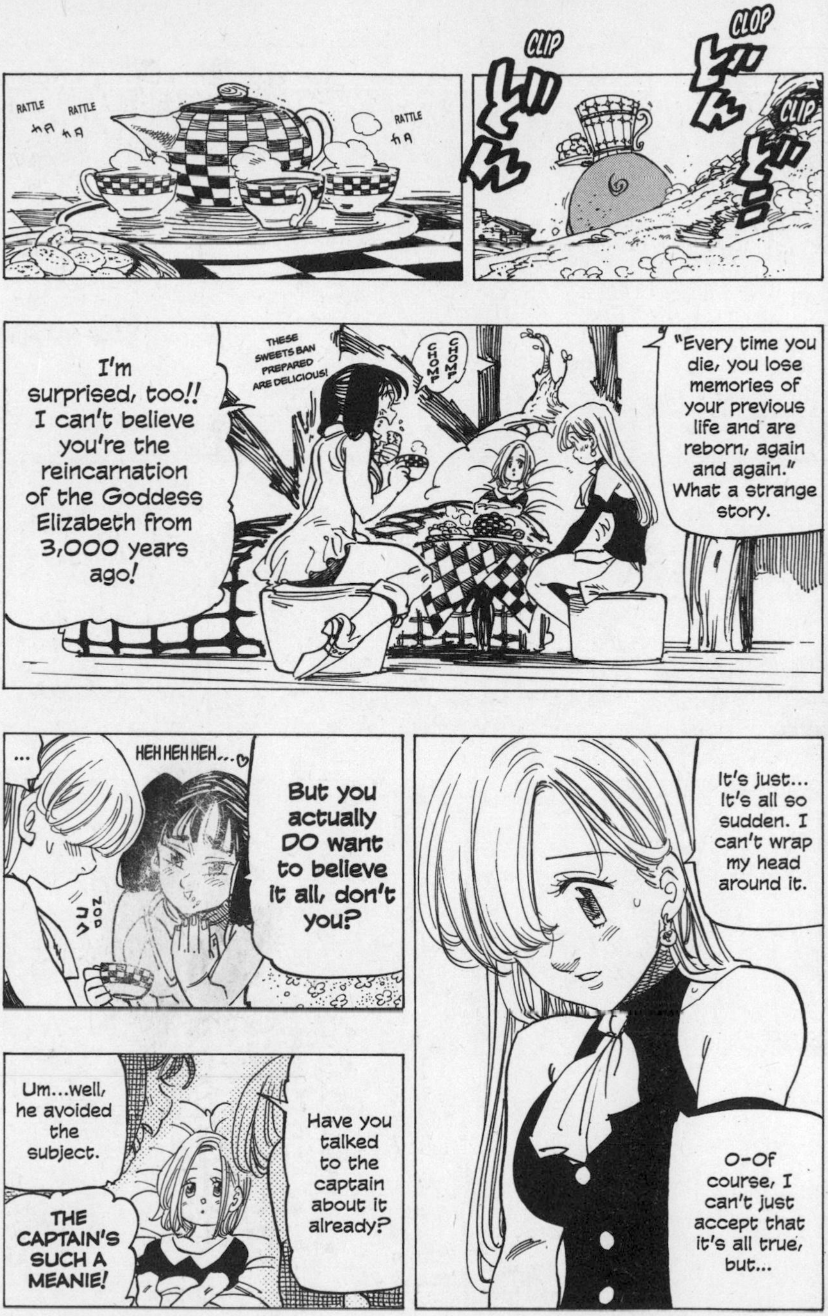
CLOP
CLIP
CLIP
RATTLE
RATTLE
RATTLE
"Every time you die, you lose memories of your previous life and are reborn, again and again." What a strange story.
CHOMP CHOMP
THESE SWEETS BAN PREPARED ARE DELICIOUS!
I'm surprised, too!! I can't believe you're the reincarnation of the Goddess Elizabeth from 3,000 years ago!
It's just... It's all so sudden. I can't wrap my head around it.
O-Of course, I can't just accept that it's all true, but...
But you actually DO want to believe it all, don't you?
HEH HEH HEH...♡
NOD
...
Have you talked to the captain about it already?
Um...well, he avoided the subject.
THE CAPTAIN'S SUCH A MEANIE!

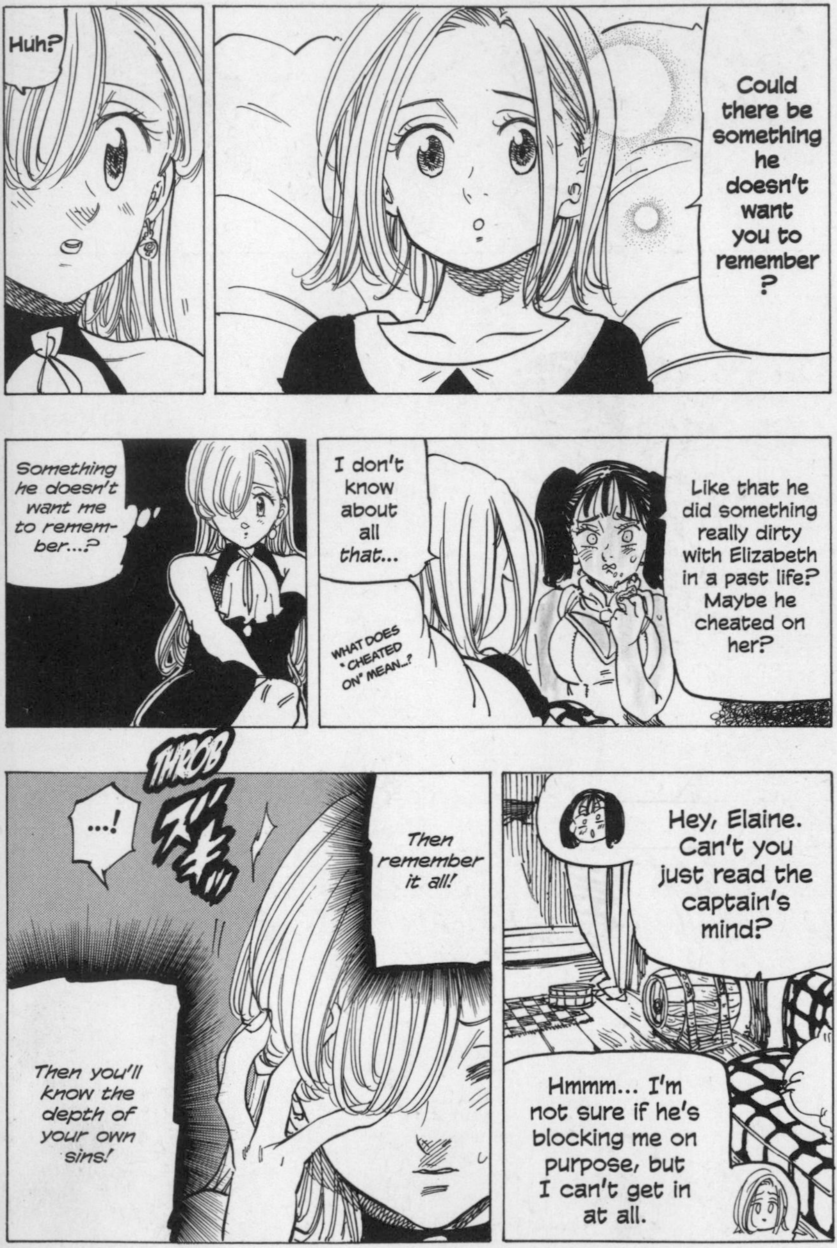
Could there be something he doesn't want you to remember?
Huh?
Like that he did something really dirty with Elizabeth in a past life? Maybe he cheated on her?
I don't know about all that...
WHAT DOES "CHEATED ON" MEAN...?
Something he doesn't want me to remember...?
Hey, Elaine. Can't you just read the captain's mind?
Hmmm... I'm not sure if he's blocking me on purpose, but I can't get in at all.
Then remember it all!
THROB
...!
Then you'll know the depth of your own sins!

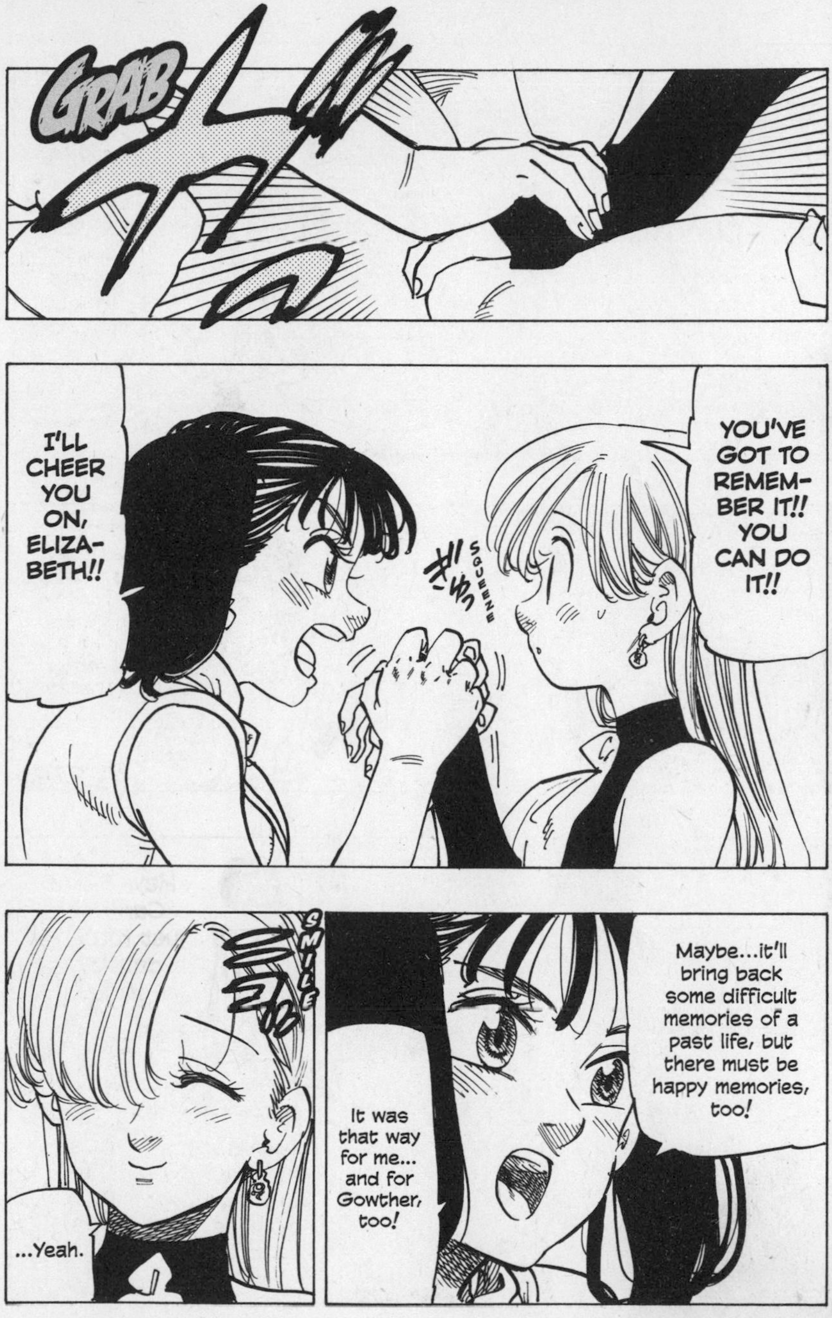
GRAB
YOU'VE GOT TO REMEMBER IT!! YOU CAN DO IT!!
ぎゅう
SQUEEZE
I'LL CHEER YOU ON, ELIZABETH!!
Maybe...it'll bring back some difficult memories of a past life, but there must be happy memories, too!
It was that way for me... and for Gowther, too!
SMILE
...Yeah.

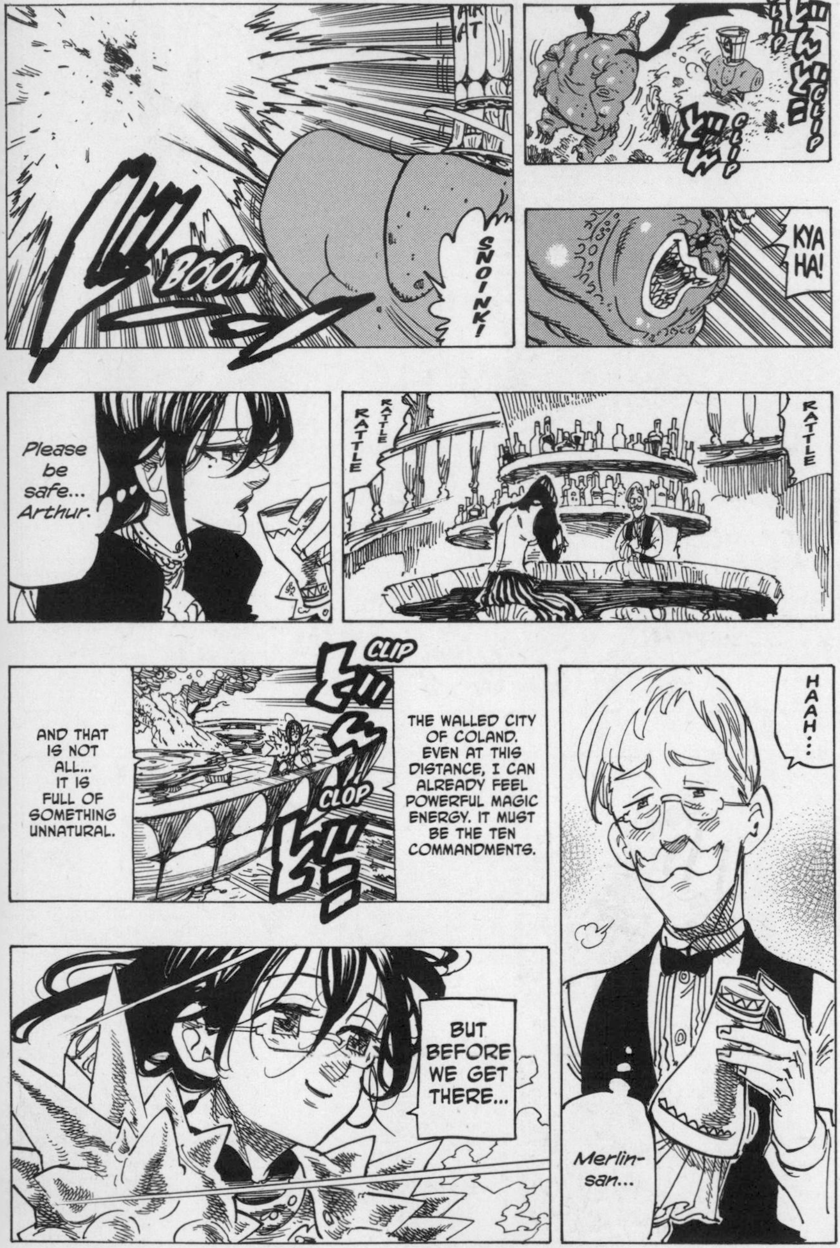
CLIP
CLIP
CLIP
KYA HA!
SNOINK!
BOOM
RATTLE
RATTLE
RATTLE
Please be safe... Arthur.
HAAAH...
Merlin-san...
THE WALLED CITY OF COLAND. EVEN AT THIS DISTANCE, I CAN ALREADY FEEL POWERFUL MAGIC ENERGY. IT MUST BE THE TEN COMMANDMENTS.
CLIP
CLOP
AND THAT IS NOT ALL... IT IS FULL OF SOMETHING UNNATURAL.
BUT BEFORE WE GET THERE...

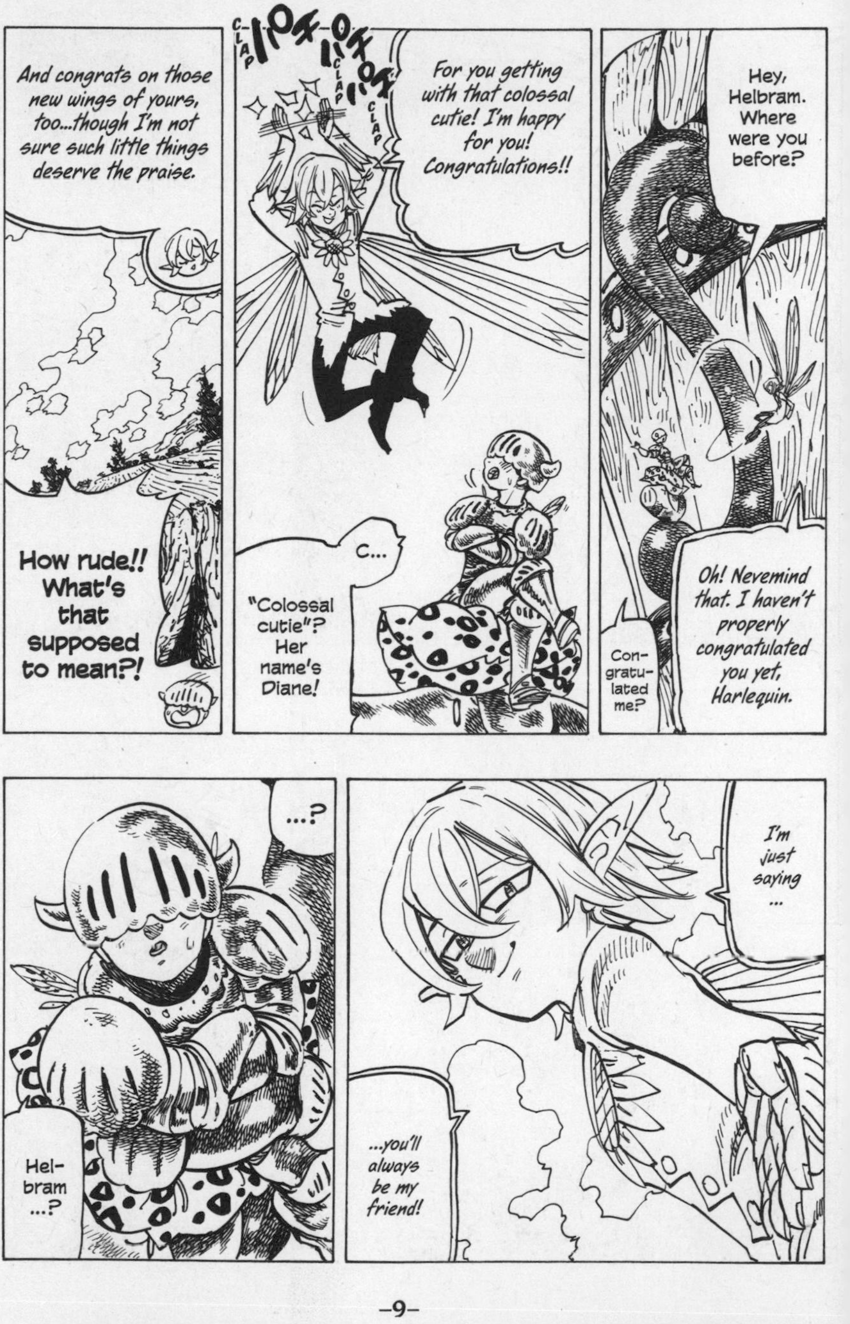
Hey, Helbram. Where were you before?
Oh! Nevemind that. I haven't properly congratulated you yet, Harlequin.
Con-gratu-lated me?
CLAP CLAP CLAP
For you getting with that colossal cutie! I'm happy for you! Congratulations!!
C...
"Colossal cutie"? Her name's Diane!
And congrats on those new wings of yours, too...though I'm not sure such little things deserve the praise.
How rude!! What's that supposed to mean?!
I'm just saying ...
...you'll always be my friend!
...?
Hel-bram ...?

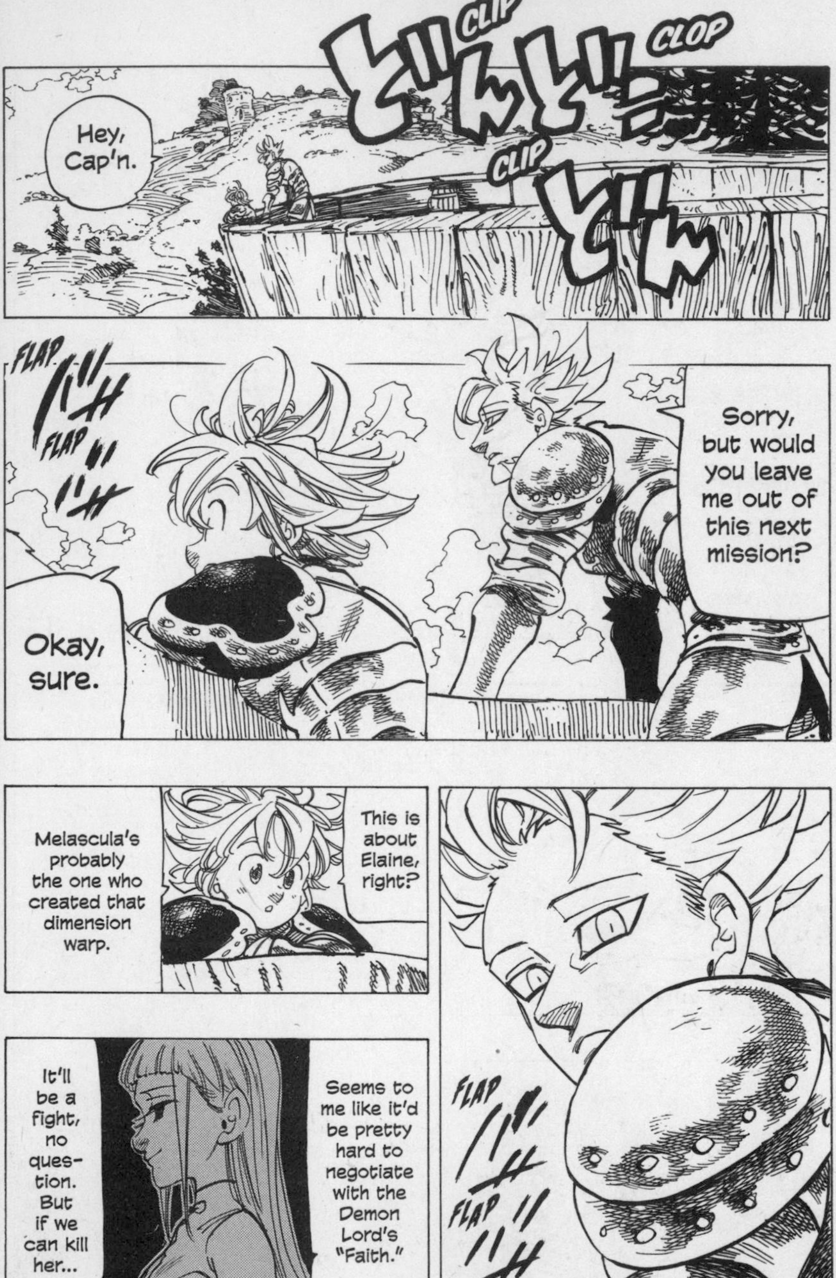

CLIP
CLOP
CLIP
Hey, Cap'n.
Sorry, but would you leave me out of this next mission?
FLAP
FLAP
Okay, sure.
FLAP
FLAP
This is about Elaine, right?
Melascula's probably the one who created that dimension warp.
Seems to me like it'd be pretty hard to negotiate with the Demon Lord's "Faith."
It'll be a fight, no question. But if we can kill her...

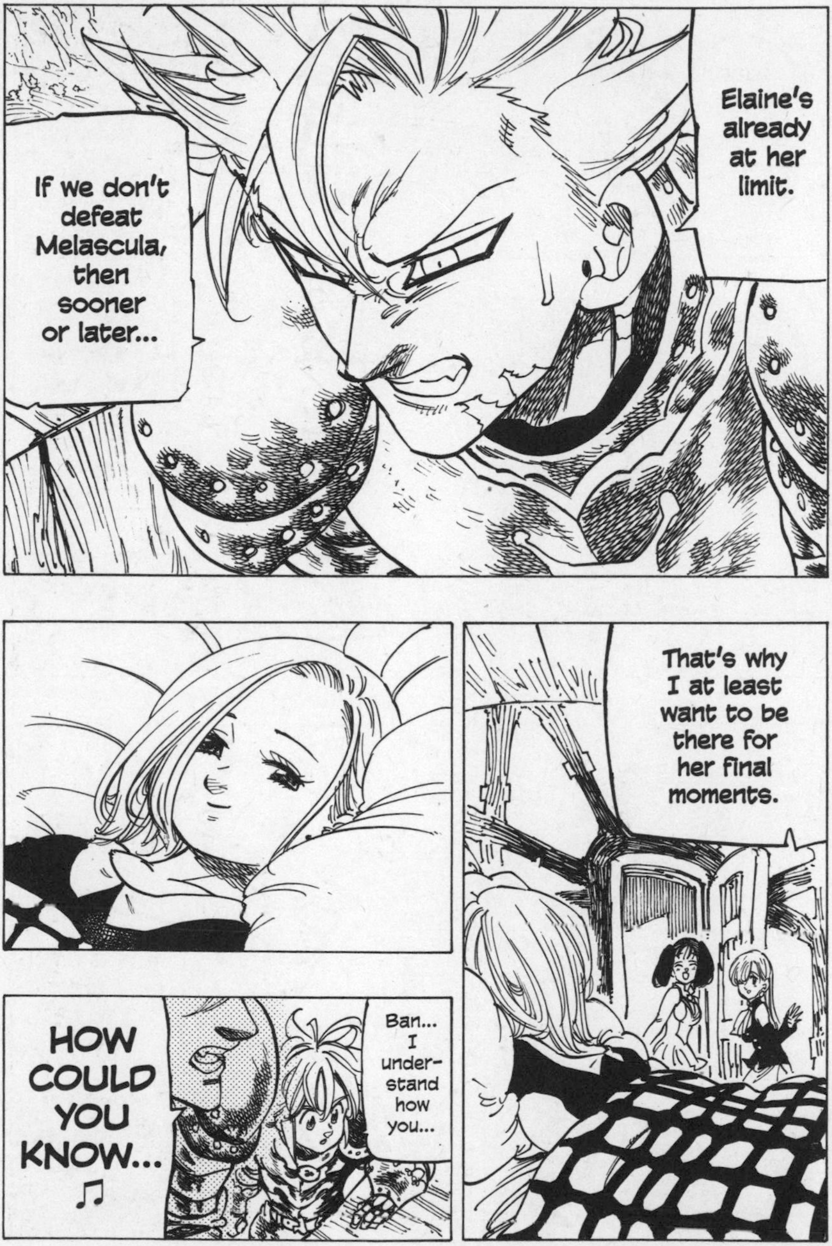
Elaine's already at her limit.
If we don't defeat Melascula, then sooner or later...
That's why I at least want to be there for her final moments.
Ban... I understand how you...
HOW COULD YOU KNOW... ♫

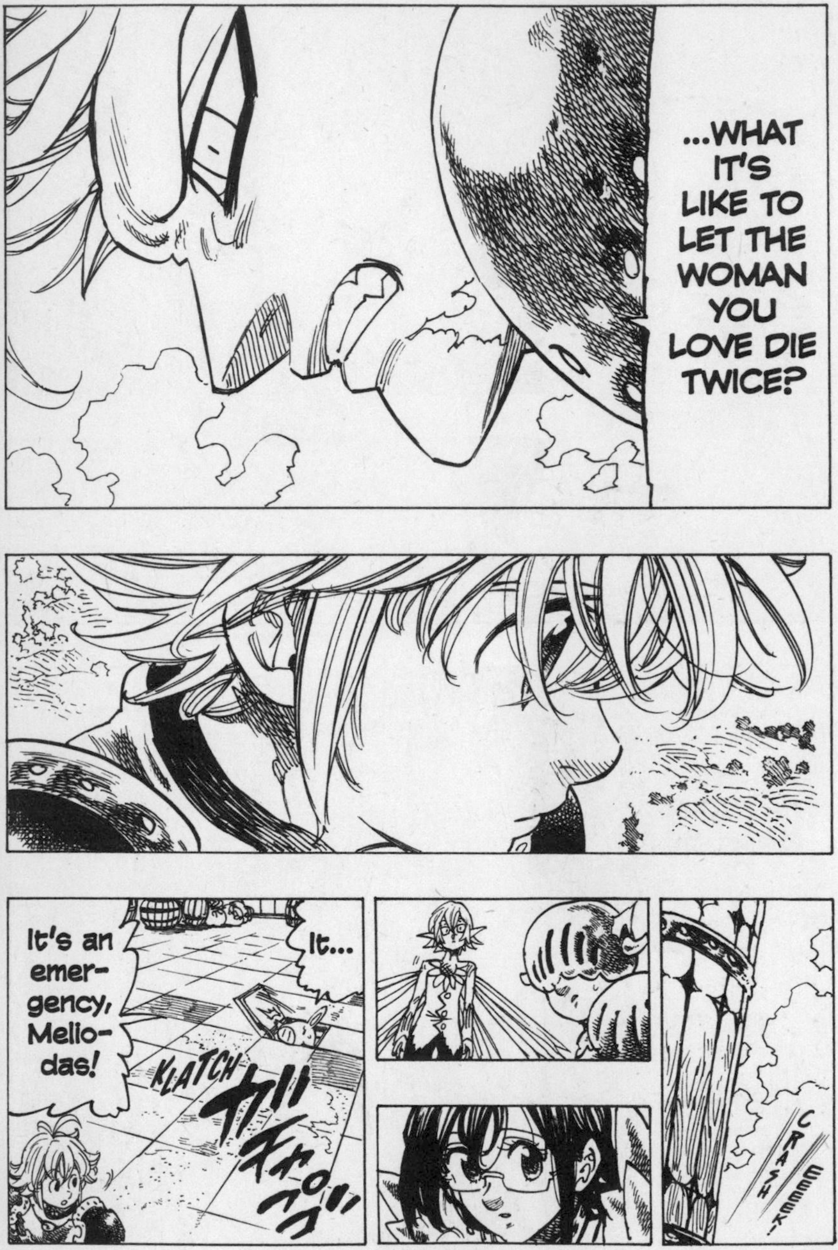
...WHAT IT'S LIKE TO LET THE WOMAN YOU LOVE DIE TWICE?
CRASH
CREEEK!
It...
It's an emergency, Melio-das!
KLATCH

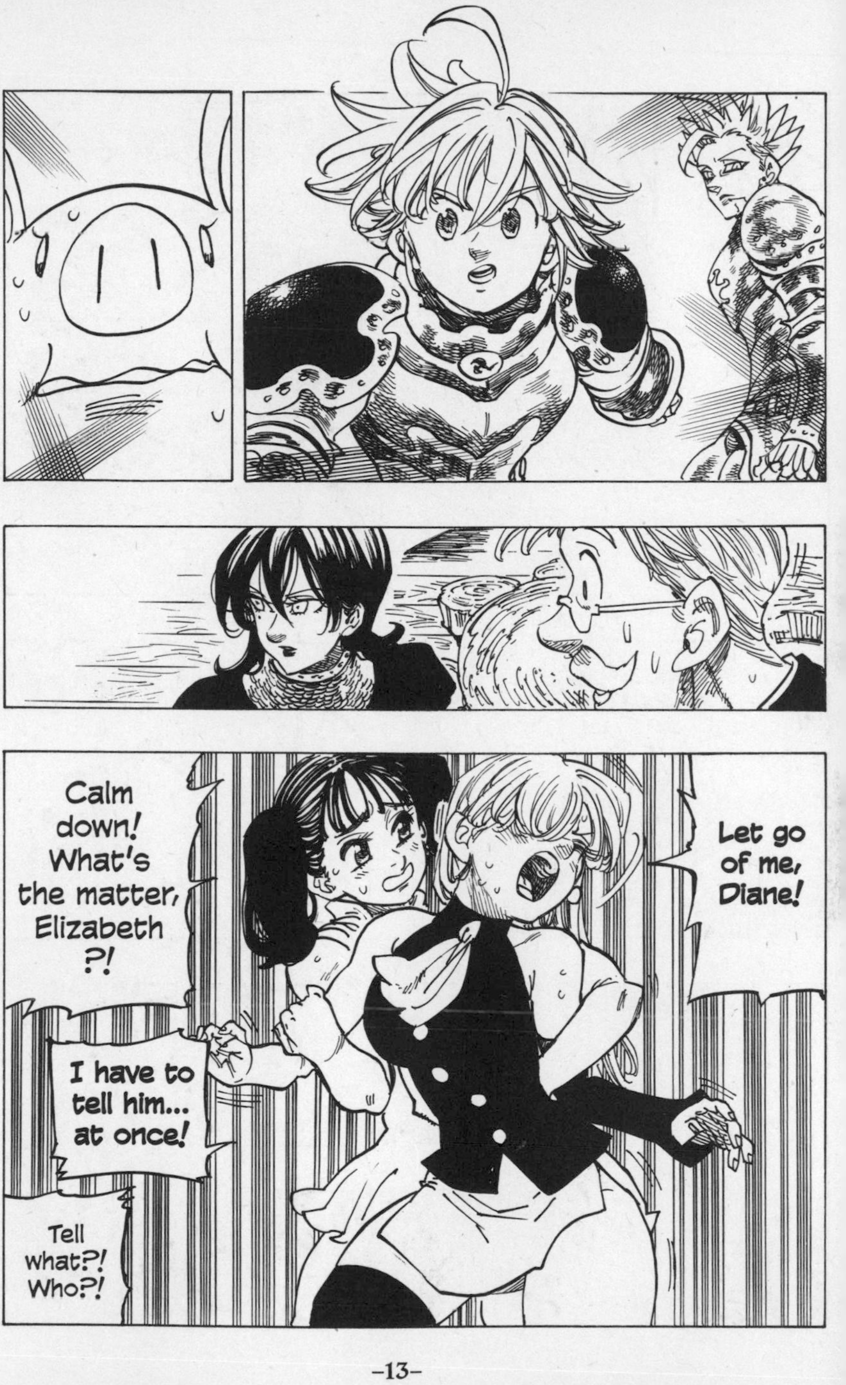
Let go of me, Diane!
Calm down! What's the matter, Elizabeth?!
I have to tell him... at once!
Tell what?! Who?!

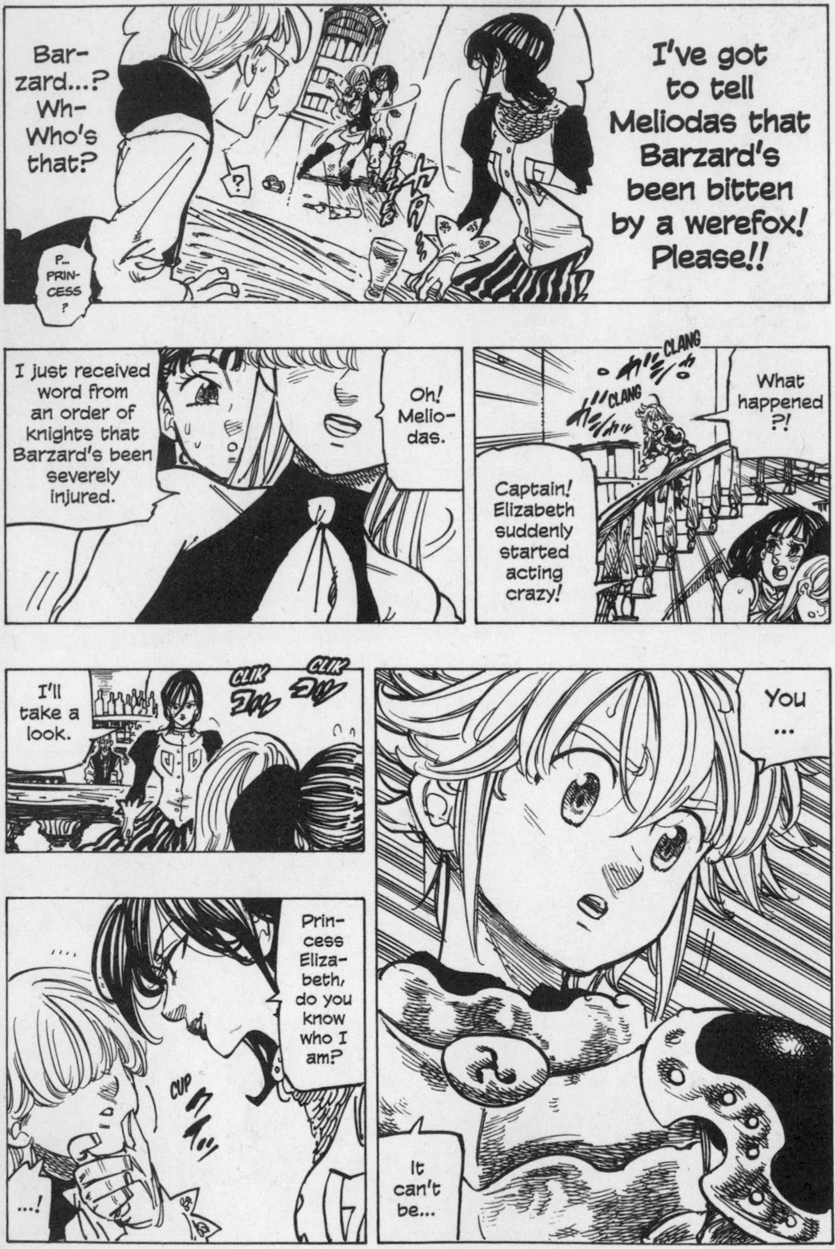

I've got to tell Meliodas that Barzard's been bitten by a werefox! Please!!
Bar-zard...? Wh-Who's that?
?
P... PRIN-CESS ?
CLANG
CLANG
What happened ?!
Captain! Elizabeth suddenly started acting crazy!
Oh! Melio-das.
I just received word from an order of knights that Barzard's been severely injured.
You ...
It can't be...
CLIK
CLIK
I'll take a look.
Prin-cess Eliza-beth, do you know who I am?
CUP
....
...!

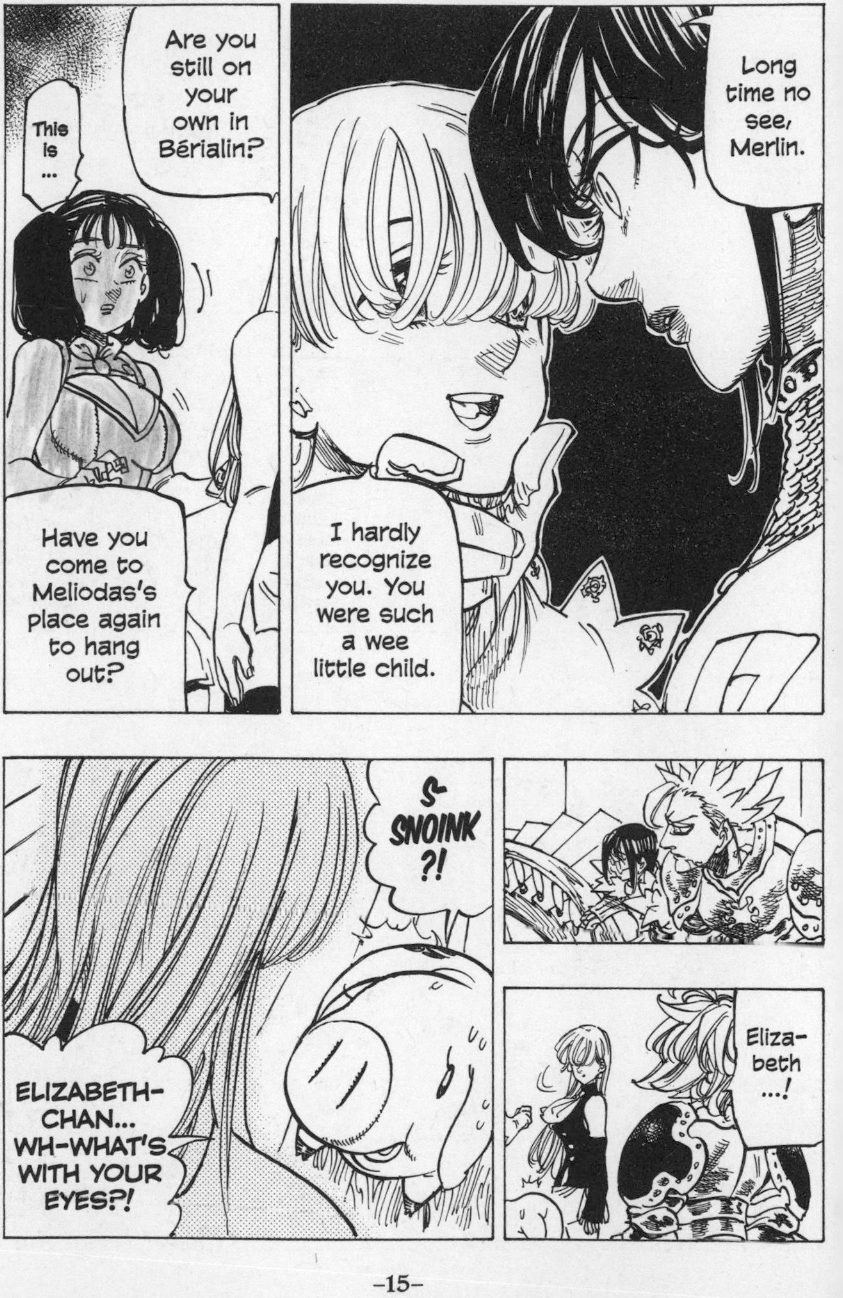
Long time no see, Merlin.
I hardly recognize you. You were such a wee little child.
Are you still on your own in Bérialin?
This is ...
Have you come to Meliodas's place again to hang out?
Eliza-beth ...!
S- SNOINK ?!
ELIZABETH-CHAN... WH-WHAT'S WITH YOUR EYES?!

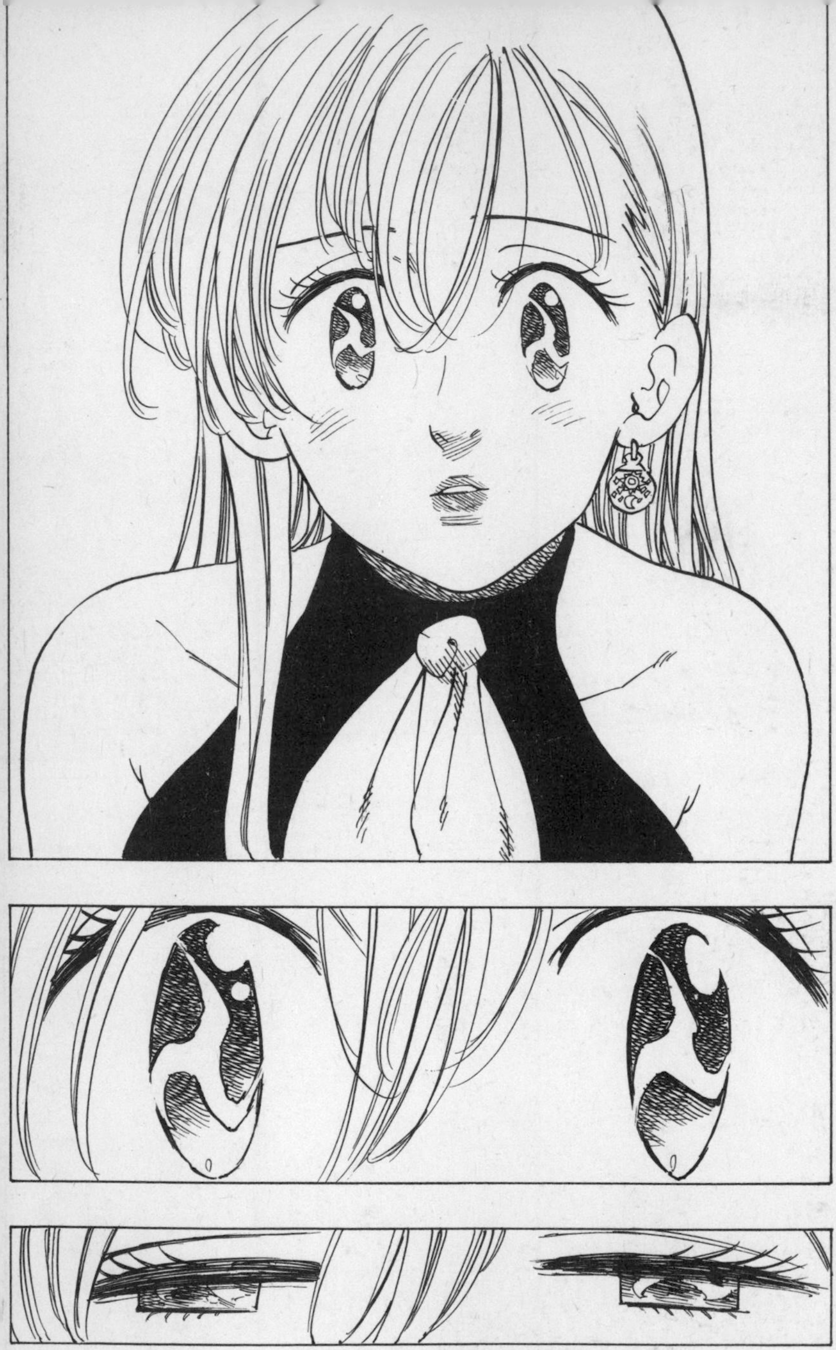

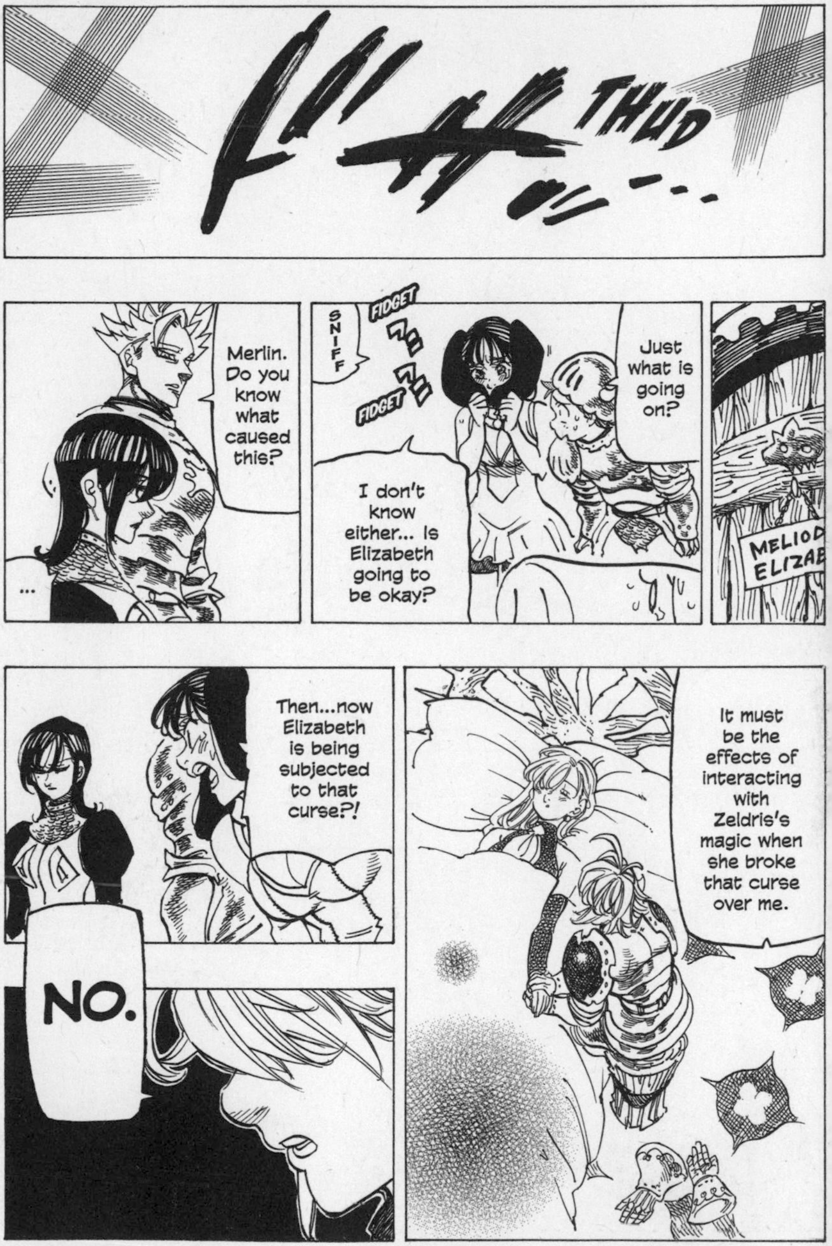
THUD
MELIOD
ELIZAB
Just what is going on?
FIDGET
SNIFF
FIDGET
I don't know either... Is Elizabeth going to be okay?
Merlin. Do you know what caused this?
...
It must be the effects of interacting with Zeldris's magic when she broke that curse over me.
Then...now Elizabeth is being subjected to that curse?!
NO.

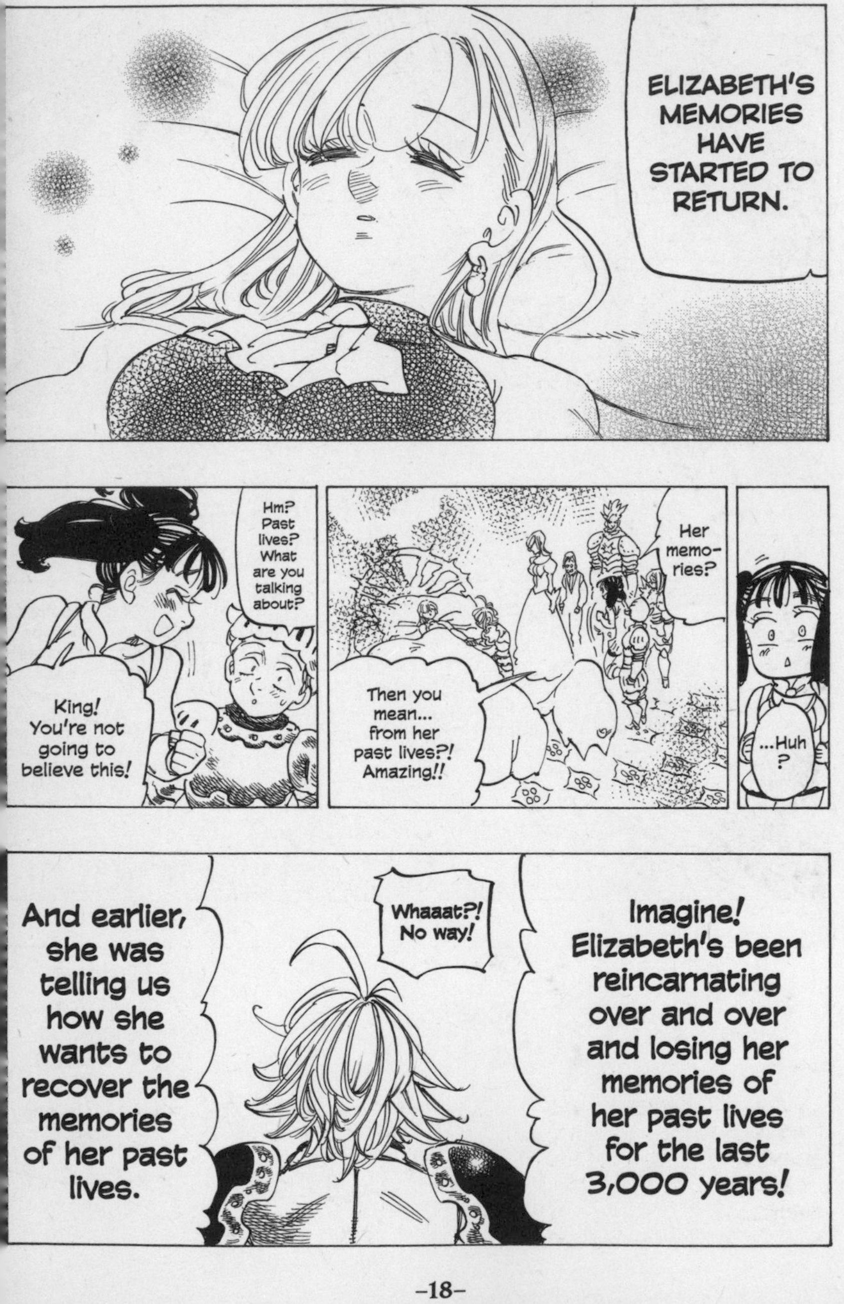
ELIZABETH'S MEMORIES HAVE STARTED TO RETURN.
...Huh?
Her memories?
Then you mean... from her past lives?! Amazing!!
Hm? Past lives? What are you talking about?
King! You're not going to believe this!
Imagine! Elizabeth's been reincarnating over and over and losing her memories of her past lives for the last 3,000 years!
Whaaat?! No way!
And earlier, she was telling us how she wants to recover the memories of her past lives.

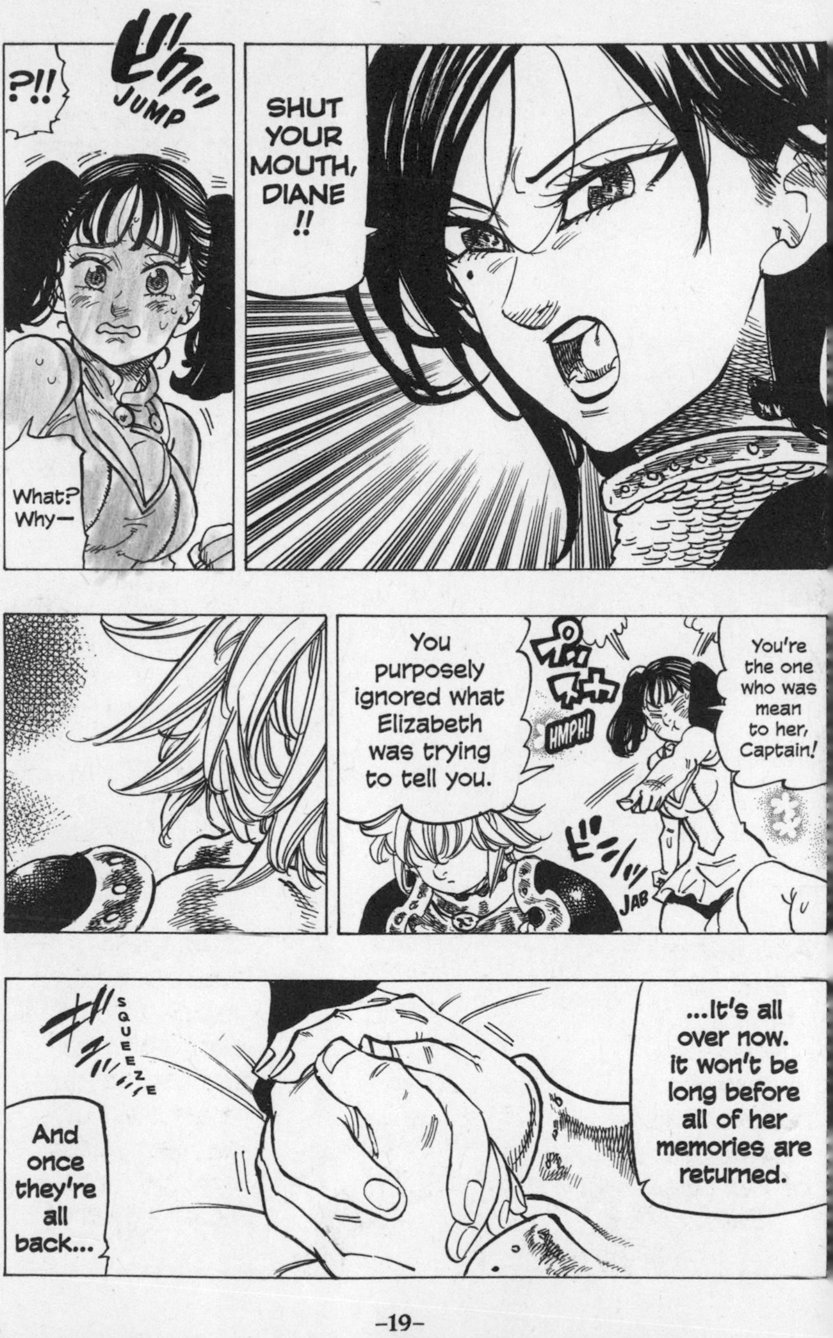
SHUT YOUR MOUTH, DIANE !!
?!!
JUMP
What? Why—
You're the one who was mean to her, Captain!
HMPH!
You purposely ignored what Elizabeth was trying to tell you.
JAB
...It's all over now. it won't be long before all of her memories are returned.
SQUEEZE
And once they're all back...

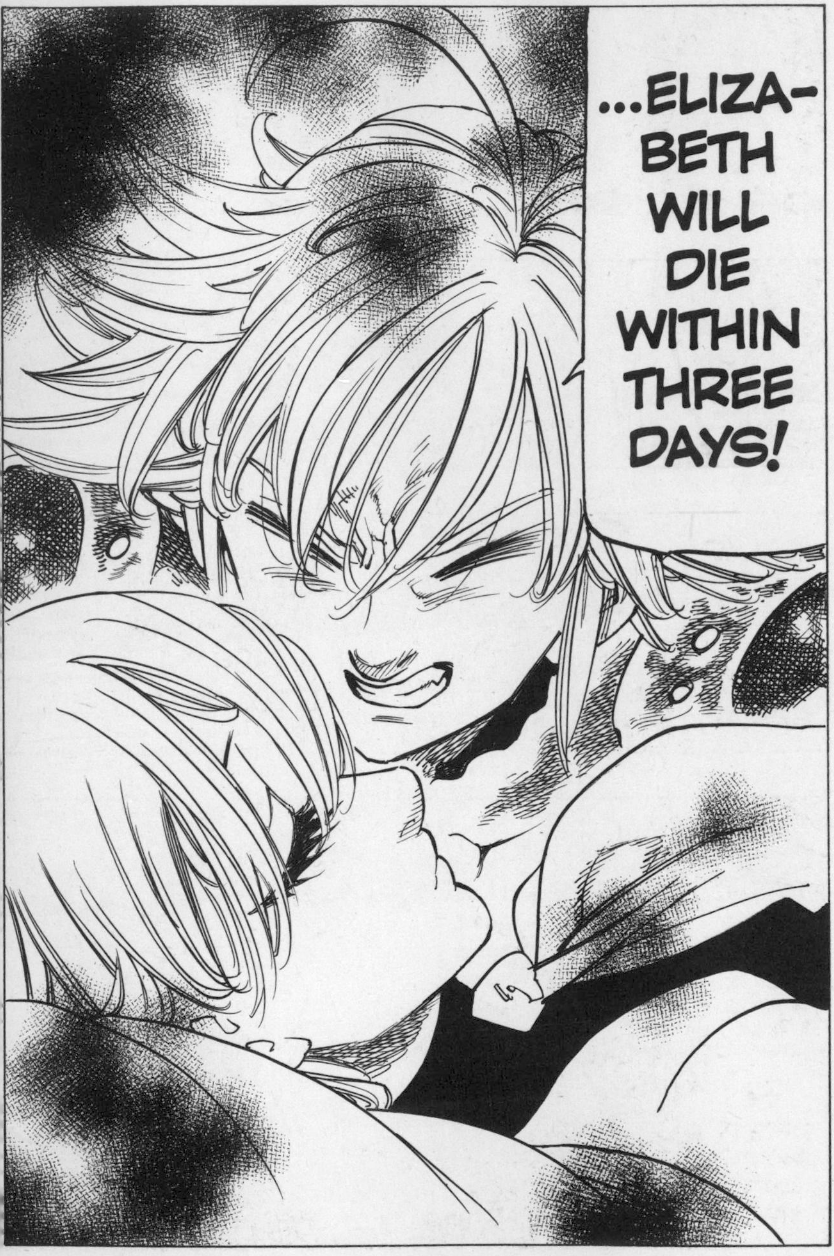
...ELIZA-BETH WILL DIE WITHIN THREE DAYS!

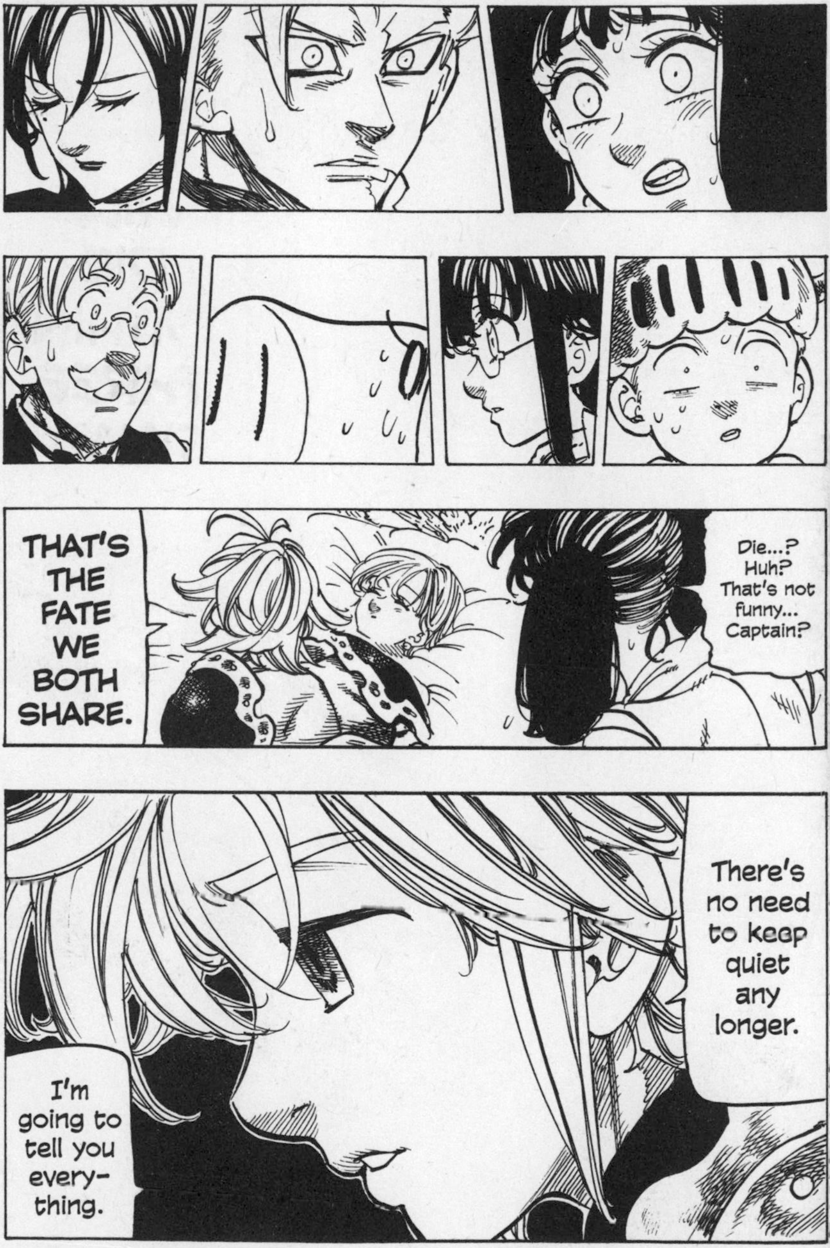
Die...? Huh? That's not funny... Captain?
THAT'S THE FATE WE BOTH SHARE.
There's no need to keep quiet any longer.
I'm going to tell you every-thing.

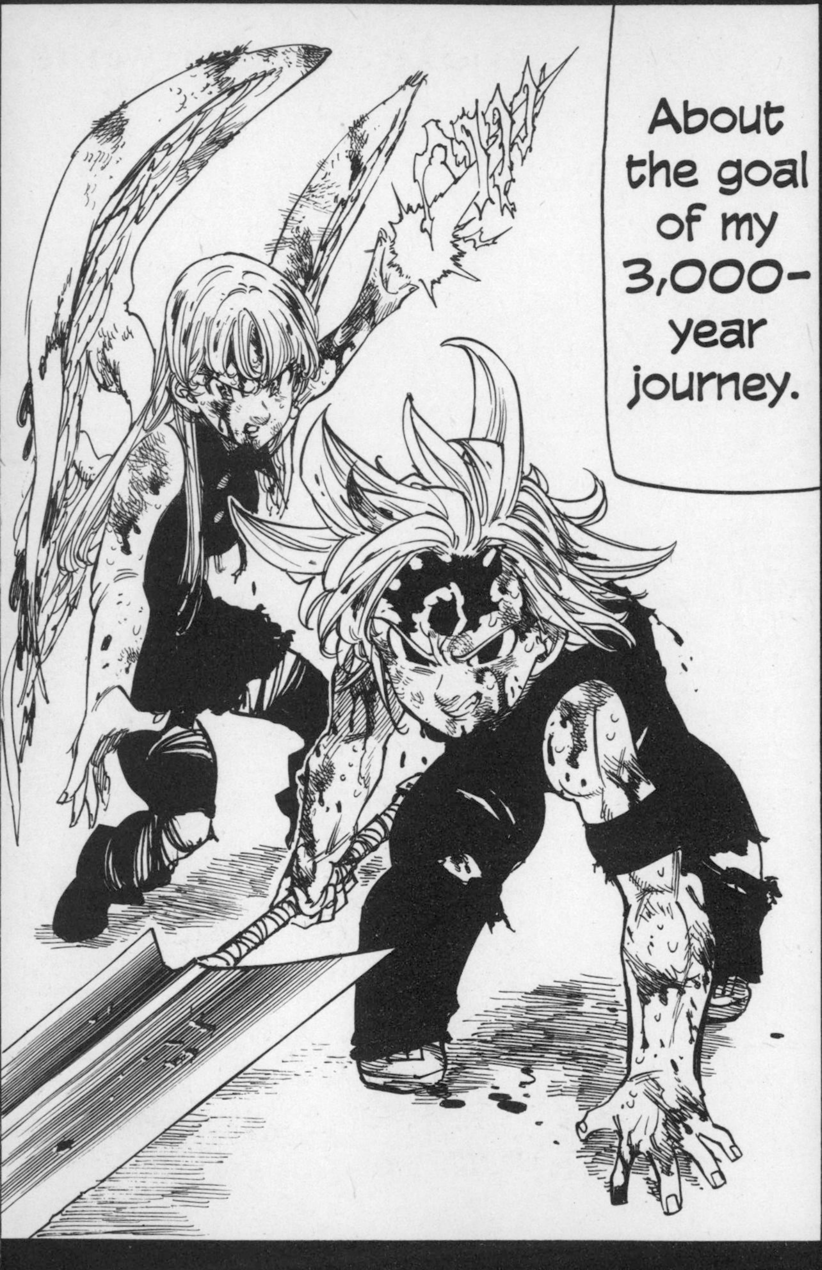
About the goal of my 3,000-year journey.

Chapter 224 - The Life We Live

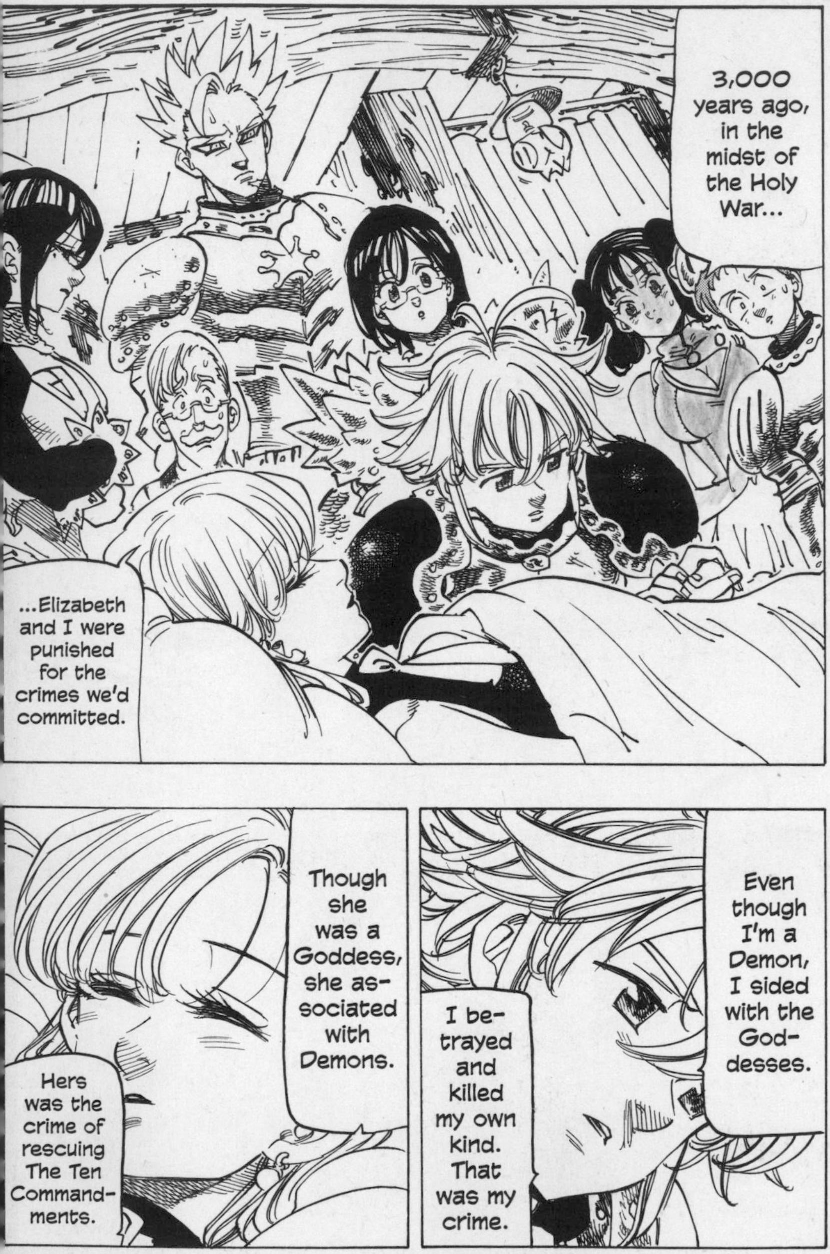
3,000 years ago, in the midst of the Holy War...
...Elizabeth and I were punished for the crimes we'd committed.
Even though I'm a Demon, I sided with the God-desses.
I be-trayed and killed my own kind. That was my crime.
Though she was a Goddess, she as-sociated with Demons.
Hers was the crime of rescuing The Ten Command-ments.

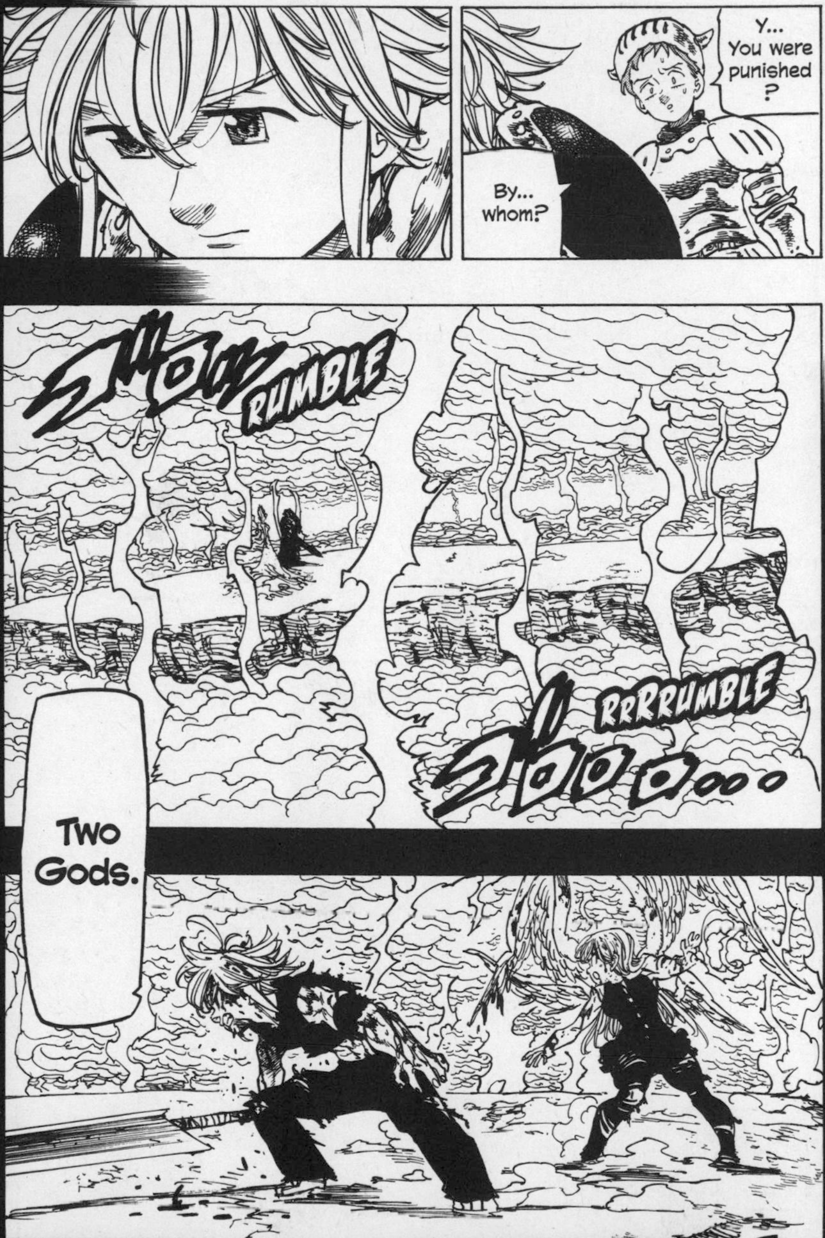
Y... You were punished?
By... whom?
RUMBLE
RRRUMBLE
Two Gods.

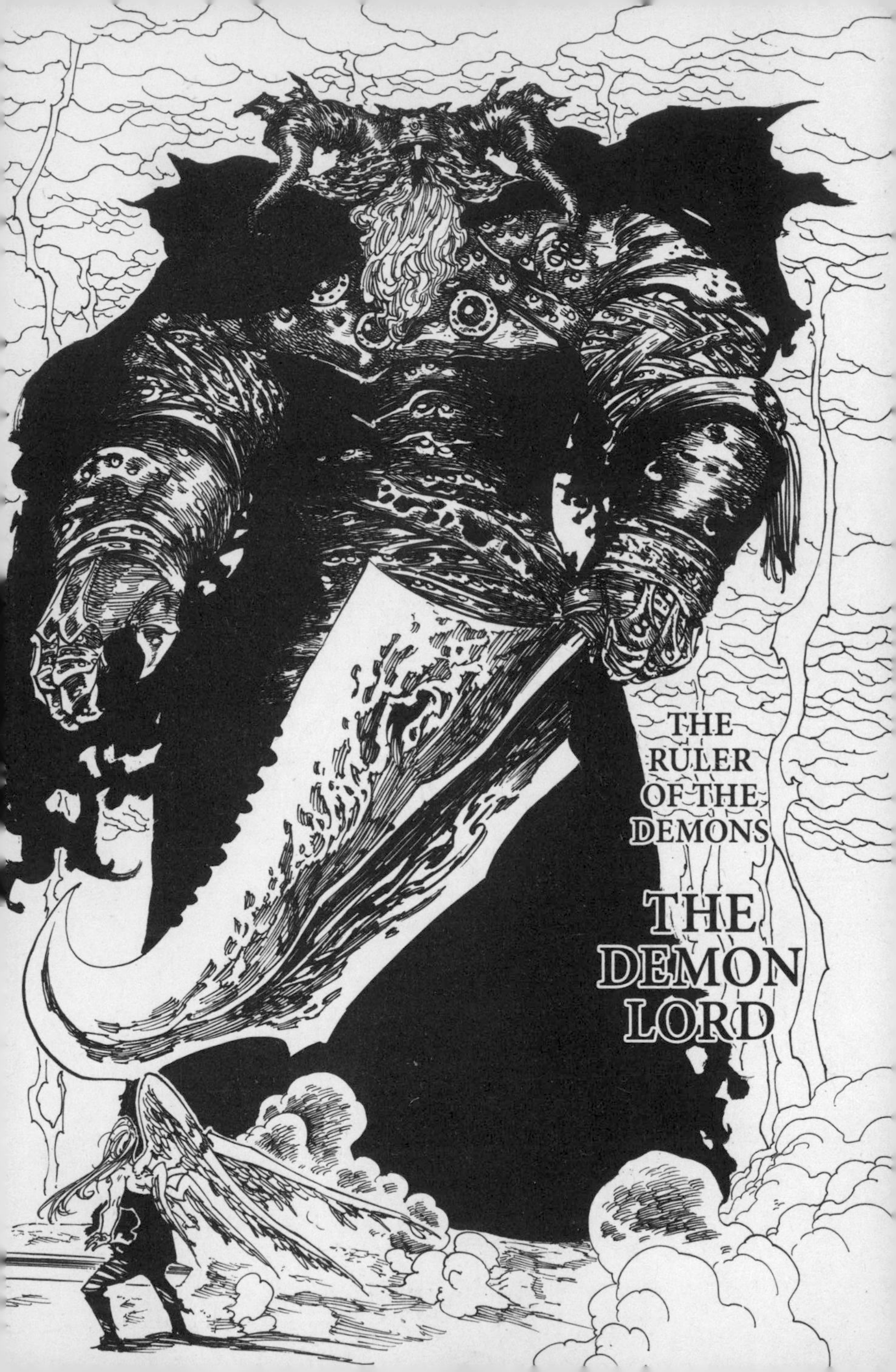
THE RULER OF THE DEMONS
THE DEMON LORD

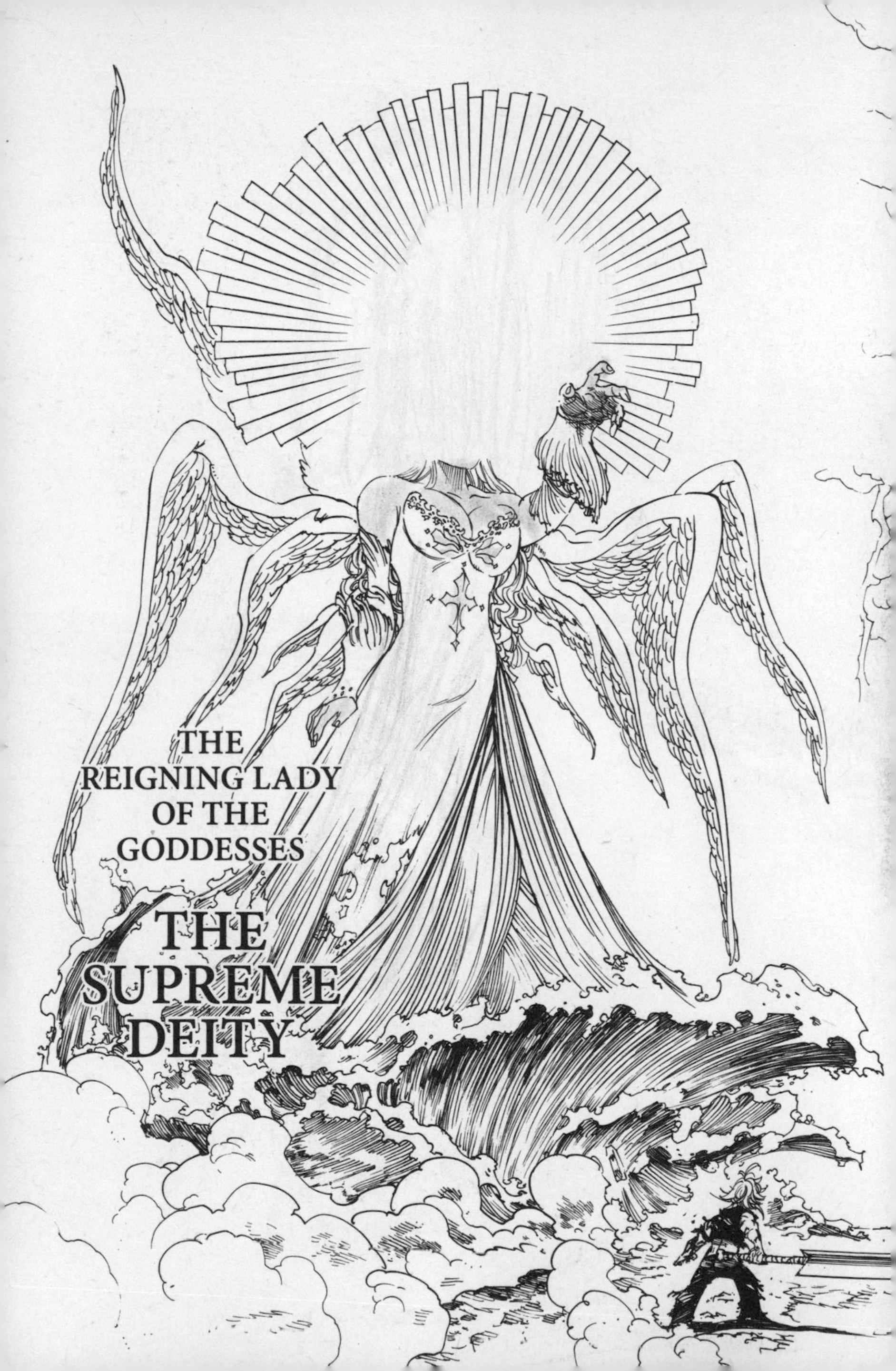
THE REIGNING LADY OF THE GODDESSES
THE SUPREME DEITY

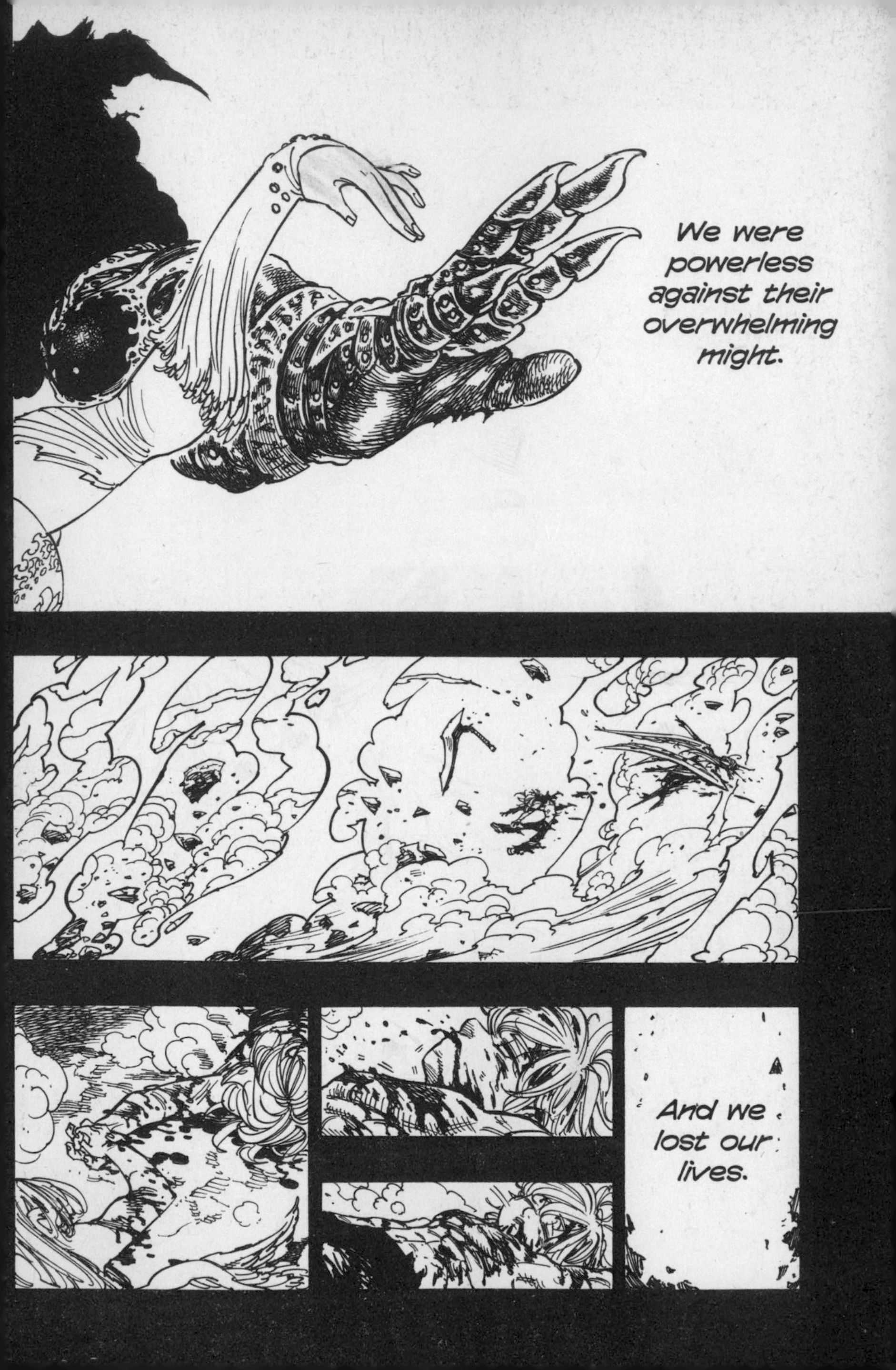
We were powerless against their overwhelming might.
And we lost our lives.

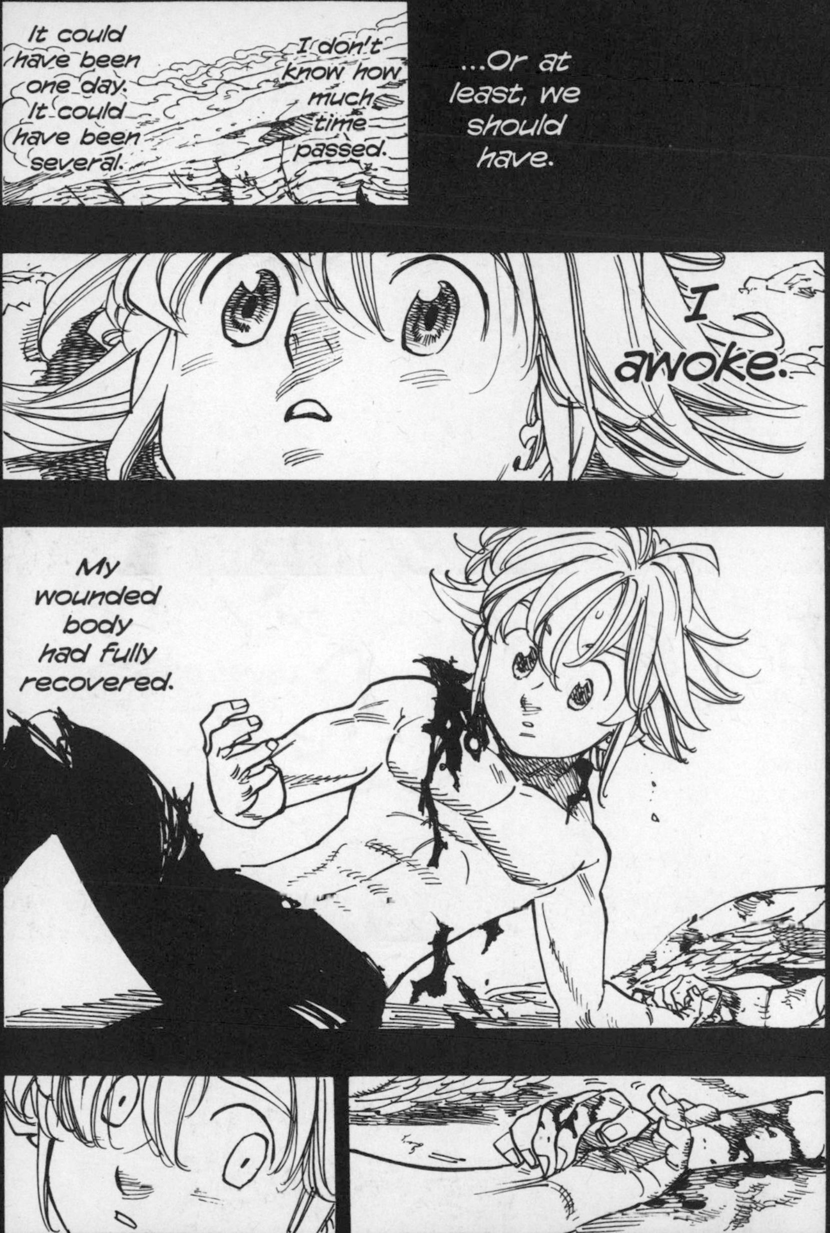
...Or at least, we should have.
I don't know how much time passed.
It could have been one day. It could have been several.
I awoke.
My wounded body had fully recovered.

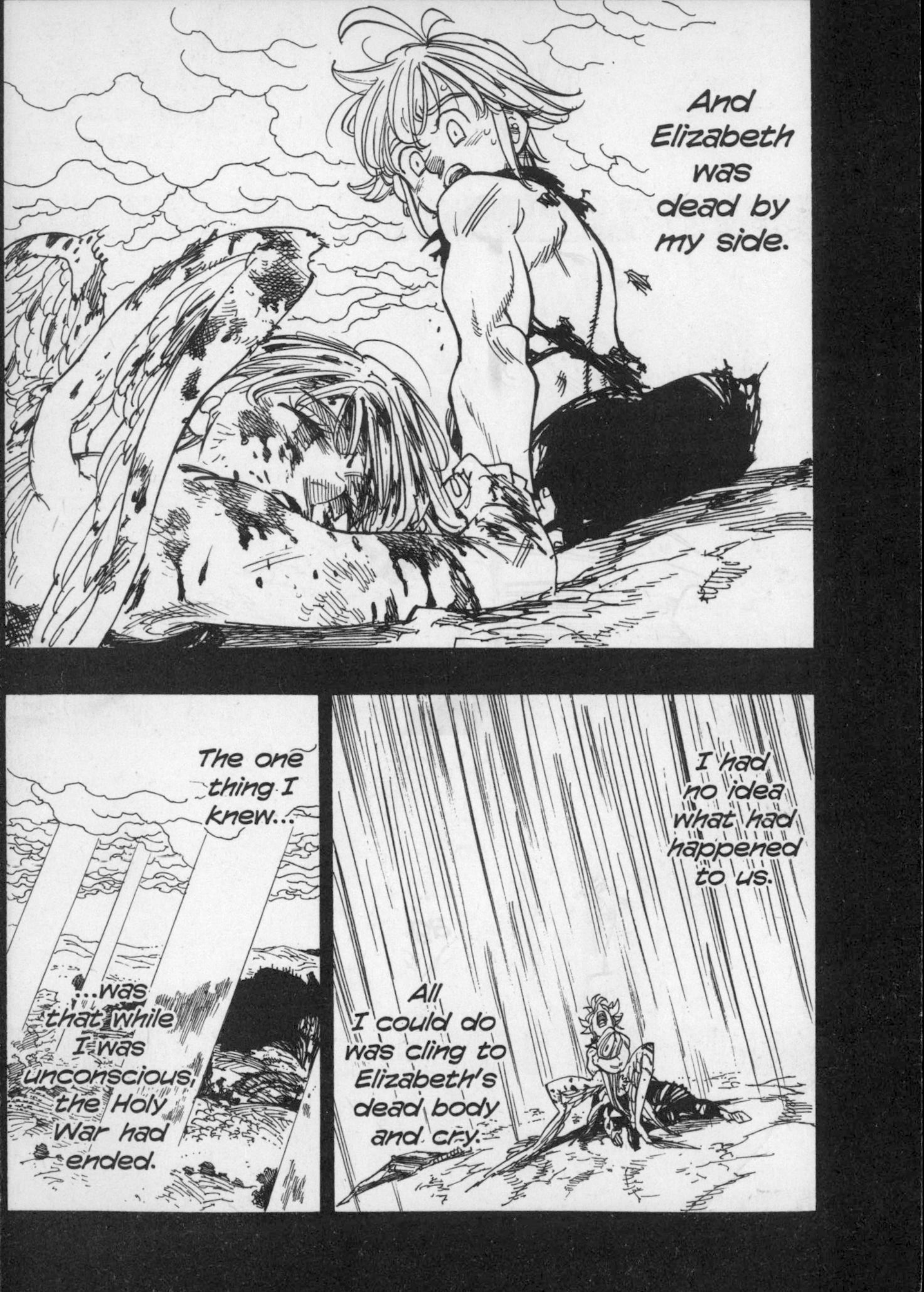
And Elizabeth was dead by my side.
I had no idea what had happened to us.
All I could do was cling to Elizabeth's dead body and cry.
The one thing I knew...
...was that while I was unconscious, the Holy War had ended.

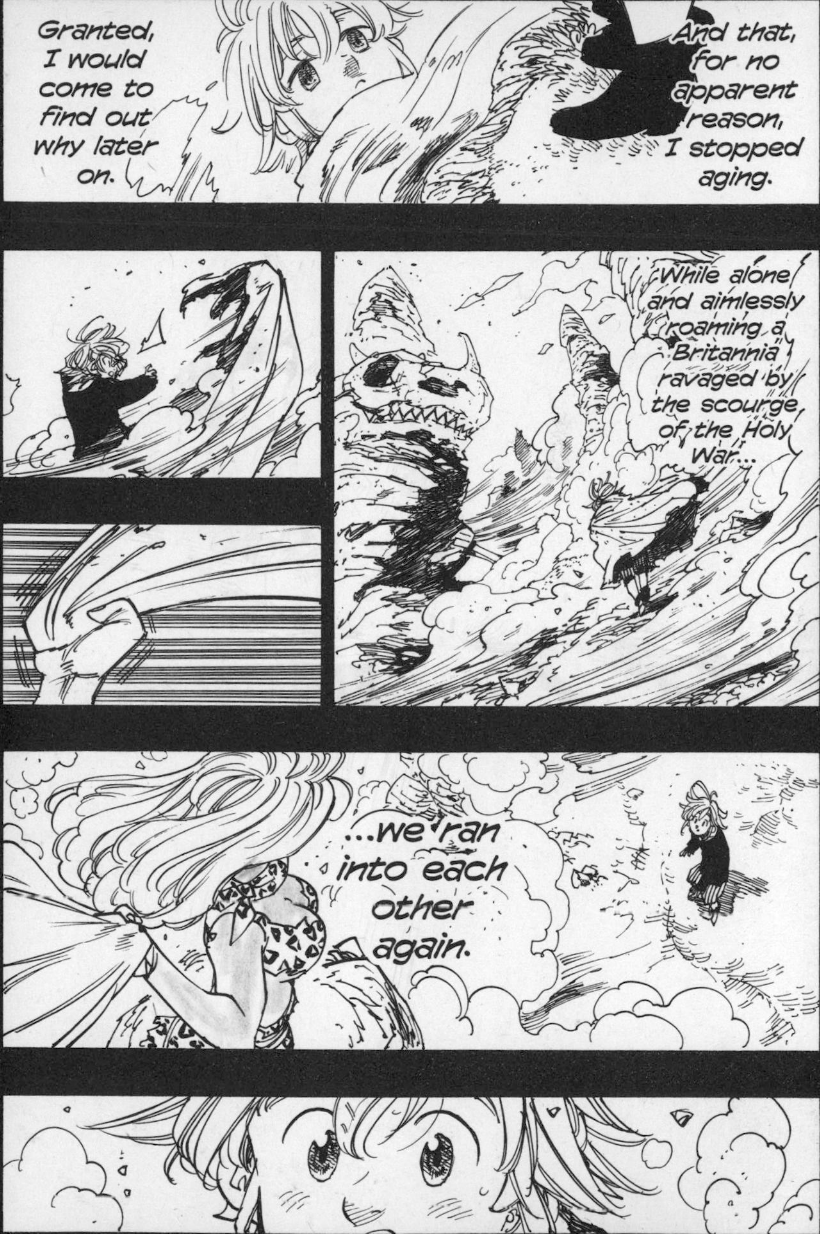
And that, for no apparent reason, I stopped aging.
Granted, I would come to find out why later on.
While alone and aimlessly roaming a Britannia ravaged by the scourge of the Holy War...
...we ran into each other again.

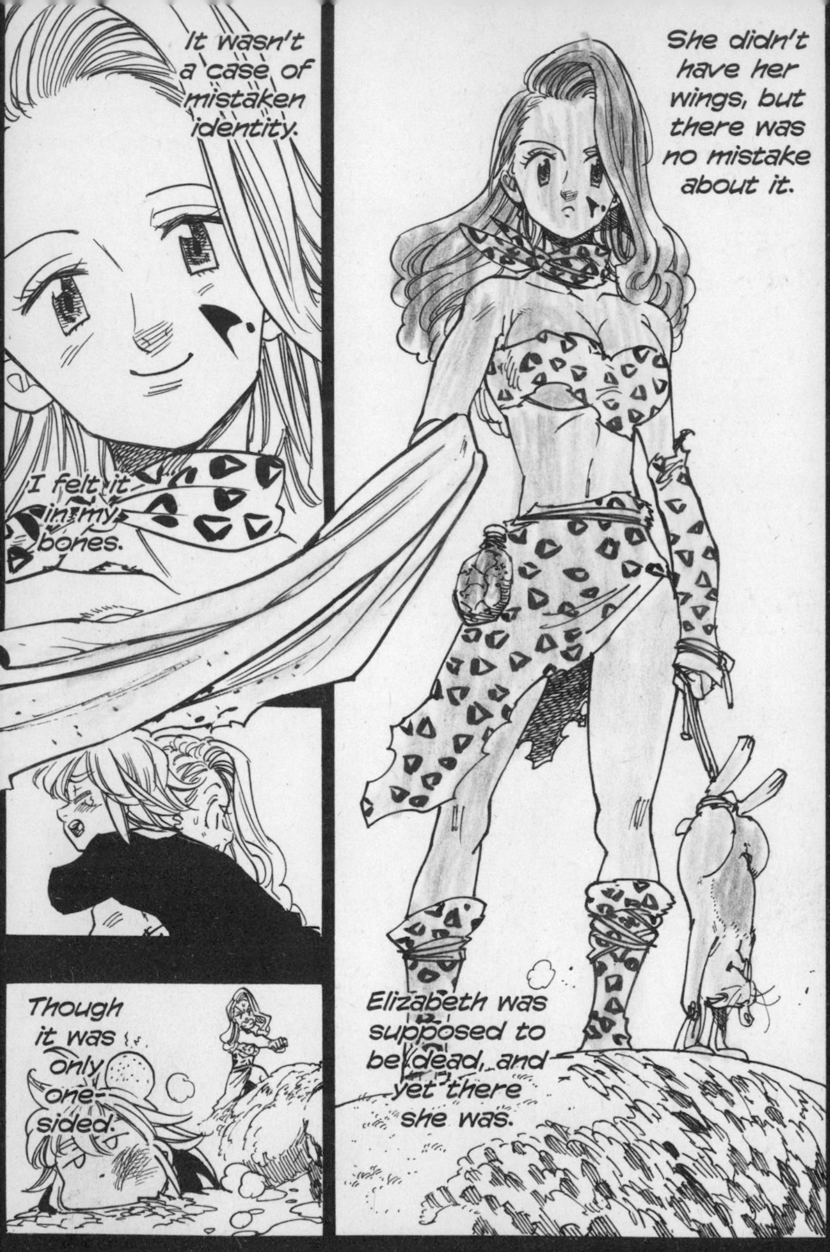
She didn't have her wings, but there was no mistake about it.
Elizabeth was supposed to be dead, and yet there she was.
It wasn't a case of mistaken identity.
I felt it in my bones.
Though it was only one-sided.

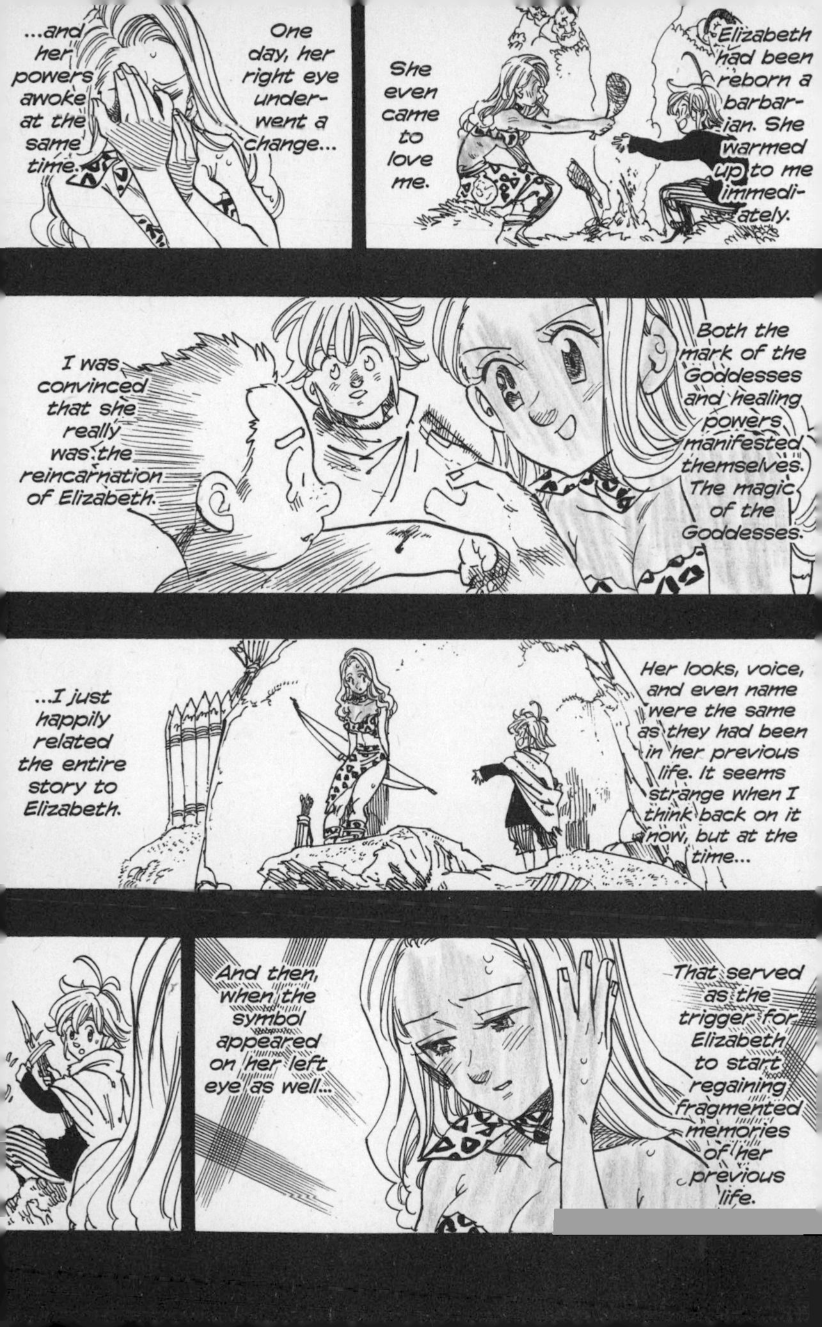
Elizabeth had been reborn a barbarian. She warmed up to me immediately.
She even came to love me.
One day, her right eye underwent a change...
...and her powers awoke at the same time.
Both the mark of the Goddesses and healing powers manifested themselves. The magic of the Goddesses.
I was convinced that she really was the reincarnation of Elizabeth.
Her looks, voice, and even name were the same as they had been in her previous life. It seems strange when I think back on it now, but at the time...
...I just happily related the entire story to Elizabeth.
And then, when the symbol appeared on her left eye as well...
That served as the trigger for Elizabeth to start regaining fragmented memories of her previous life.

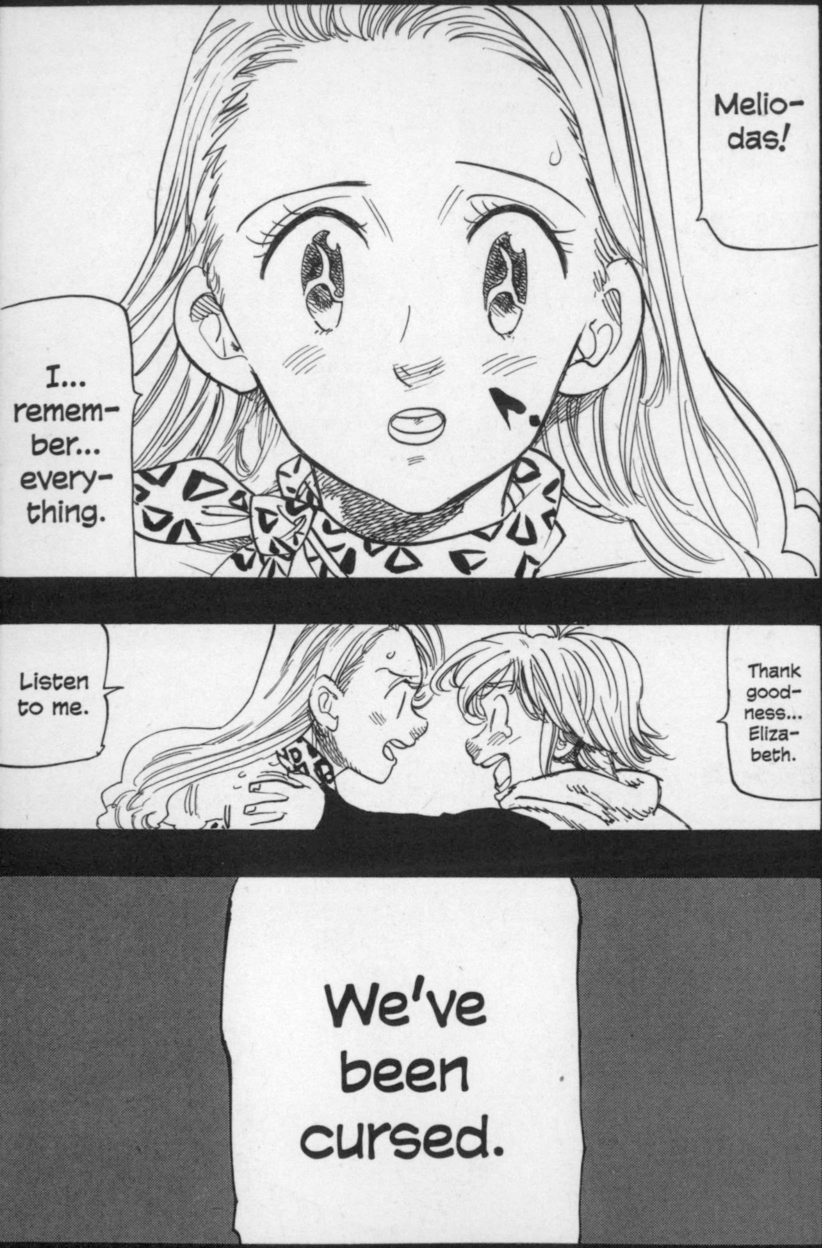
Melio-das!
I... remem-ber... every-thing.
Thank good-ness... Eliza-beth.
Listen to me.
We've been cursed.

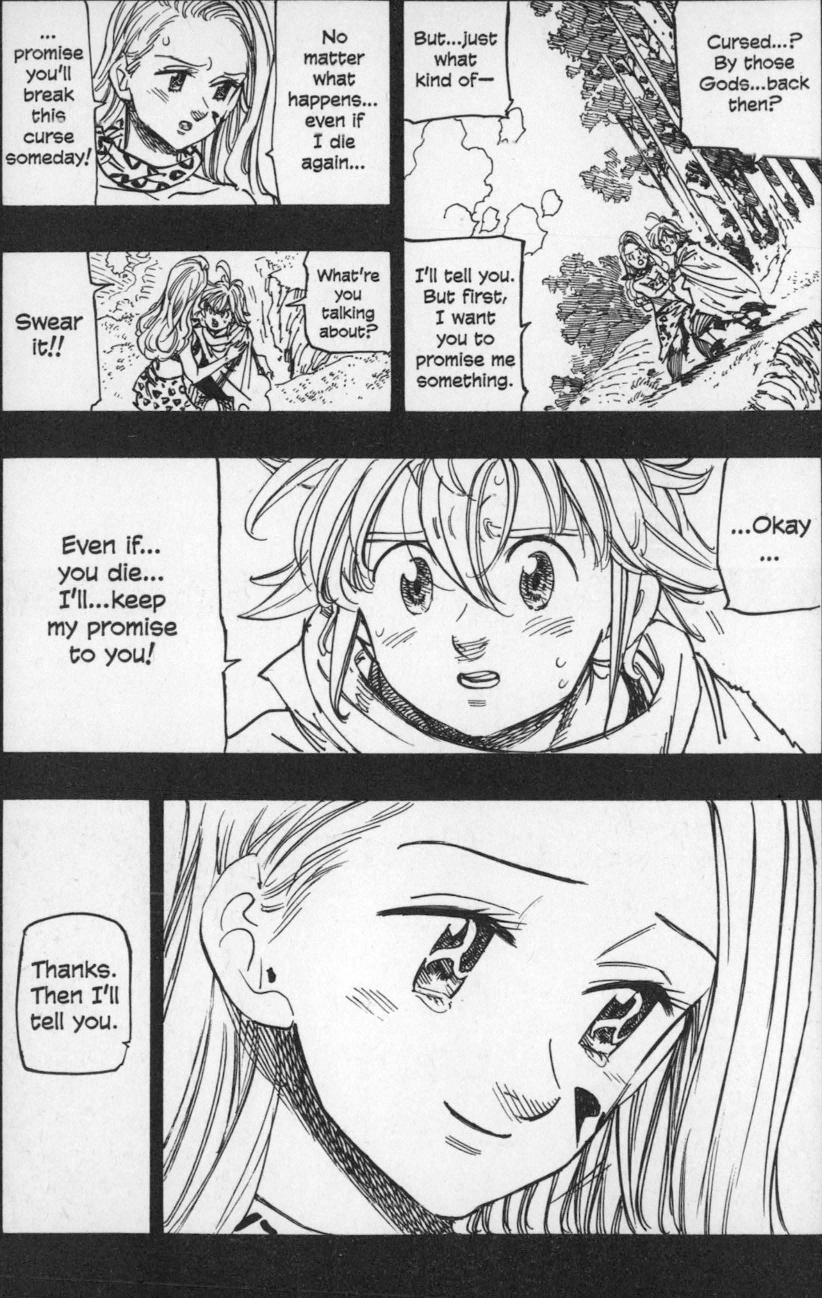
Cursed...? By those Gods...back then?
But...just what kind of—
I'll tell you. But first, I want you to promise me something.
No matter what happens... even if I die again...
... promise you'll break this curse someday!
What're you talking about?
Swear it!!
...Okay ...
Even if... you die... I'll...keep my promise to you!
Thanks. Then I'll tell you.

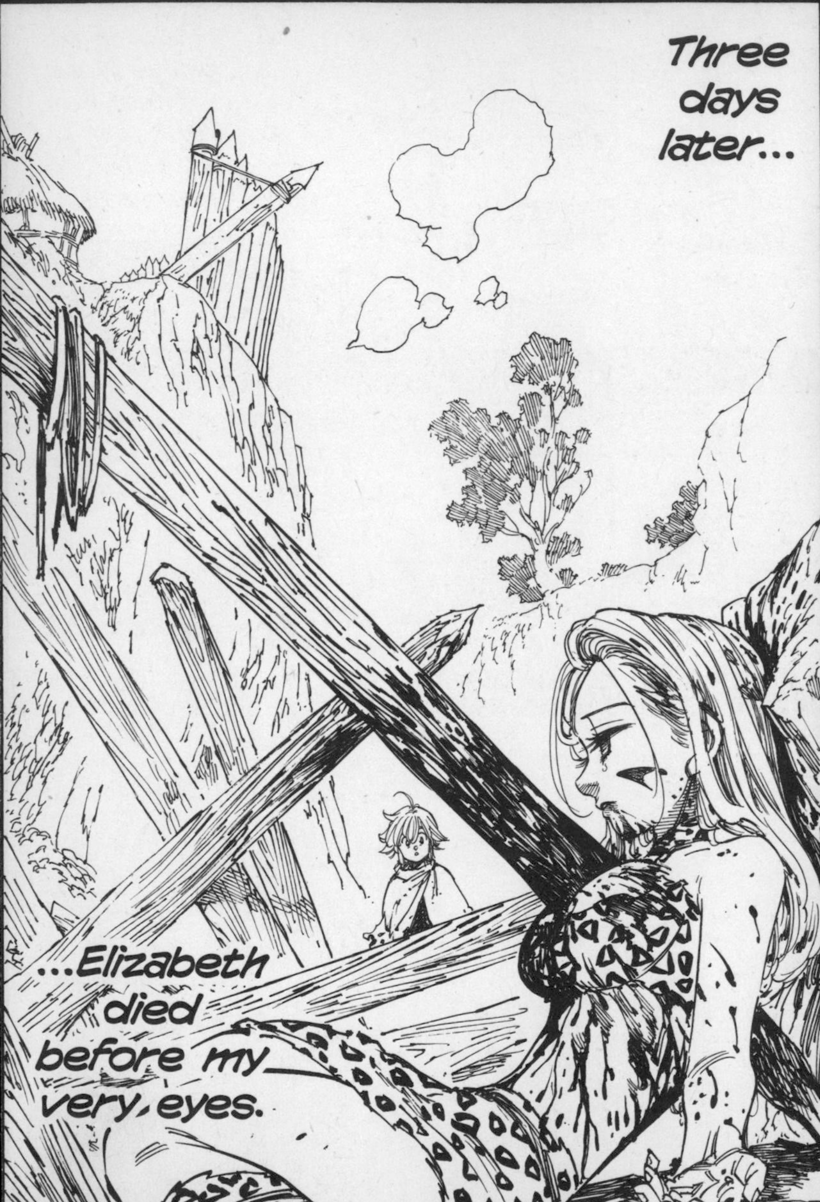
Three days later...
...Elizabeth died before my very eyes.

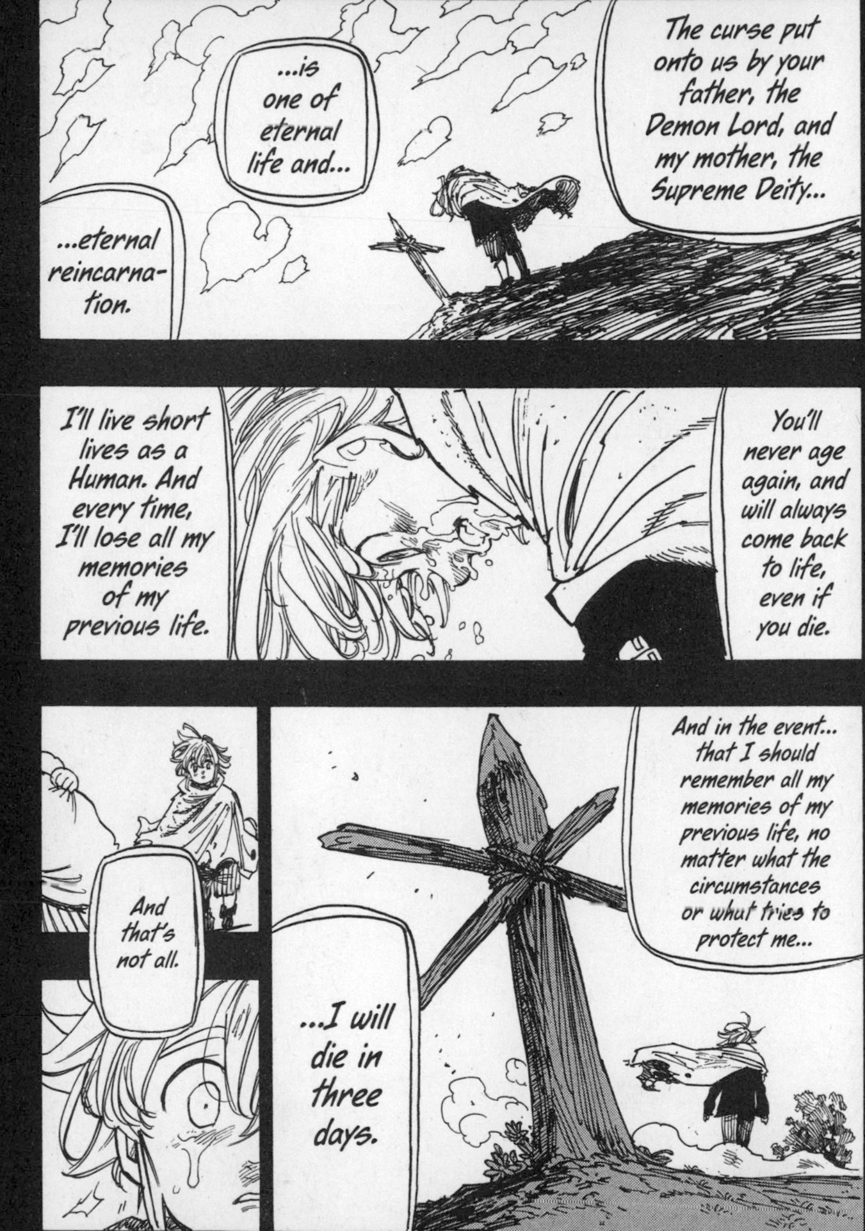
The curse put onto us by your father, the Demon Lord, and my mother, the Supreme Deity...
...is one of eternal life and...
...eternal reincarnation.
You'll never age again, and will always come back to life, even if you die.
I'll live short lives as a Human. And every time, I'll lose all my memories of my previous life.
And in the event... that I should remember all my memories of my previous life, no matter what the circumstances or what tries to protect me...
...I will die in three days.
And that's not all.

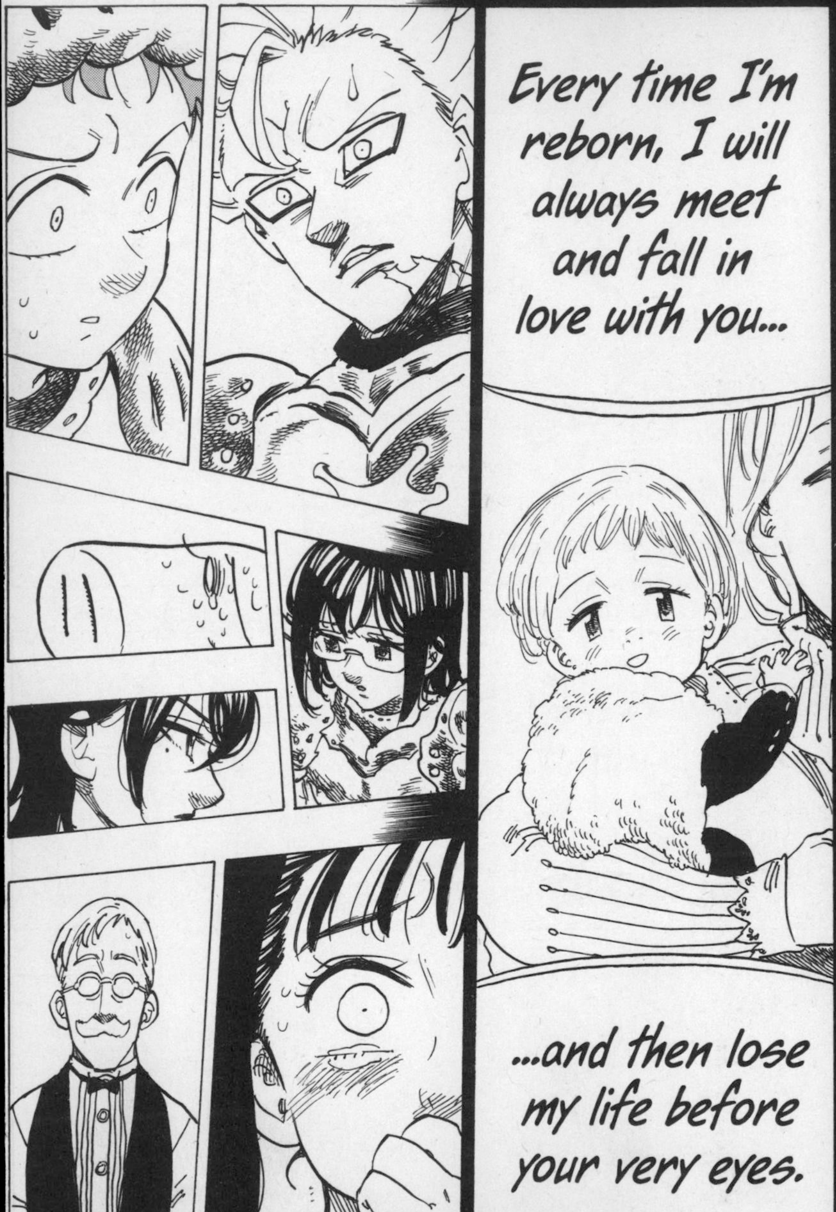

Every time I'm reborn, I will always meet and fall in love with you...
...and then lose my life before your very eyes.

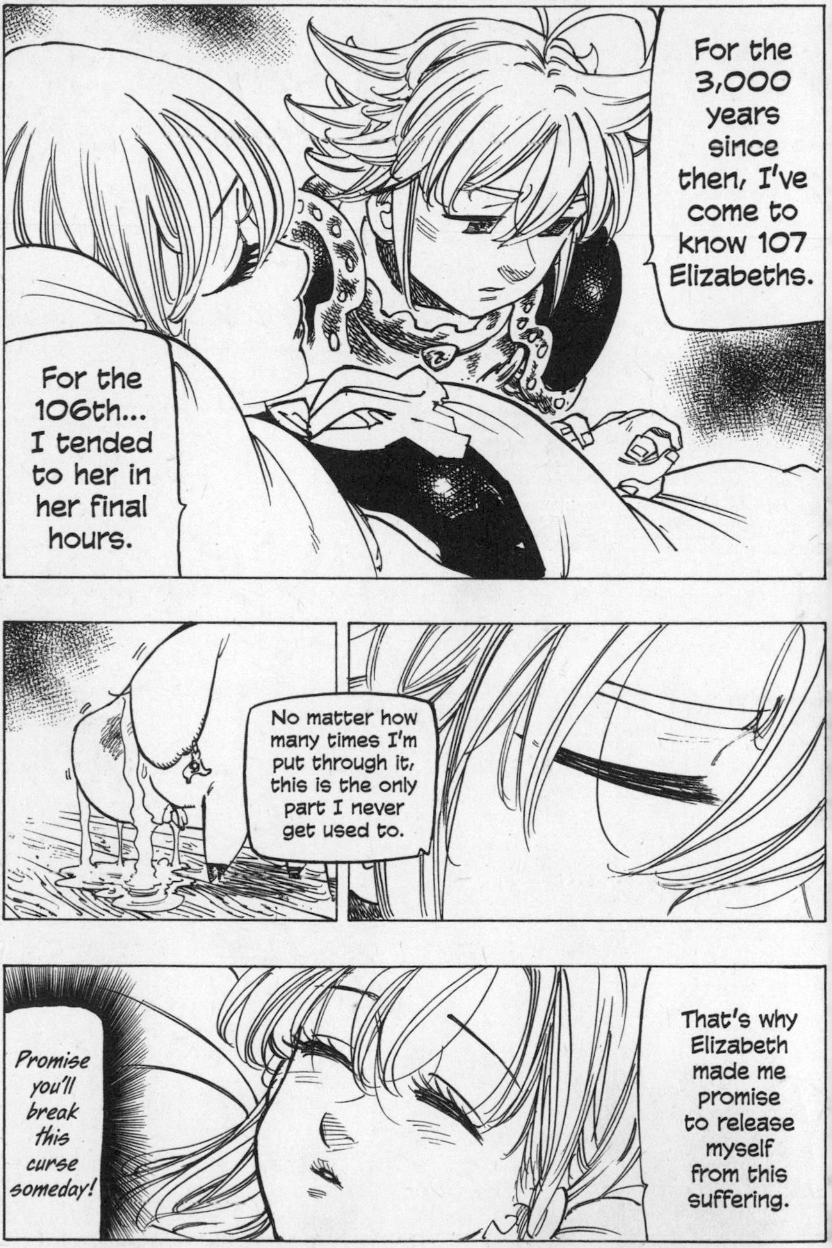
For the 3,000 years since then, I've come to know 107 Elizabeths.
For the 106th... I tended to her in her final hours.
No matter how many times I'm put through it, this is the only part I never get used to.
That's why Elizabeth made me promise to release myself from this suffering.
Promise you'll break this curse someday!

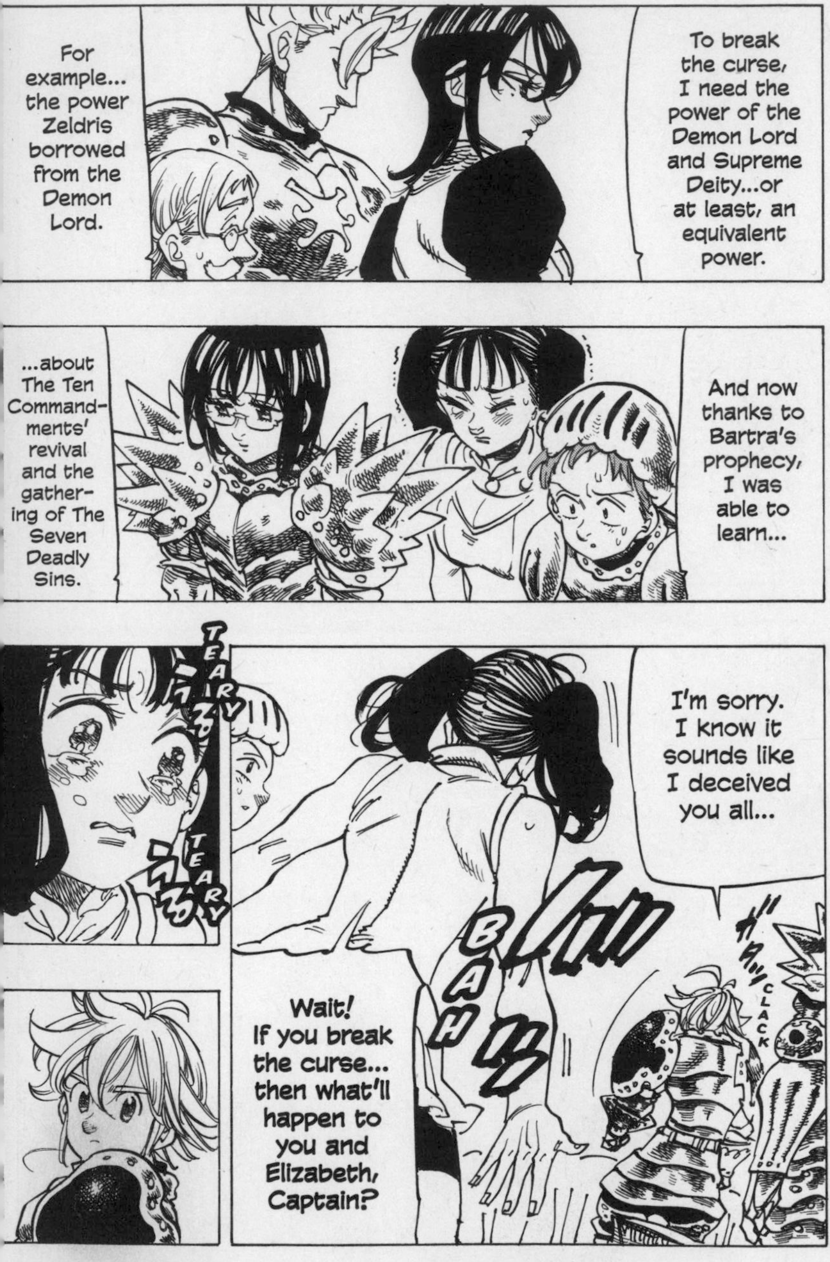
To break the curse, I need the power of the Demon Lord and Supreme Deity...or at least, an equivalent power.
For example... the power Zeldris borrowed from the Demon Lord.
And now thanks to Bartra's prophecy, I was able to learn...
...about The Ten Commandments' revival and the gathering of The Seven Deadly Sins.
I'm sorry. I know it sounds like I deceived you all...
CLACK
BAH
Wait! If you break the curse... then what'll happen to you and Elizabeth, Captain?
TEARY
TEARY

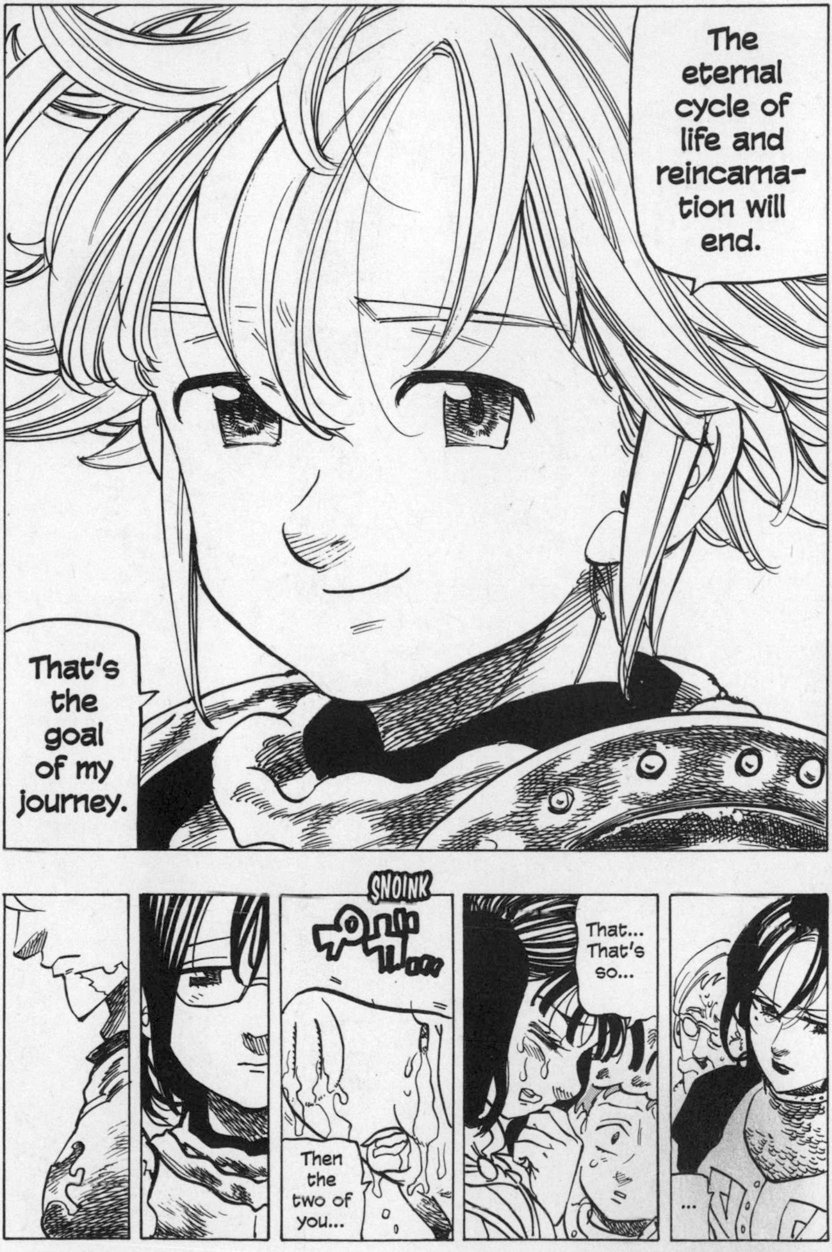
The eternal cycle of life and reincarnation will end.
That's the goal of my journey.
...
That... That's so...
SNOINK
Then the two of you...

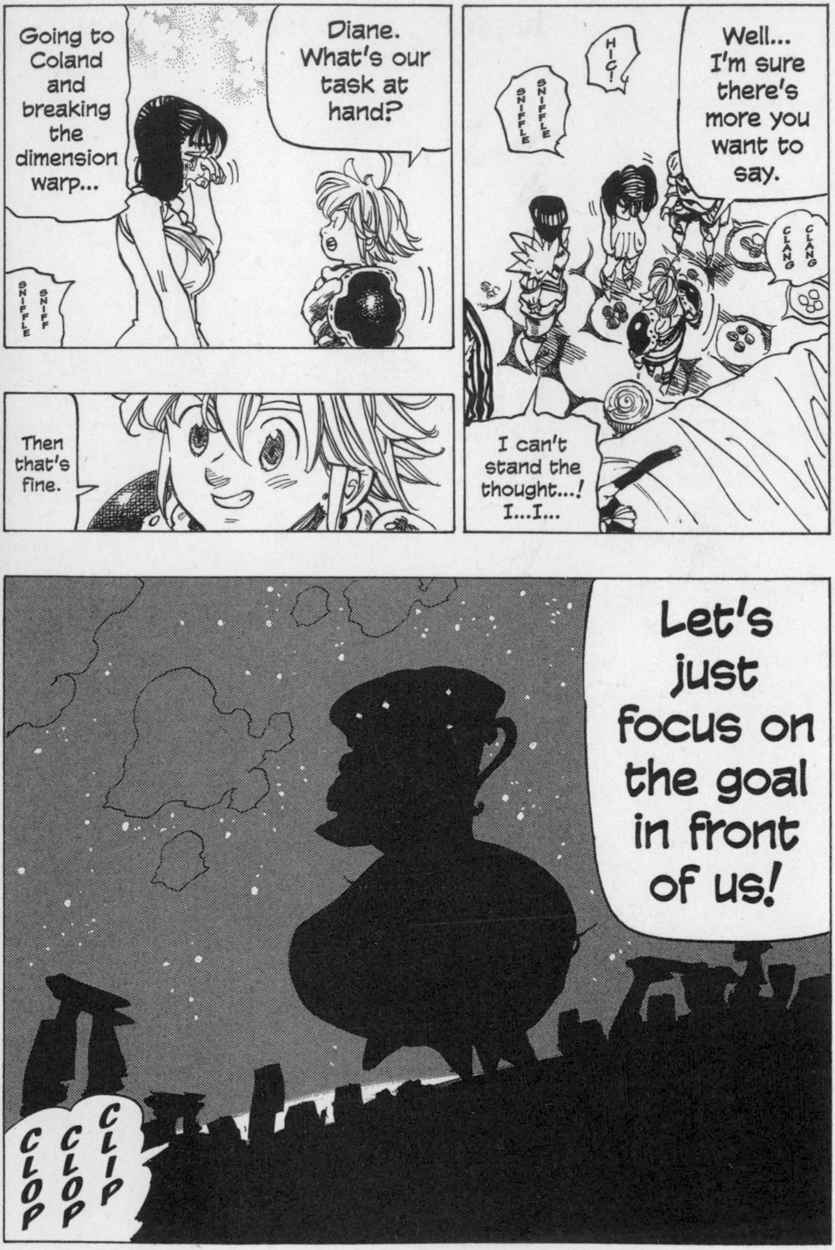
Well... I'm sure there's more you want to say.
HIC!
SNIFFLE SNIFFLE
CLANG CLANG
I can't stand the thought...! I...I...
Diane. What's our task at hand?
Going to Coland and breaking the dimension warp...
SNIFF SNIFFLE
Then that's fine.
Let's just focus on the goal in front of us!
CLIP CLOP CLOP

Chapter 225 - Troubles Between Us

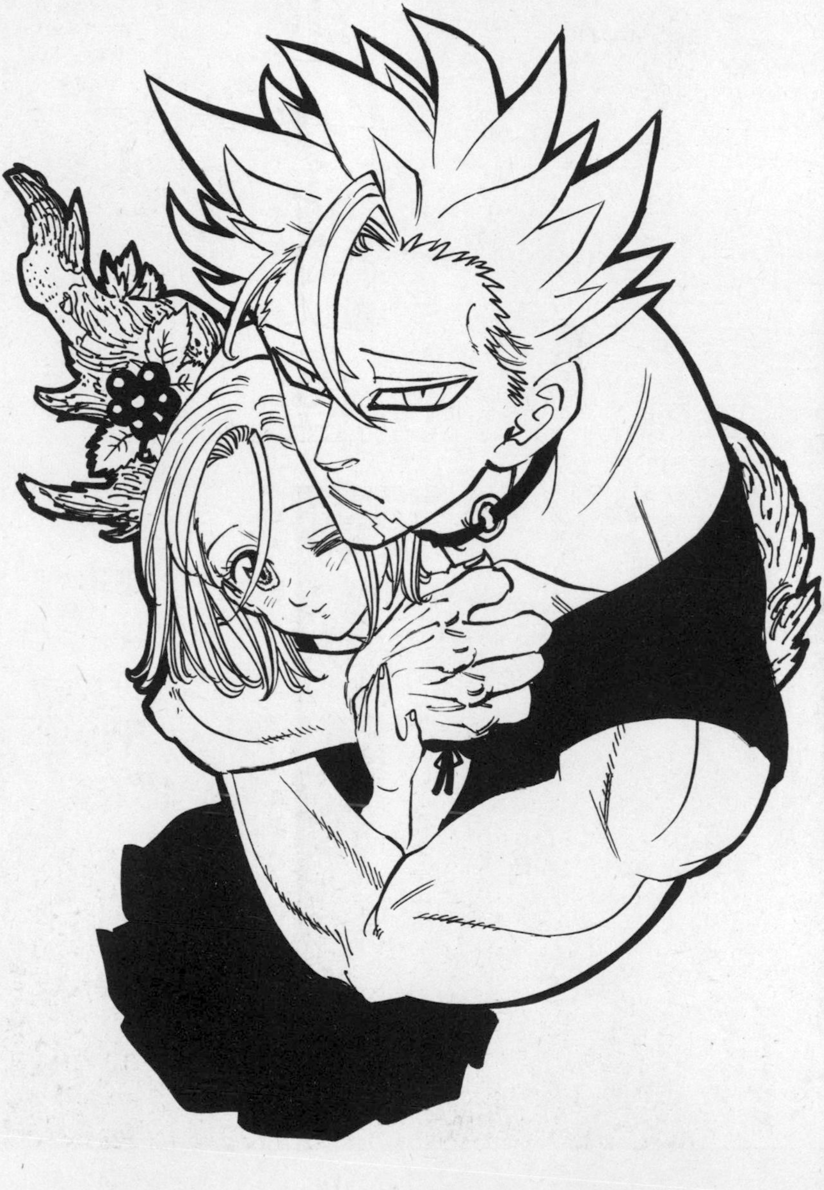

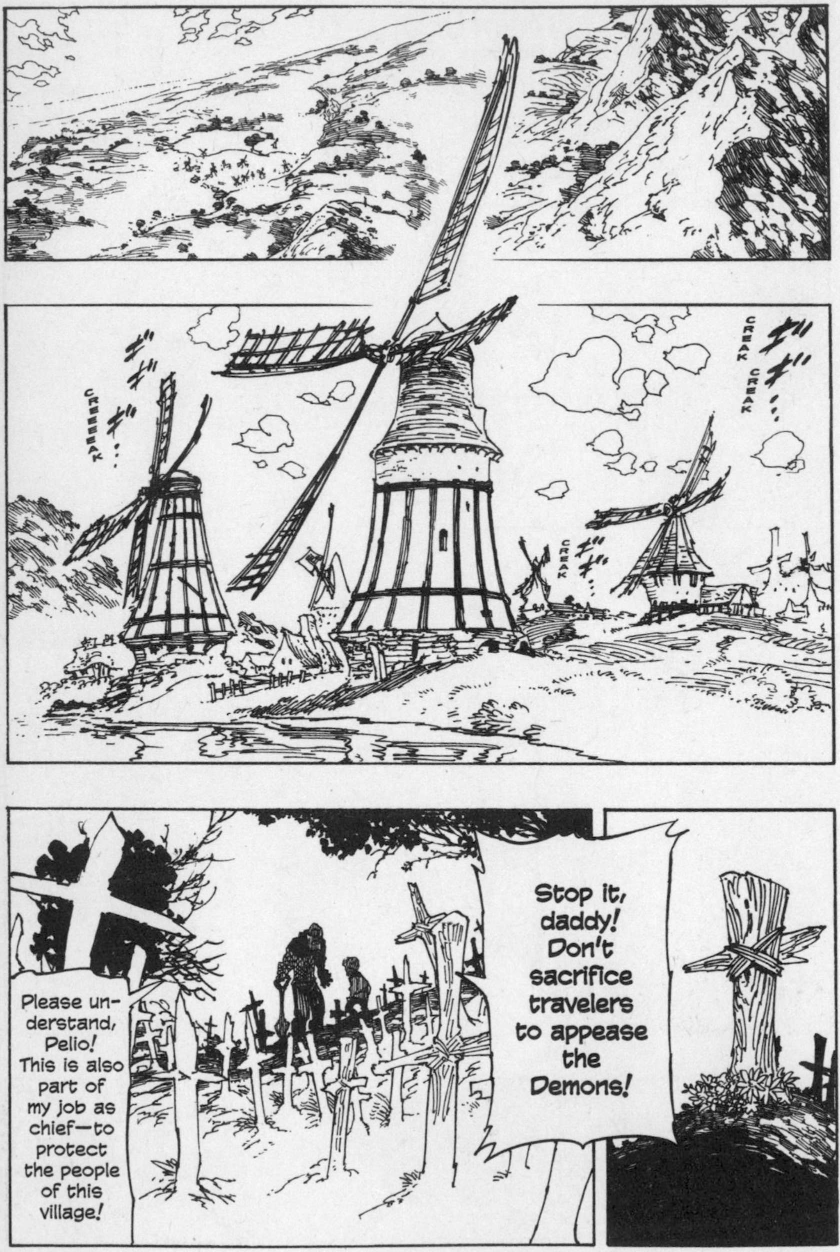
CREAK CREAK
CREAK
CREEEEAK
Stop it, daddy! Don't sacrifice travelers to appease the Demons!
Please understand, Pelio! This is also part of my job as chief—to protect the people of this village!

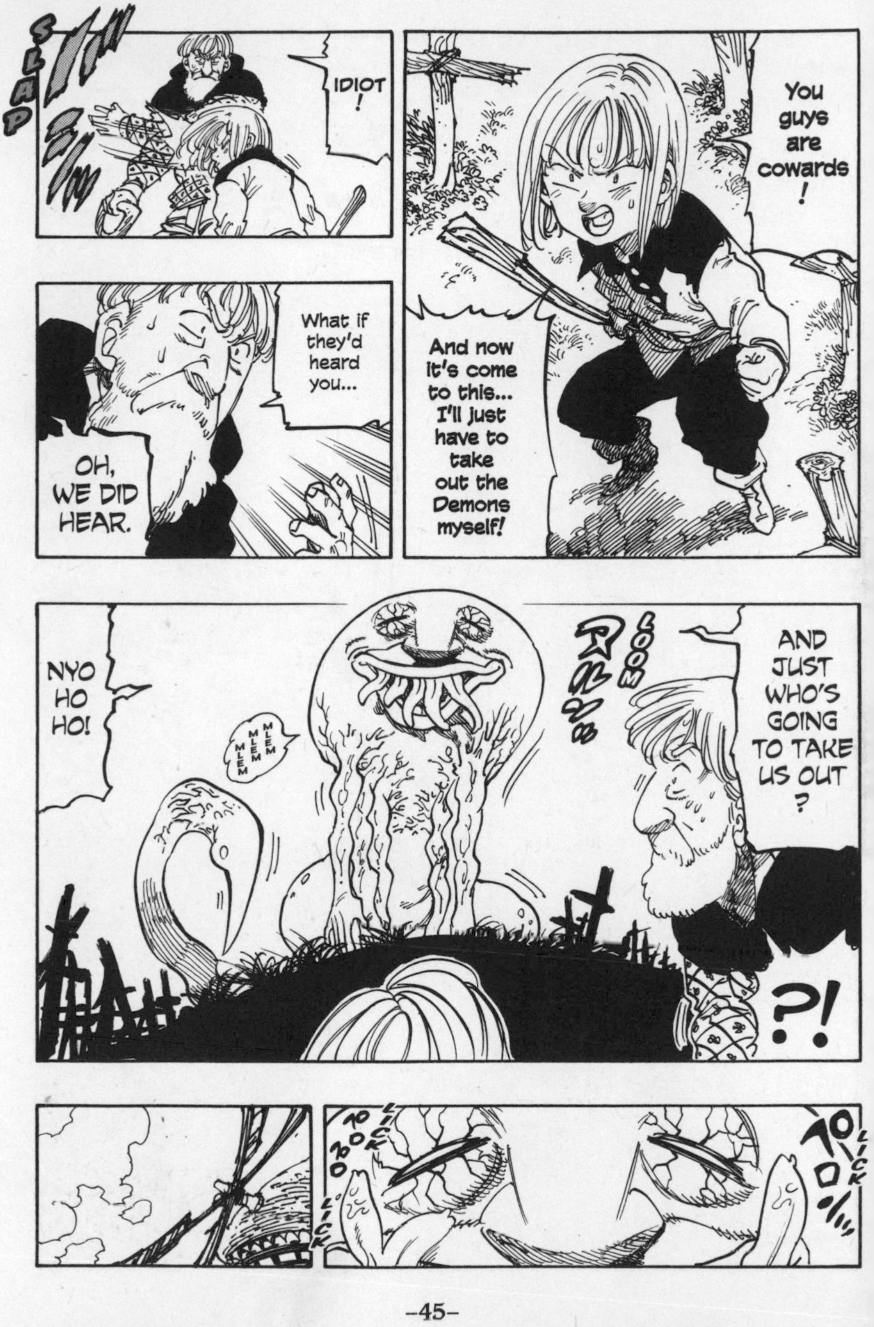
You guys are cowards!
And now it's come to this... I'll just have to take out the Demons myself!
SLAP
IDIOT!
What if they'd heard you...
OH, WE DID HEAR.
AND JUST WHO'S GOING TO TAKE US OUT?
LOOM
?!
MLEM MLEM MLEM
NYO HO HO!
LICK
LICK
LICK

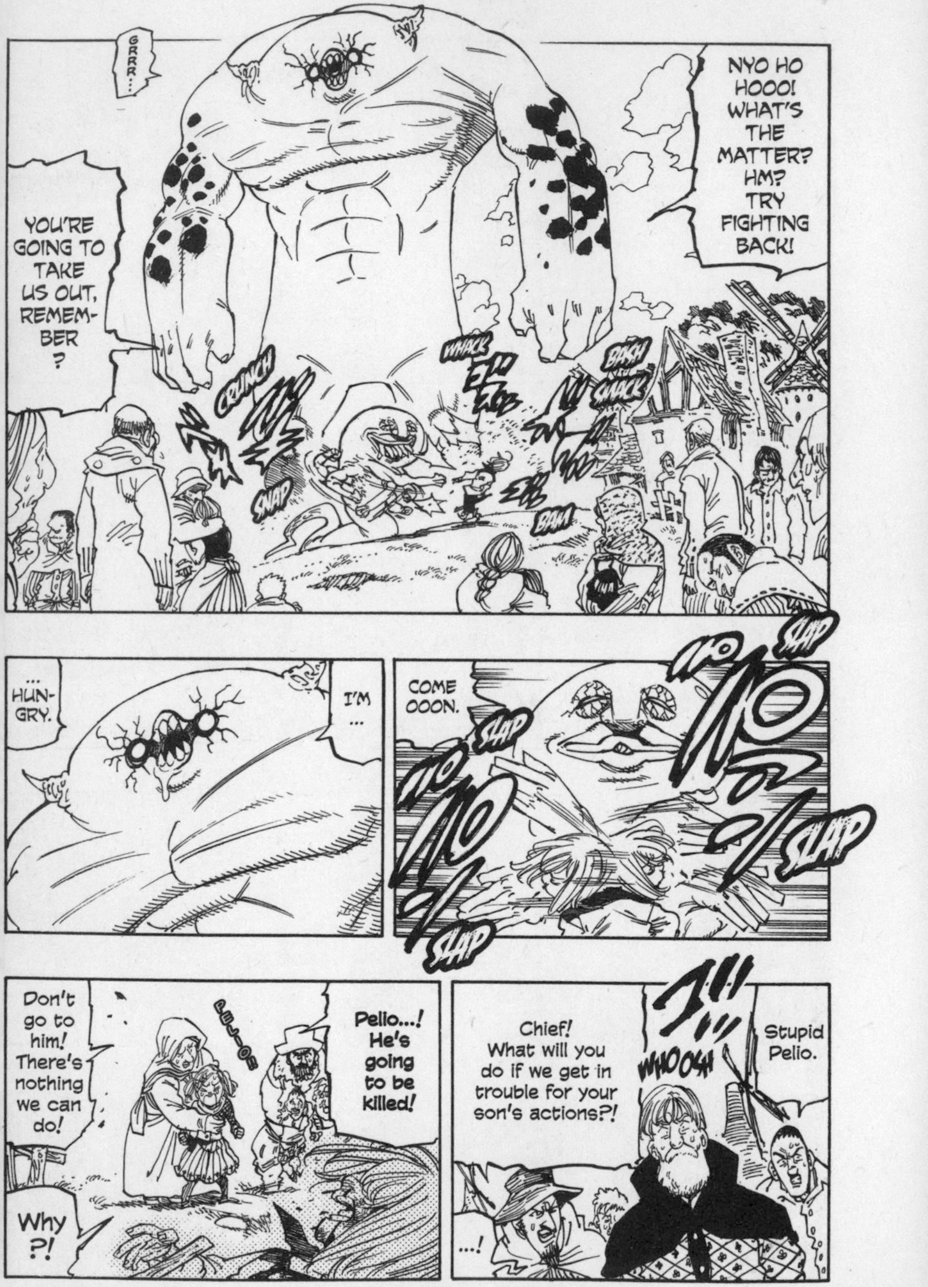
NYO HO HOOO! WHAT'S THE MATTER? HM? TRY FIGHTING BACK!
GRRR...
YOU'RE GOING TO TAKE US OUT, REMEMBER?
WHACK
BASH
SMACK
CRUNCH
SNAP
BAM
SLAP
COME OOON.
SLAP
SLAP
SLAP
I'M ...
... HUNGRY.
Stupid Pelio.
Chief! What will you do if we get in trouble for your son's actions?!
...!
Pelio...! He's going to be killed!
PELIO!!
Don't go to him! There's nothing we can do!
Why?!

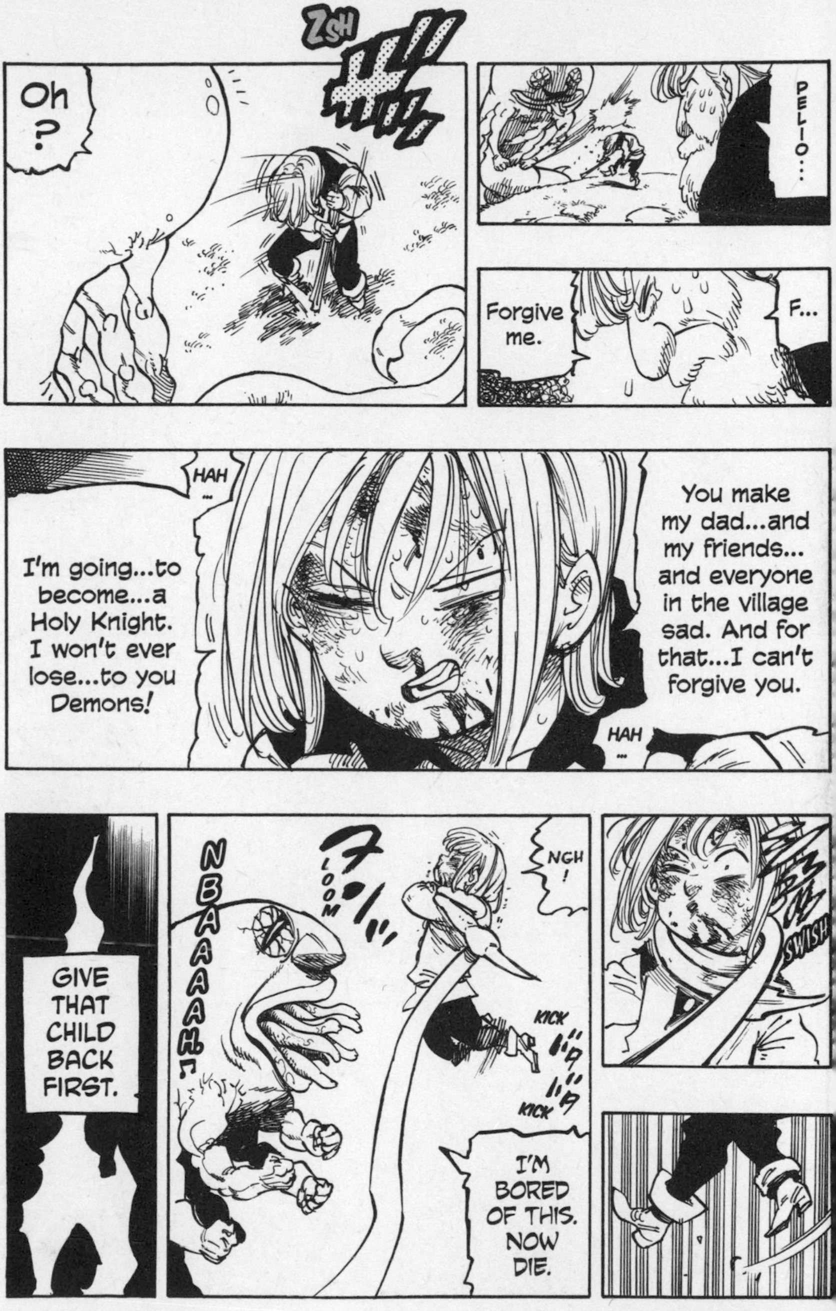
PELIO...
F...
Forgive me.
ZSH
Oh?
You make my dad...and my friends...and everyone in the village sad. And for that...I can't forgive you.
HAH...
I'm going...to become...a Holy Knight. I won't ever lose...to you Demons!
HAH...
SWISH
NGH!
FLOOM
NBAAAAAAH!
KICK
KICK
I'M BORED OF THIS. NOW DIE.
GIVE THAT CHILD BACK FIRST.

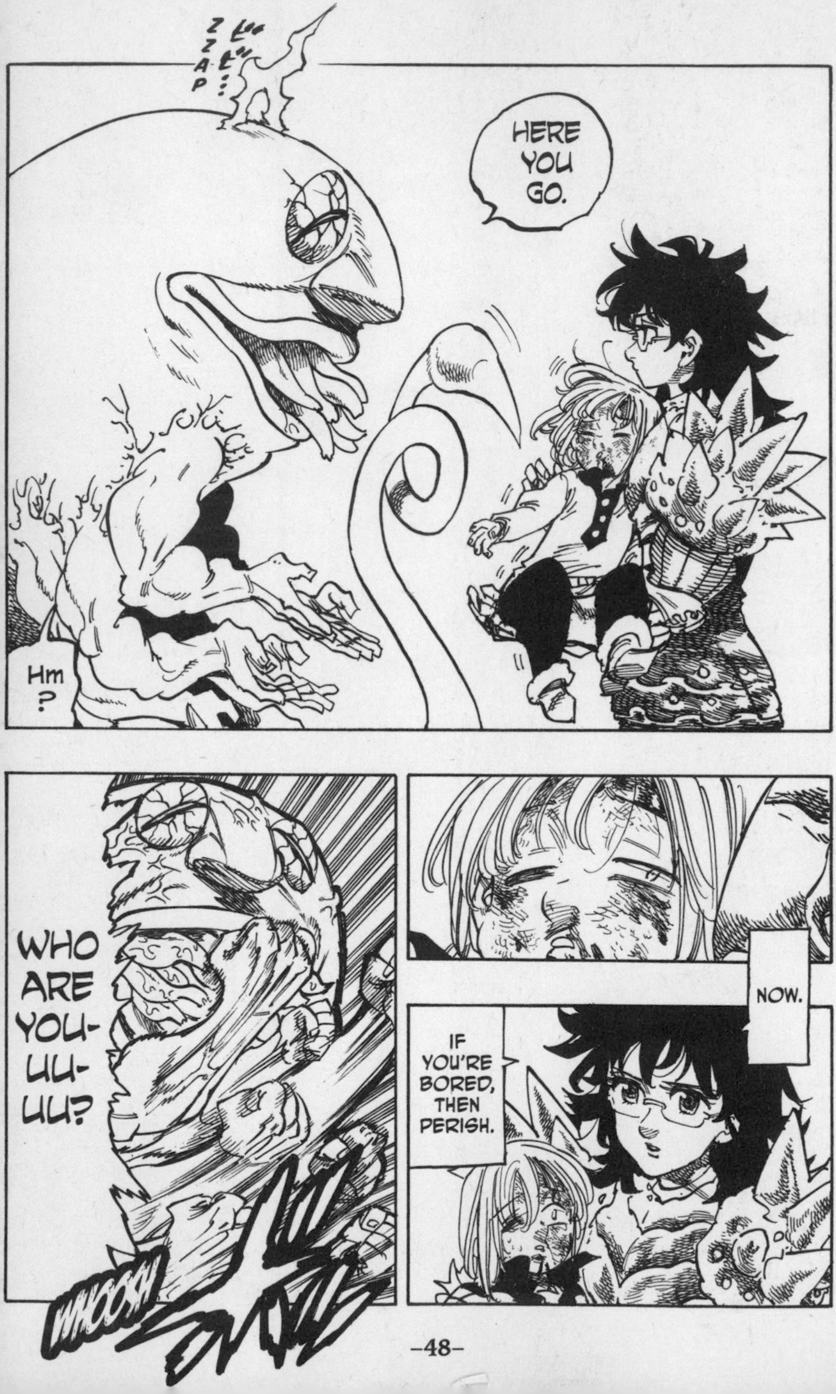

ZZZAP
HERE YOU GO.
Hm?
NOW.
IF YOU'RE BORED, THEN PERISH.
WHO ARE YOU-UU-UU?
WHOOSH

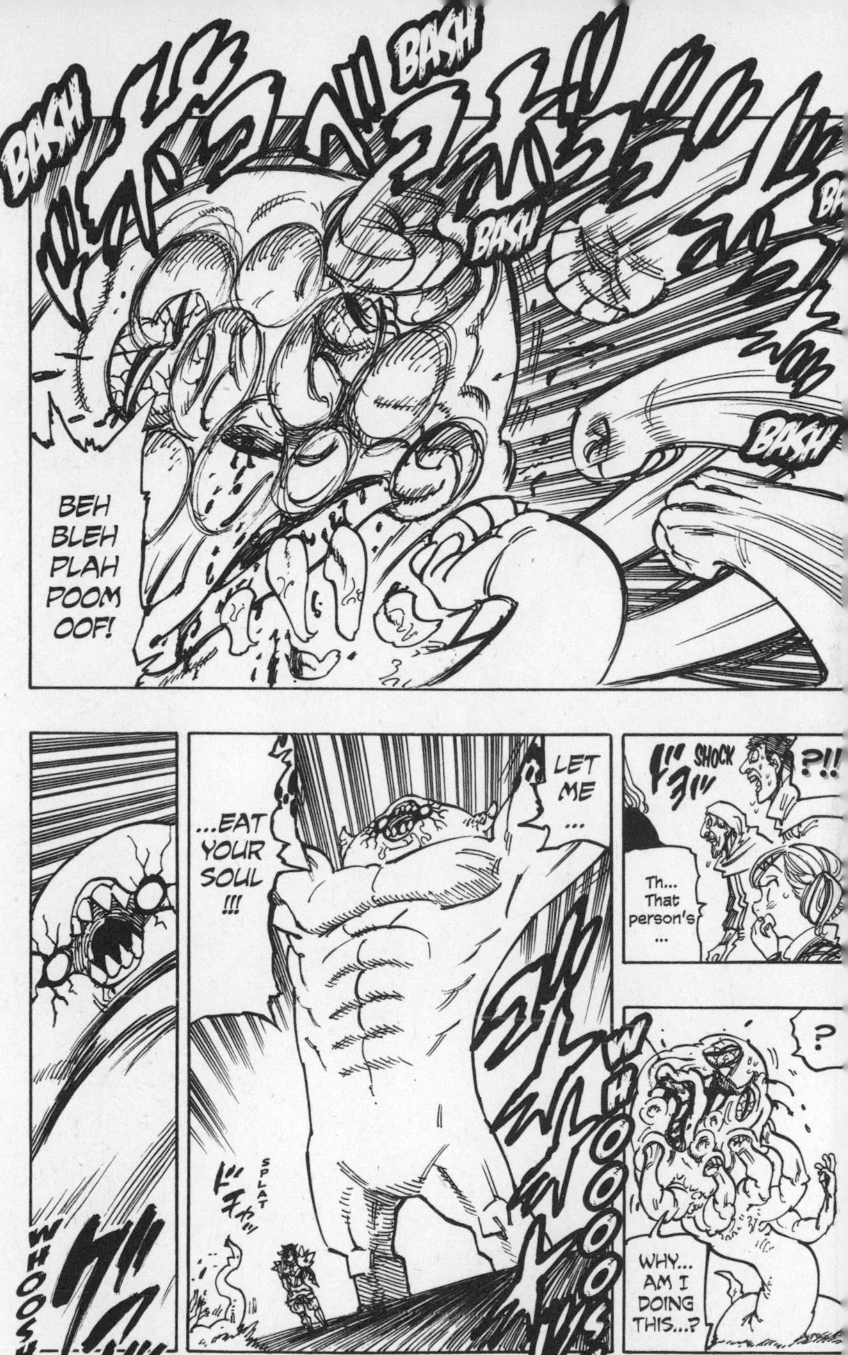
BASH
BASH
BASH
BASH
BEH BLEH PLAH POOM OOF!
SHOCK
?!!
Th... That person's ...
?
WHY... AM I DOING THIS...?
LET ME ...
...EAT YOUR SOUL !!!
WHOOOOOOOSH
SPLAT
WHOOSH

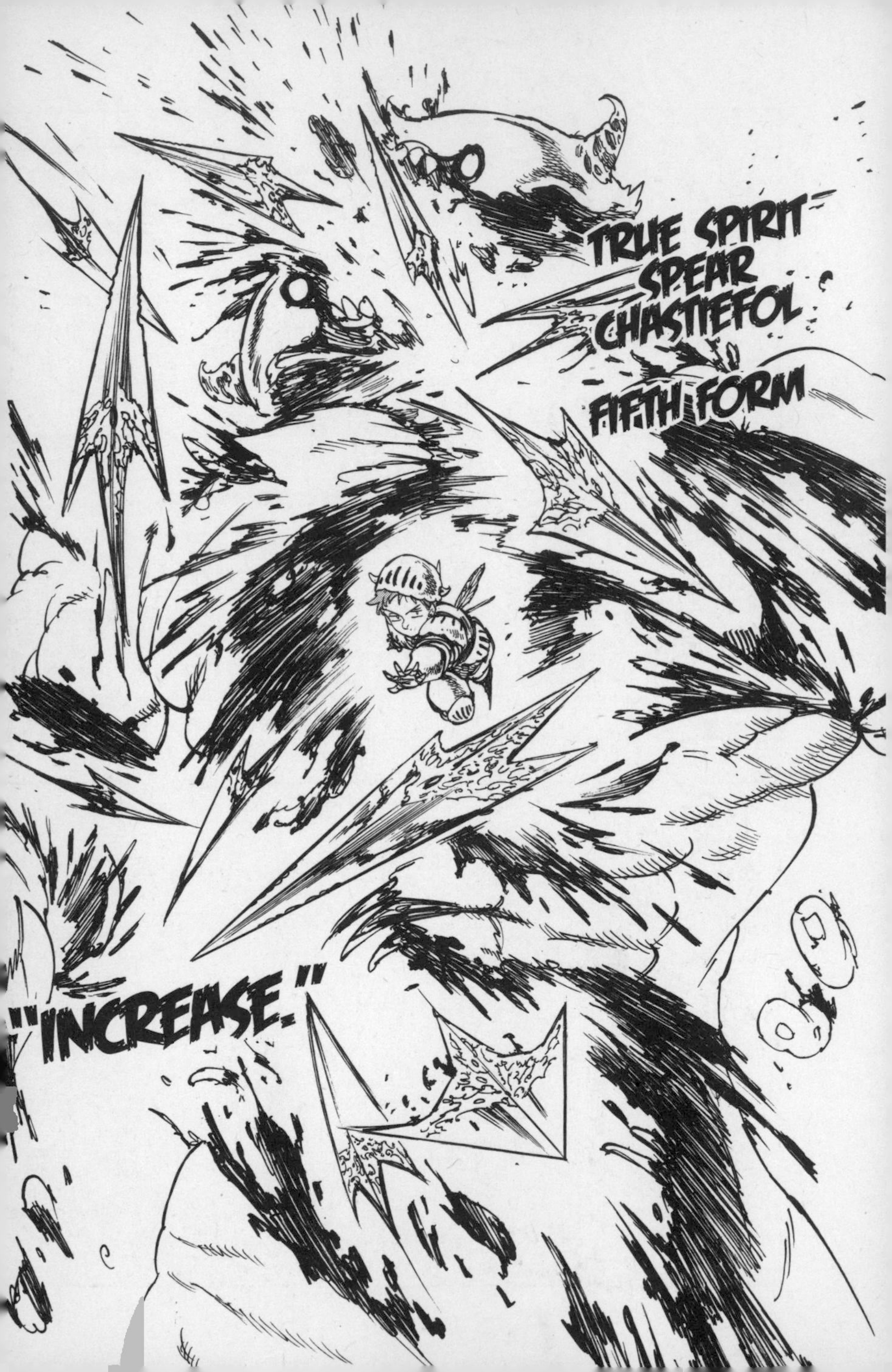
TRUE SPIRIT SPEAR CHASTIEFOL
FIFTH FORM
"INCREASE."

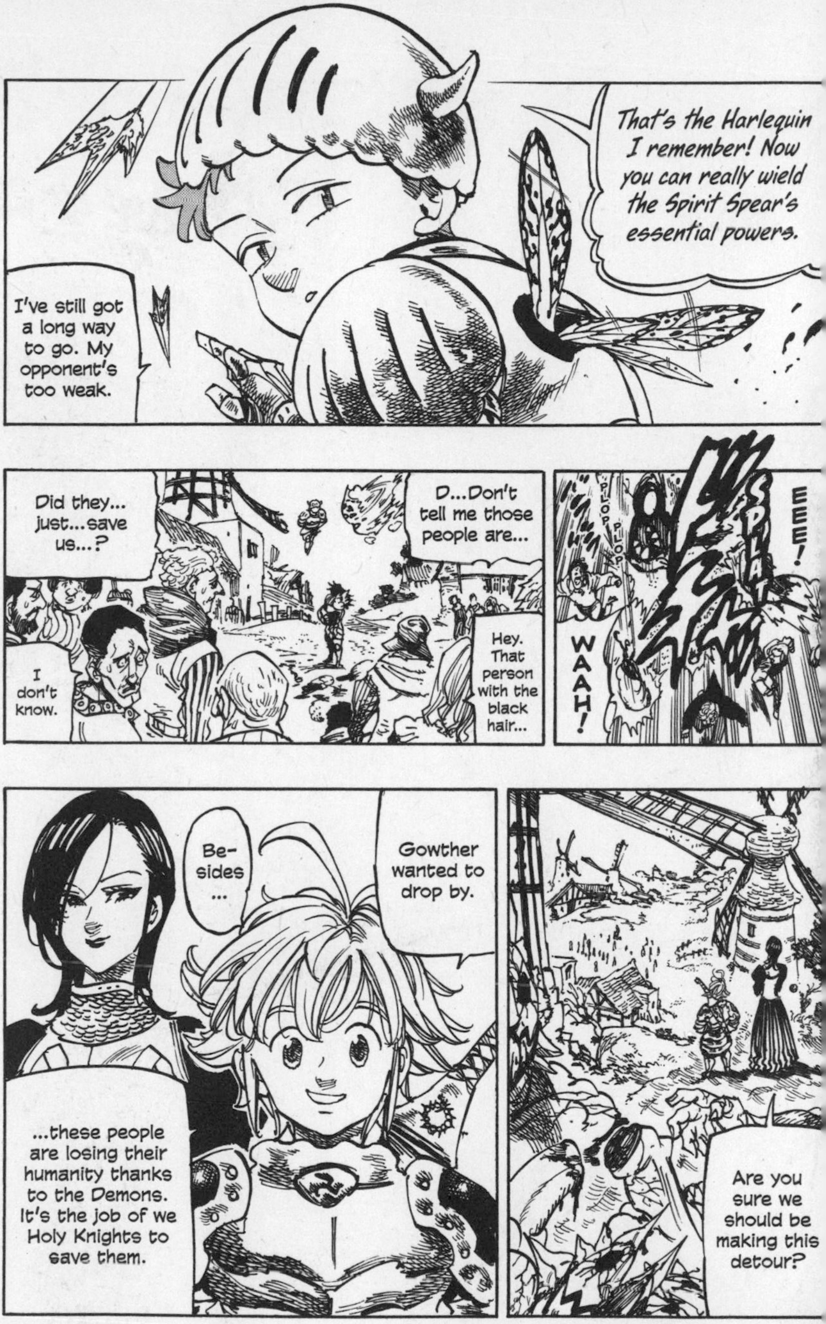

That's the Harlequin I remember! Now you can really wield the Spirit Spear's essential powers.
I've still got a long way to go. My opponent's too weak.
EEE!
SPLAT
PLOP PLOP
WAAH!
D...Don't tell me those people are...
Did they... just...save us...?
Hey. That person with the black hair...
I don't know.
Are you sure we should be making this detour?
Gowther wanted to drop by.
Be-sides ...
...these people are losing their humanity thanks to the Demons. It's the job of we Holy Knights to save them.

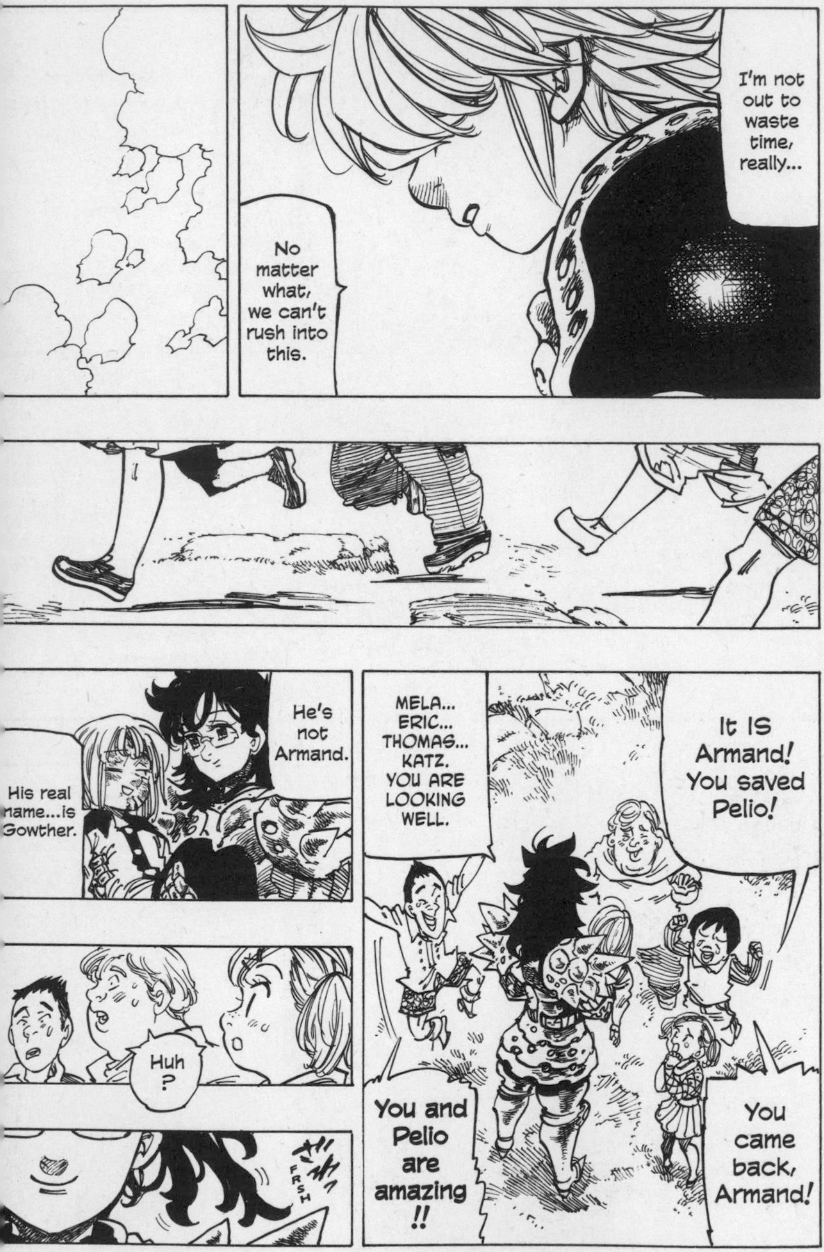
I'm not out to waste time, really...
No matter what, we can't rush into this.
It IS Armand! You saved Pelio!
MELA... ERIC... THOMAS... KATZ. YOU ARE LOOKING WELL.
You came back, Armand!
You and Pelio are amazing!!
He's not Armand.
His real name...is Gowther.
Huh?
FRSH

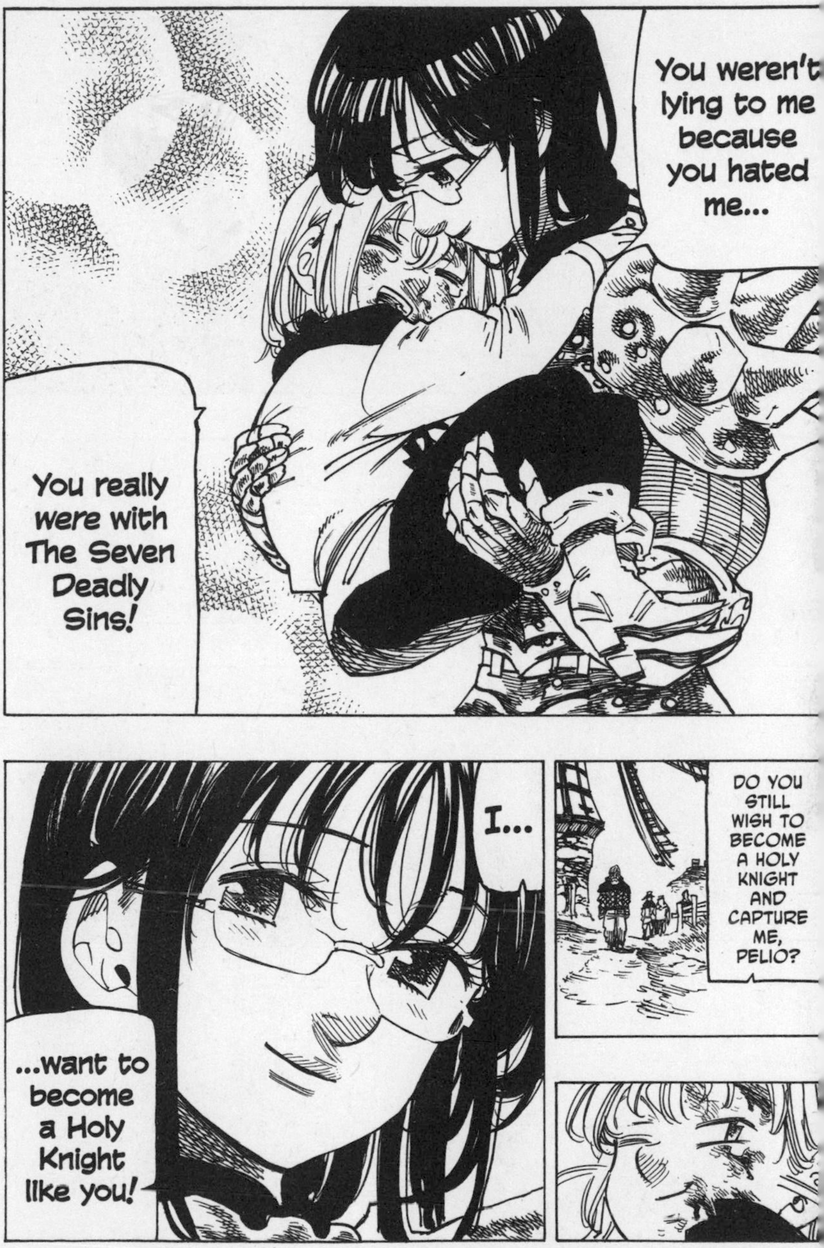
You weren't lying to me because you hated me...
You really were with The Seven Deadly Sins!
DO YOU STILL WISH TO BECOME A HOLY KNIGHT AND CAPTURE ME, PELIO?
I...
...want to become a Holy Knight like you!

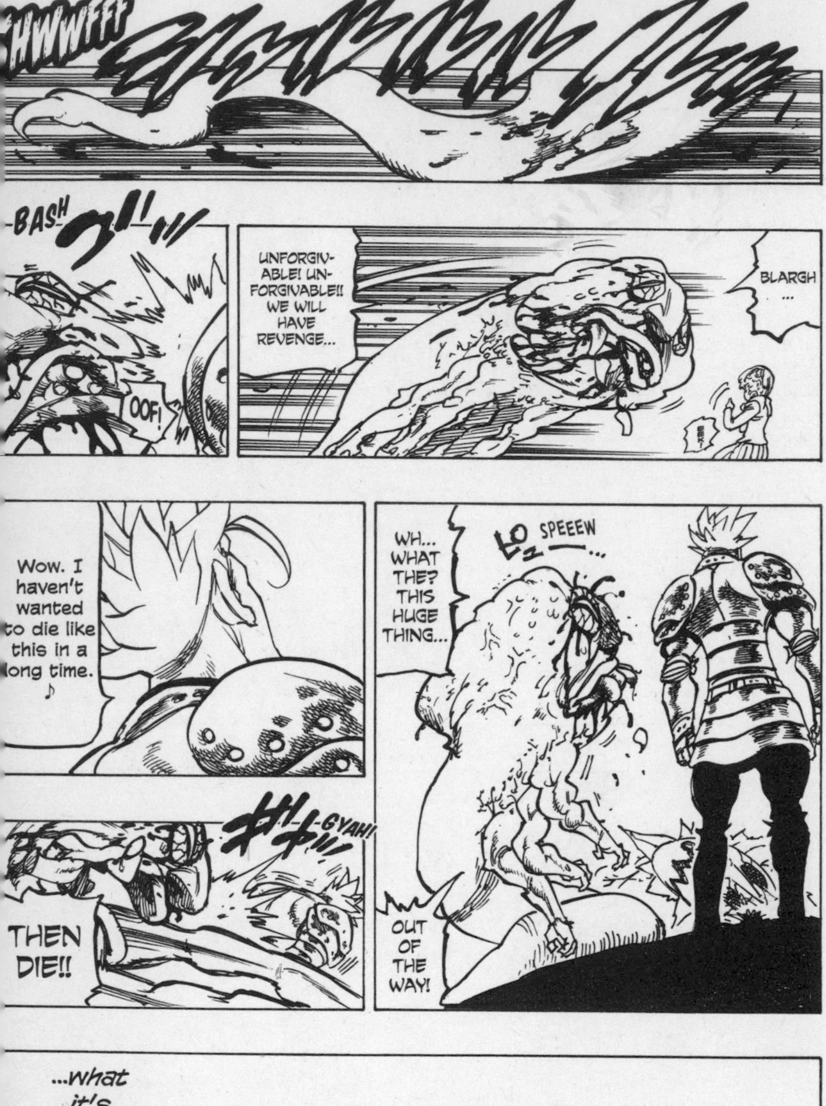
HWWFFF
BLARGH ...
UNFORGIVABLE! UNFORGIVABLE!! WE WILL HAVE REVENGE...
BASH
OOF!
SPEEEW...
WH... WHAT THE? THIS HUGE THING...
OUT OF THE WAY!
Wow. I haven't wanted to die like this in a long time. ♪
GYAH!
THEN DIE!!
How could you know... ♫
...what it's like to let the woman you love die twice?

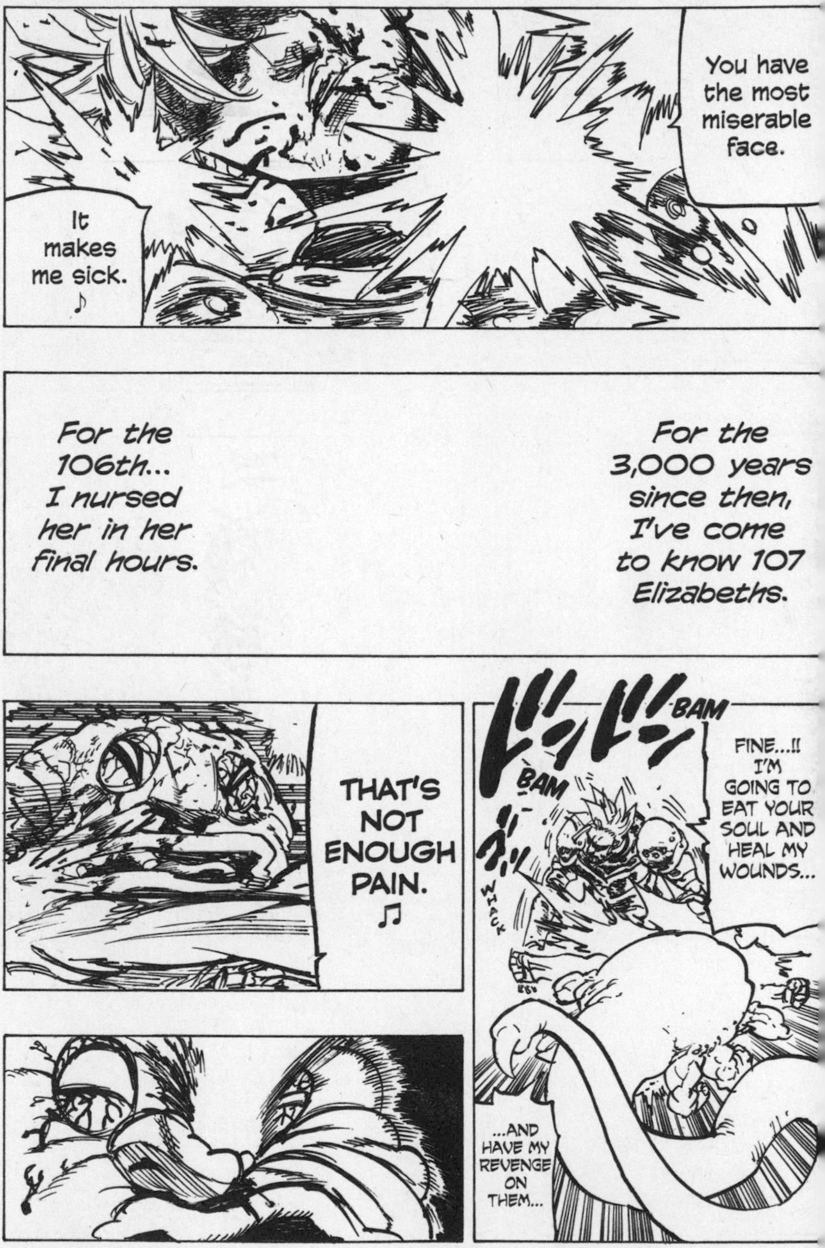

You have the most miserable face.
It makes me sick. ♪
For the 3,000 years since then, I've come to know 107 Elizabeths.
For the 106th... I nursed her in her final hours.
BAM
BAM
FINE...!! I'M GOING TO EAT YOUR SOUL AND HEAL MY WOUNDS...
WHACK
...AND HAVE MY REVENGE ON THEM...
THAT'S NOT ENOUGH PAIN. ♫

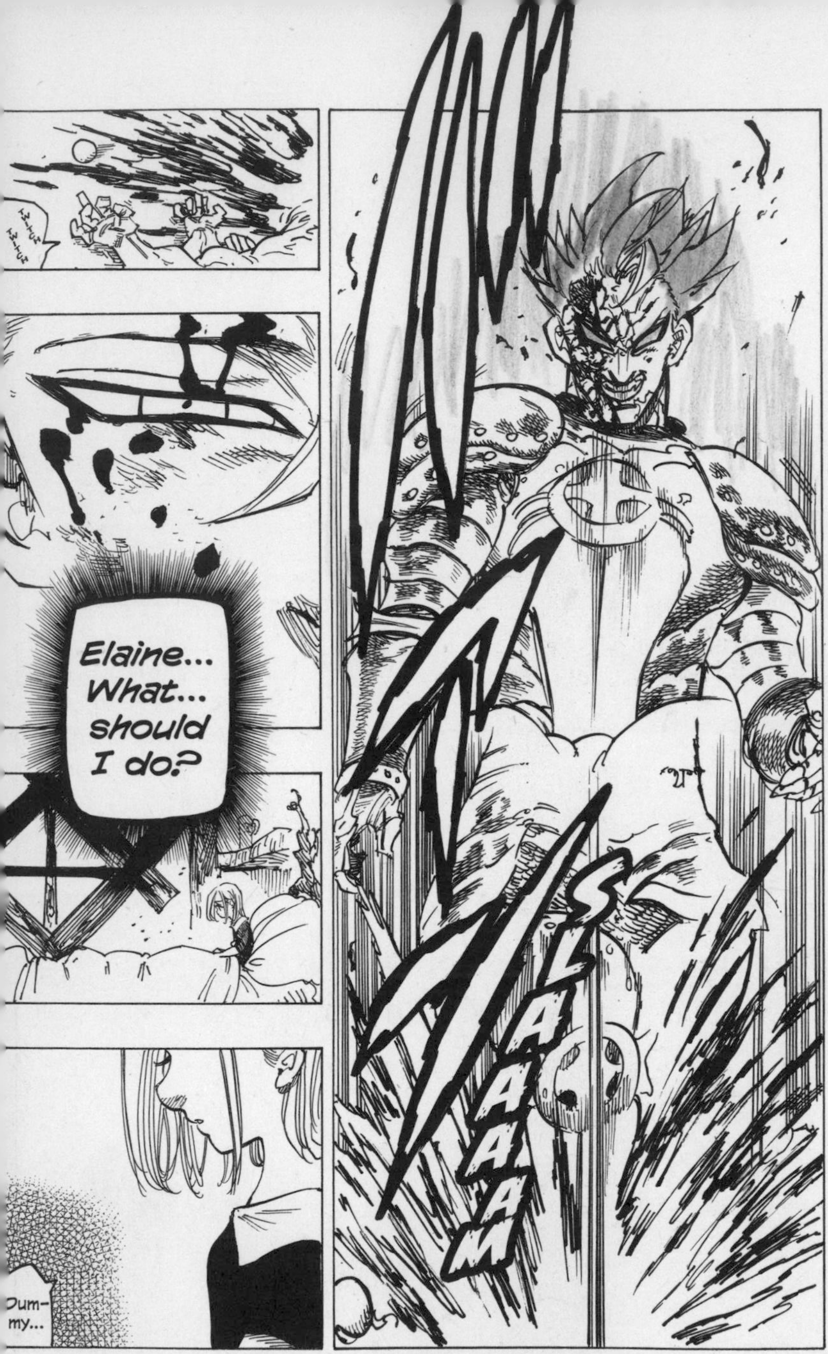
SLAAAAAAM
TWITCH TWITCH
Elaine... What... should I do?
Dum-my...

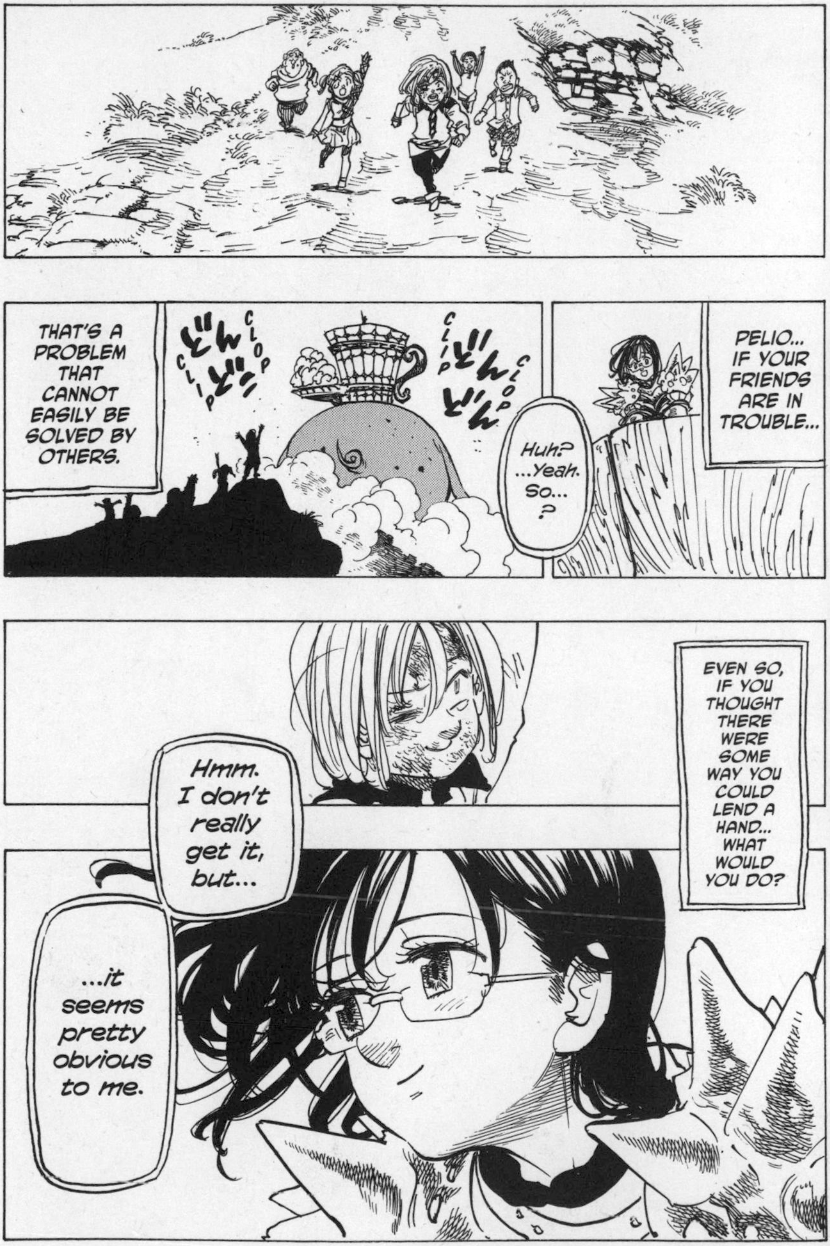
PELIO... IF YOUR FRIENDS ARE IN TROUBLE...
Huh? ...Yeah. So... ?
CLIP CLOP
CLIP CLOP
THAT'S A PROBLEM THAT CANNOT EASILY BE SOLVED BY OTHERS.
EVEN SO, IF YOU THOUGHT THERE WERE SOME WAY YOU COULD LEND A HAND... WHAT WOULD YOU DO?
Hmm. I don't really get it, but...
...it seems pretty obvious to me.

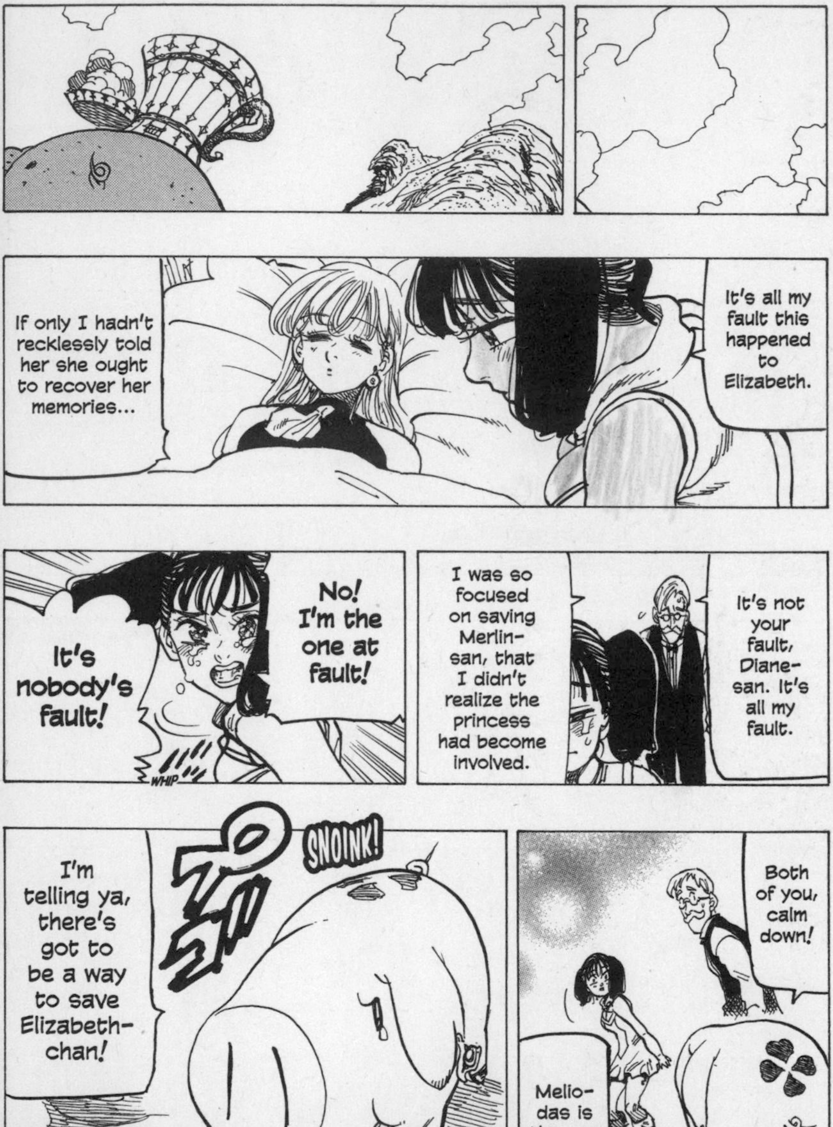

It's all my fault this happened to Elizabeth.
If only I hadn't recklessly told her she ought to recover her memories...
It's not your fault, Diane-san. It's all my fault.
I was so focused on saving Merlin-san, that I didn't realize the princess had become involved.
No! I'm the one at fault!
It's nobody's fault!
WHIP
Both of you, calm down!
Melio-das is the one really suffer-ing.
SNOINK!
I'm telling ya, there's got to be a way to save Elizabeth-chan!

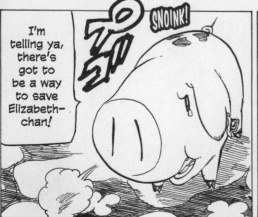

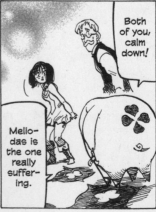

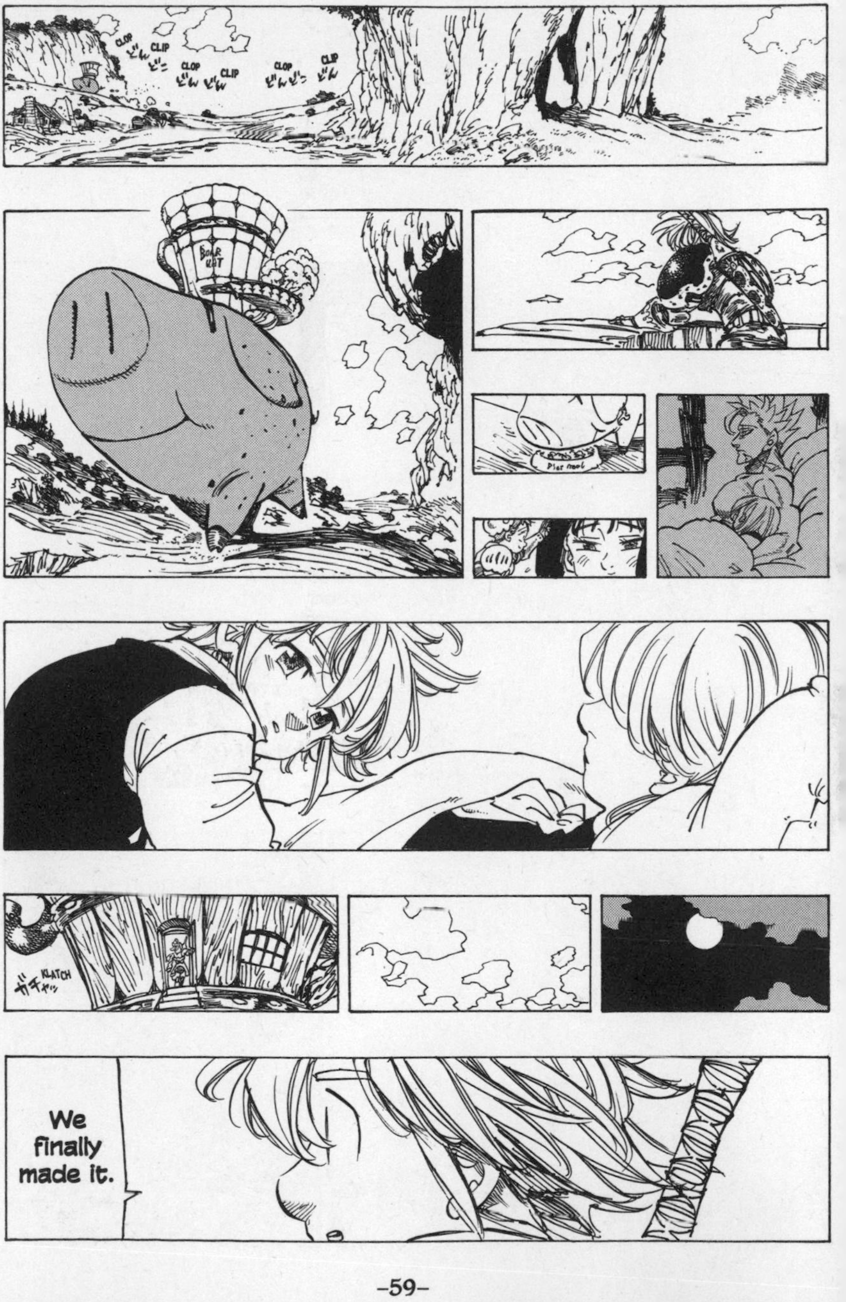
CLIP
CLOP
CLIP
CLOP
CLIP
CLOP
BOAR HAT
KLATCH
ガチャッ
We finally made it.

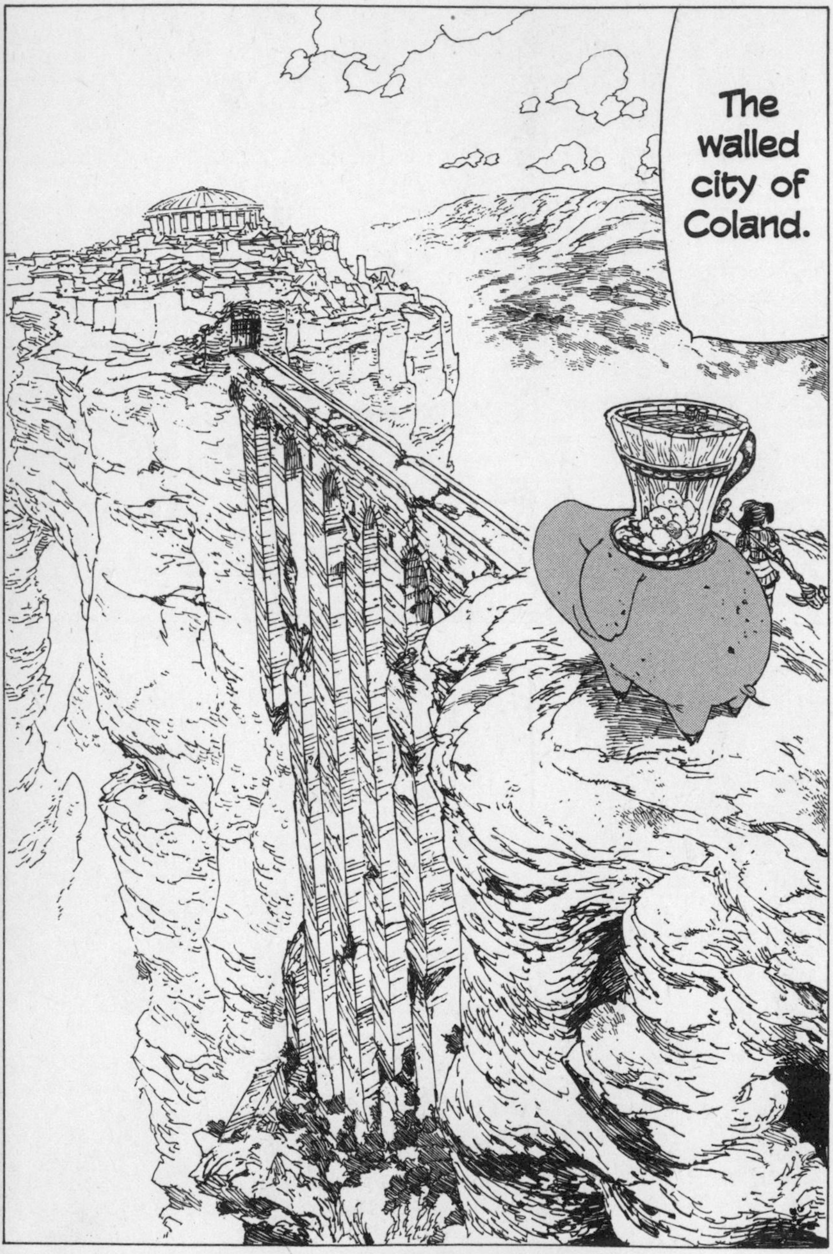
The walled city of Coland.

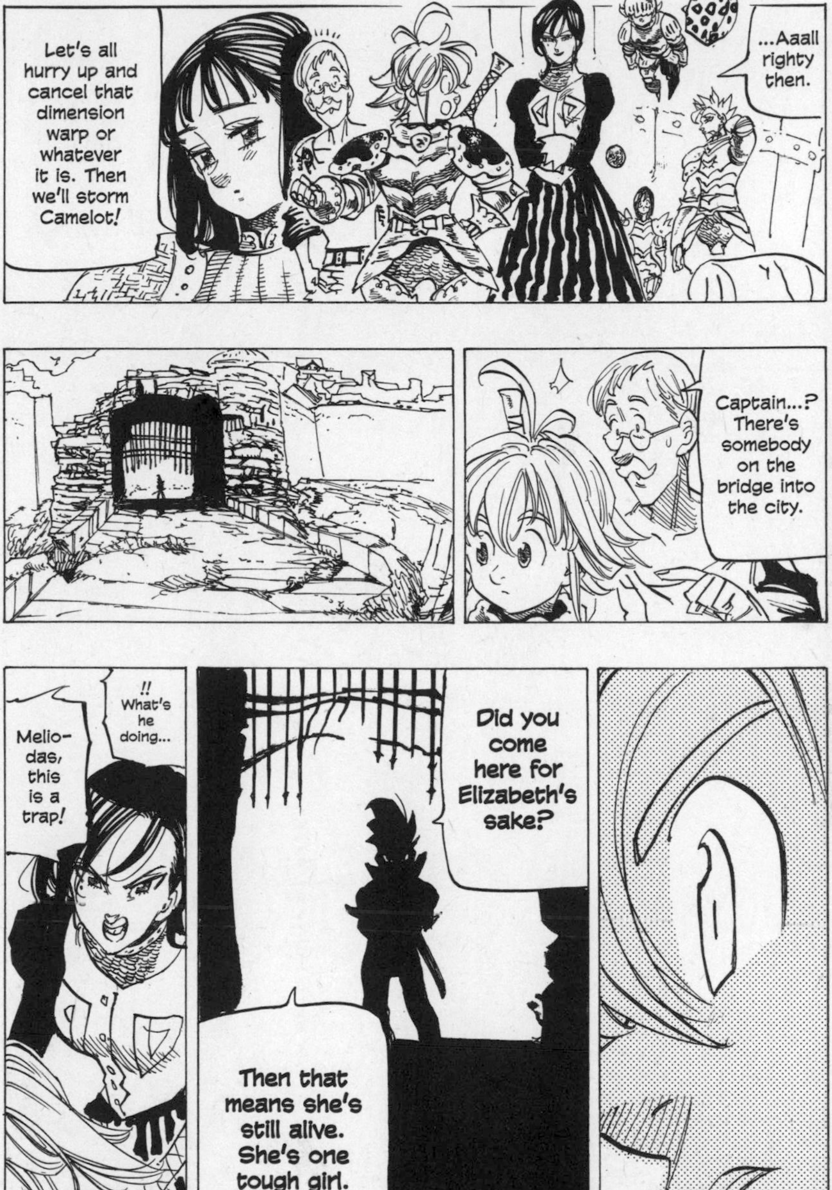
...Aaall righty then.
Let's all hurry up and cancel that dimension warp or whatever it is. Then we'll storm Camelot!
Captain...? There's somebody on the bridge into the city.
Did you come here for Elizabeth's sake?
Then that means she's still alive. She's one tough girl.
!! What's he doing...
Melio-das, this is a trap!

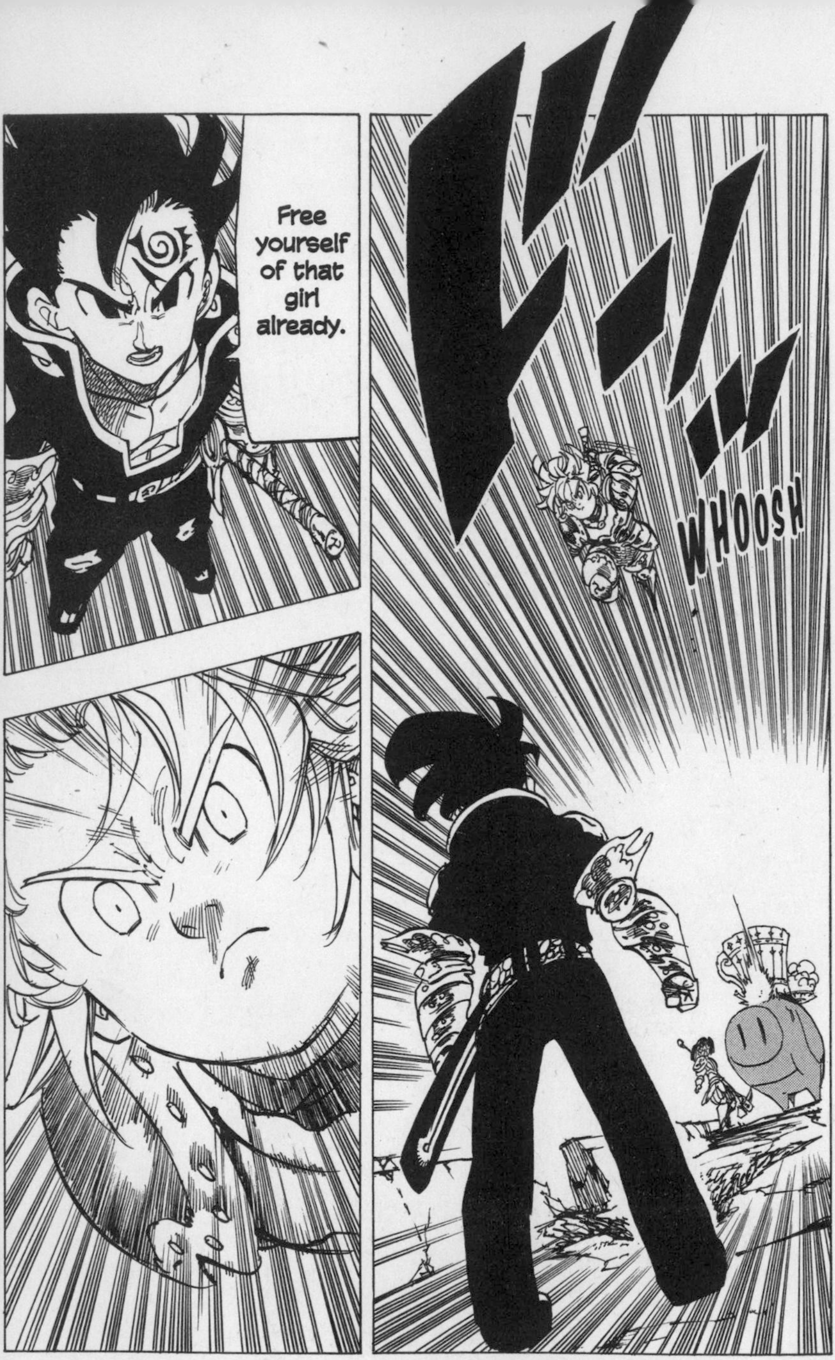

WHOOSH
Free yourself of that girl already.

Chapter 226 - Untamed

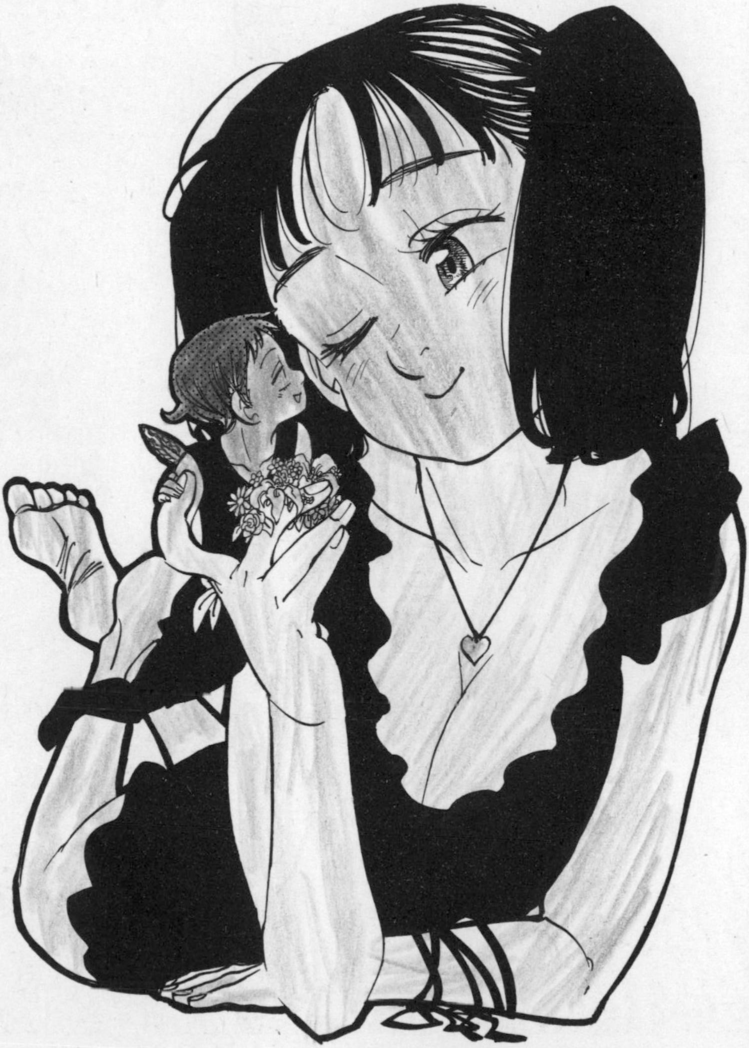

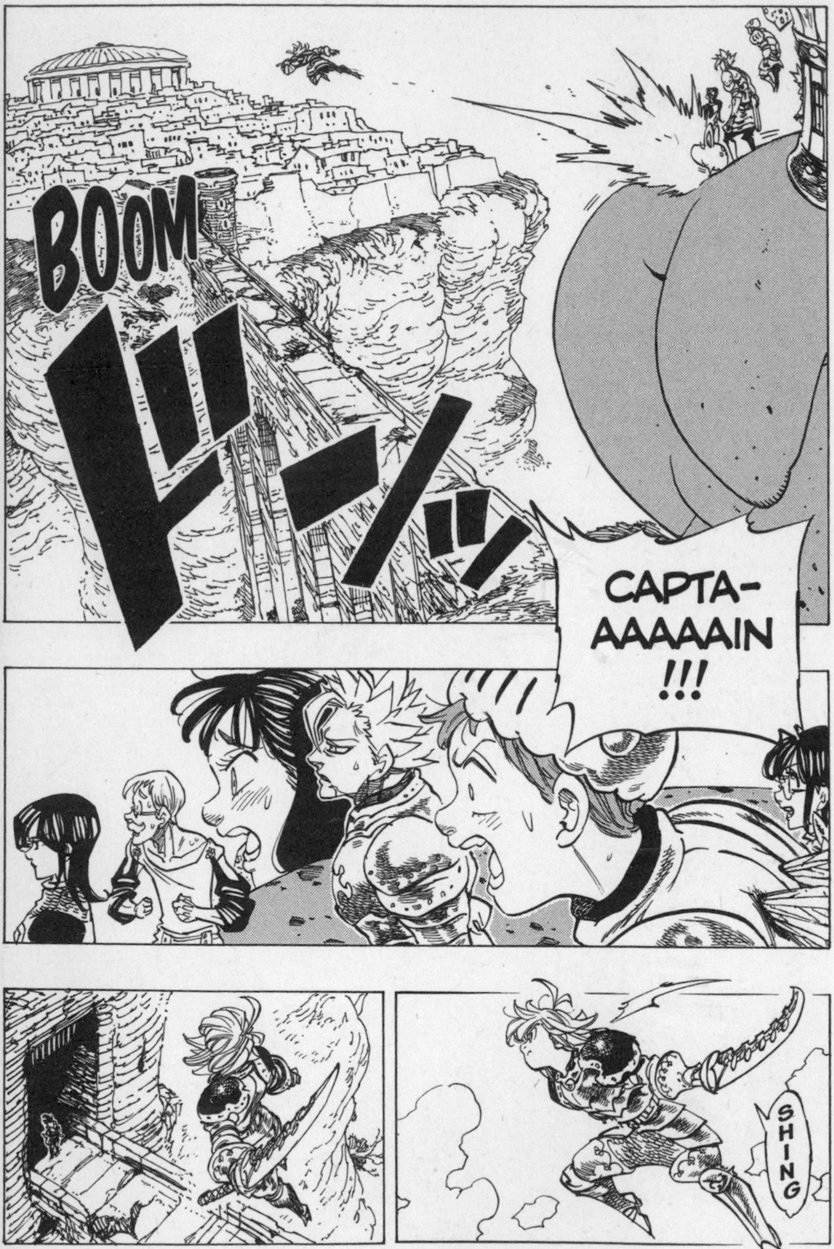
BOOM
ドーンッ
CAPTA-AAAAAIN!!!
SHING

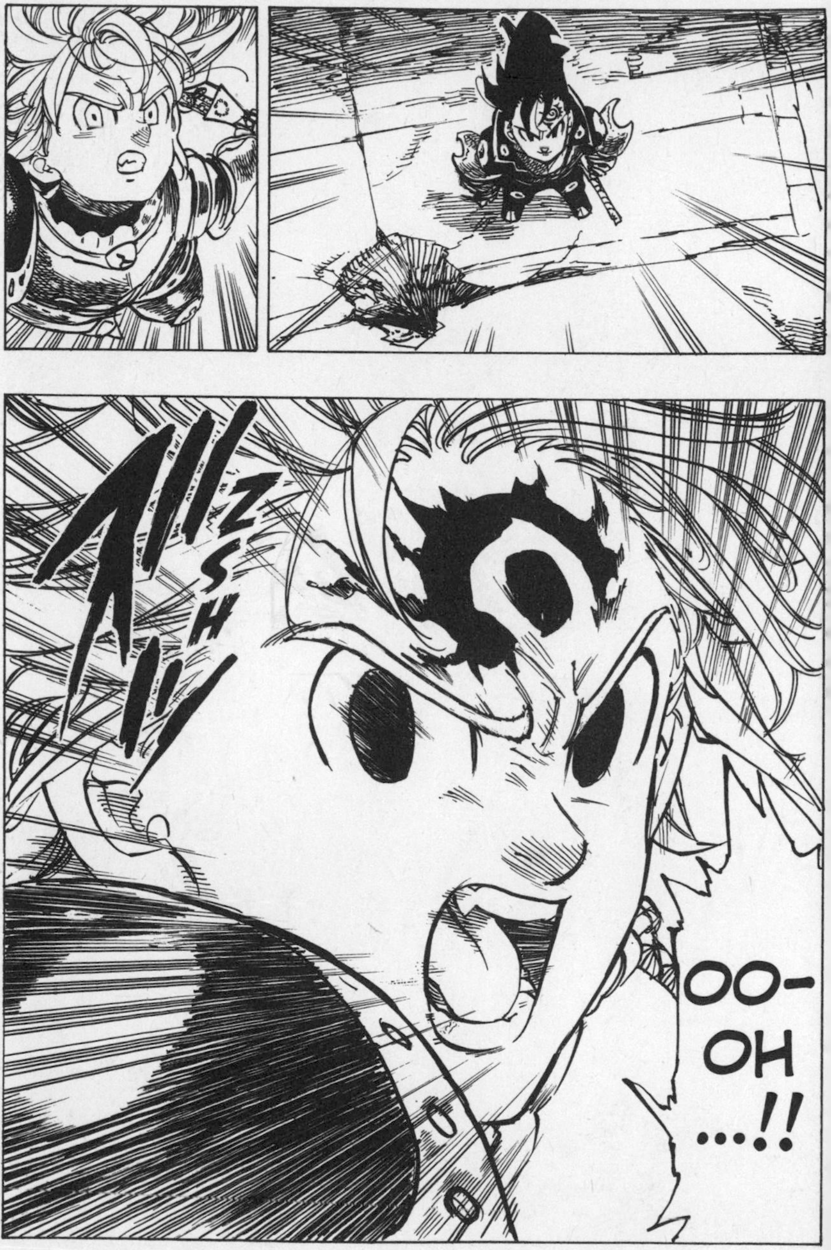
ZSH
OO-OH...!!

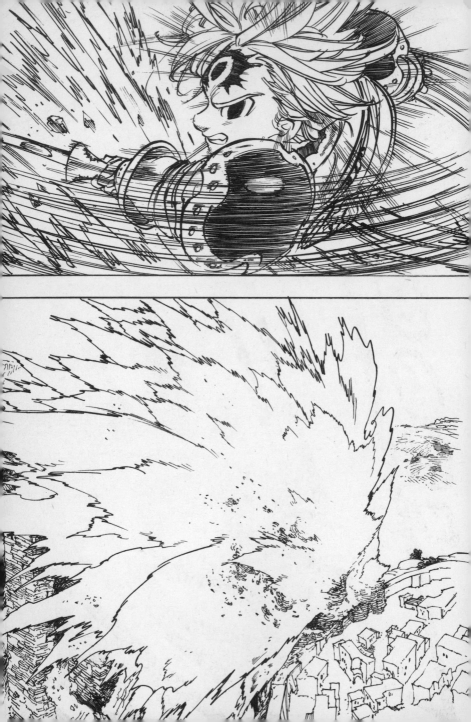

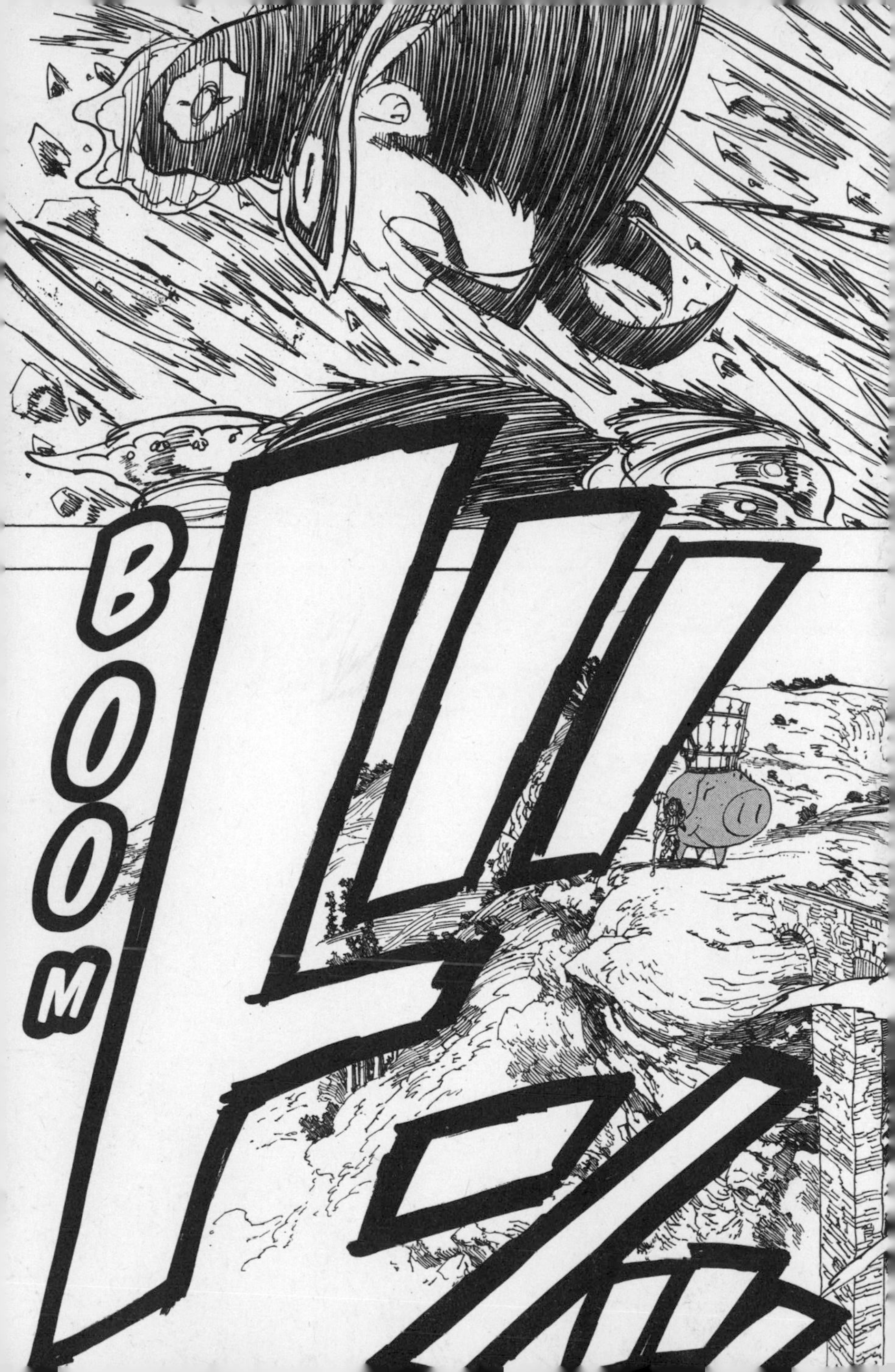
BOOM

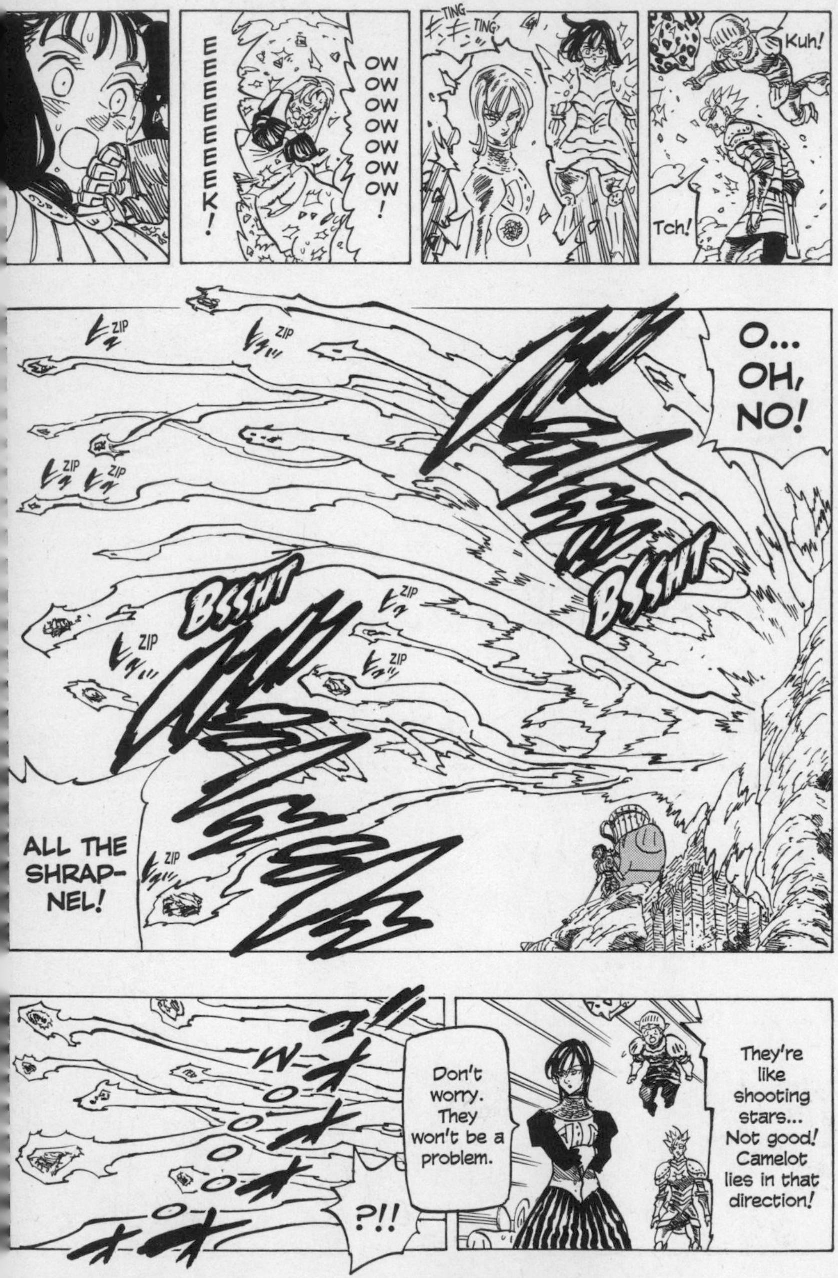
Kuh!
Tch!
TING
TING
OW OW OW OW OW OW OW!
EEEEEEEK!
O... OH, NO!
BSSHT
ZIP
ZIP
BSSHT
ZIP
ZIP
ZIP
ZIP
ZIP
ALL THE SHRAP-NEL!
They're like shooting stars... Not good! Camelot lies in that direction!
Don't worry. They won't be a problem.
?!!

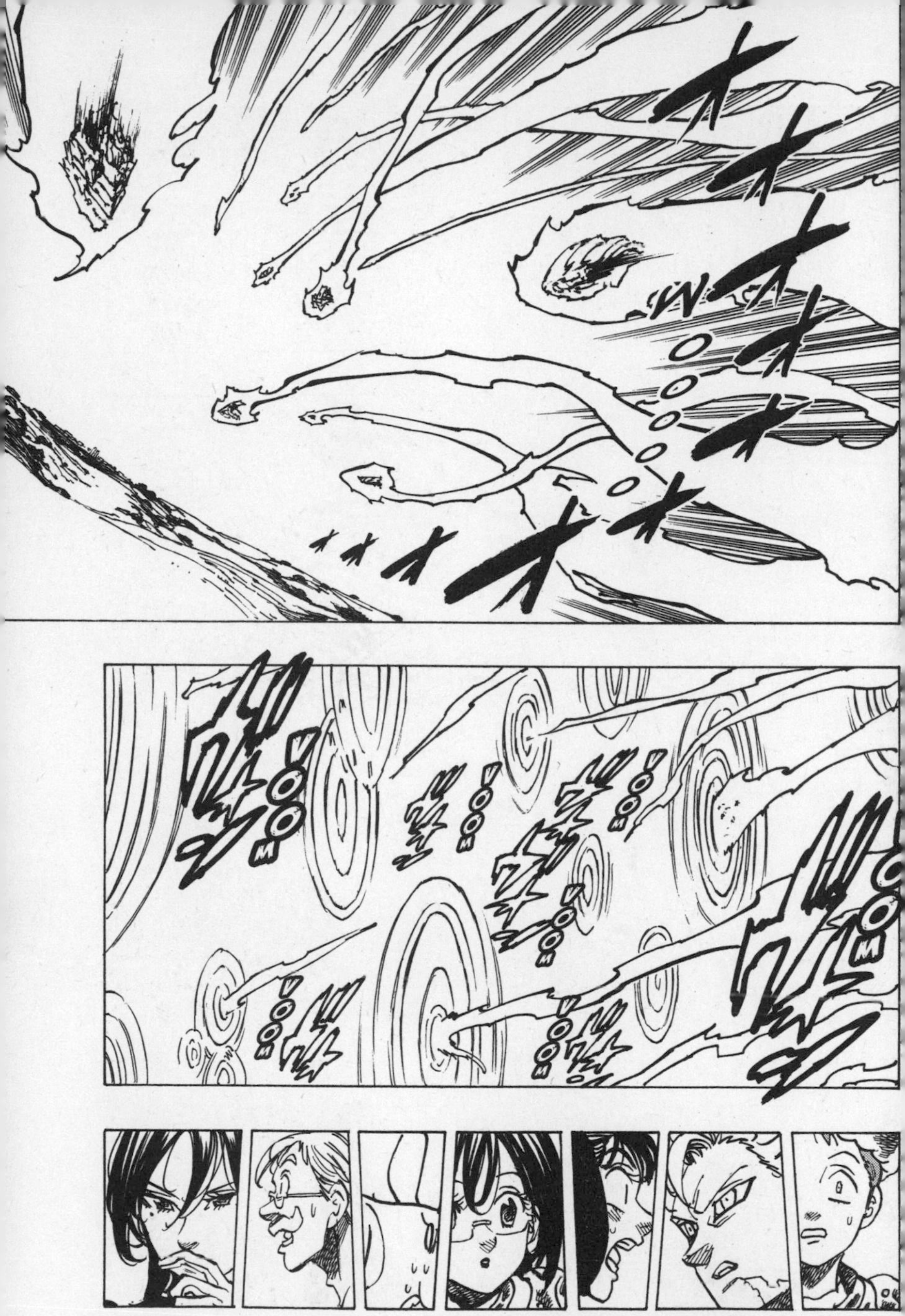
WOOOOO
VOOOM
VOOOM
VOOOM
VOOOM
VOOOM
VOOOM
VOOOM

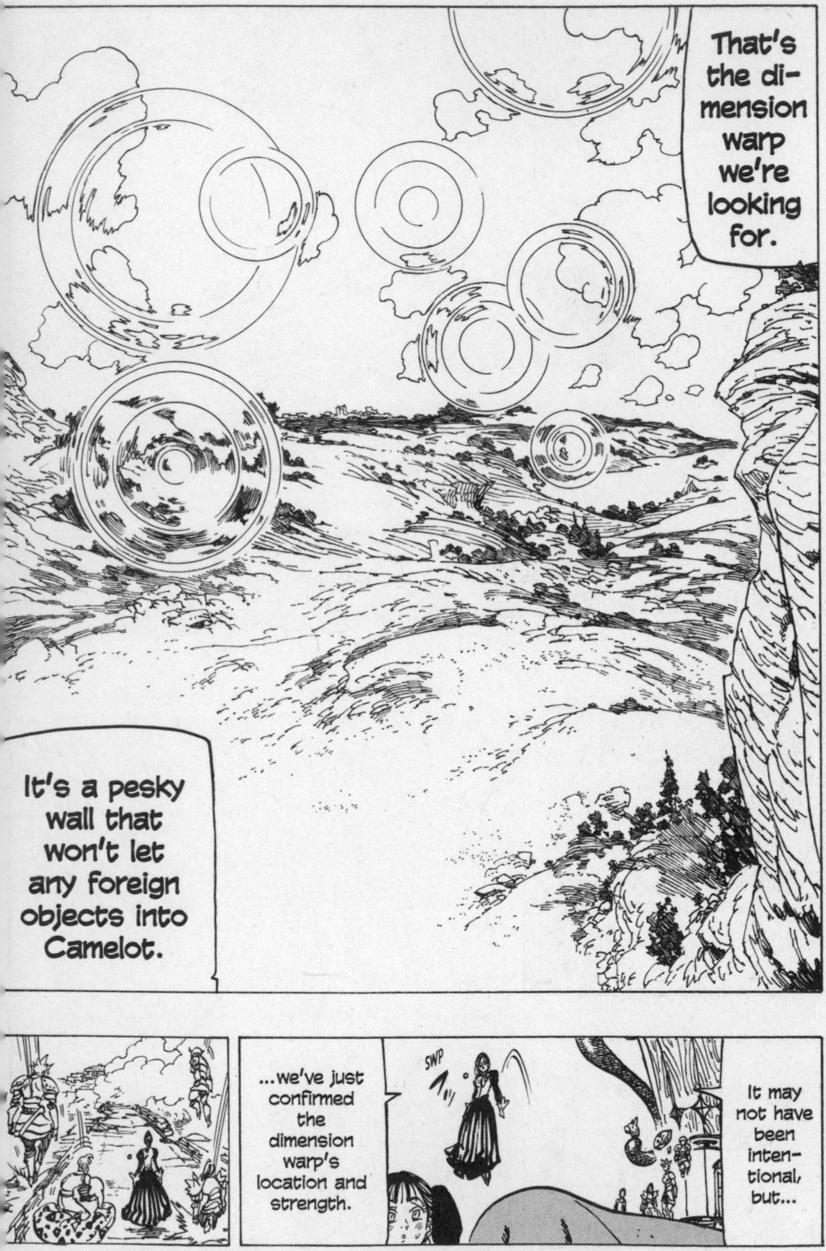
That's the dimension warp we're looking for.
It's a pesky wall that won't let any foreign objects into Camelot.
It may not have been intentional, but...
SWP
...we've just confirmed the dimension warp's location and strength.

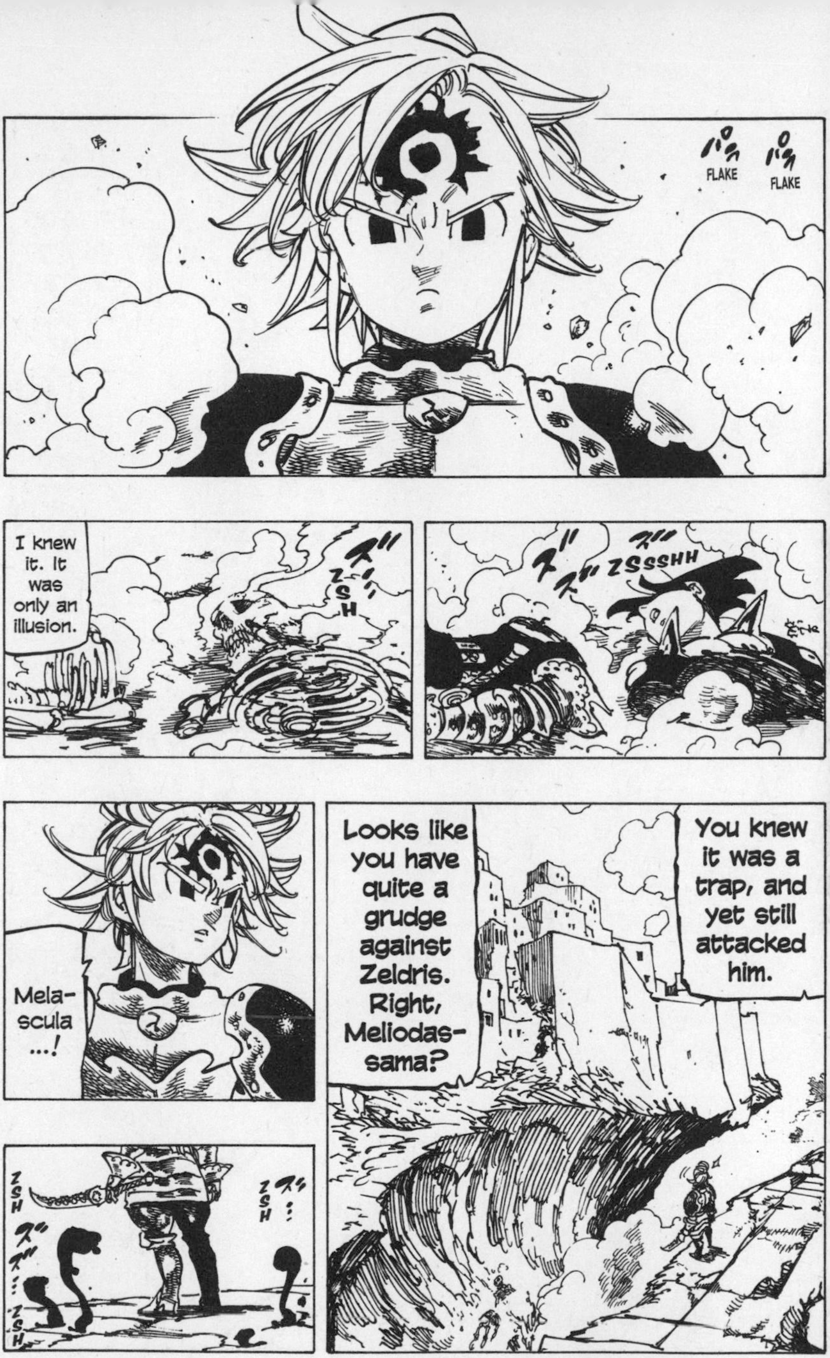
FLAKE
FLAKE
ZSSSHH
I knew it. It was only an illusion.
ZSH
You knew it was a trap, and yet still attacked him.
Looks like you have quite a grudge against Zeldris. Right, Meliodas-sama?
Mela-scula ....!
ZSH
ZSH
ZSH

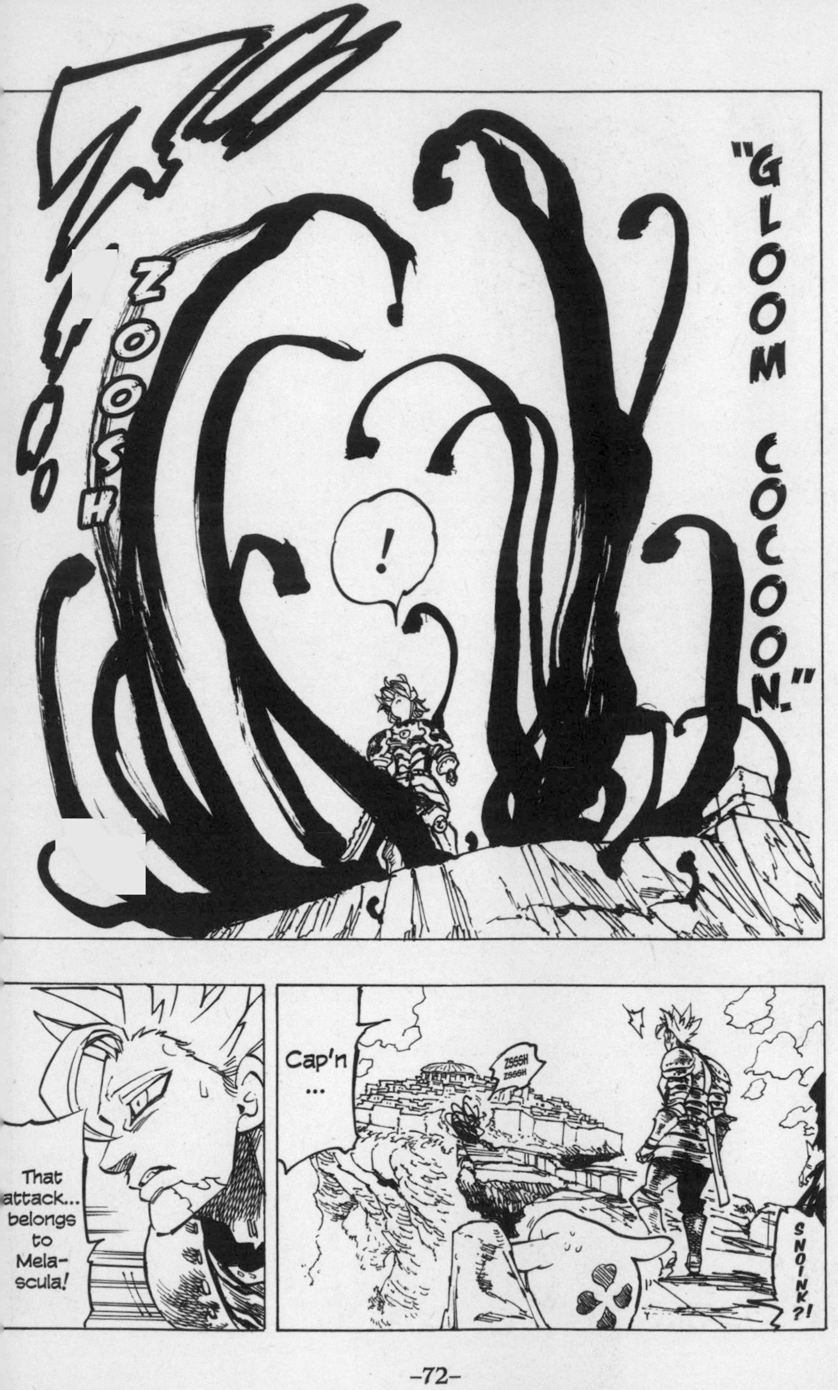
"GLOOM COCOON."
!
ZOOOSH
Cap'n ...
ZSSSH ZSSSH
SNOINK?!
That attack... belongs to Melascula!

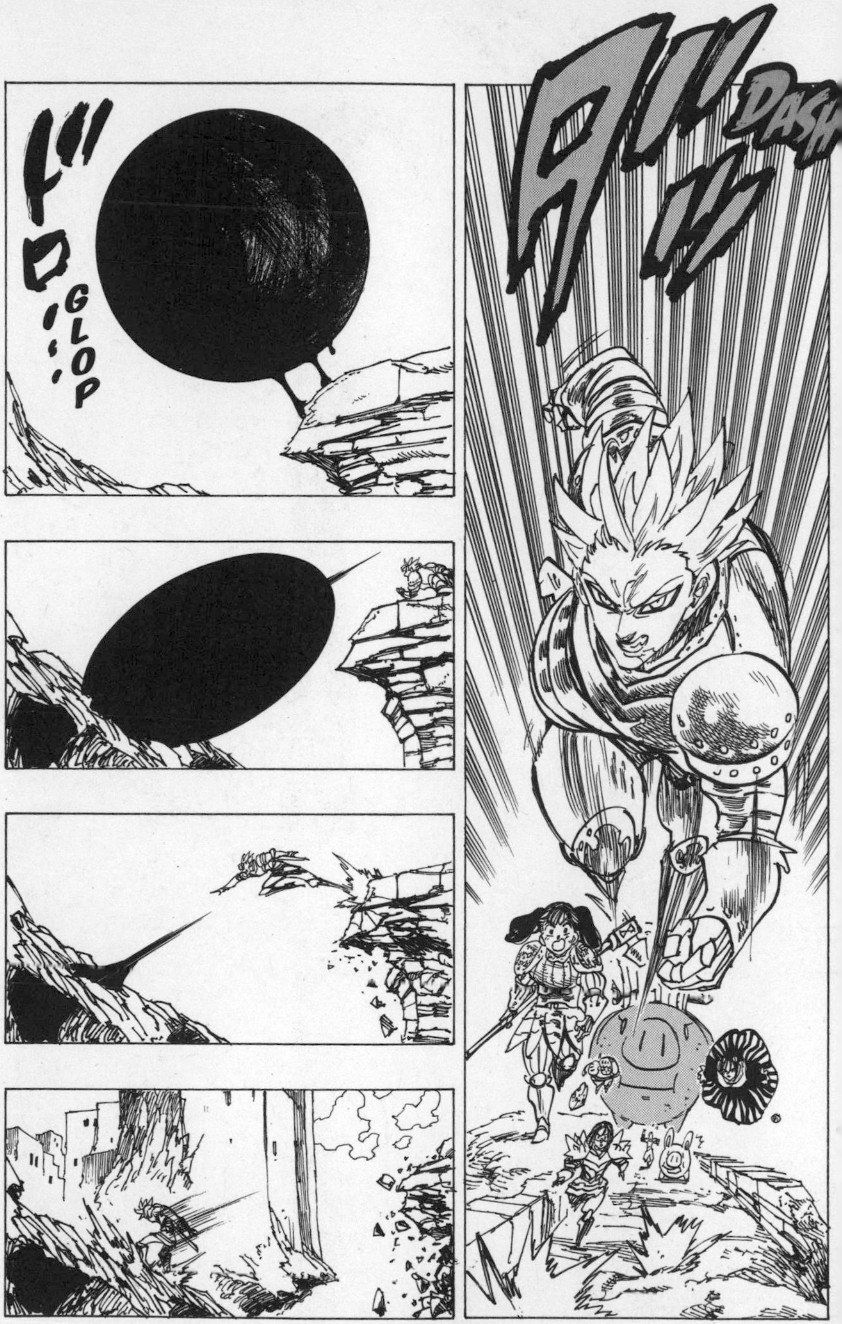
ダッ
DASH
ドロ
GLOP

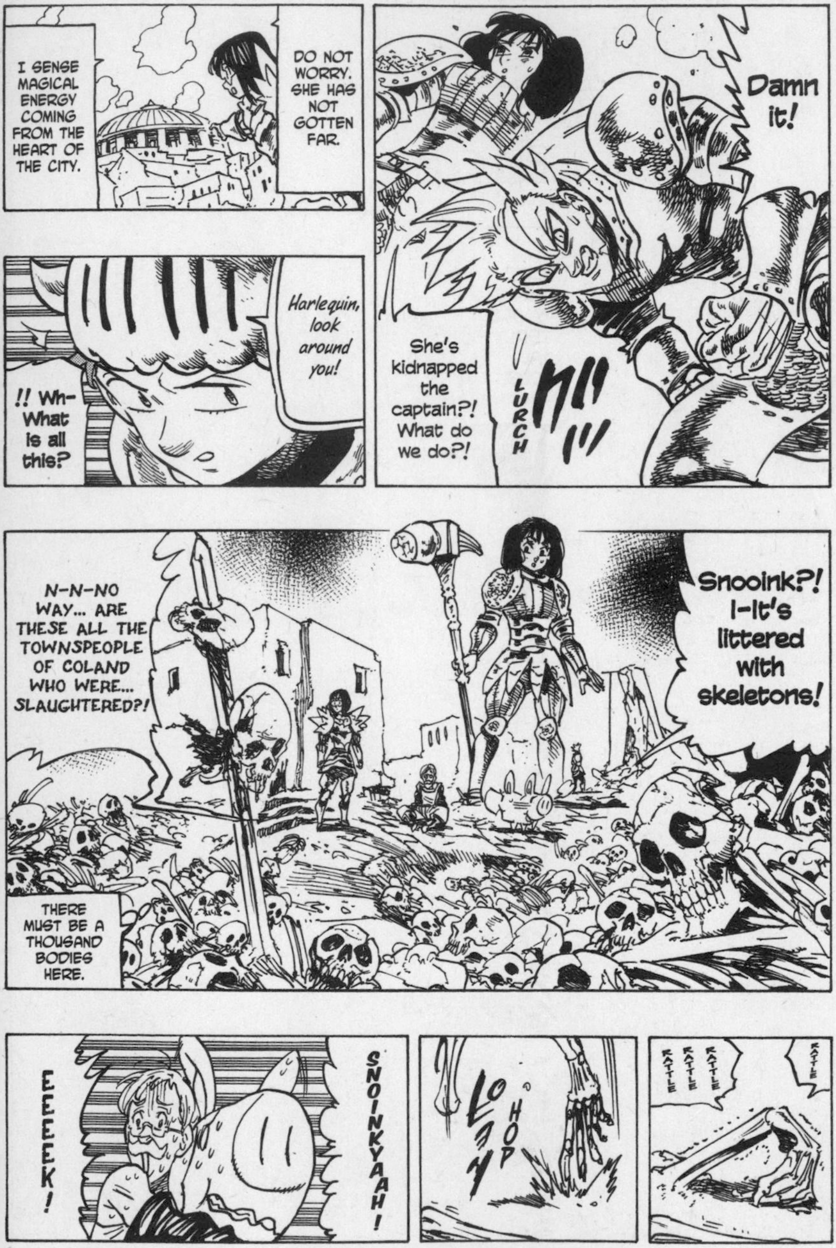
Damn it!
She's kidnapped the captain?! What do we do?!
LURCH
DO NOT WORRY. SHE HAS NOT GOTTEN FAR.
I SENSE MAGICAL ENERGY COMING FROM THE HEART OF THE CITY.
Harlequin, look around you!
!! Wh-What is all this?
Snooink?! I-It's littered with skeletons!
N-N-NO WAY... ARE THESE ALL THE TOWNSPEOPLE OF COLAND WHO WERE... SLAUGHTERED?!
THERE MUST BE A THOUSAND BODIES HERE.
RATTLE
RATTLE
RATTLE
RATTLE
HOP
SNOINKYAAH!
EEEEEK!

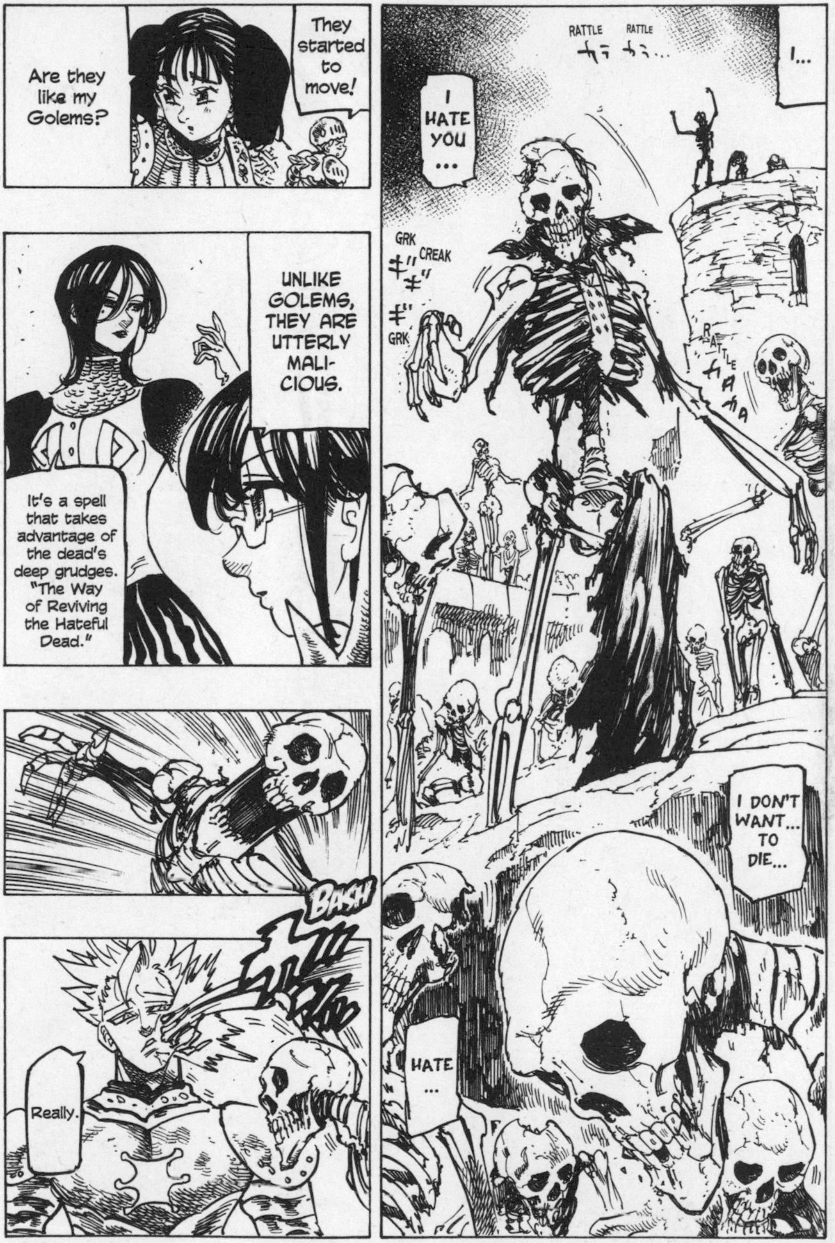
I...
RATTLE RATTLE
I HATE YOU...
GRK CREAK
RATTLE
GRK
I DON'T WANT... TO DIE...
HATE...
They started to move!
Are they like my Golems?
UNLIKE GOLEMS, THEY ARE UTTERLY MALICIOUS.
It's a spell that takes advantage of the dead's deep grudges. "The Way of Reviving the Hateful Dead."
BASH
Really.

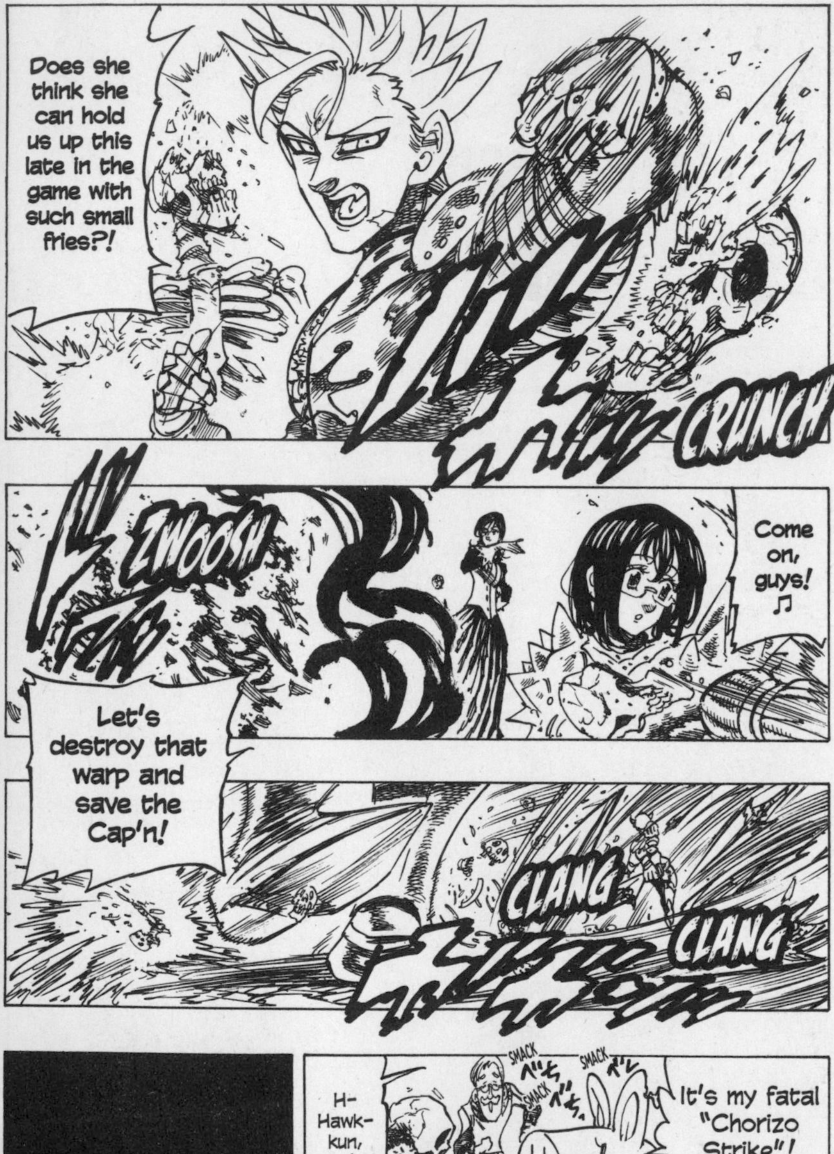
Does she think she can hold us up this late in the game with such small fries?!
CRUNCH
Come on, guys! ♫
ZWOOSH
Let's destroy that warp and save the Cap'n!
CLANG
CLANG
SMACK
SMACK
SMACK
It's my fatal "Chorizo Strike"! Hwa ta ta ta taaaa!
H-Hawk-kun, you're amaz-ing!!

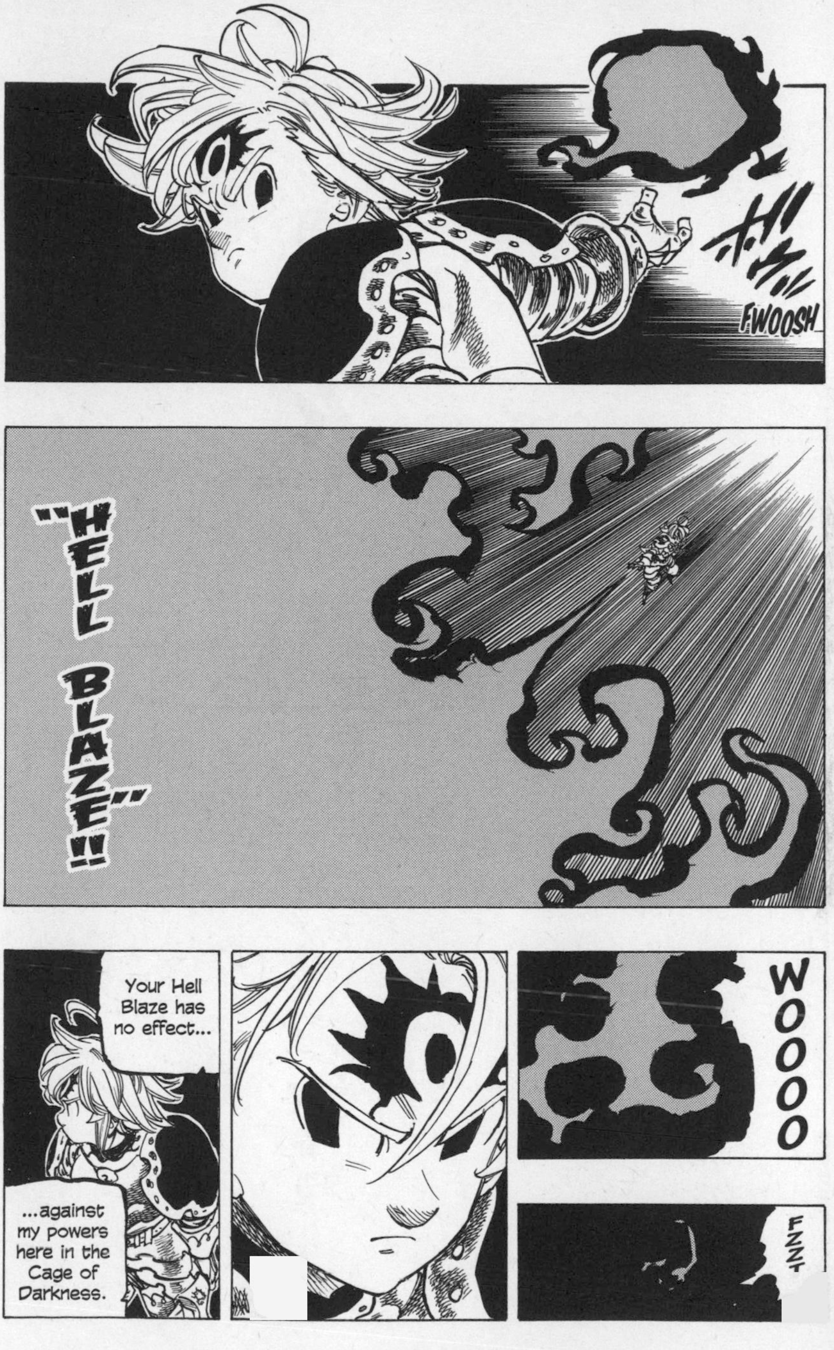
FWOOSH
"HELL BLAZE"!!
WOOOO
FZZT
Your Hell Blaze has no effect...
...against my powers here in the Cage of Darkness.

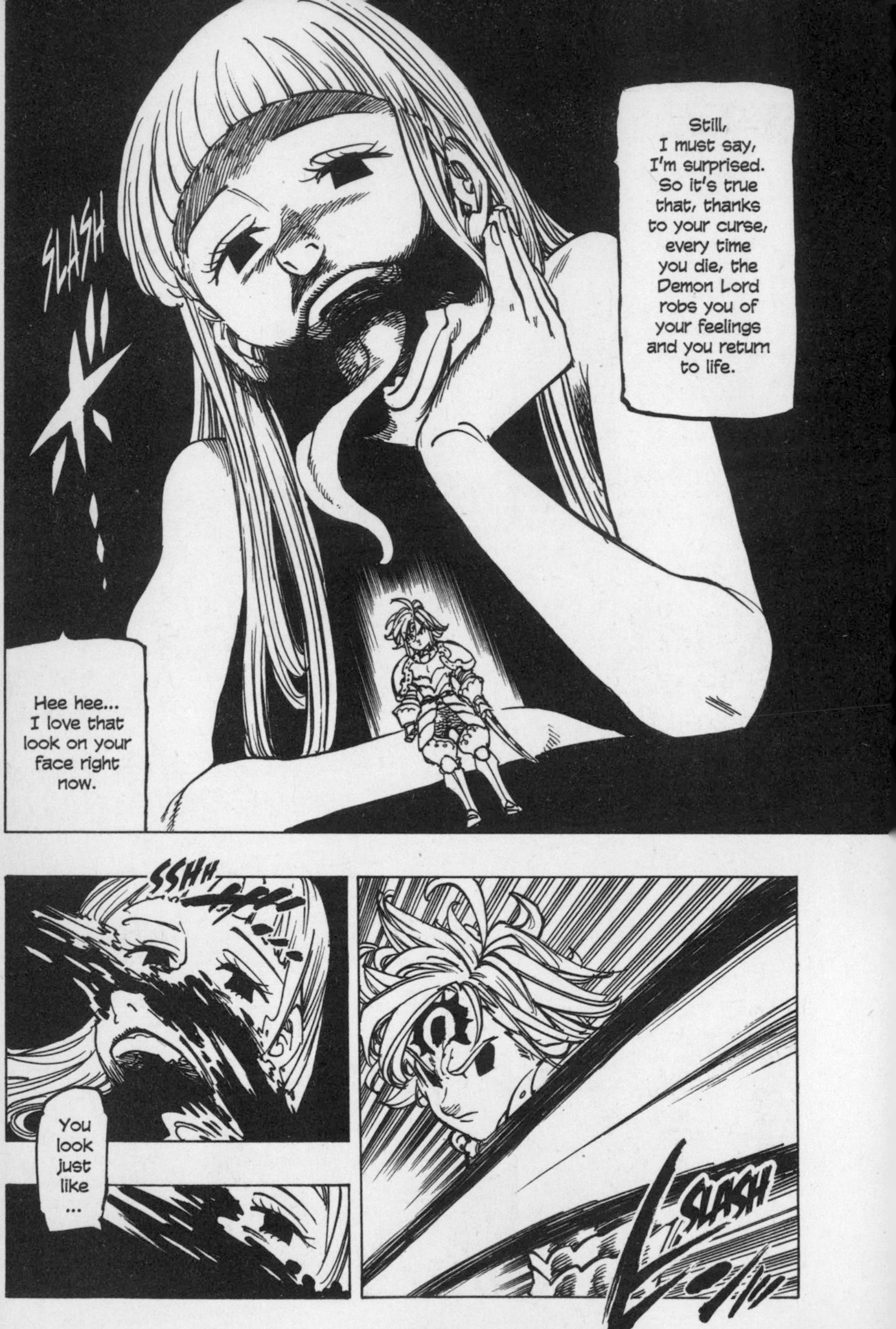
Still, I must say, I'm surprised. So it's true that, thanks to your curse, every time you die, the Demon Lord robs you of your feelings and you return to life.
SLASH
Hee hee... I love that look on your face right now.
SLASH
SSHH...
You look just like ...

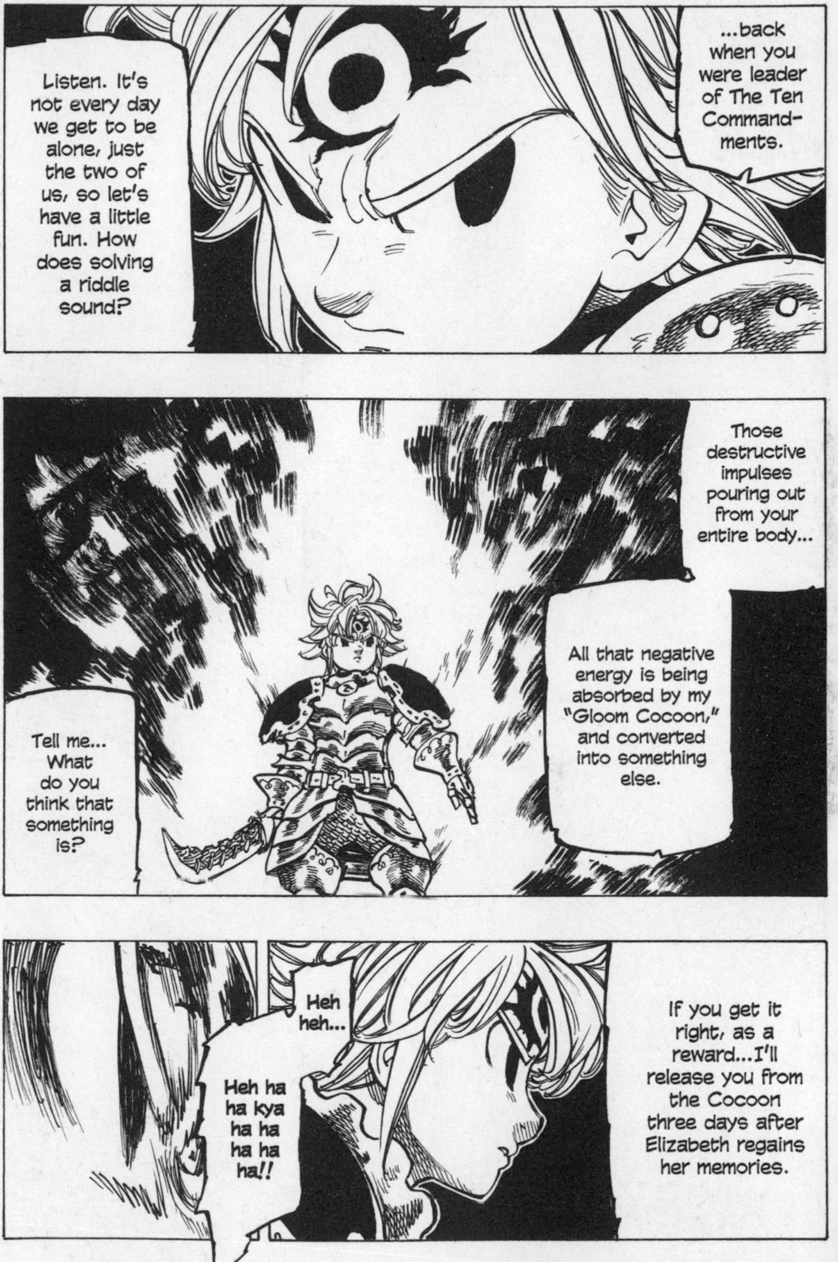
...back when you were leader of The Ten Command-ments.
Listen. It's not every day we get to be alone, just the two of us, so let's have a little fun. How does solving a riddle sound?
Those destructive impulses pouring out from your entire body...
All that negative energy is being absorbed by my "Gloom Cocoon," and converted into something else.
Tell me... What do you think that something is?
If you get it right, as a reward...I'll release you from the Cocoon three days after Elizabeth regains her memories.
Heh heh...
Heh ha ha kya ha ha ha ha ha!!

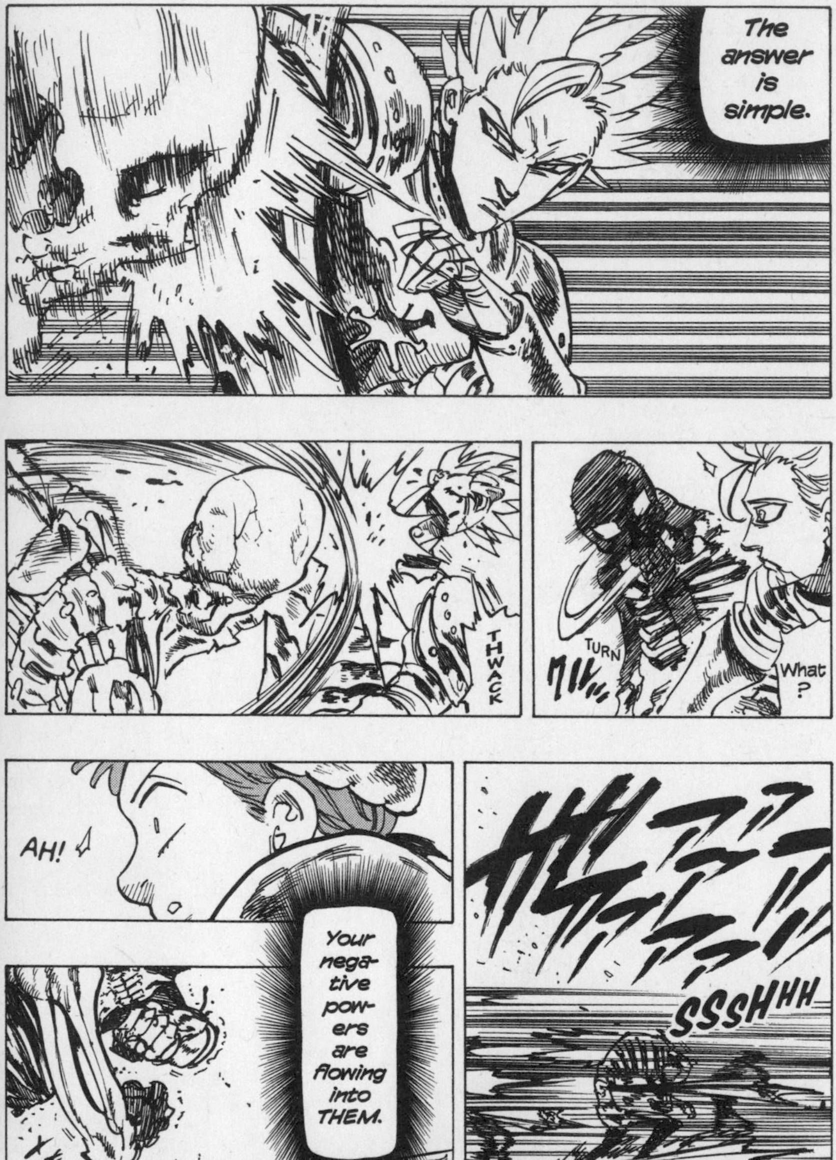
The answer is simple.
TURN
What?
THWACK
SSSHHH
AH!
Your negative powers are flowing into THEM.
CRICK
CRICK

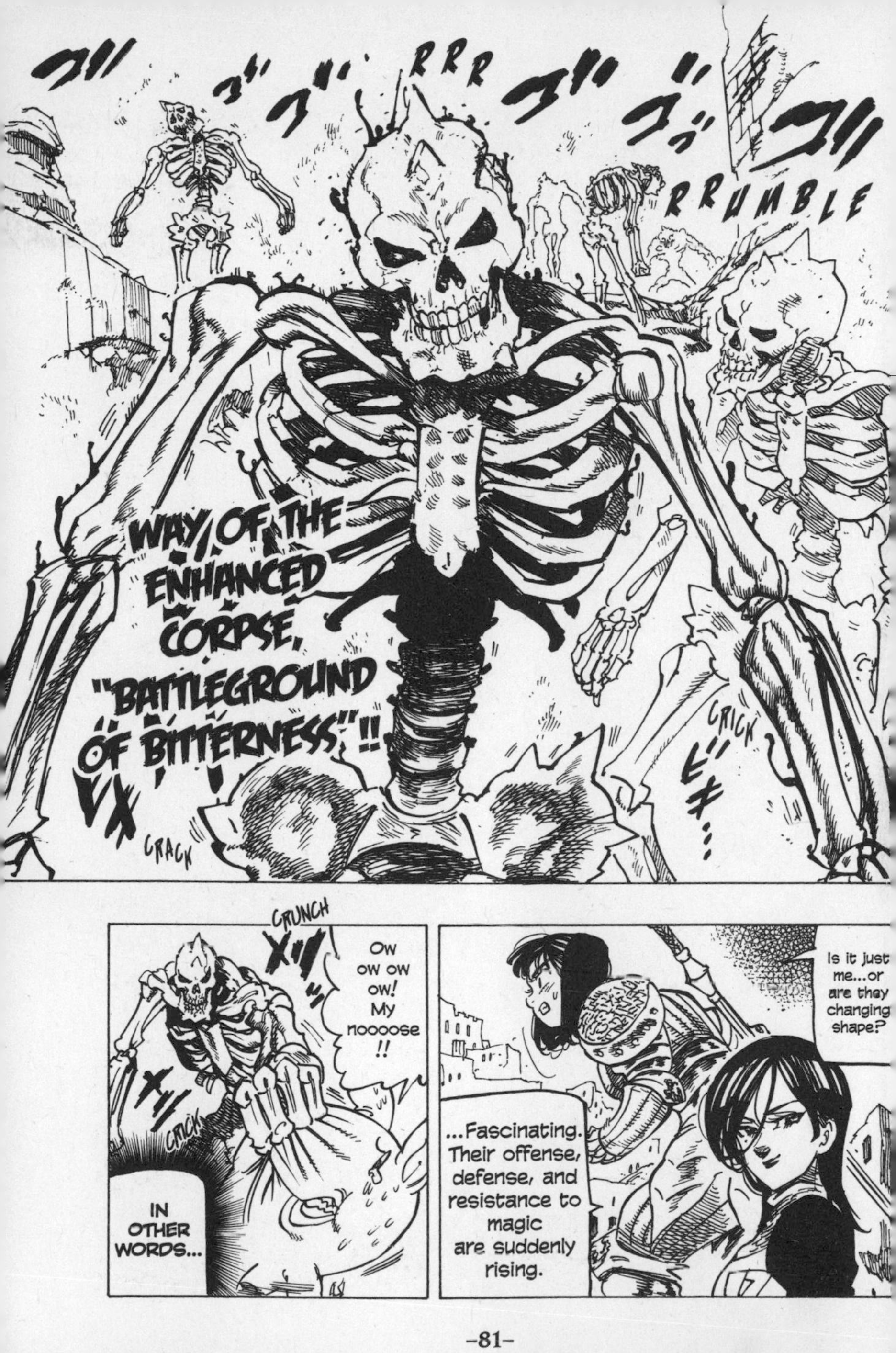
RRR
RRUMBLE
WAY OF THE ENHANCED CORPSE, "BATTLEGROUND OF BITTERNESS"!!
CRICK
CRACK
Is it just me...or are they changing shape?
...Fascinating. Their offense, defense, and resistance to magic are suddenly rising.
CRUNCH
Ow ow ow ow! My noooose !!
CRICK
IN OTHER WORDS...

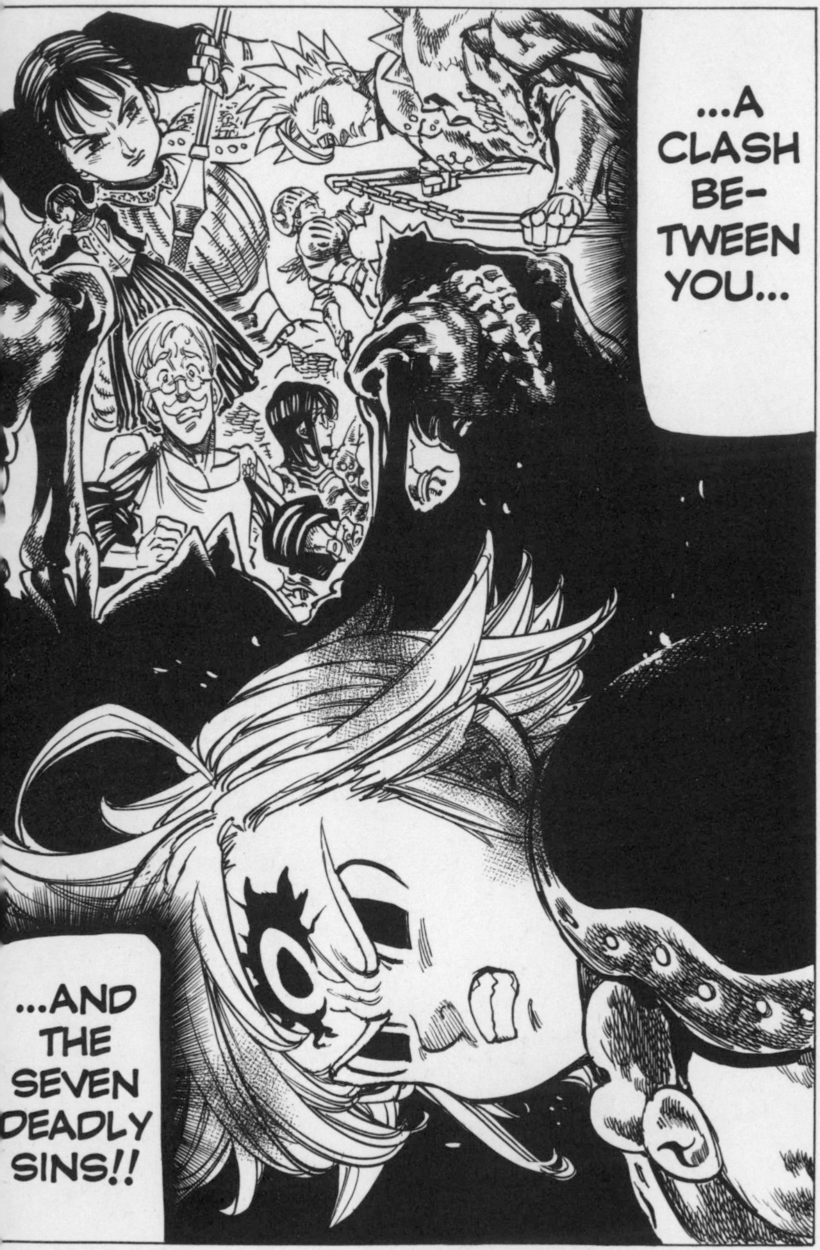
...A CLASH BE-TWEEN YOU...
...AND THE SEVEN DEADLY SINS!!

Chapter 227 - The Hateful Cannot Rest

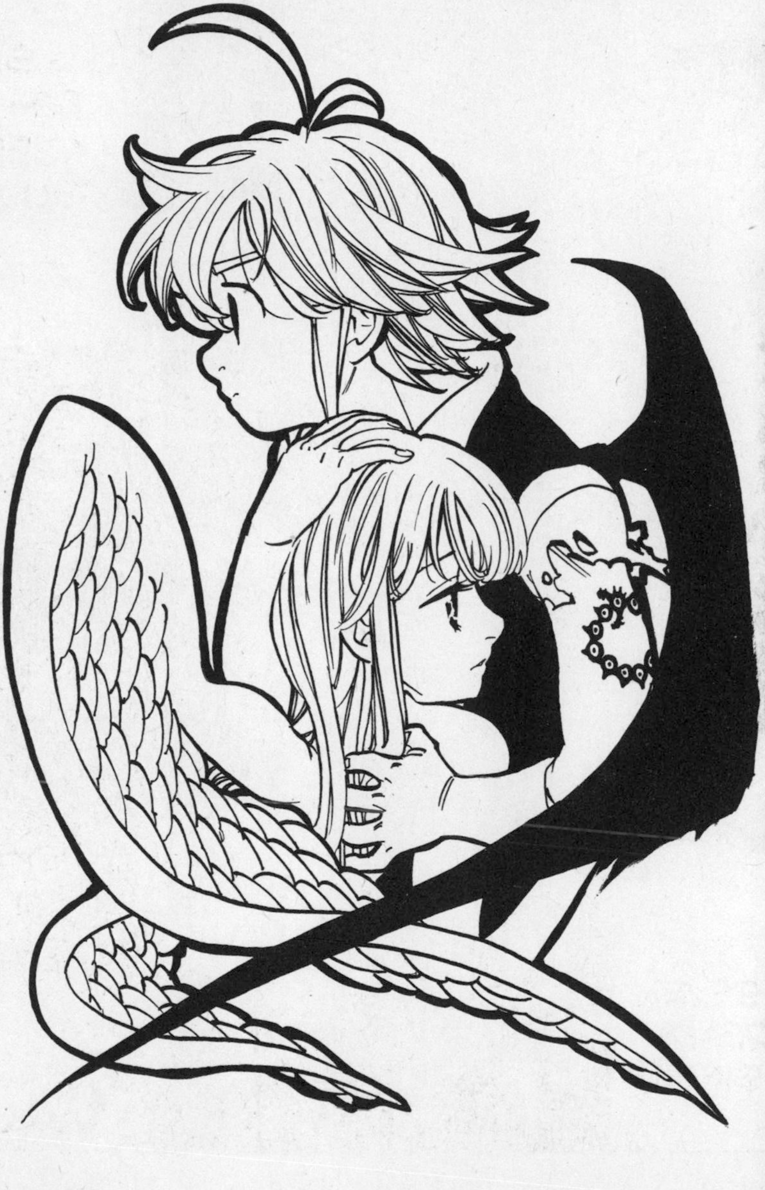

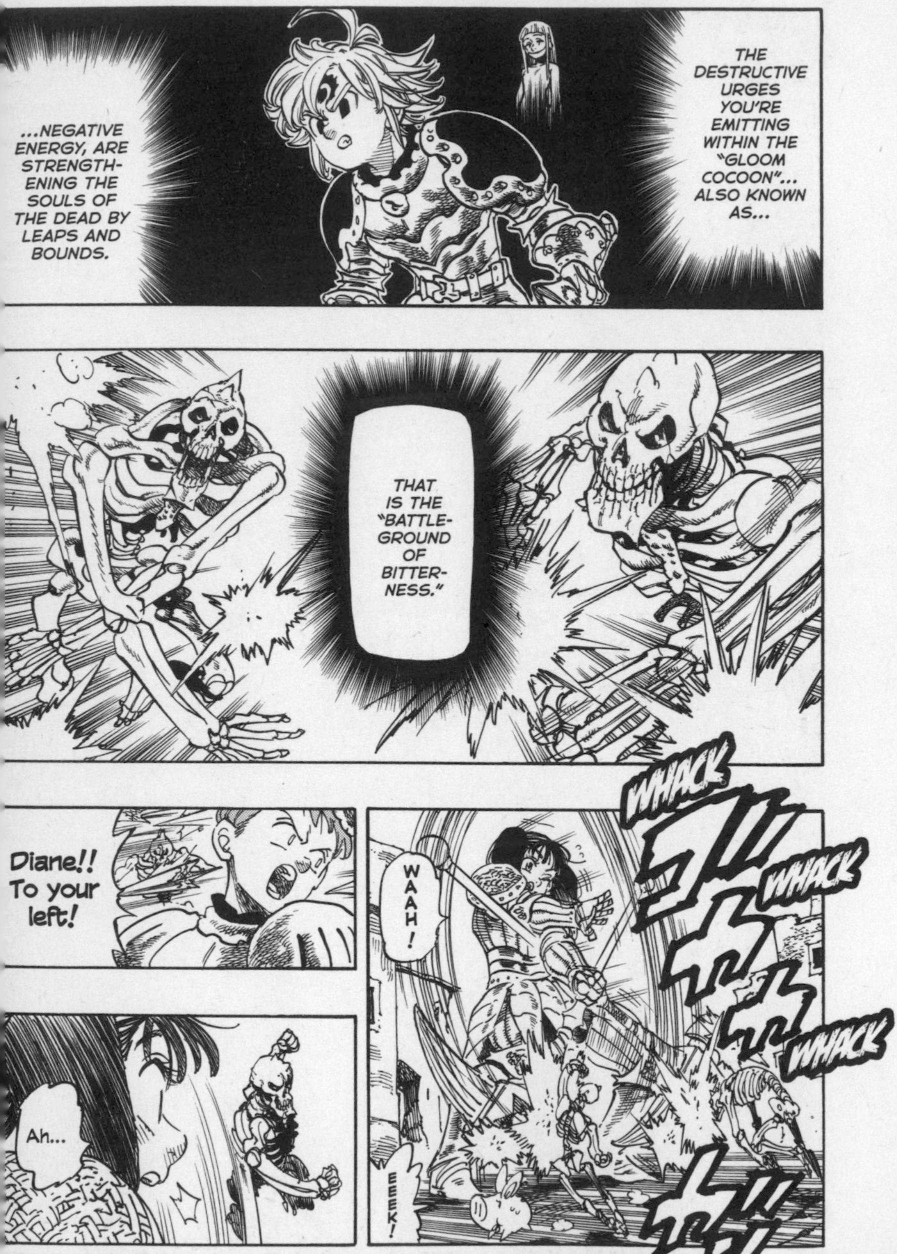
THE DESTRUCTIVE URGES YOU'RE EMITTING WITHIN THE "GLOOM COCOON"... ALSO KNOWN AS...
...NEGATIVE ENERGY, ARE STRENGTHENING THE SOULS OF THE DEAD BY LEAPS AND BOUNDS.
THAT IS THE "BATTLEGROUND OF BITTERNESS."
WHACK
WHACK
WAAH!
WHACK
EEEK!
WHACK
Diane!! To your left!
Ah...

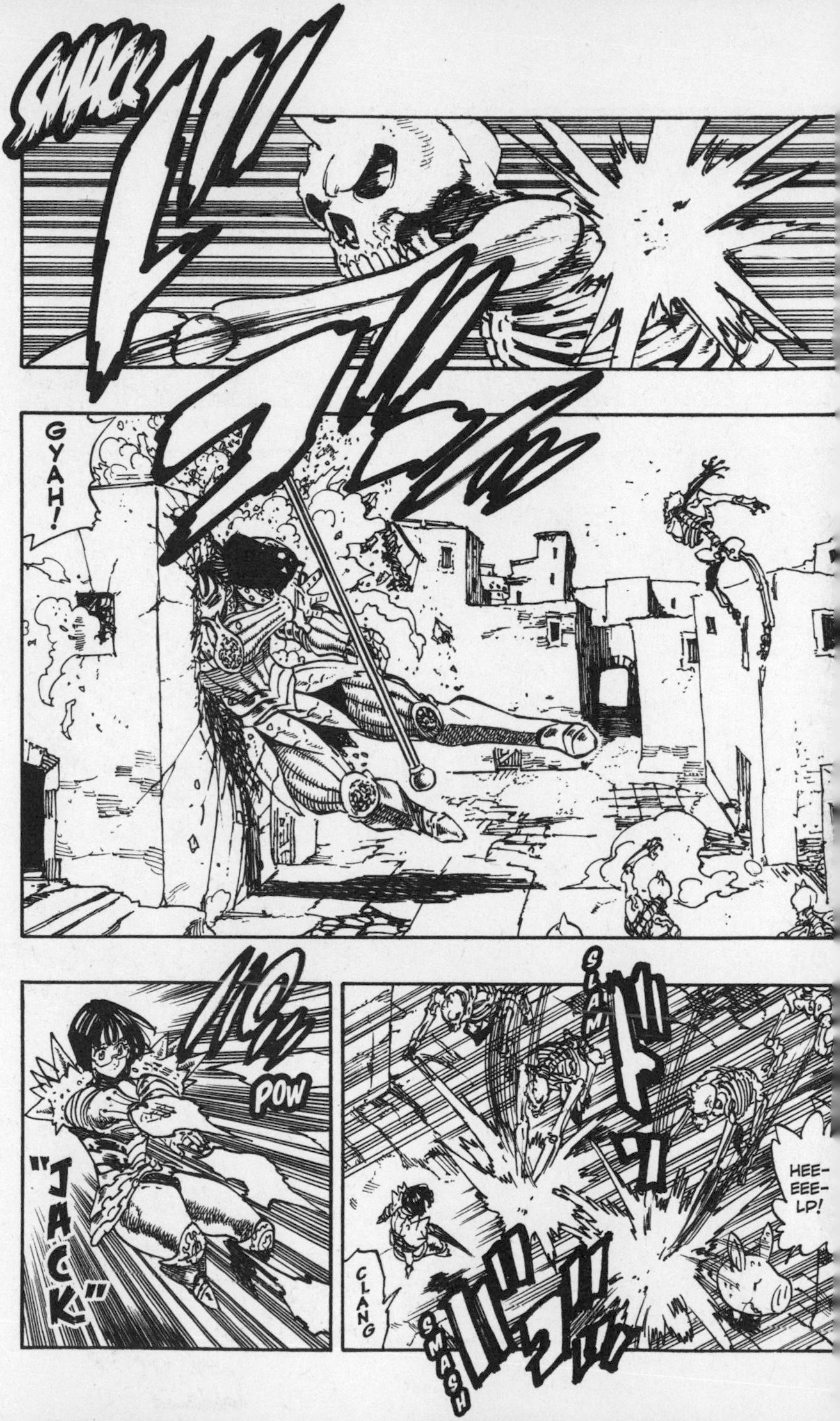
GYAH!
SLAM
HEEEEELP!
CLANG
SMASH
POW
"JACK"

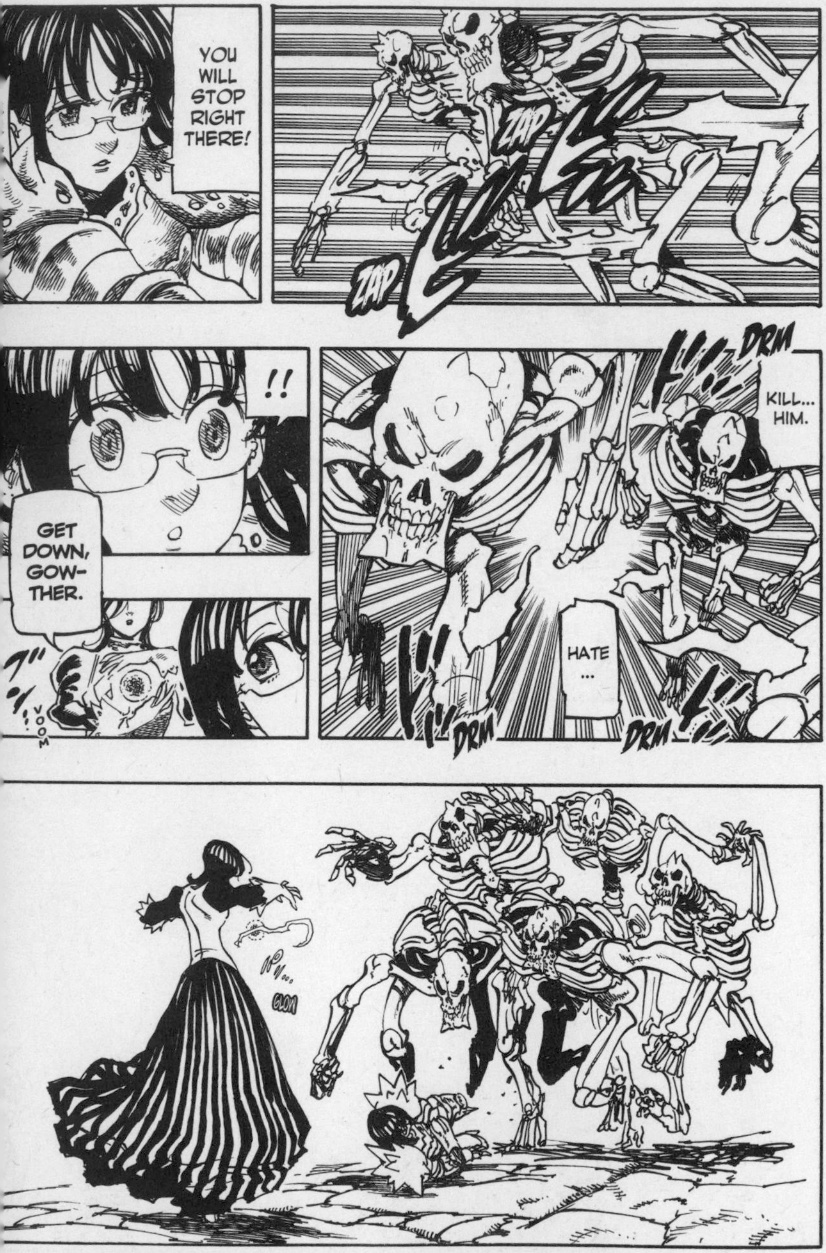
ZAP
ZAP
YOU WILL STOP RIGHT THERE!
DRM
KILL... HIM.
HATE...
DRM
DRM
!!
GET DOWN, GOW-THER.
VOOM
CLON

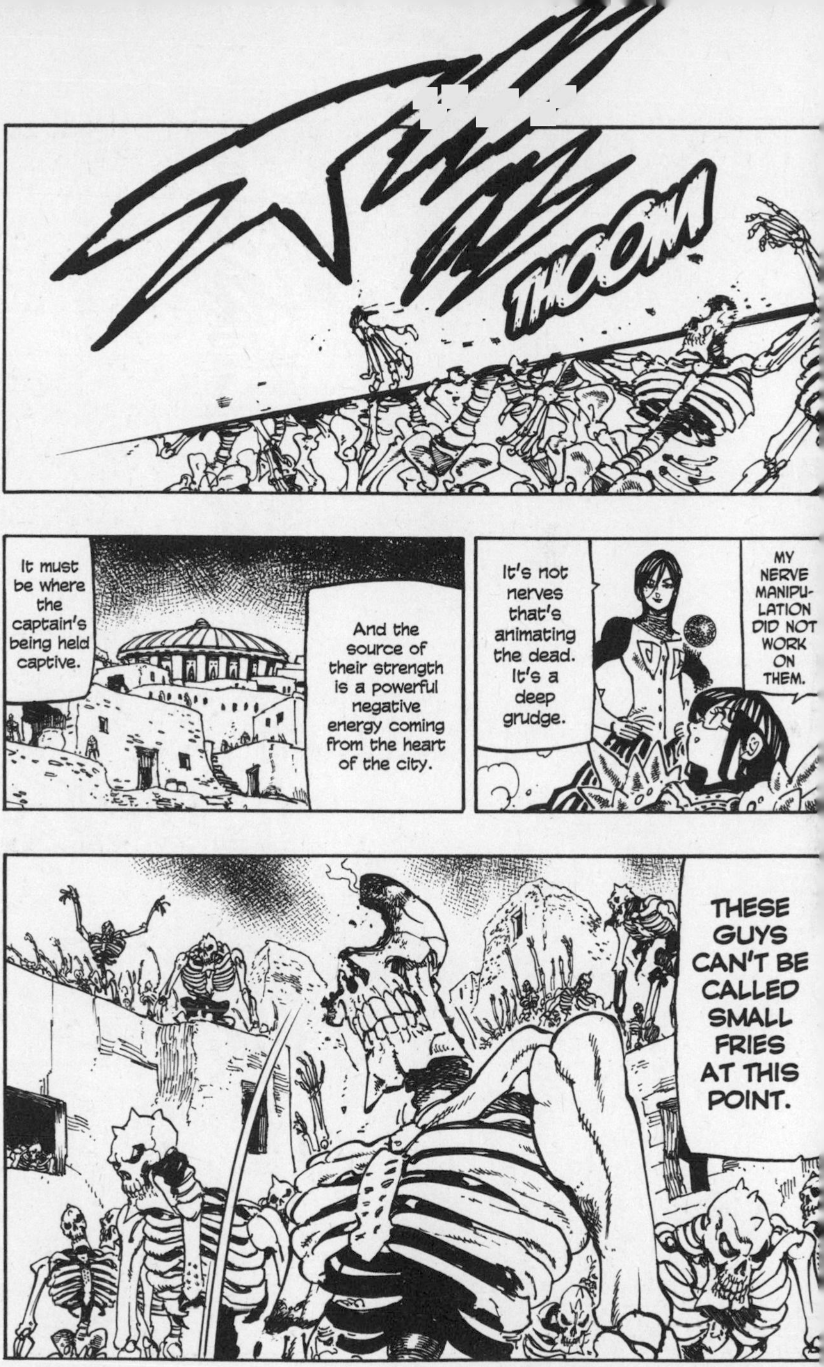
THOOM
MY NERVE MANIPU-LATION DID NOT WORK ON THEM.
It's not nerves that's animating the dead. It's a deep grudge.
And the source of their strength is a powerful negative energy coming from the heart of the city.
It must be where the captain's being held captive.
THESE GUYS CAN'T BE CALLED SMALL FRIES AT THIS POINT.

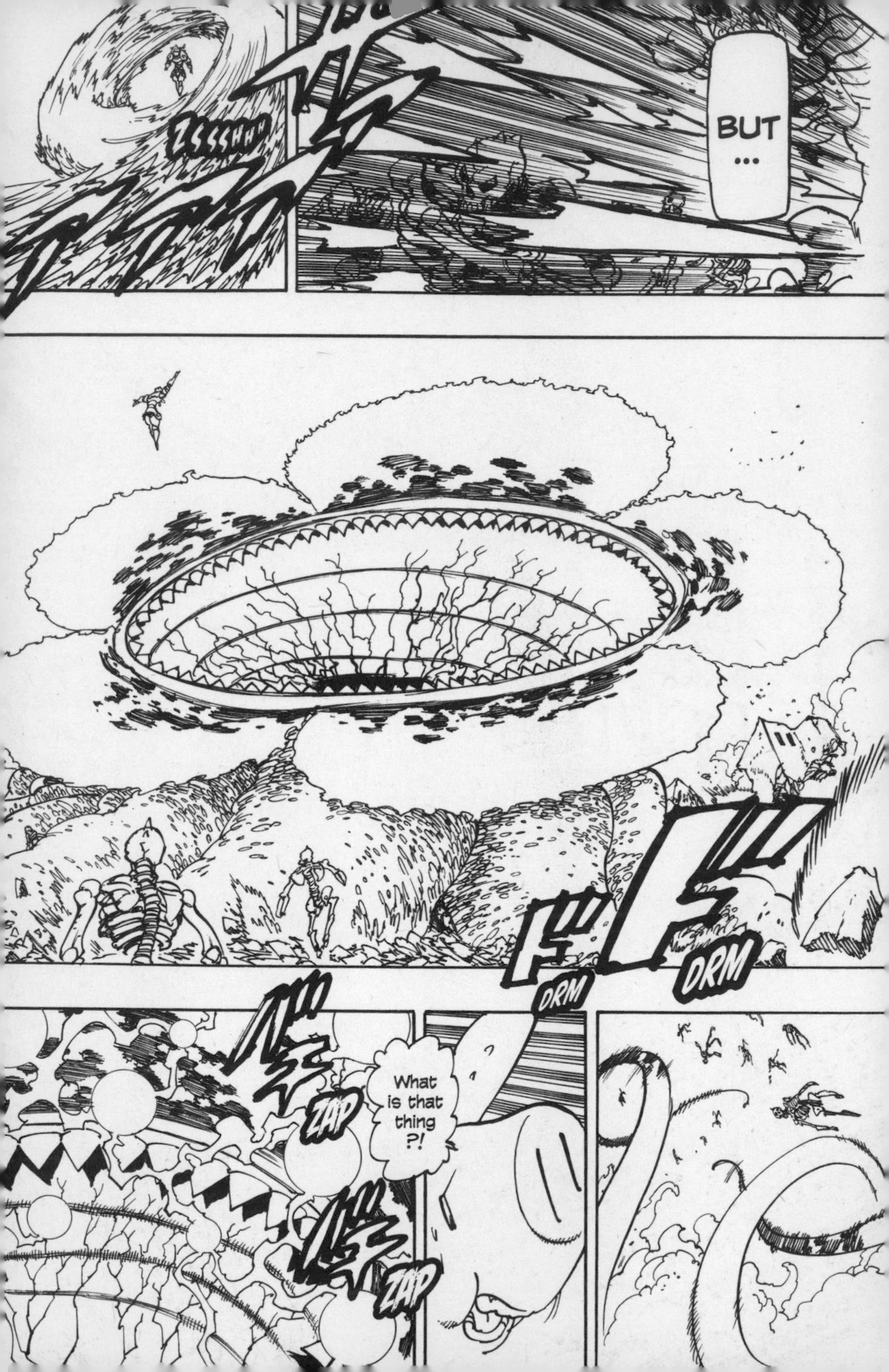
BUT ...
ZSSSHHH
DRM
DRM
What is that thing ?!
ZAP
ZAP

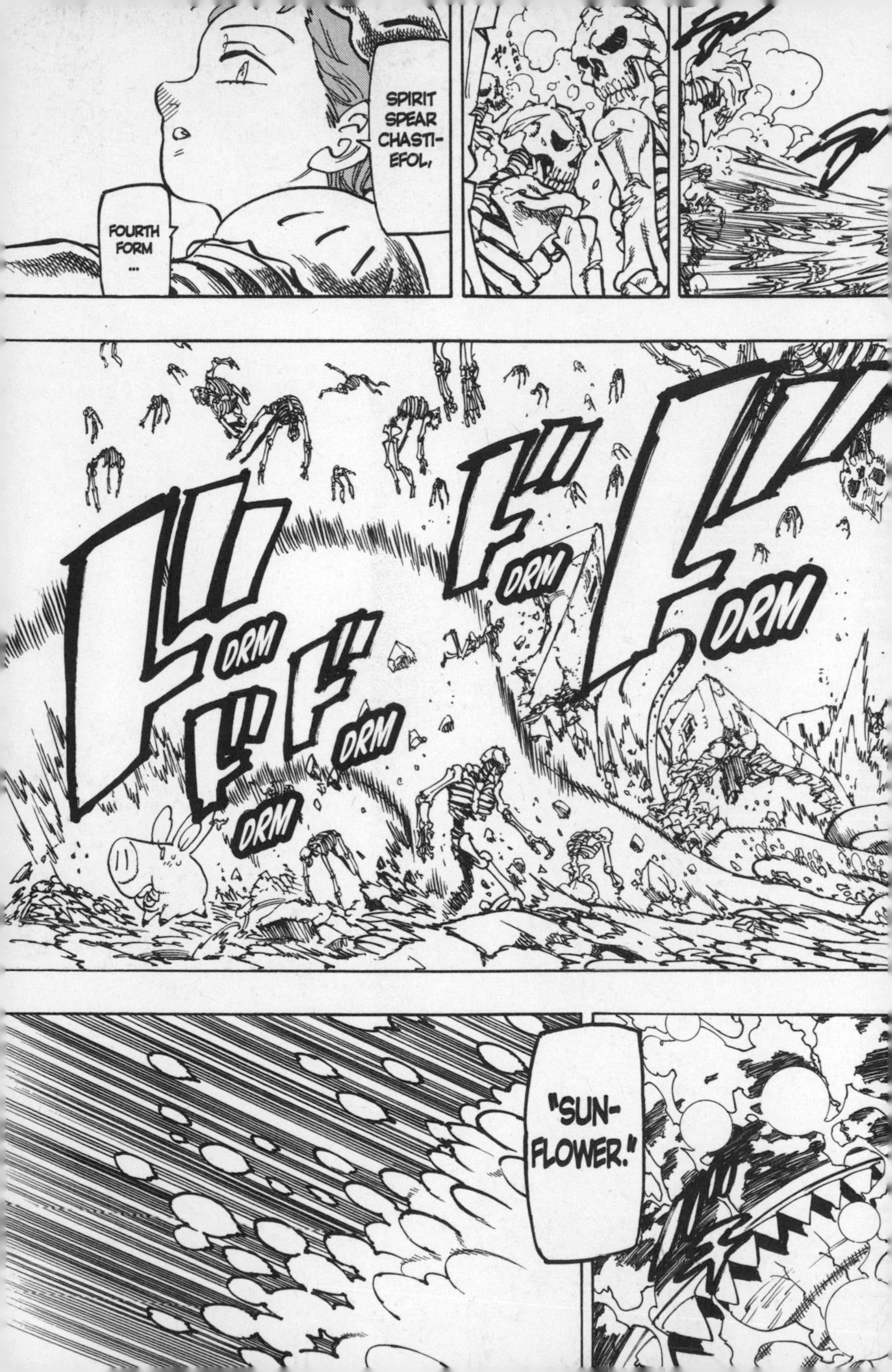
GLARE
SPIRIT SPEAR CHASTIEFOL,
FOURTH FORM ...
FORM
FORM
FORM
FORM
FORM
"SUNFLOWER."

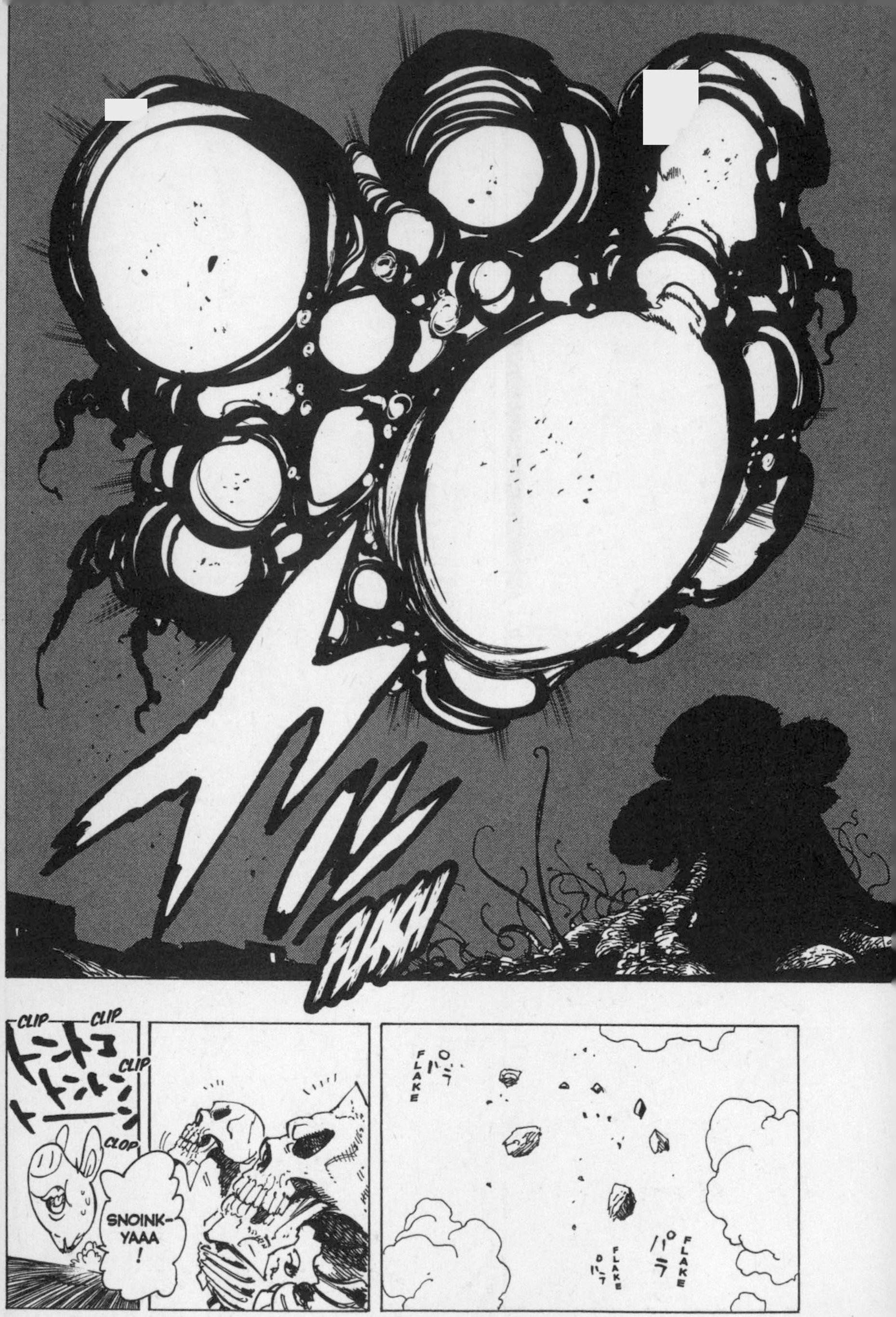
FLASH
FLAKE
FLAKE
FLAKE
CLIP
CLIP
CLIP
CLOP
SNOINK-YAAA!

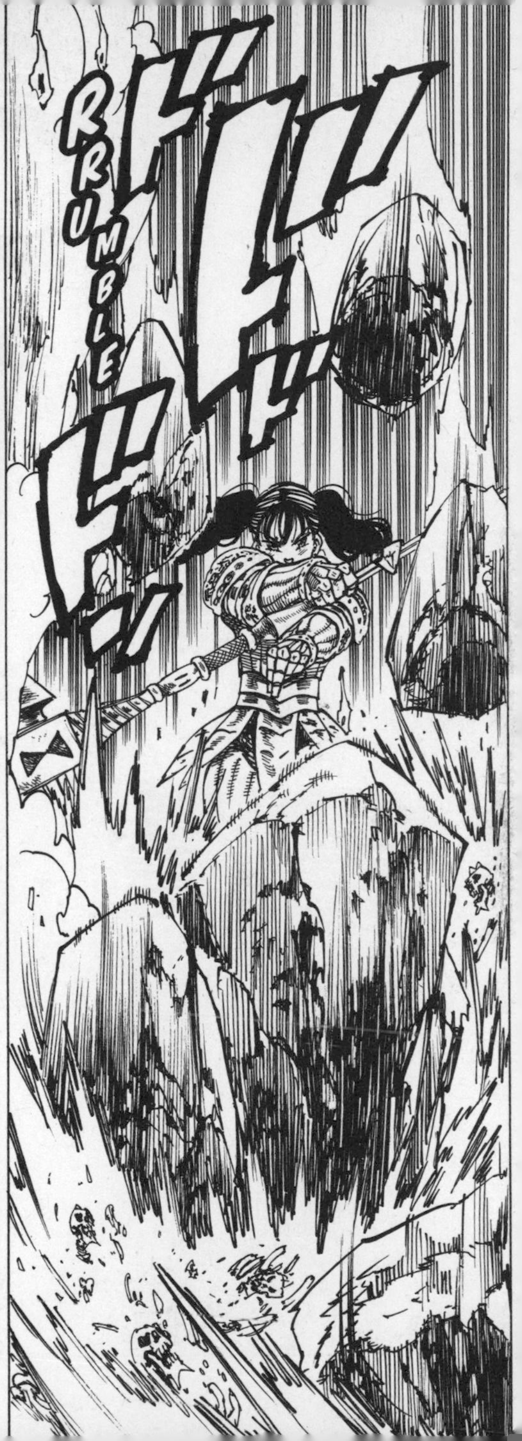
RRUMBLE
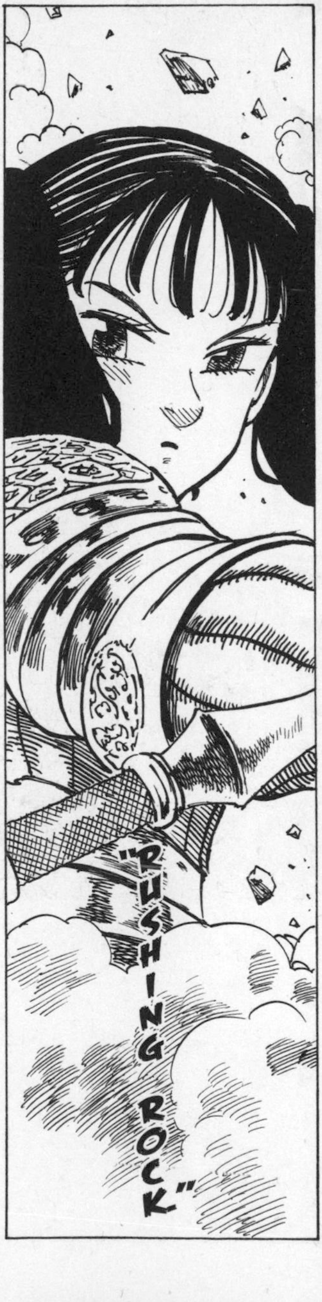
"RUSHING ROCK"

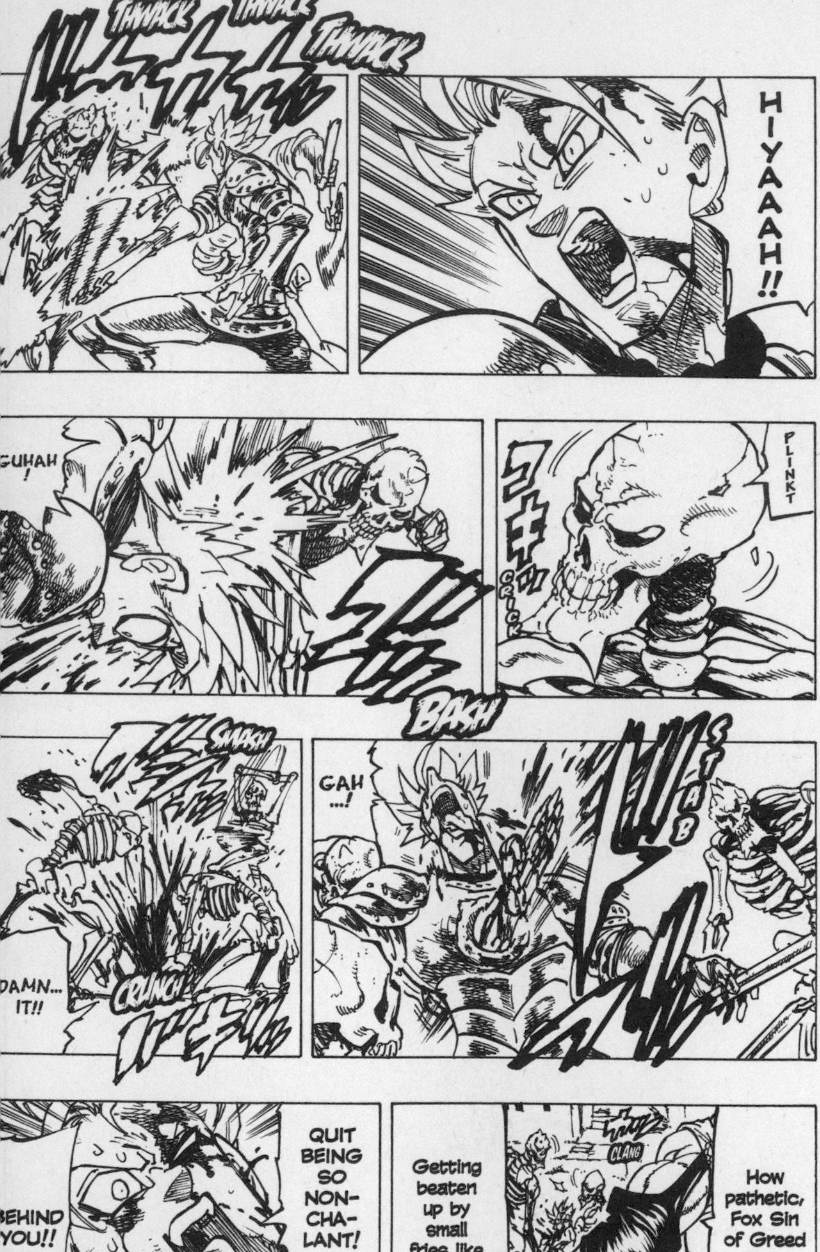
HIYAAAH!!
THWACK
THWACK
THWACK
PLINKT
CRICK
GUHAH!
BASH
GAH...!
STAB
SMASH
DAMN... IT!!
CRUNCH
How pathetic, Fox Sin of Greed Ban.
Getting beaten up by small fries like them.
CLANG
QUIT BEING SO NON-CHALANT!
BEHIND YOU!!

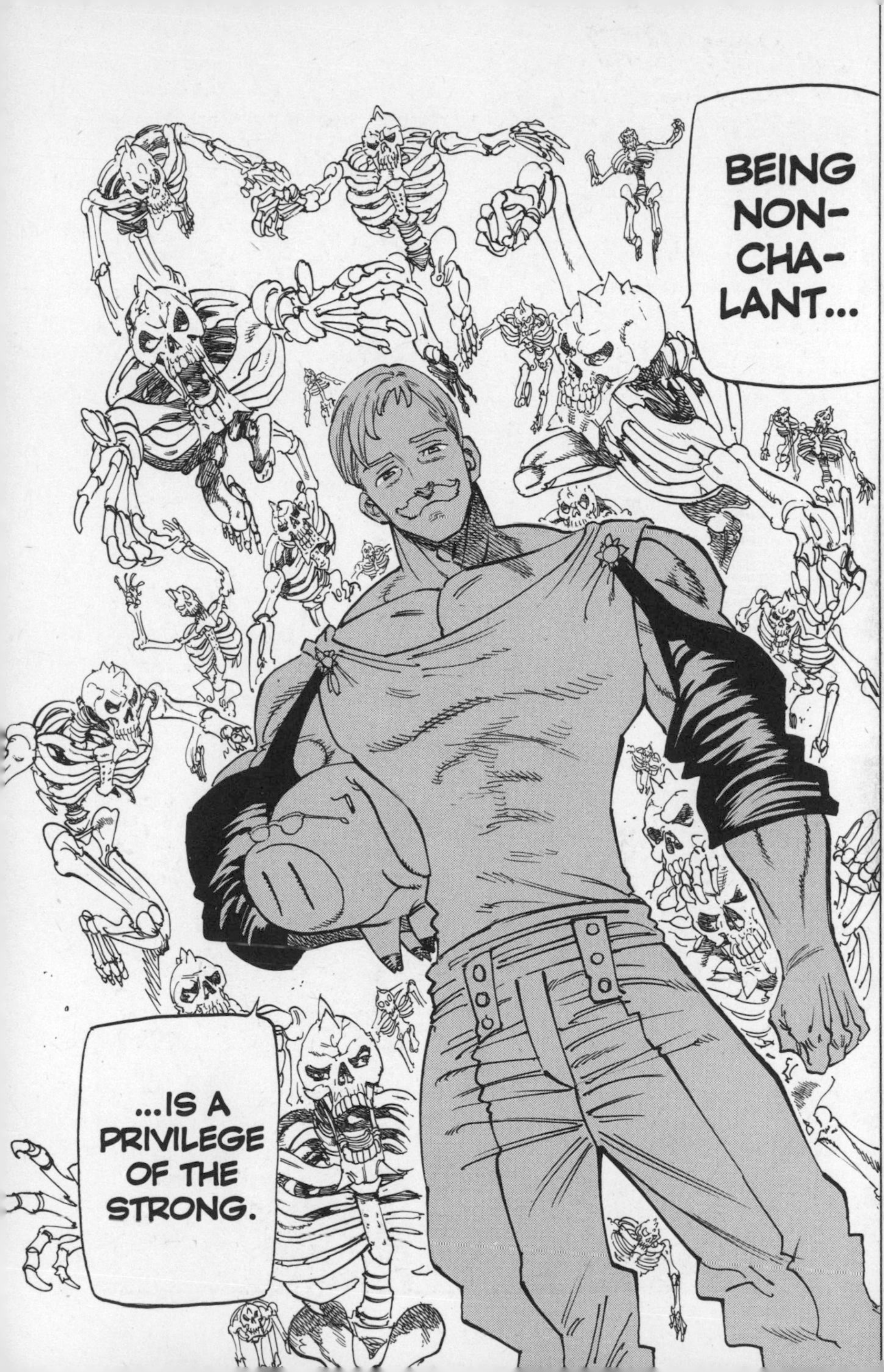
BEING NON-CHA-LANT...
...IS A PRIVILEGE OF THE STRONG.

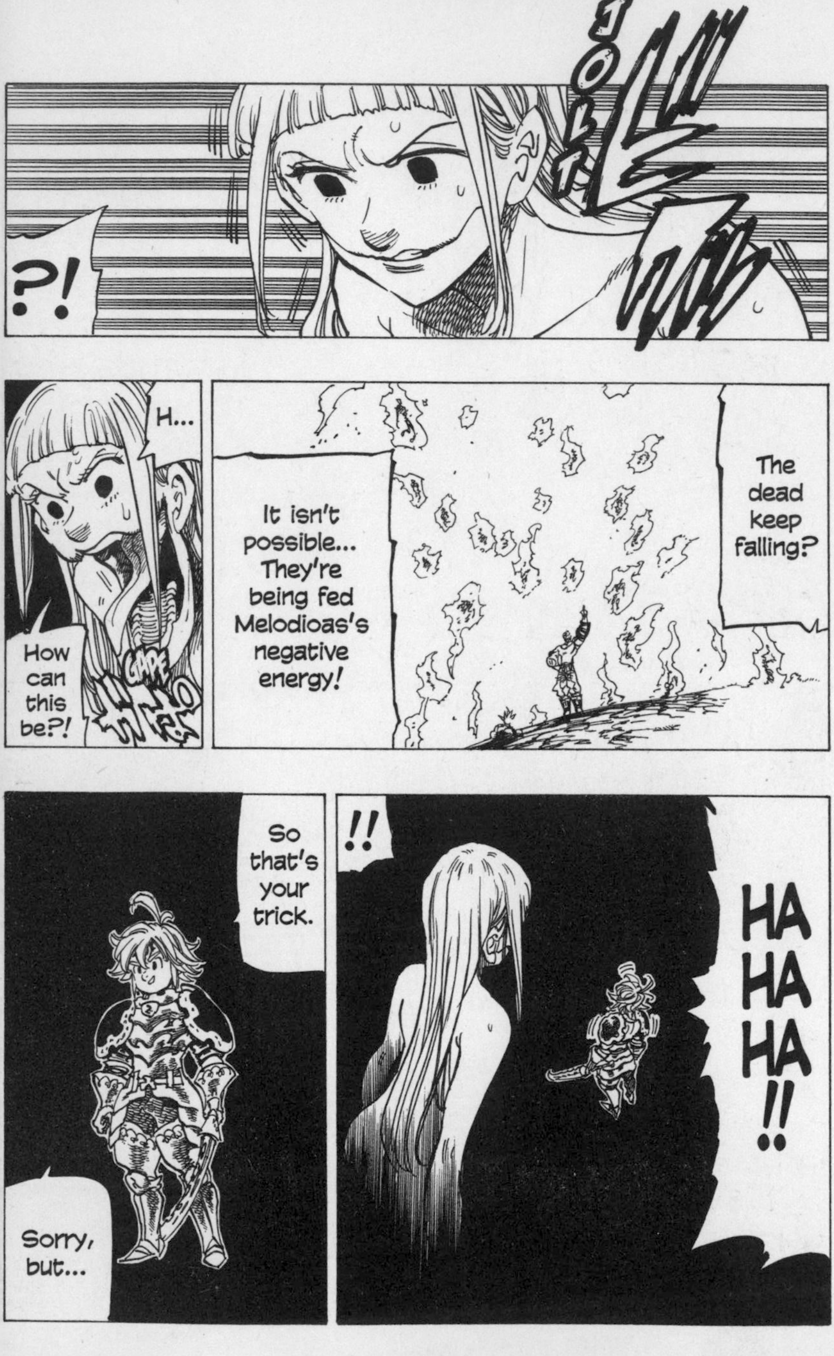
JOLT
?!
The dead keep falling?
It isn't possible... They're being fed Melodioas's negative energy!
H...
How can this be?!
GAPE
!!
HA HA HA!!
So that's your trick.
Sorry, but...

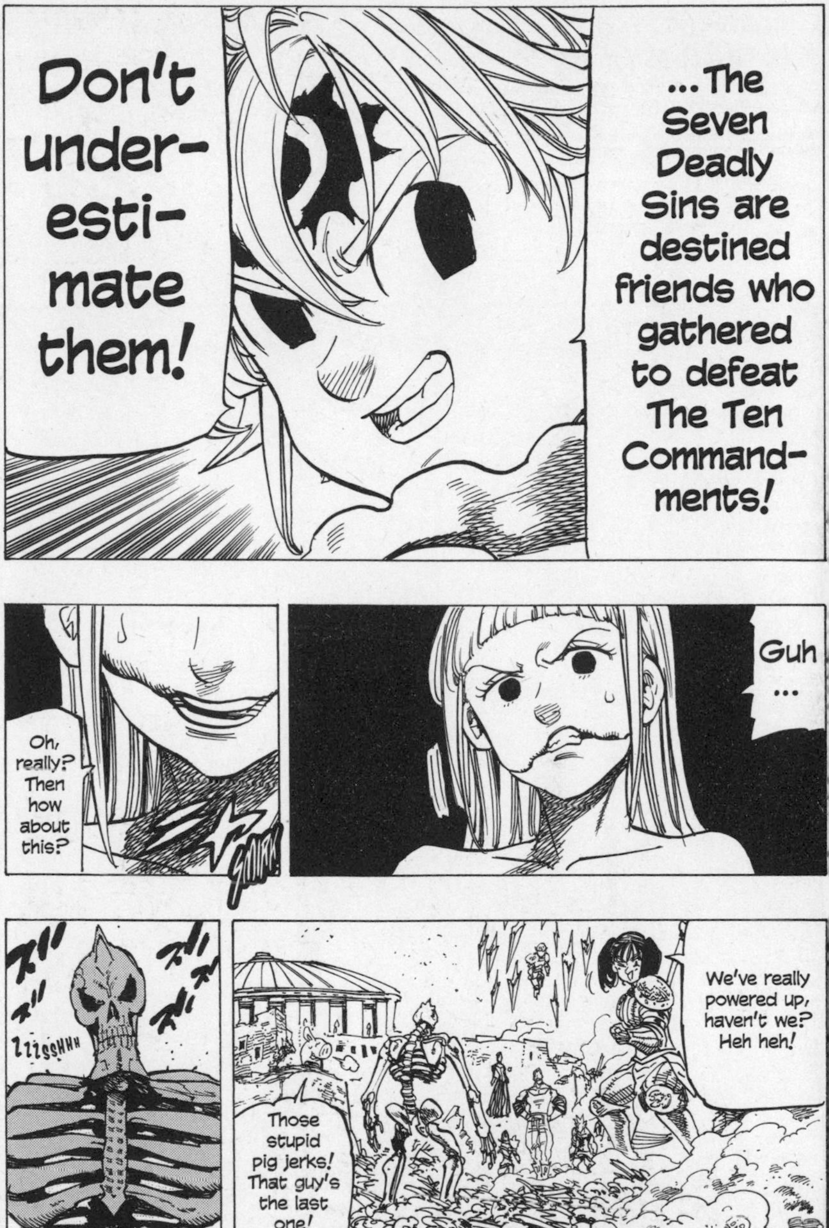
...The Seven Deadly Sins are destined friends who gathered to defeat The Ten Command-ments!
Don't under-esti-mate them!
Guh ...
Oh, really? Then how about this?
SMIRK
We've really powered up, haven't we? Heh heh!
Those stupid pig jerks! That guy's the last one!
ZZZSSHHH

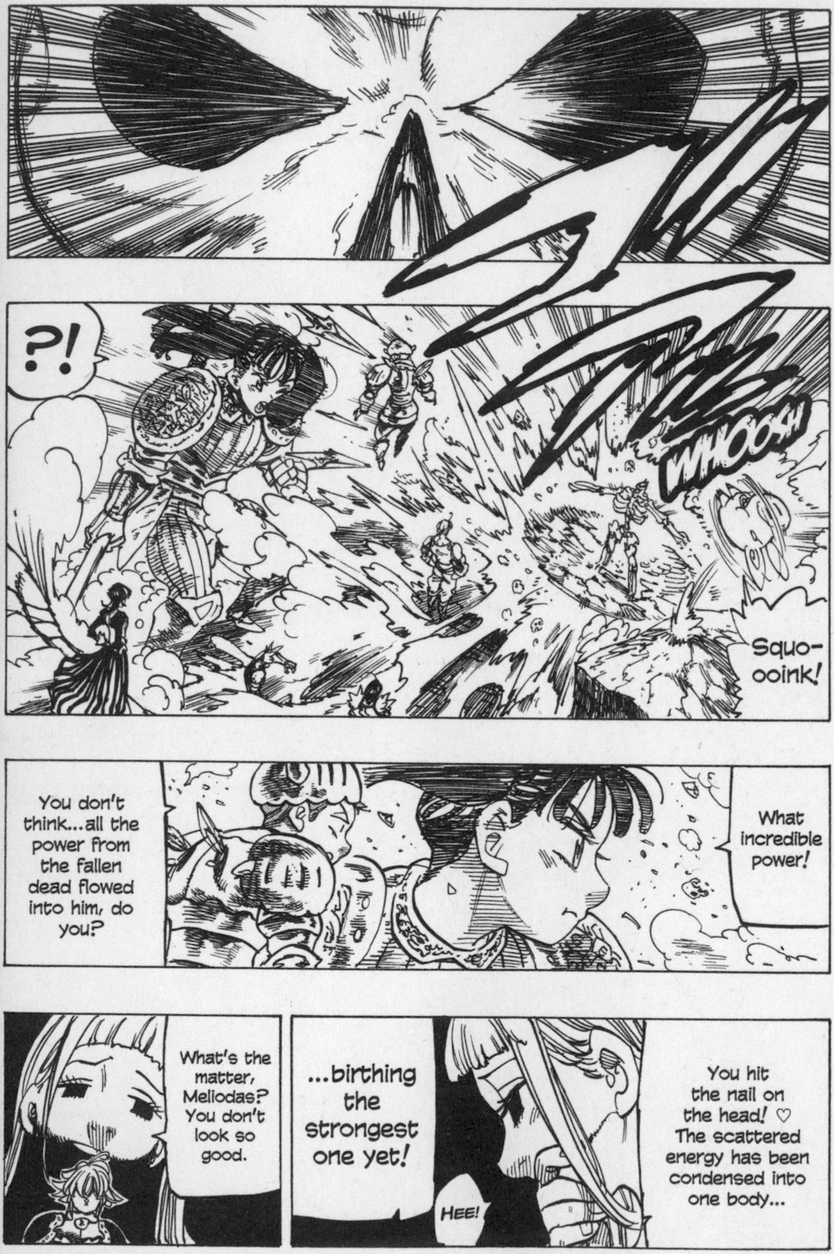
WHOO
Squo-ooink!
?!
What incredible power!
You don't think...all the power from the fallen dead flowed into him, do you?
You hit the nail on the head! ♡ The scattered energy has been condensed into one body...
HEE!
...birthing the strongest one yet!
What's the matter, Meliodas? You don't look so good.

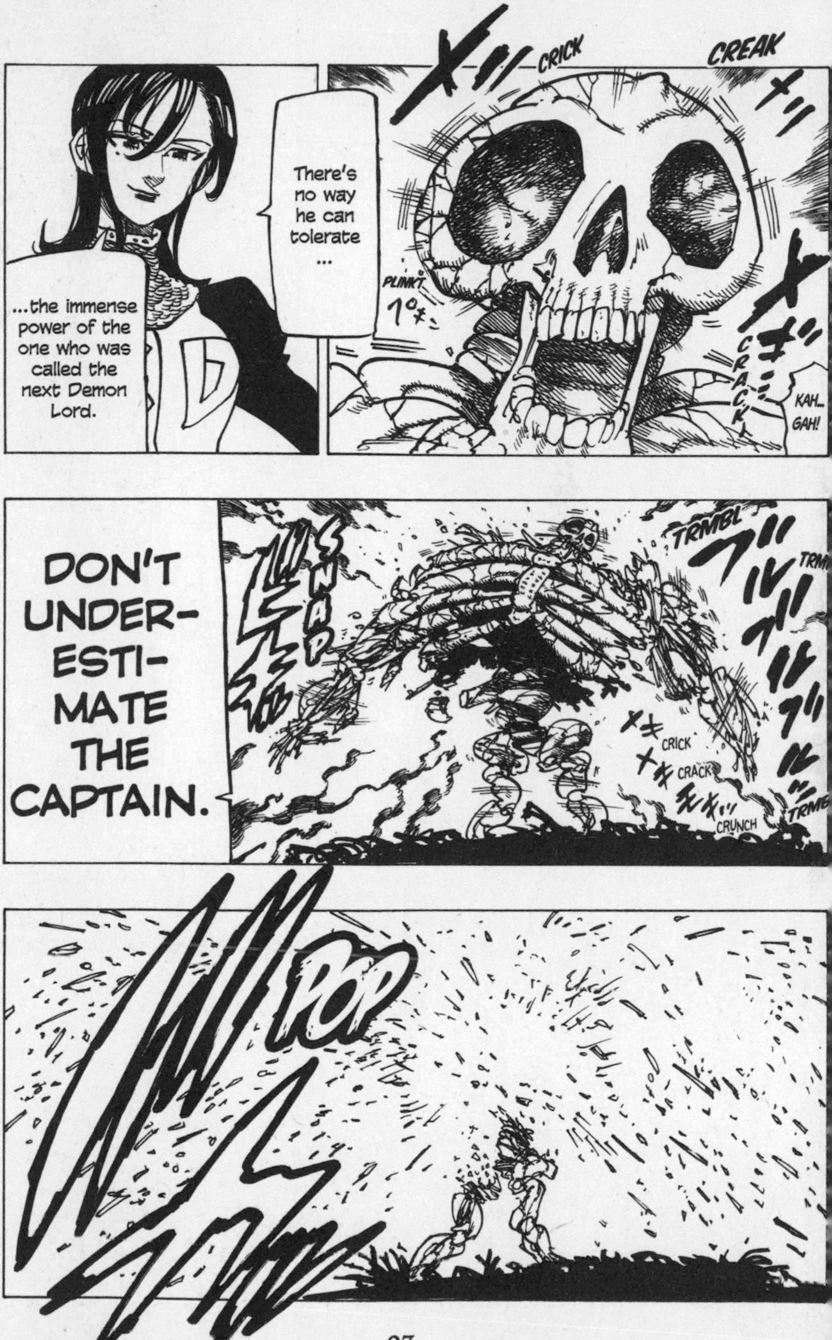
CREAK
CRICK
CRACK
KAH... GAH!
PLINK!
There's no way he can tolerate ...
...the immense power of the one who was called the next Demon Lord.
TRMBL
SNAP
CRICK
CRACK
CRUNCH
DON'T UNDER-ESTI-MATE THE CAPTAIN.
POP

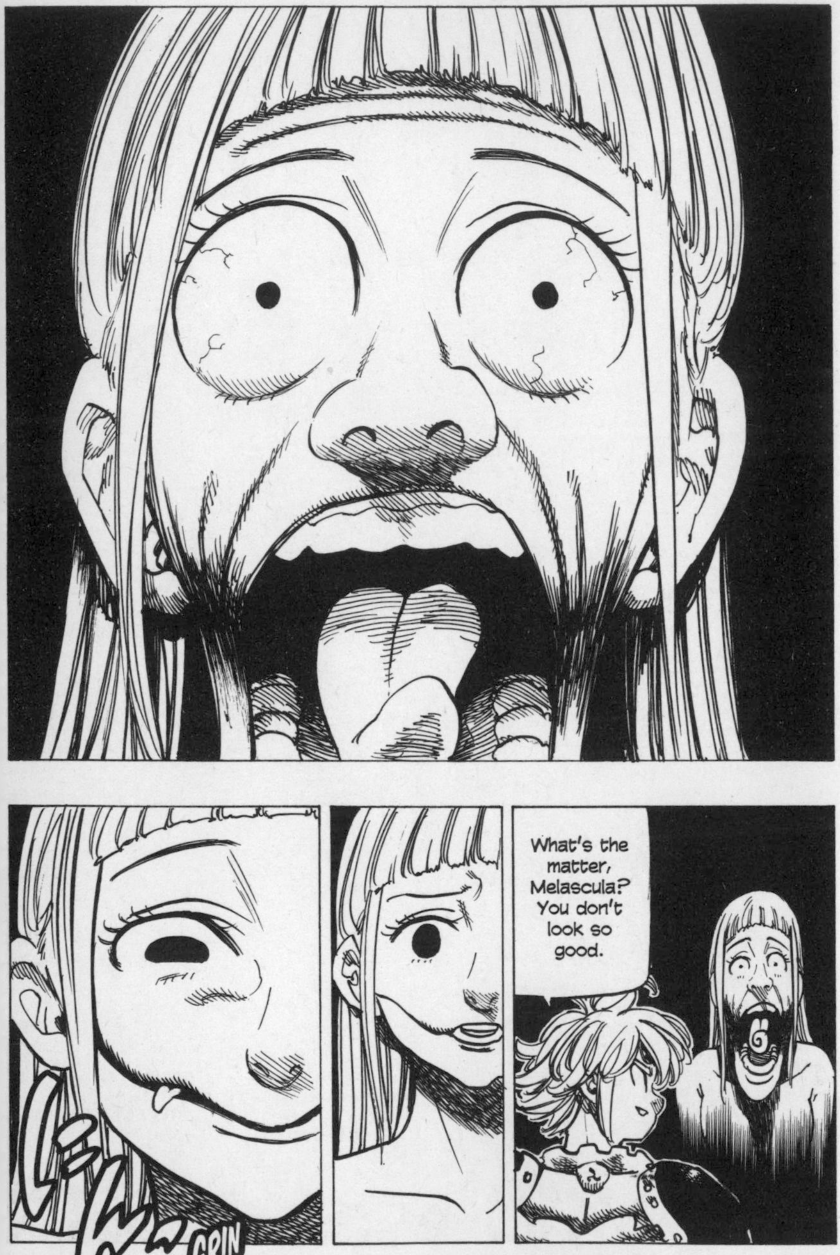
What's the matter, Melascula? You don't look so good.
GRIN

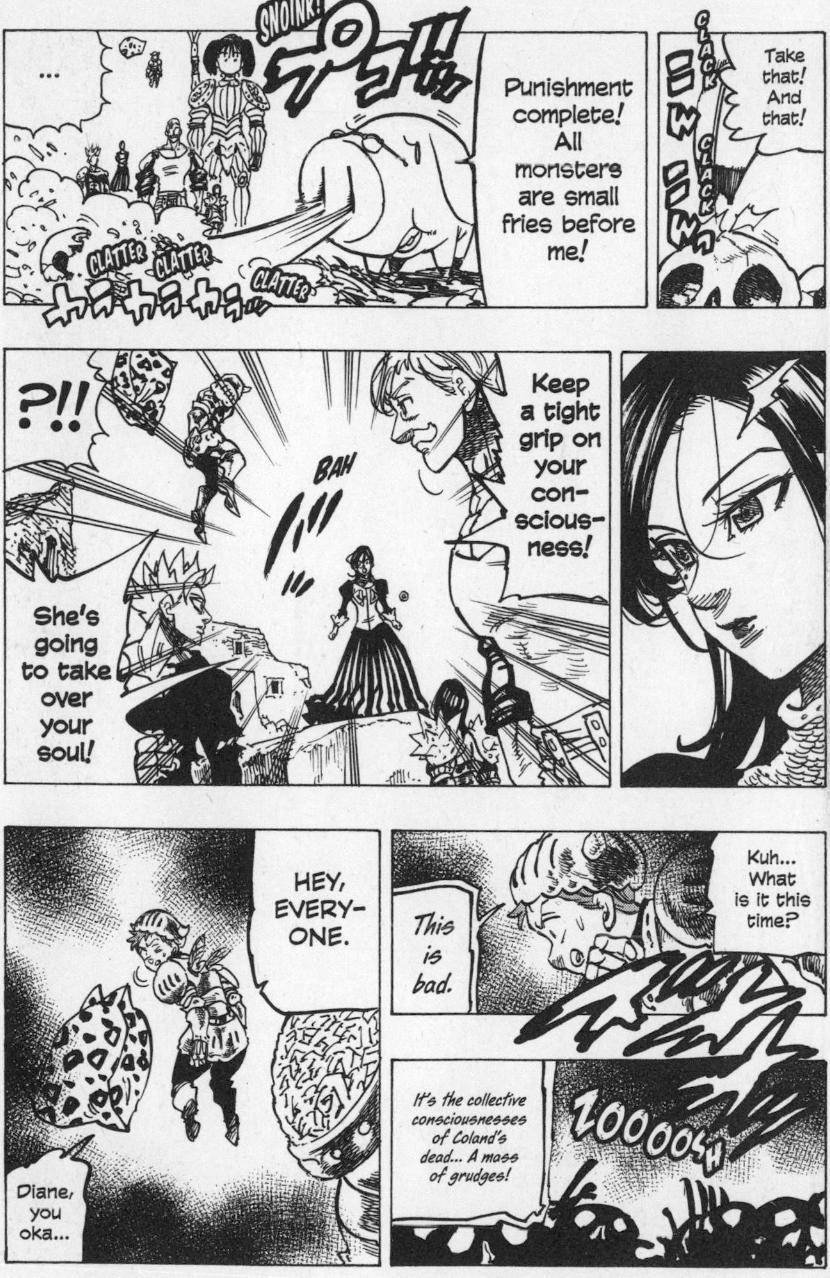
CLACK
CLACK
CLACK
Take that! And that!
SNOINK!
...
Punishment complete! All monsters are small fries before me!
CLATTER
CLATTER
CLATTER
Keep a tight grip on your consciousness!
BAH
?!!
She's going to take over your soul!
Kuh... What is it this time?
This is bad.
ZOOOOSH
It's the collective consciousnesses of Coland's dead... A mass of grudges!
HEY, EVERYONE.
Diane, you oka...

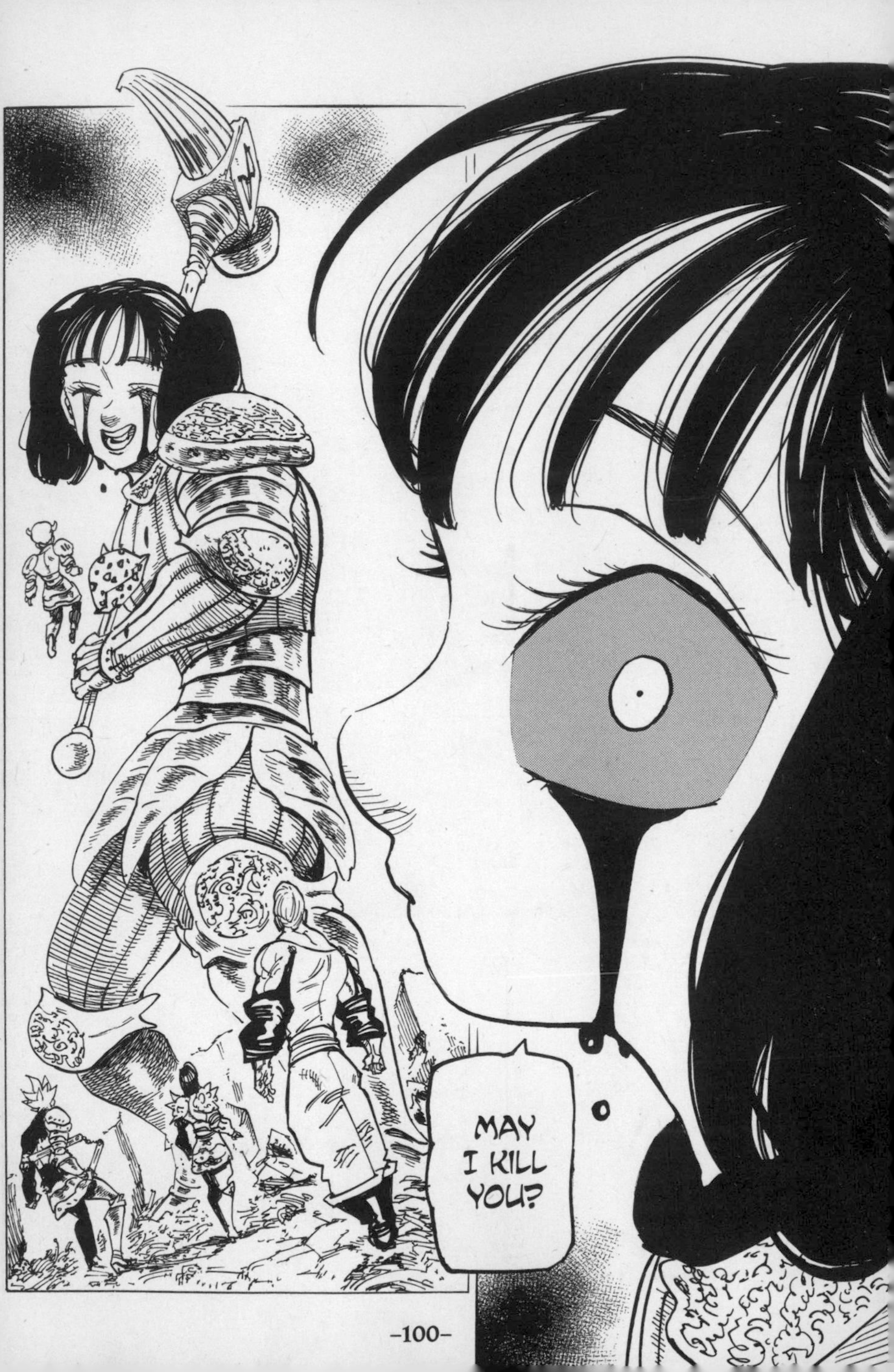
MAY I KILL YOU?

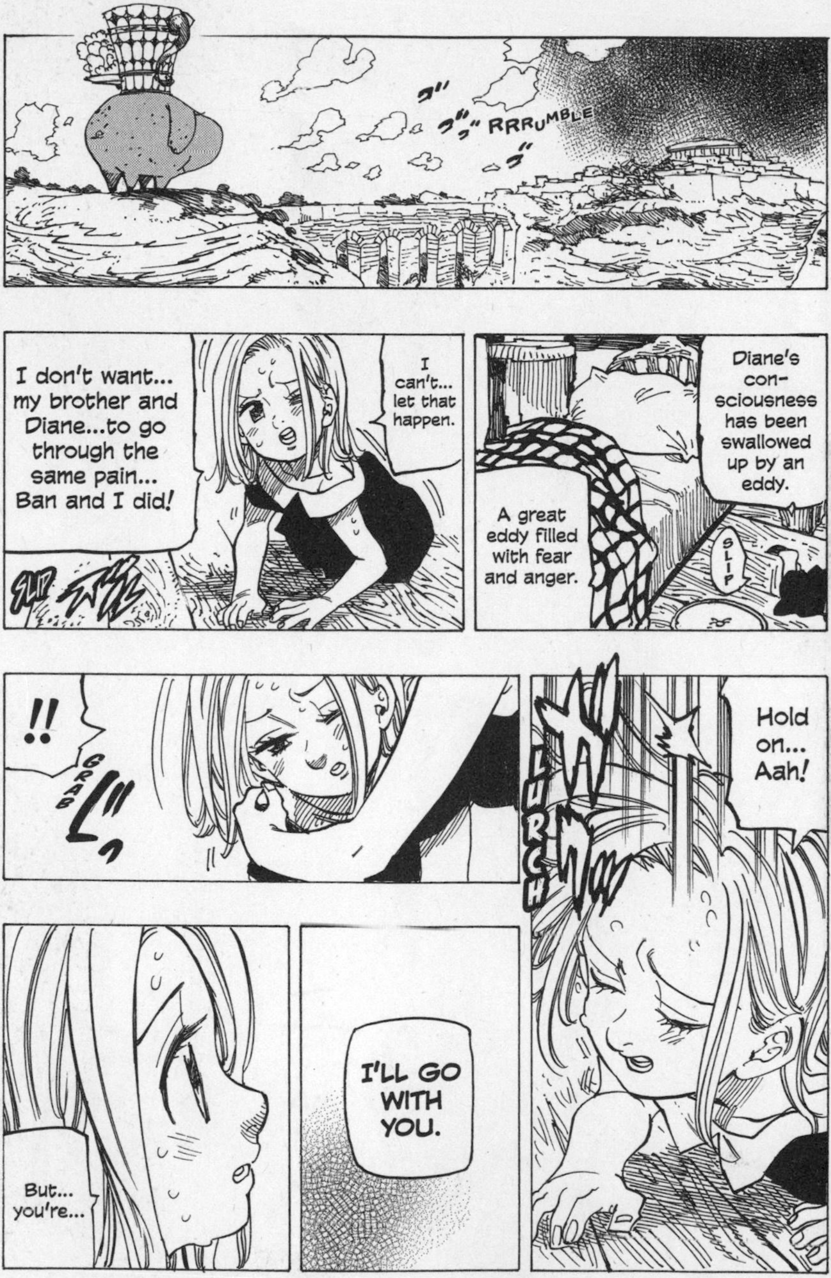
RRRUMBLE
Diane's con-sciousness has been swallowed up by an eddy.
A great eddy filled with fear and anger.
SLIP
I can't... let that happen.
I don't want... my brother and Diane...to go through the same pain... Ban and I did!
SLIP
Hold on... Aah!
LURCH
!!
GRAB
I'LL GO WITH YOU.
But... you're...

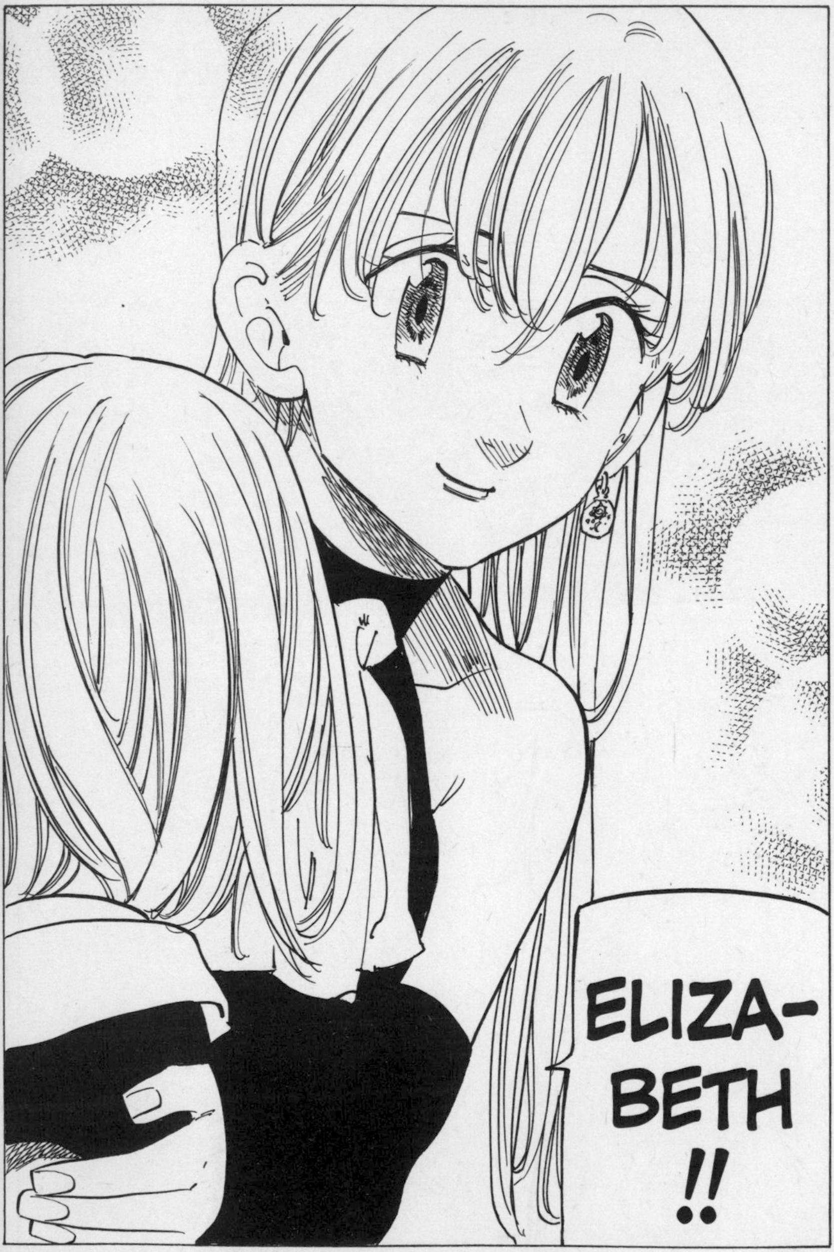
ELIZA-
BETH
!!

Chapter 228 - The Goddess and the Saint

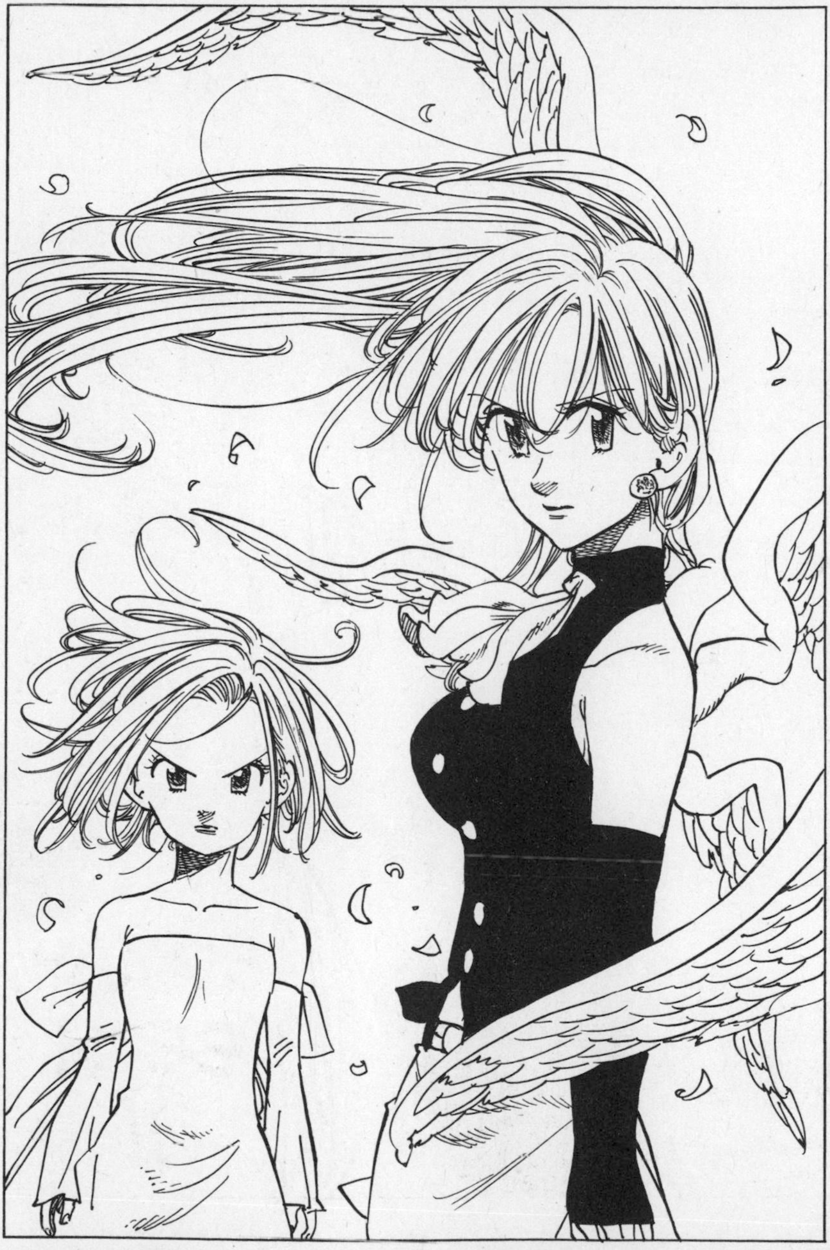

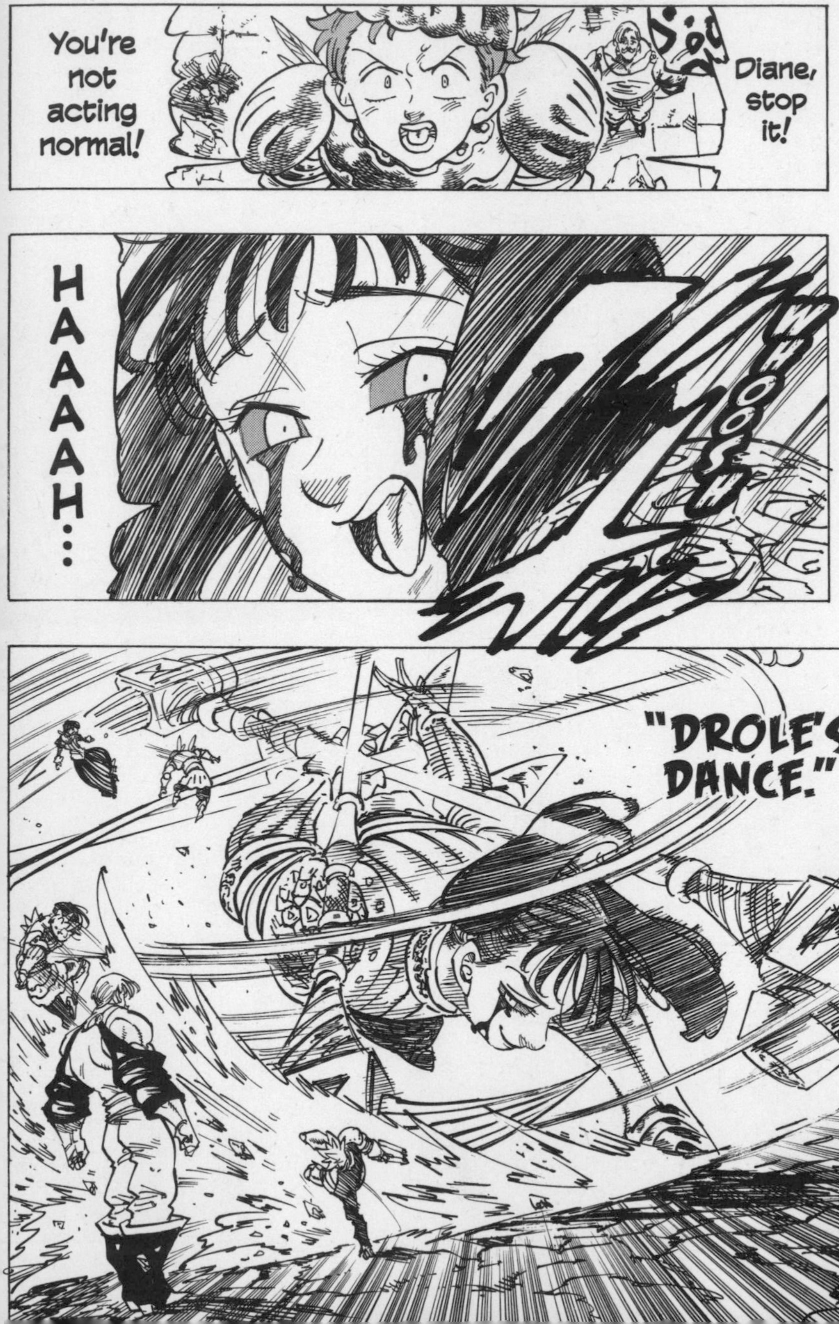
Diane, stop it!
You're not acting normal!
WHOOSH
HAAAAAH...
"DROLE'S DANCE."

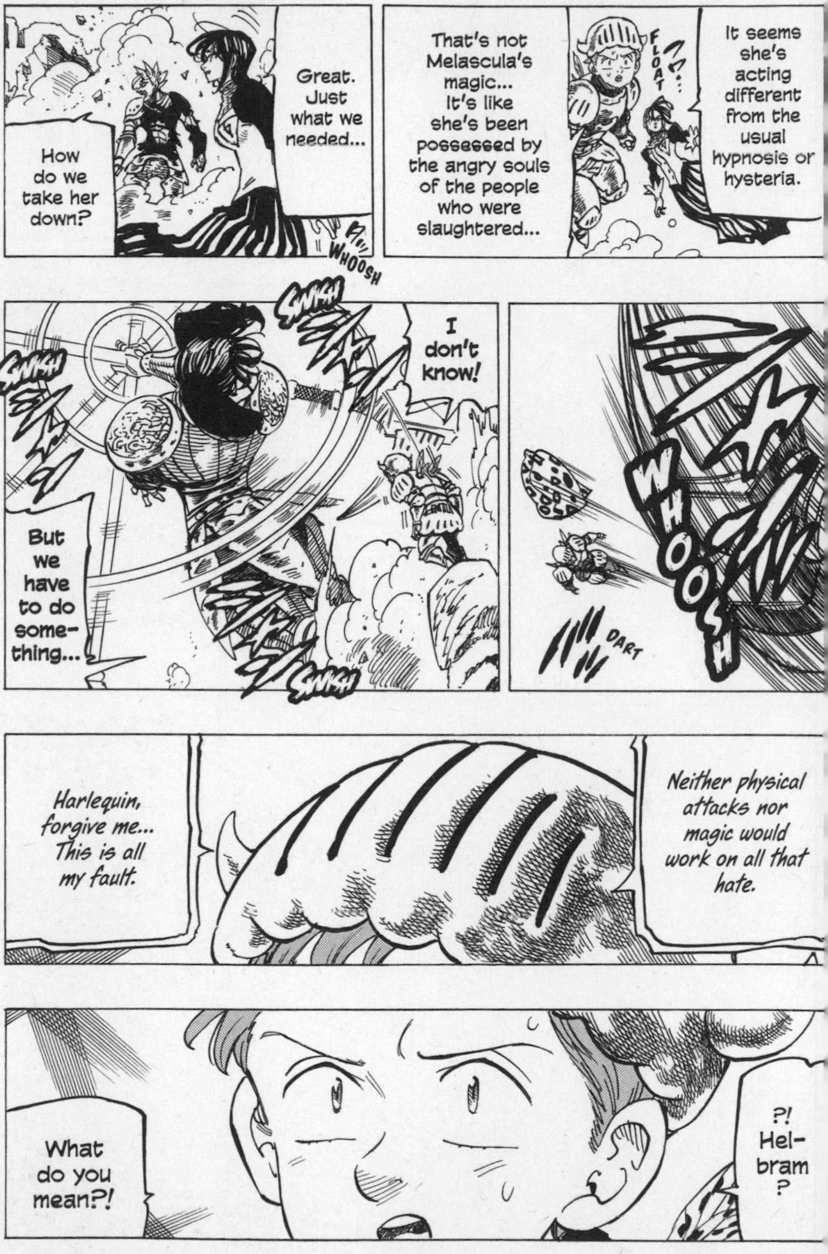
It seems she's acting different from the usual hypnosis or hysteria.
FLOAT
That's not Melascula's magic... It's like she's been possessed by the angry souls of the people who were slaughtered...
Great. Just what we needed...
How do we take her down?
WHOOSH
WHOOSH
DART
SWISH
I don't know!
SWISH
But we have to do some-thing...
SWISH
Neither physical attacks nor magic would work on all that hate.
Harlequin, forgive me... This is all my fault.
?! Hel-bram?
What do you mean?!

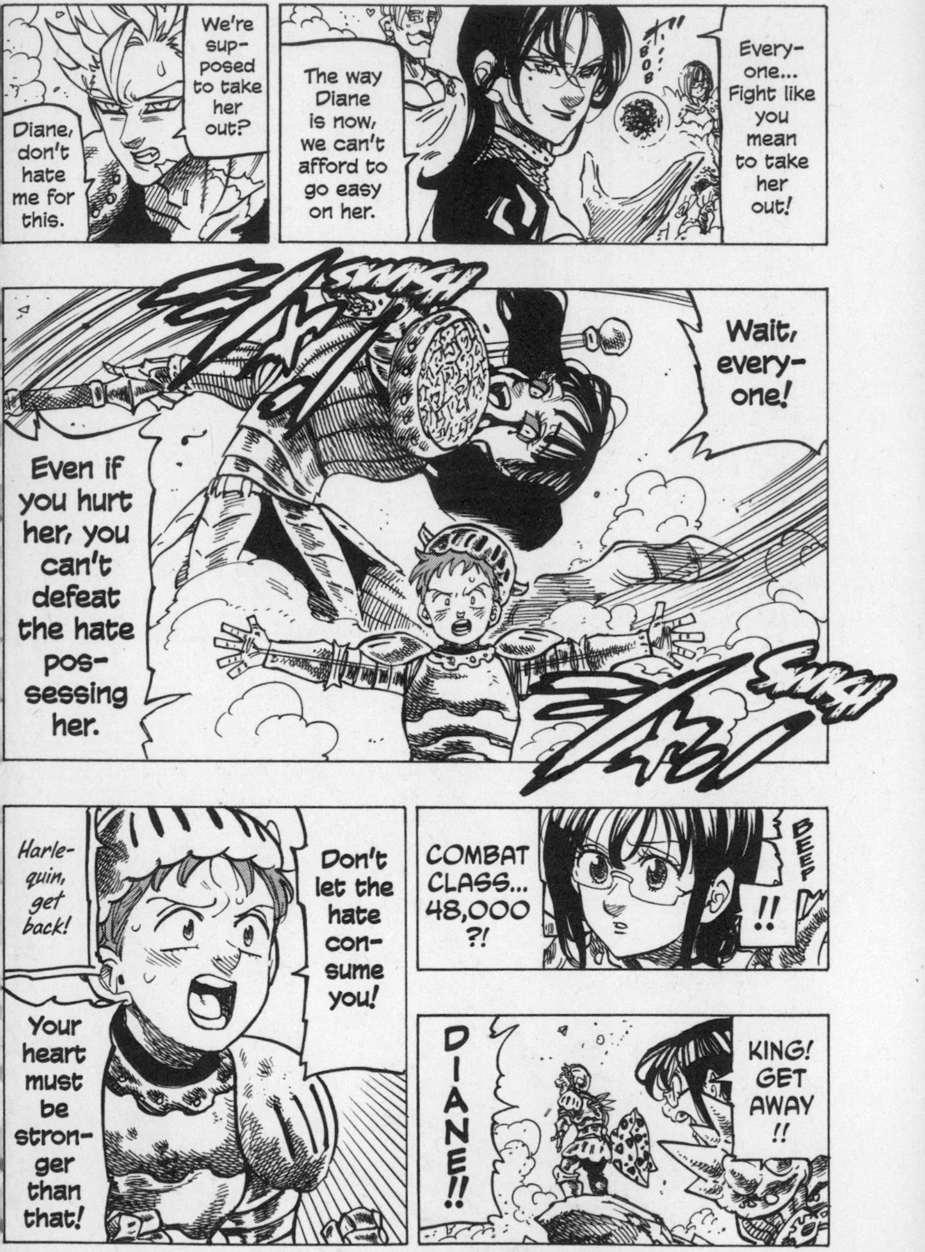
Every-one... Fight like you mean to take her out!
BOB
The way Diane is now, we can't afford to go easy on her.
We're sup-posed to take her out?
Diane, don't hate me for this.
Wait, every-one!
Even if you hurt her, you can't defeat the hate pos-sessing her.
BEEP
!!
COMBAT CLASS... 48,000 ?!
KING! GET AWAY !!
DIANE!!
Don't let the hate con-sume you!
Harle-quin, get back!
Your heart must be stron-ger than that!

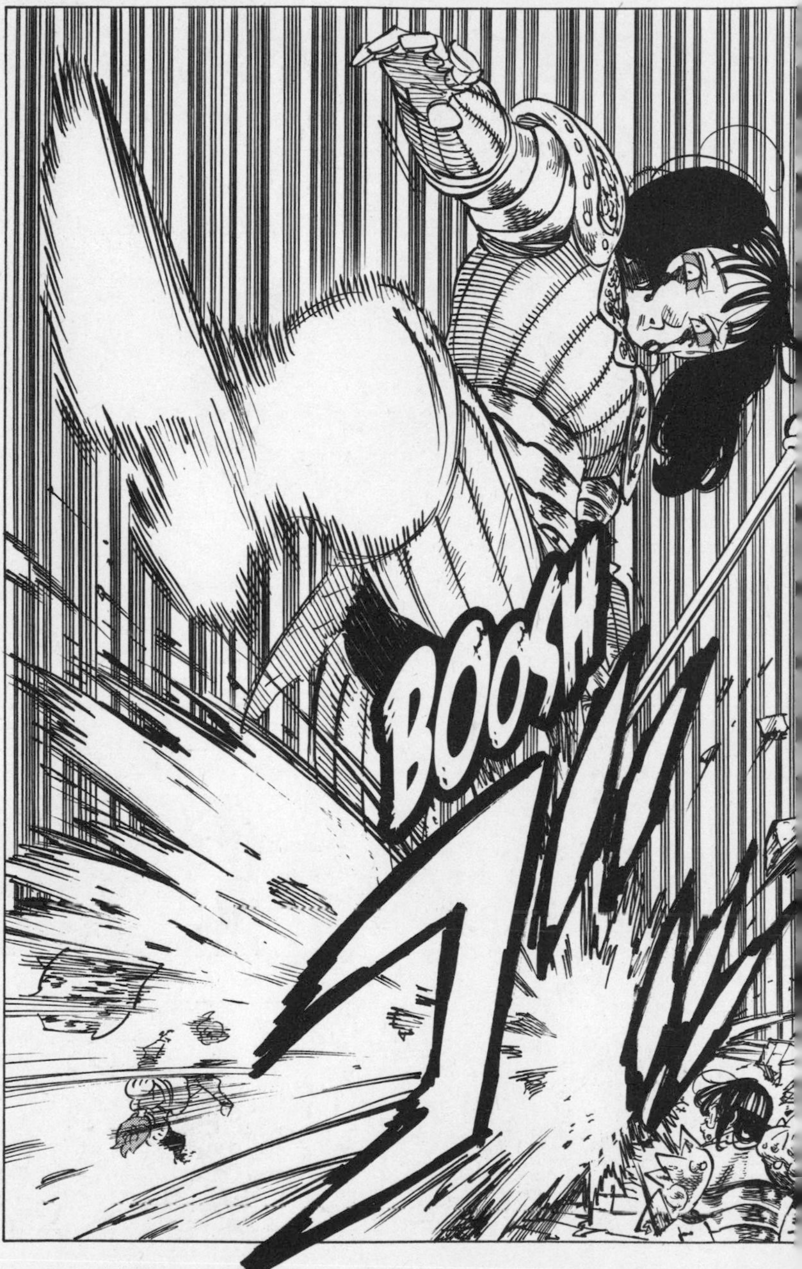
BOOSH

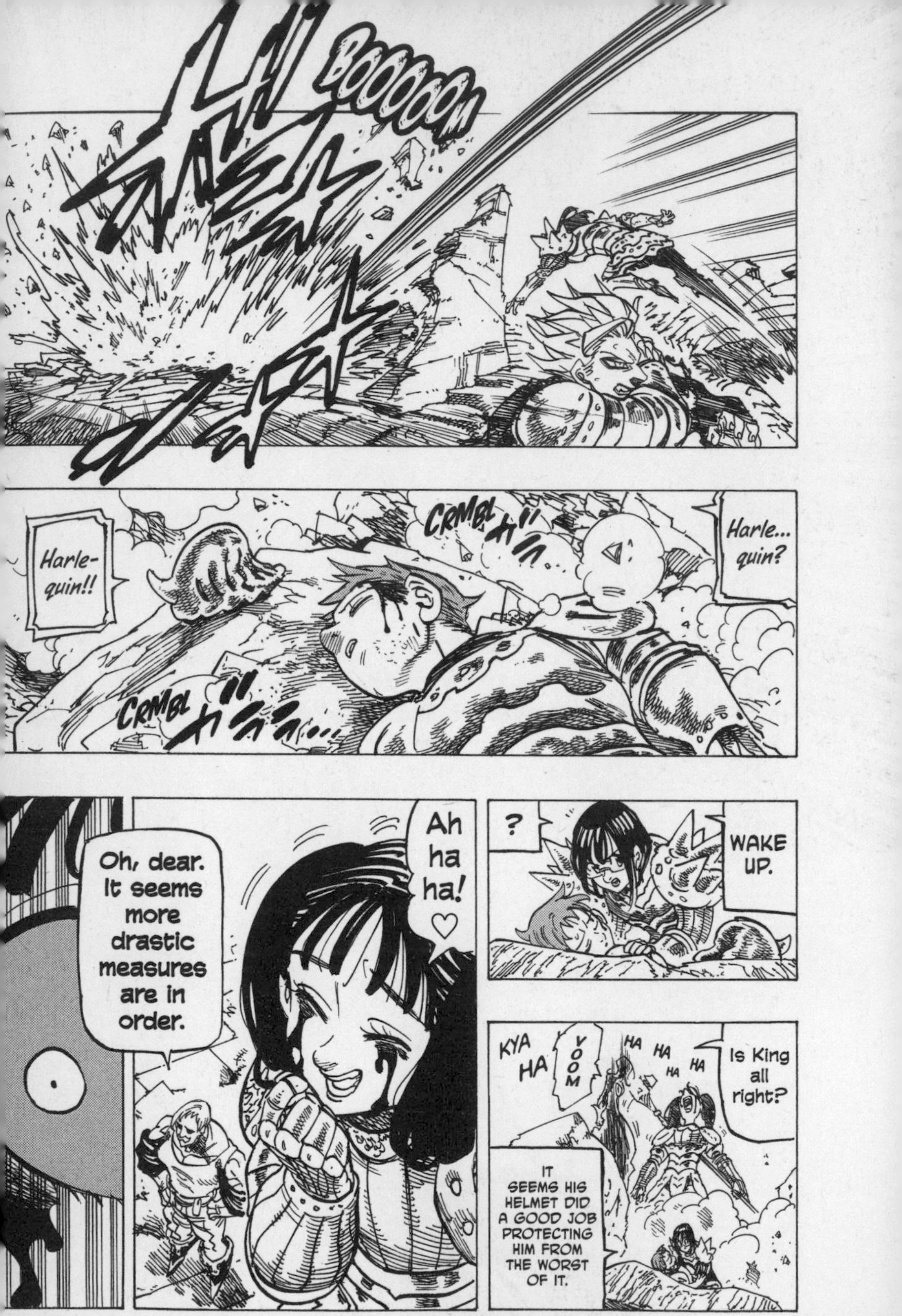
BOOOOOM
Harle... quin?
CRMBL
Harle-quin!!
CRMBL
WAKE UP.
?
Is King all right?
HA HA HA HA
VOOM
KYA HA
IT SEEMS HIS HELMET DID A GOOD JOB PROTECTING HIM FROM THE WORST OF IT.
Ah ha ha! ♡
Oh, dear. It seems more drastic measures are in order.

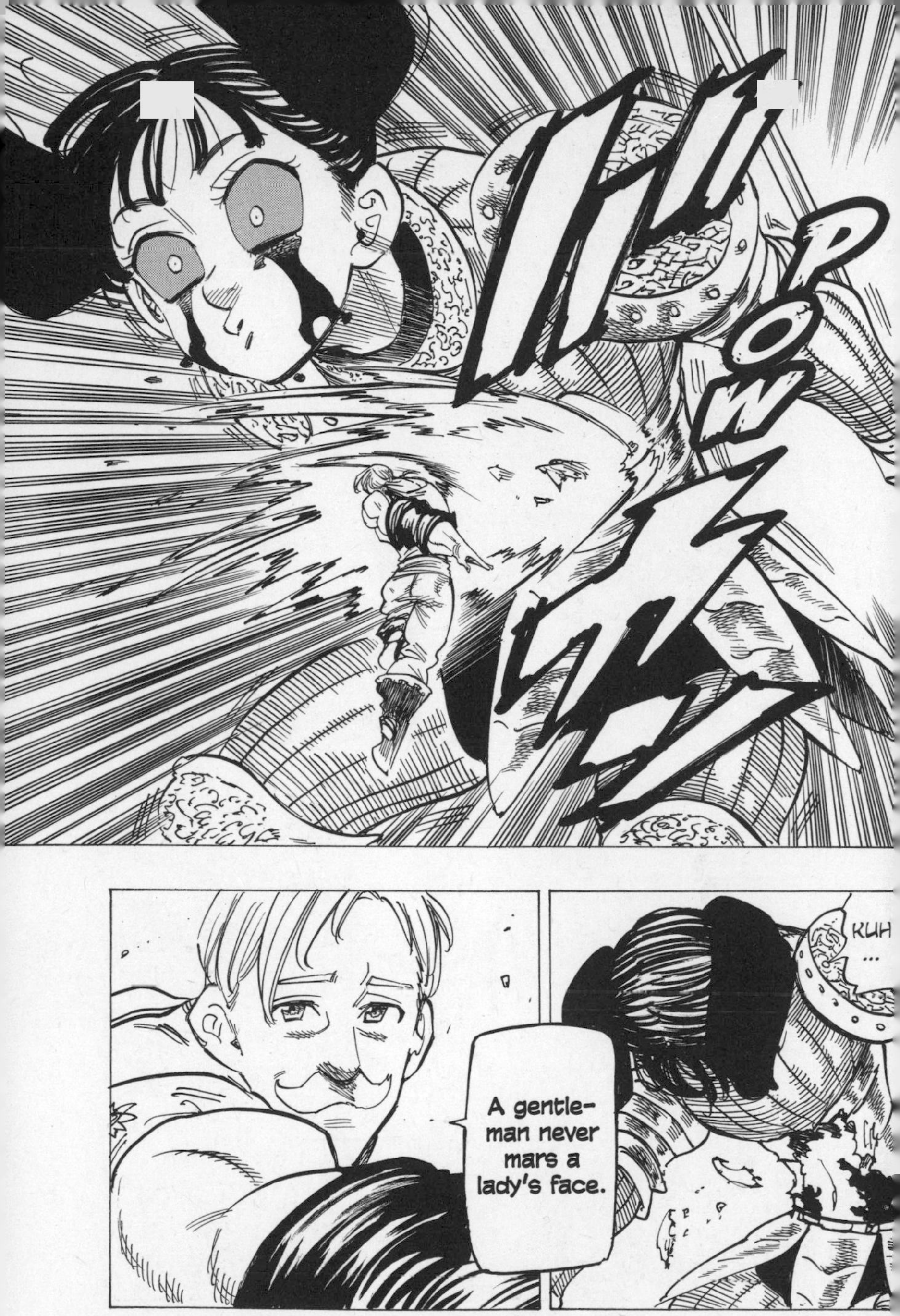
POW
KUH ...
A gentle-
man never
mars a
lady's face.

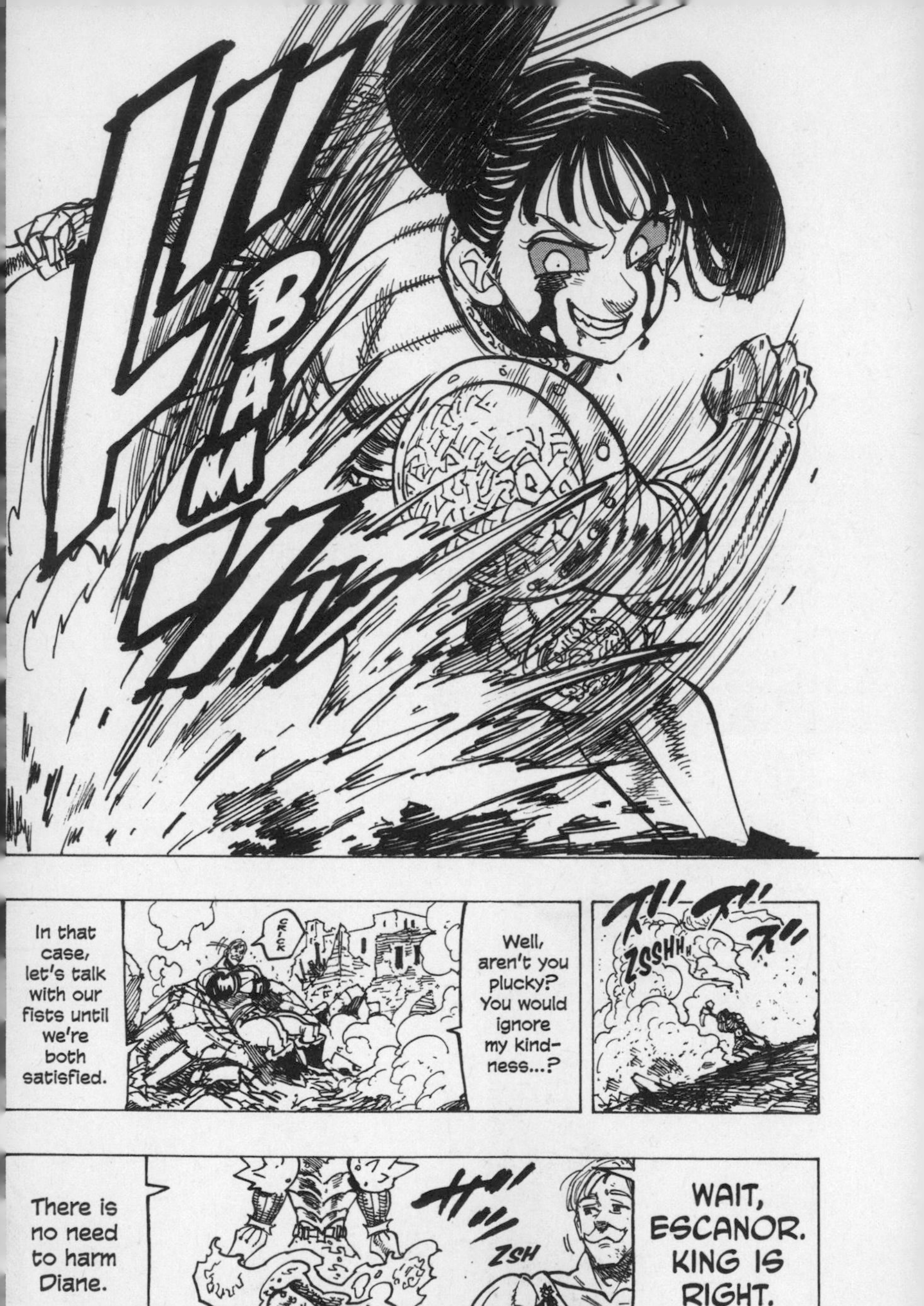
BAM
ZSSHH
Well, aren't you plucky? You would ignore my kind-ness...?
CRICK
In that case, let's talk with our fists until we're both satisfied.
WAIT, ESCANOR. KING IS RIGHT.
ZSH
There is no need to harm Diane.

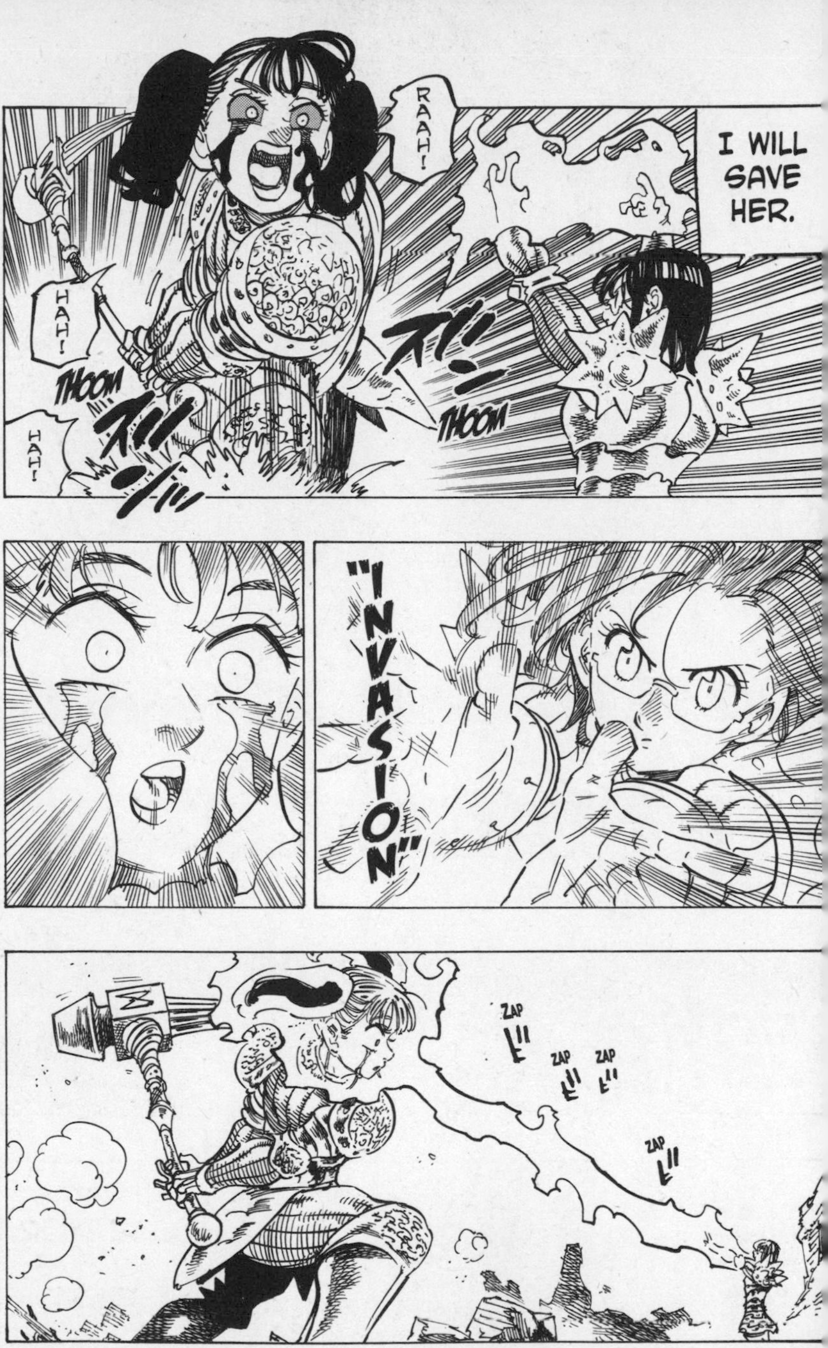
I WILL SAVE HER.
RAAH!
THOOM
HAH!
THOOM
HAH!
"INVASION"
ZAP
ZAP
ZAP
ZAP

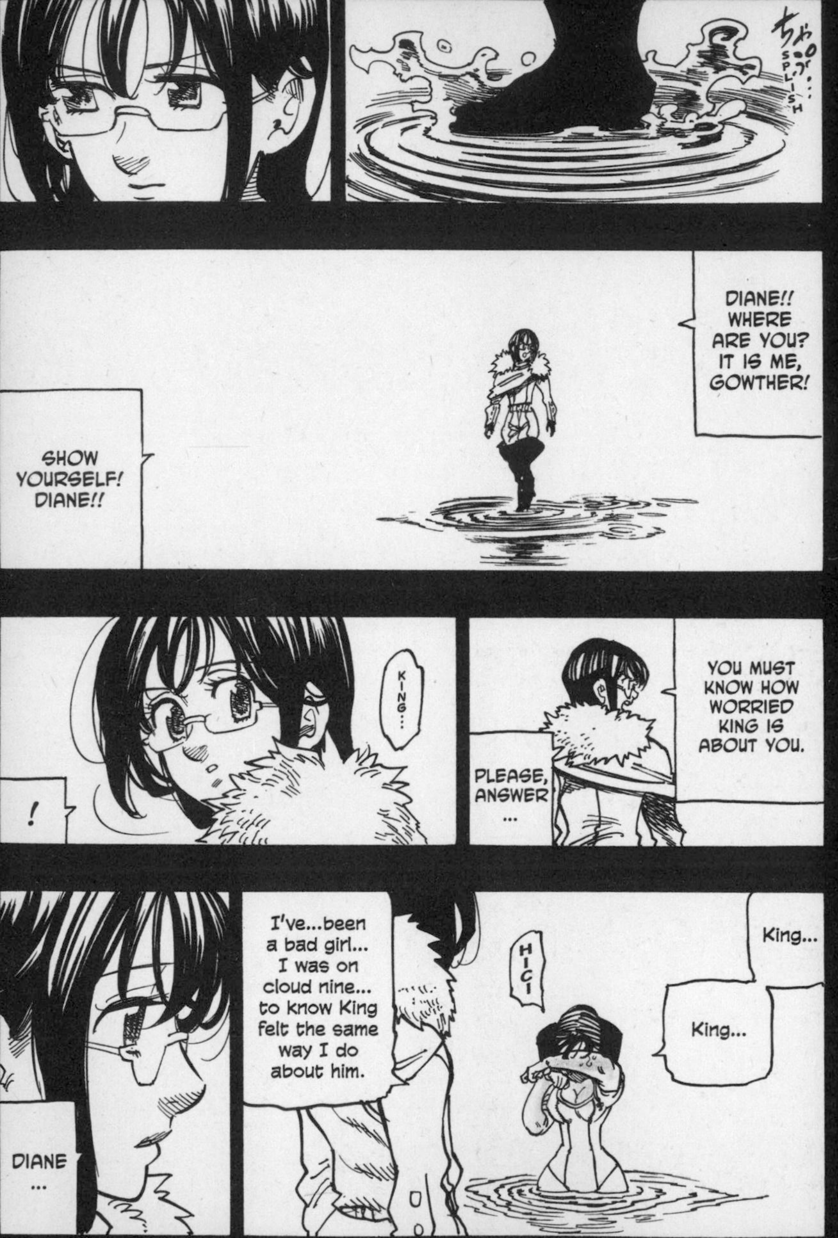
SPLISH
DIANE!! WHERE ARE YOU? IT IS ME, GOWTHER!
SHOW YOURSELF! DIANE!!
YOU MUST KNOW HOW WORRIED KING IS ABOUT YOU.
PLEASE, ANSWER...
KING...
!
King...
King...
HIC
I've...been a bad girl... I was on cloud nine... to know King felt the same way I do about him.
DIANE...

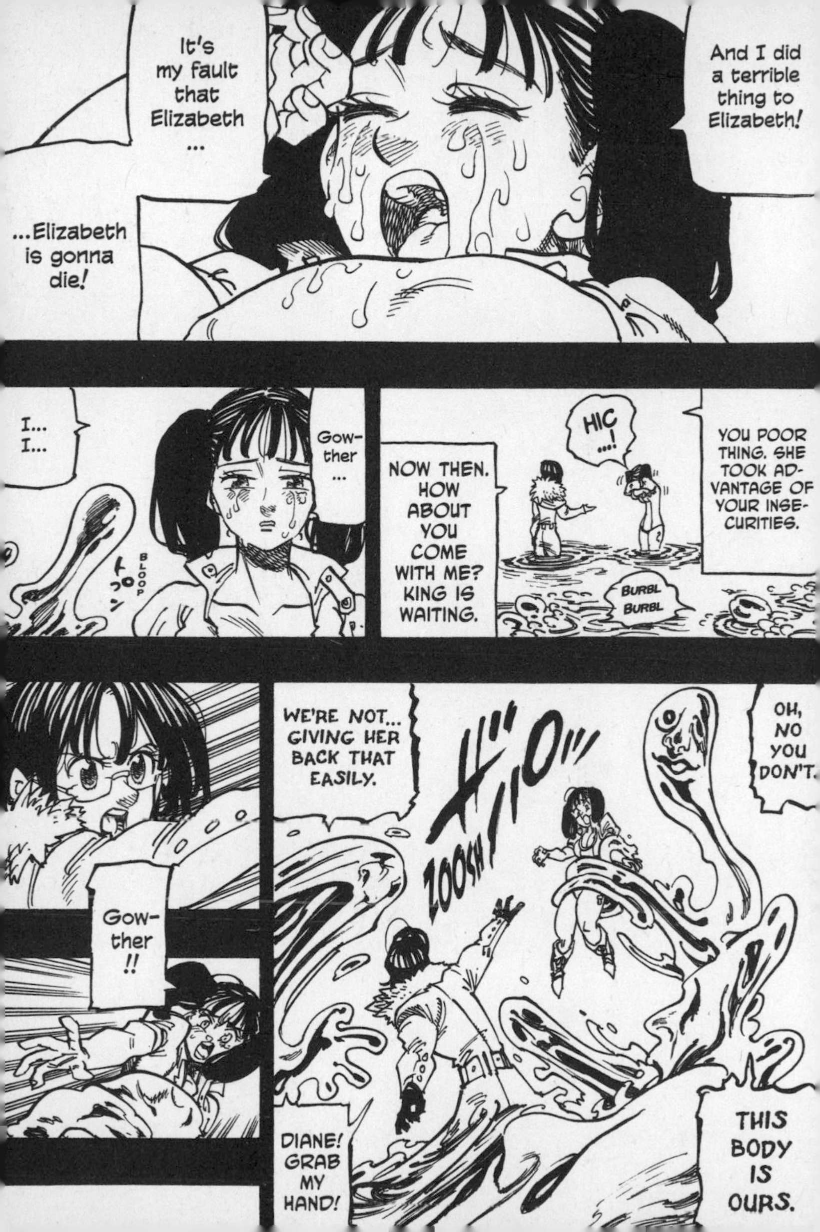
And I did a terrible thing to Elizabeth!
It's my fault that Elizabeth ...
...Elizabeth is gonna die!
YOU POOR THING. SHE TOOK ADVANTAGE OF YOUR INSECURITIES.
HIC ...!
NOW THEN. HOW ABOUT YOU COME WITH ME? KING IS WAITING.
BURBL BURBL
Gow-ther ...
I... I...
BLOOP
OH, NO YOU DON'T.
WE'RE NOT... GIVING HER BACK THAT EASILY.
ZOOSH
THIS BODY IS OURS.
DIANE! GRAB MY HAND!
Gow-ther !!

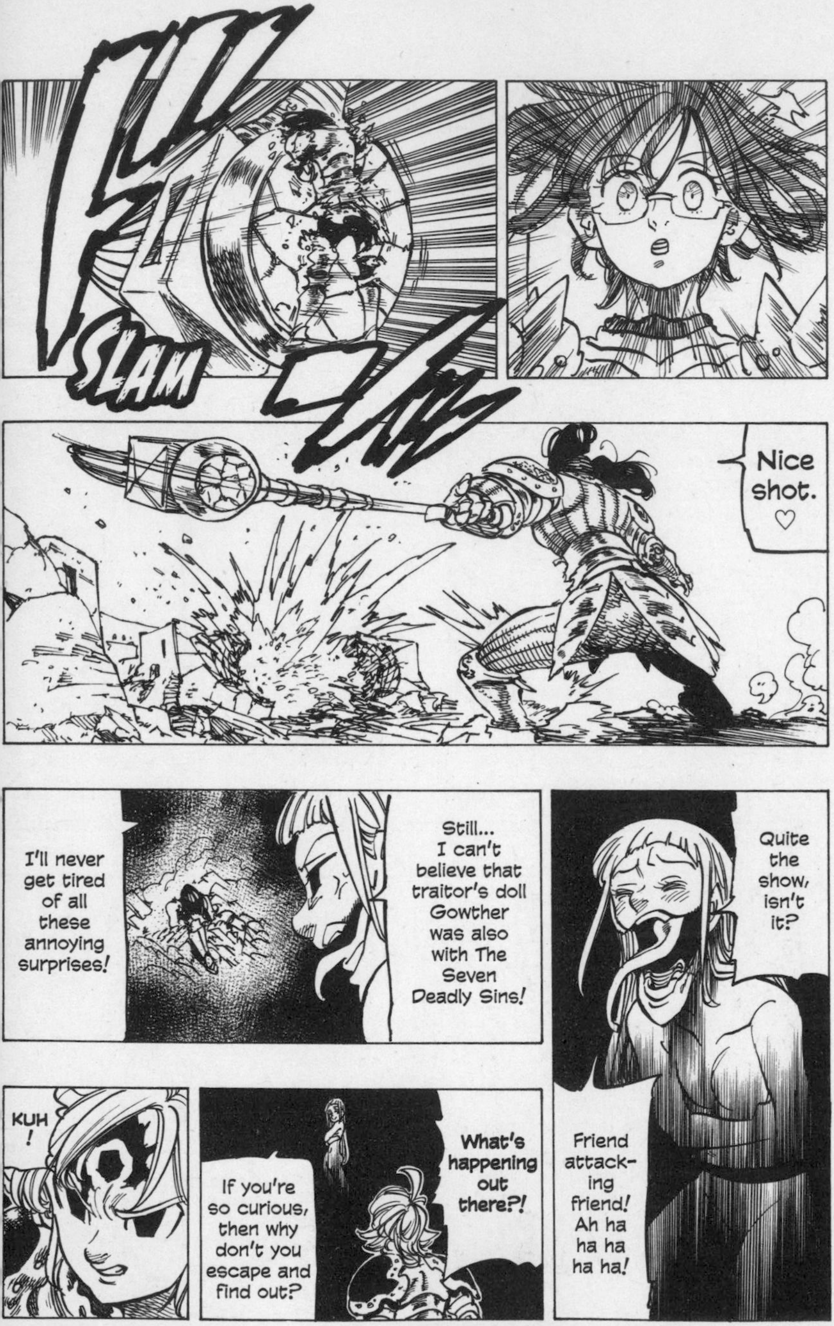
SLAM
Nice shot. ♡
Quite the show, isn't it?
Friend attacking-ing friend! Ah ha ha ha ha ha!
Still... I can't believe that traitor's doll Gowther was also with The Seven Deadly Sins!
I'll never get tired of all these annoying surprises!
What's happening out there?!
If you're so curious, then why don't you escape and find out?
KUH!

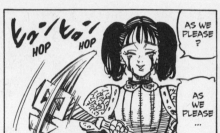

THAT BODY BELONG TO OU PRECIO FRIEND
CRMBL
WE WILL NOT LET YOU DO AS YOU PLEASE WITH IT!
AS WE PLEASE ?
HOP
HOP
AS WE PLEASE ...
LIKE THIS ?
STAB
STO IT!
"SNATCH!!"
OH? DI DO SO THIN WRON
STAB
PULL
KUH !
Dia... ne!
Enough.

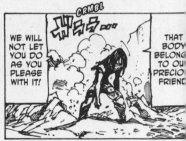

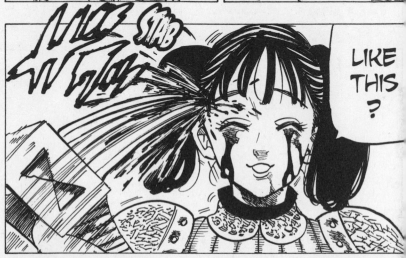

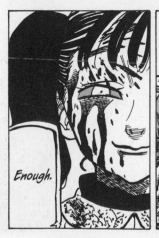

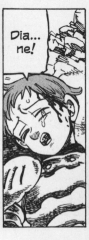

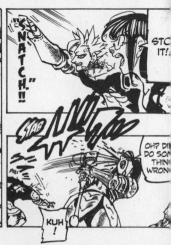

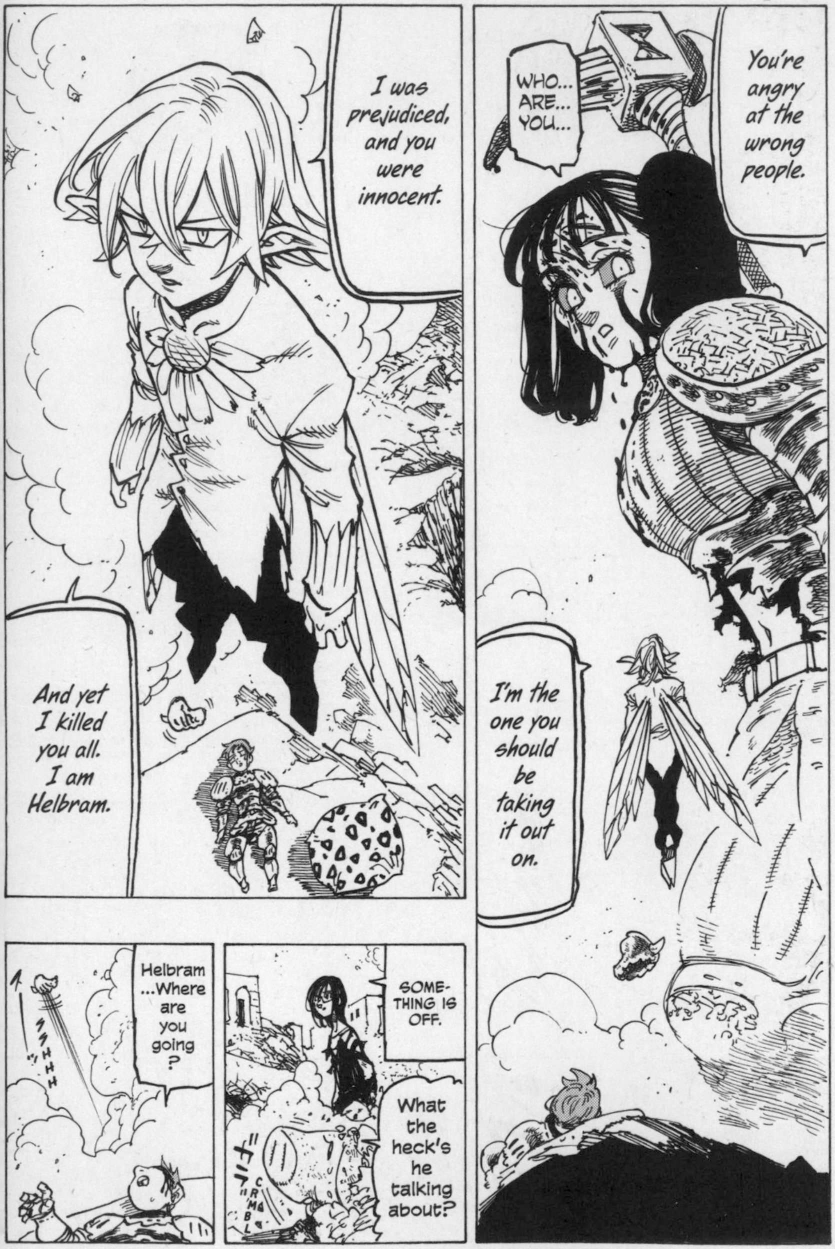
You're angry at the wrong people.
WHO... ARE... YOU...
I'm the one you should be taking it out on.
I was prejudiced, and you were innocent.
And yet I killed you all. I am Helbram.
SOME-THING IS OFF.
What the heck's he talking about?
CRMBL
Helbram ...Where are you going?
SHHH

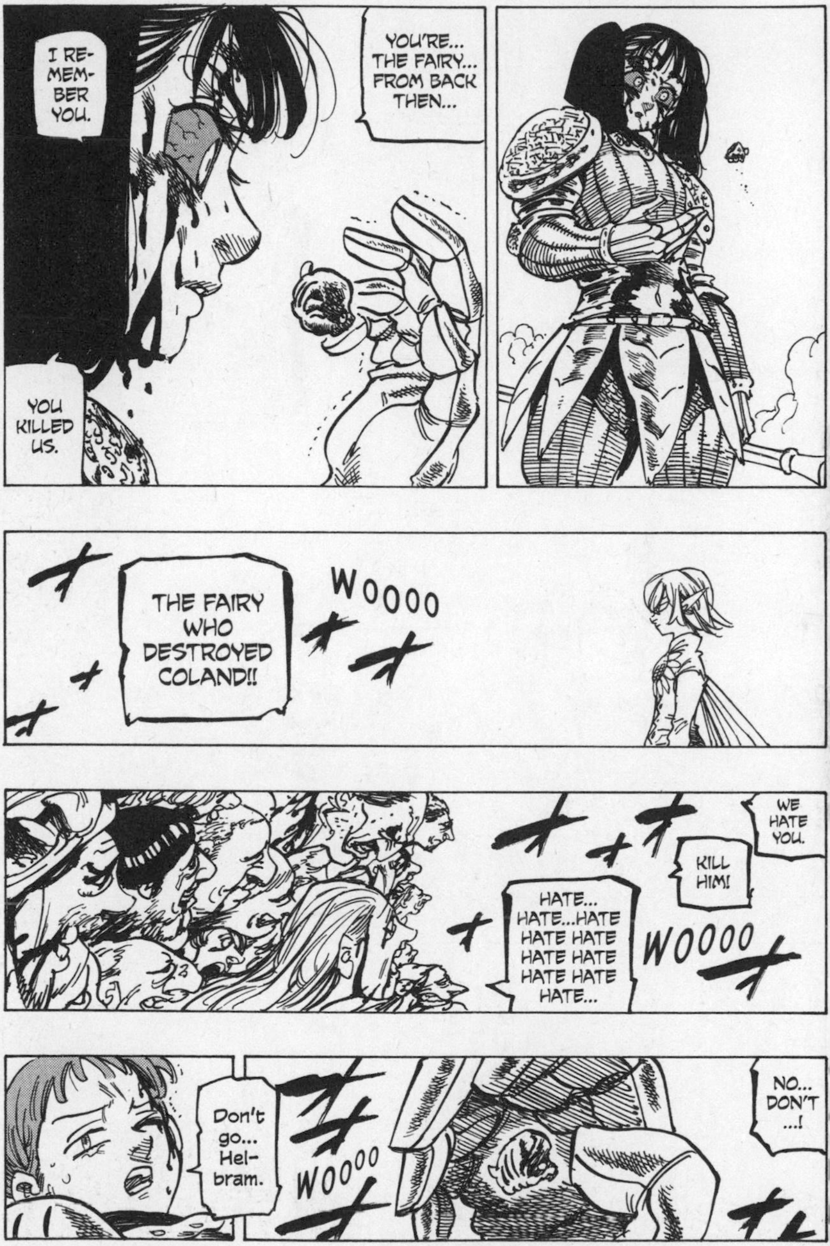
YOU'RE... THE FAIRY... FROM BACK THEN...
I RE-MEMBER YOU.
YOU KILLED US.
WOOOO
THE FAIRY WHO DESTROYED COLAND!!
WE HATE YOU.
KILL HIM!
HATE... HATE...HATE HATE HATE HATE HATE HATE HATE HATE...
WOOOO
NO... DON'T ...!
WOOOO
Don't go... Hel-bram.

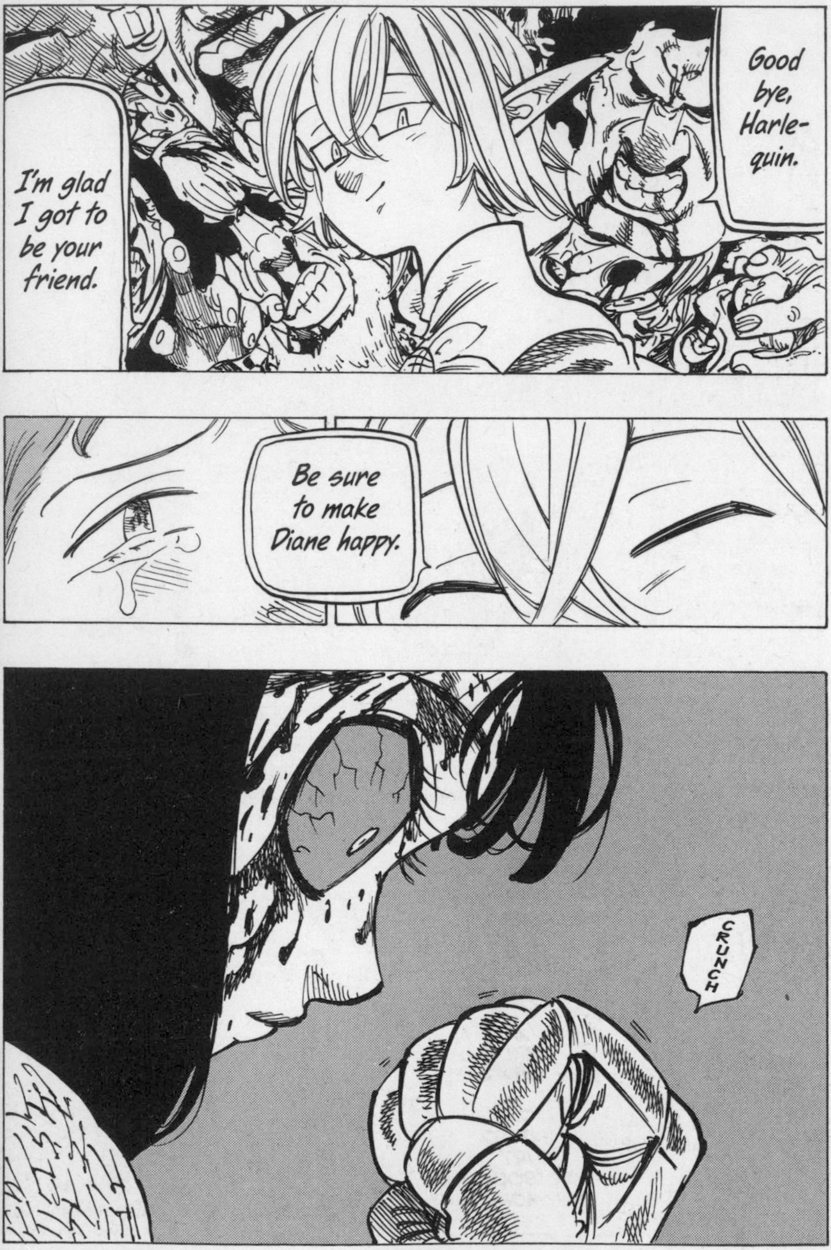
Good bye, Harle-quin.
I'm glad I got to be your friend.
Be sure to make Diane happy.
CRUNCH

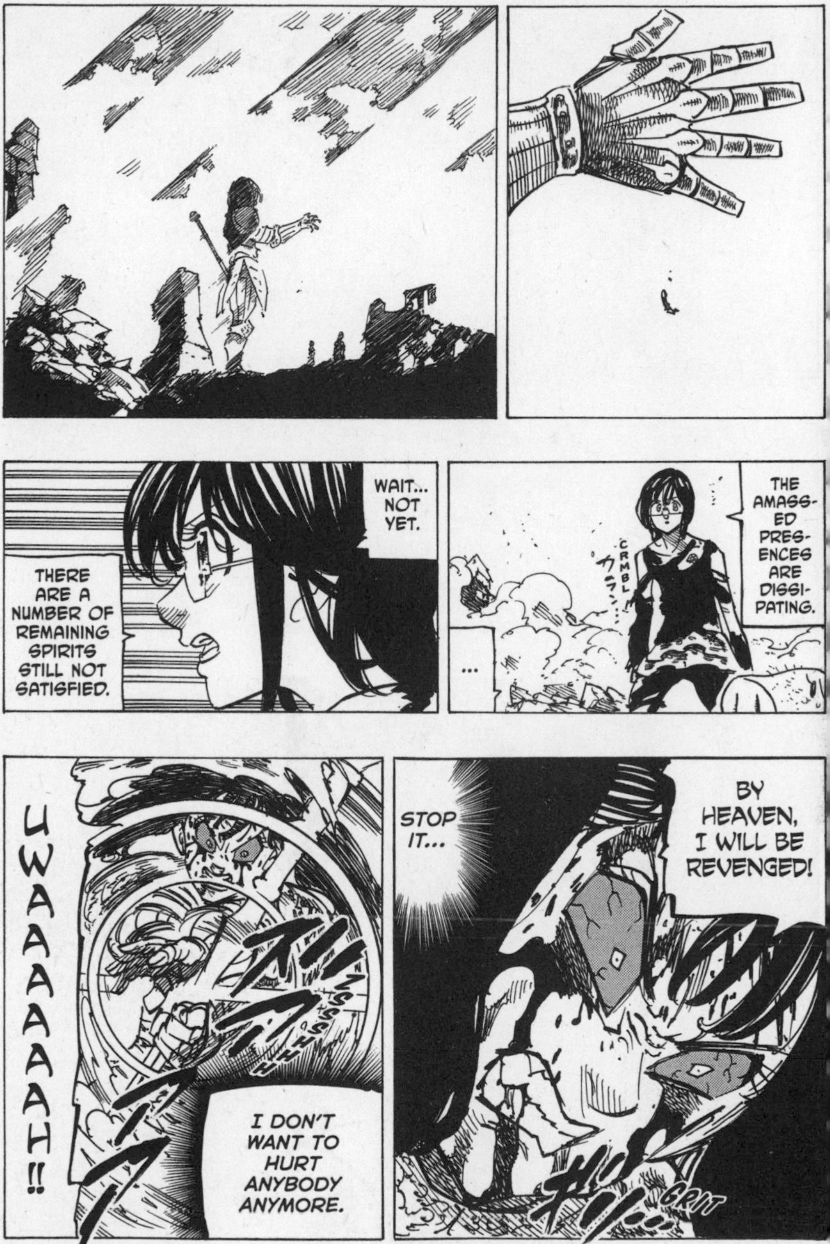
THE AMASSED PRESENCES ARE DISSIPATING.
CRMBL
...
WAIT... NOT YET.
THERE ARE A NUMBER OF REMAINING SPIRITS STILL NOT SATISFIED.
BY HEAVEN, I WILL BE REVENGED!
STOP IT...
GRIT
UWAAAAAAAH!!
I DON'T WANT TO HURT ANYBODY ANYMORE.

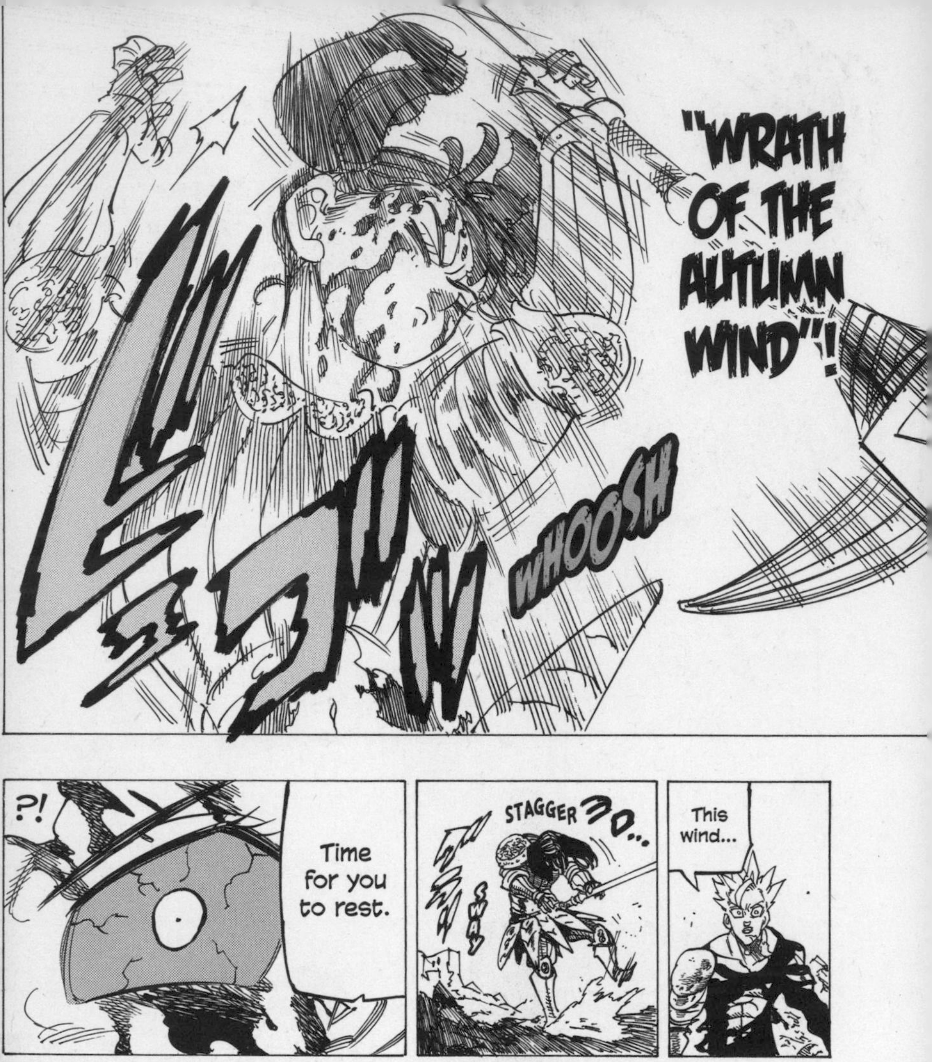

"WRATH OF THE AUTUMN WIND"!
WHOOSH
This wind...
STAGGER
SWAY
Time for you to rest.
?!
"LET THERE BE LIGHT."

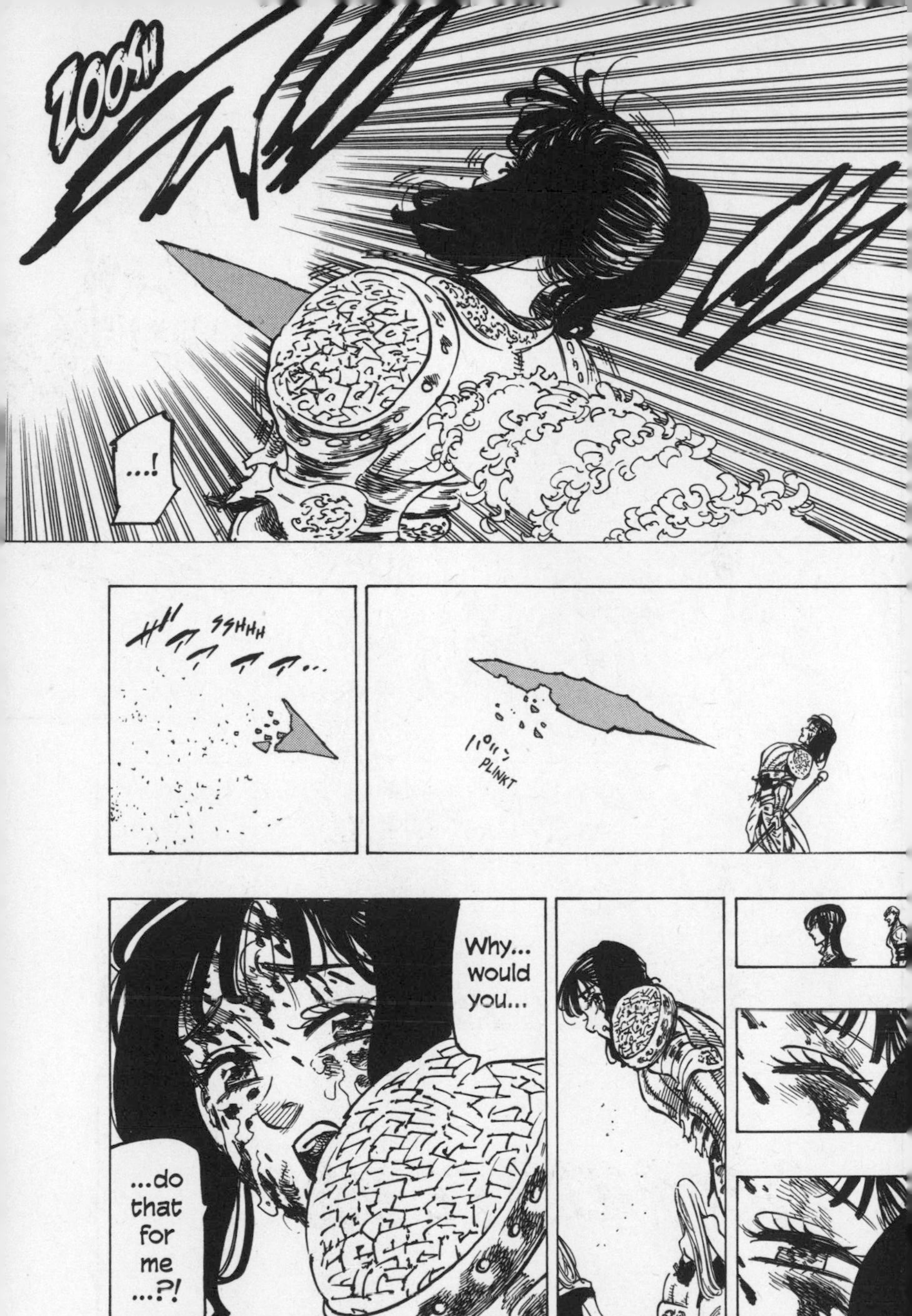
ZOOSH
...!
PLINKT
SSHHH
Why... would you...
...do that for me ...?!

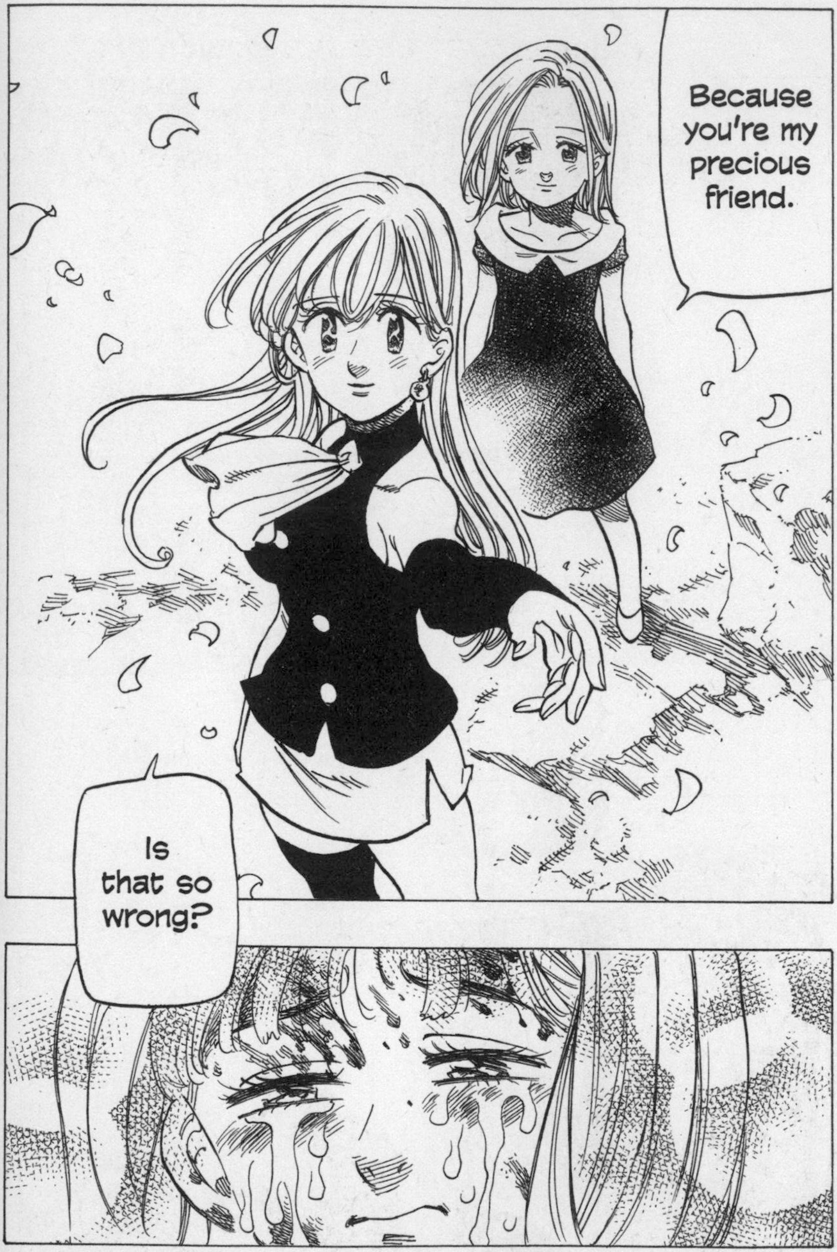
Because you're my precious friend.
Is that so wrong?

Chapter 229 - Love is a Maiden's Power

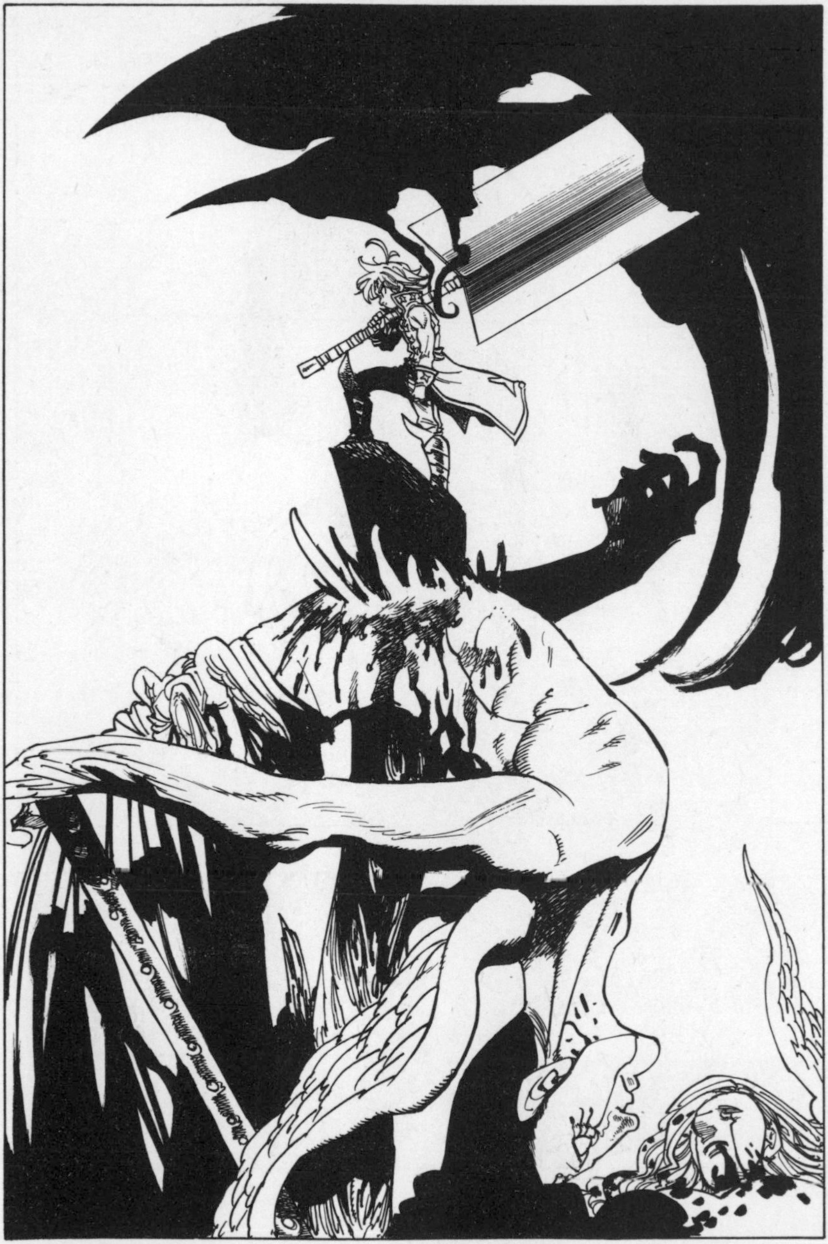

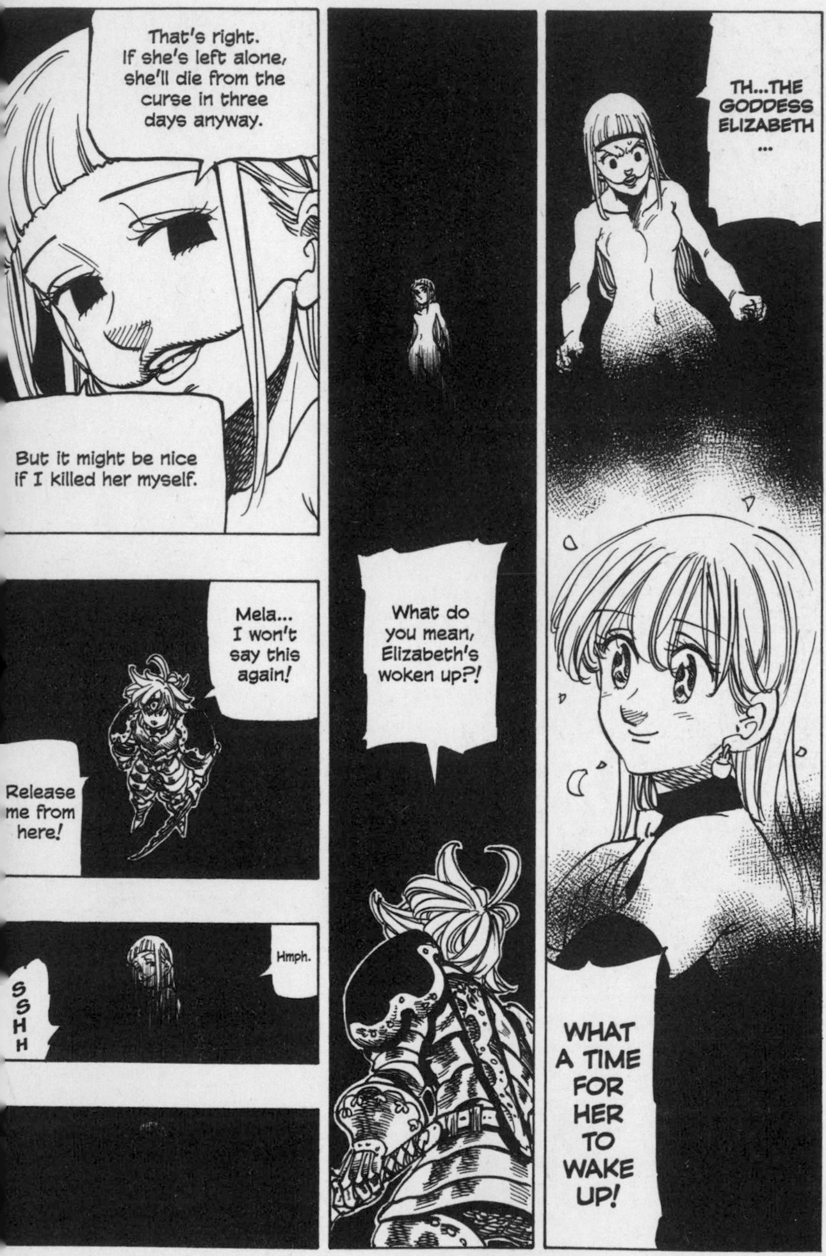
TH...THE GODDESS ELIZABETH ...
WHAT A TIME FOR HER TO WAKE UP!
What do you mean, Elizabeth's woken up?!
That's right. If she's left alone, she'll die from the curse in three days anyway.
But it might be nice if I killed her myself.
Mela... I won't say this again!
Release me from here!
Hmph.
SSHH

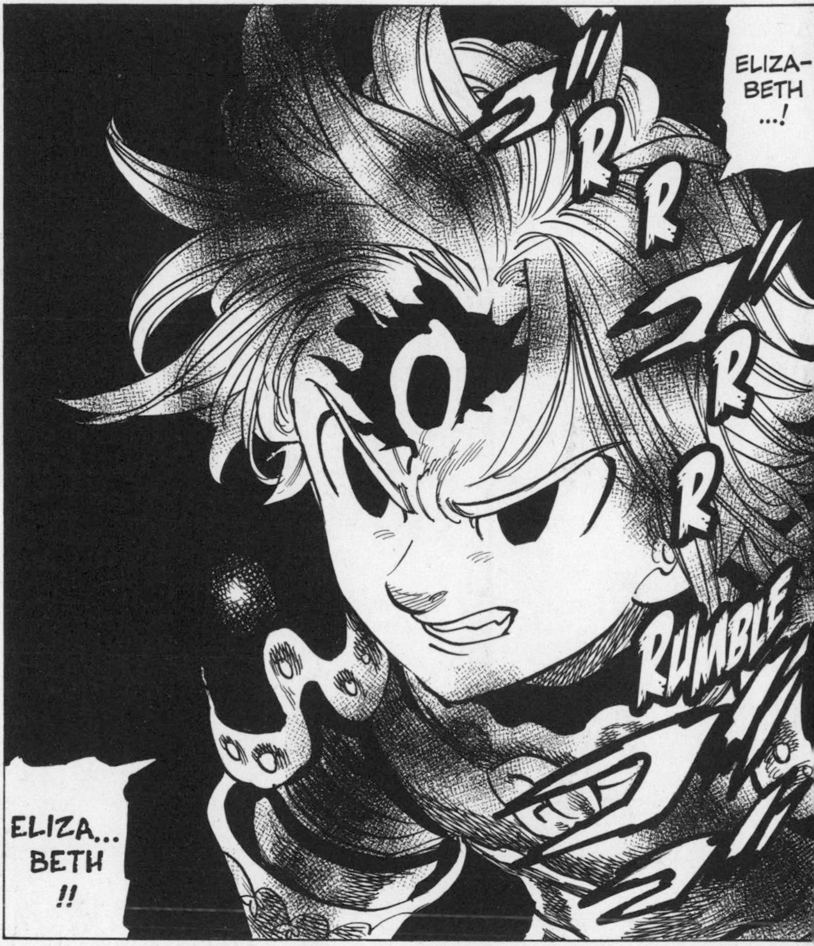
ELIZA-BETH ...!
RRRR
RUMBLE
ELIZA... BETH !!

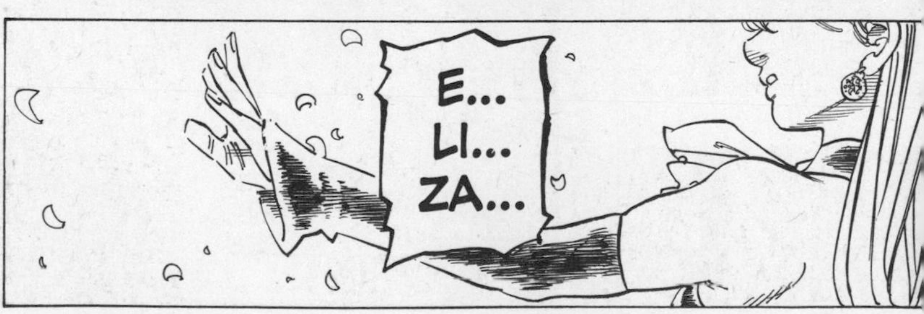
E... LI... ZA...

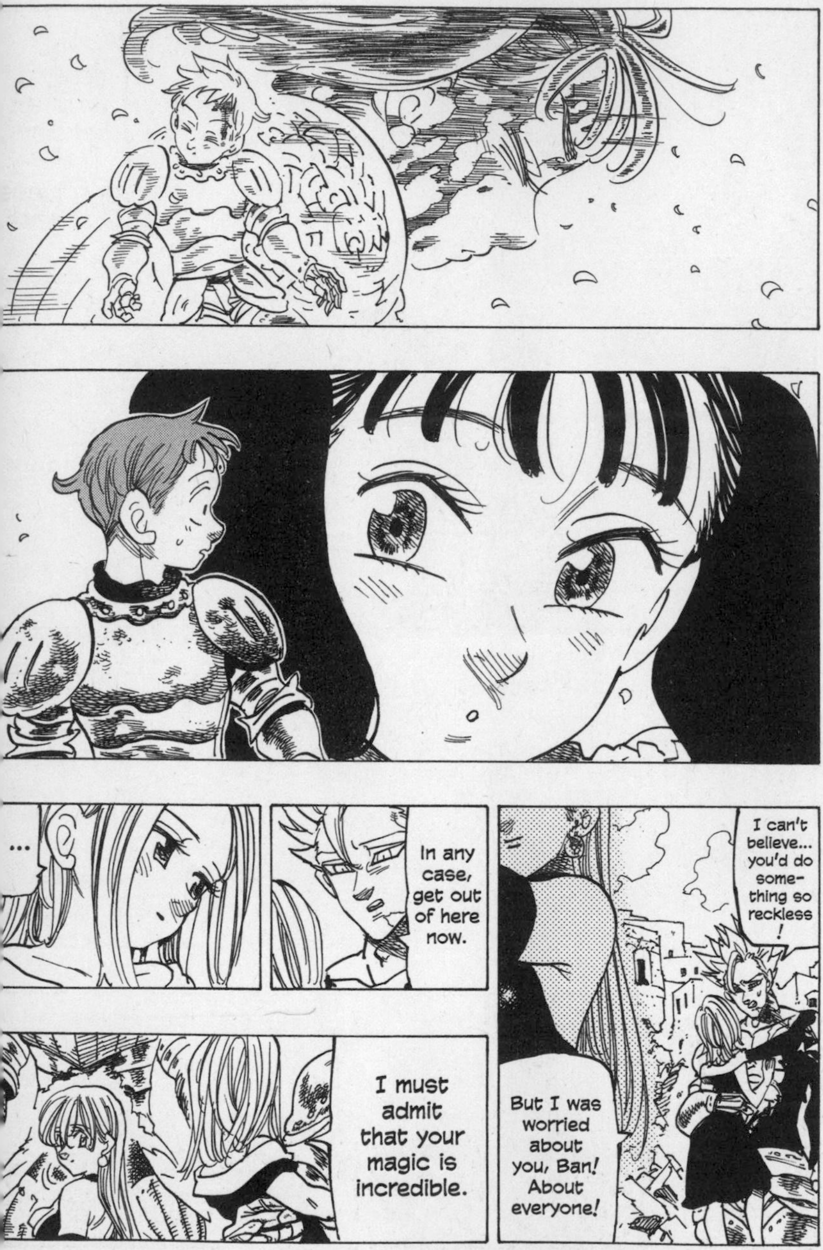
I can't believe... you'd do some-thing so reckless!
But I was worried about you, Ban! About everyone!
In any case, get out of here now.
...
I must admit that your magic is incredible.

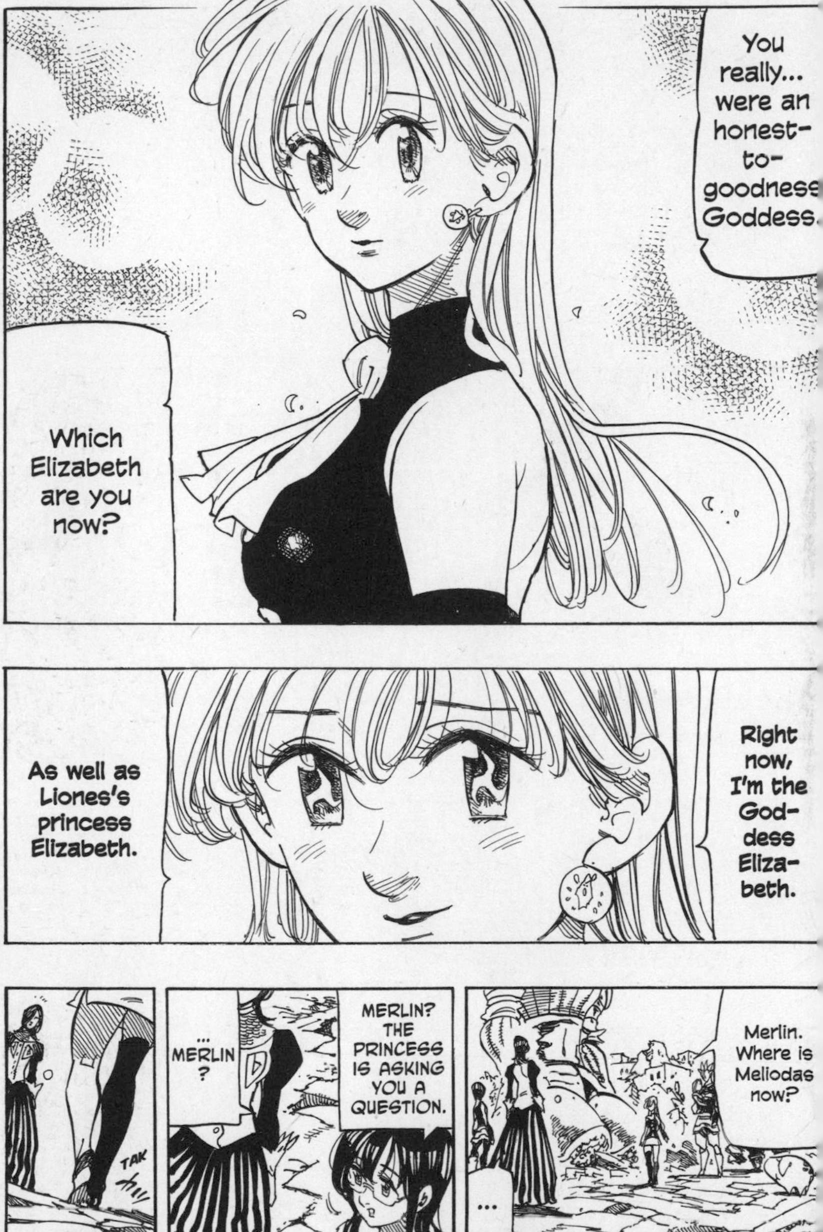
You really... were an honest-to-goodness Goddess.
Which Elizabeth are you now?
Right now, I'm the God-dess Eliza-beth.
As well as Liones's princess Elizabeth.
Merlin. Where is Meliodas now?
...
MERLIN? THE PRINCESS IS ASKING YOU A QUESTION.
... MERLIN ?
TAK

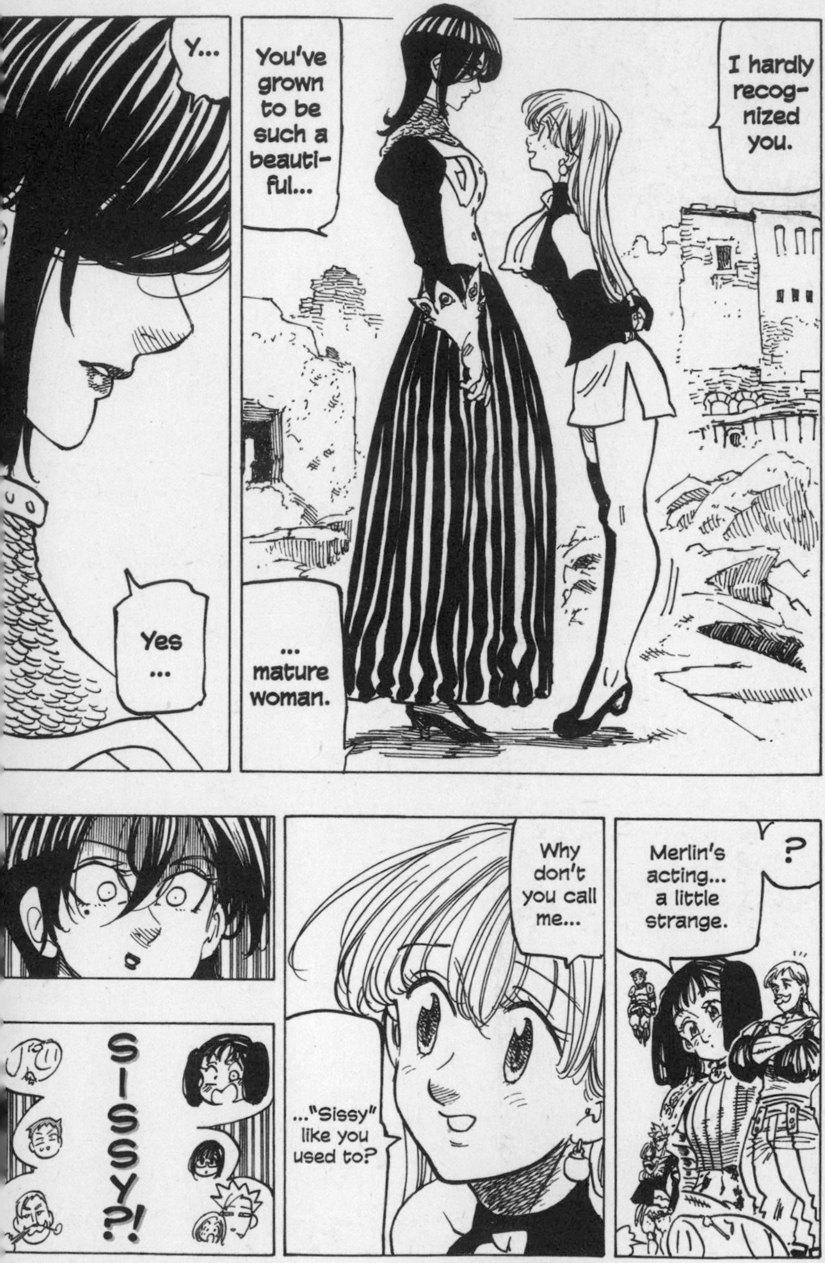
I hardly recog-nized you.
You've grown to be such a beauti-ful...
... mature woman.
Y...
Yes ...
?
Merlin's acting... a little strange.
Why don't you call me...
..."Sissy" like you used to?
SISSY?!

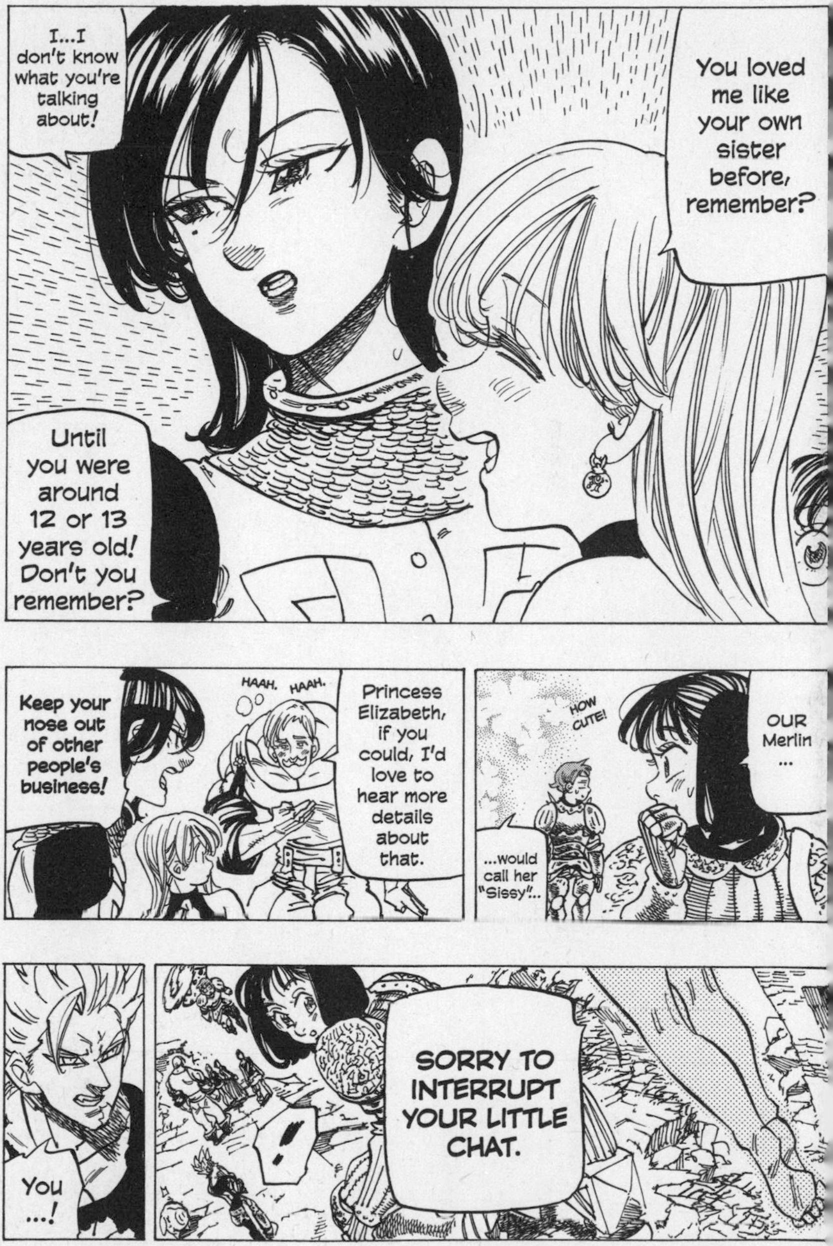
You loved me like your own sister before, remember?
I...I don't know what you're talking about!
Until you were around 12 or 13 years old! Don't you remember?
OUR Merlin ...
HOW CUTE!
...would call her "Sissy"!...
Princess Elizabeth, if you could, I'd love to hear more details about that.
HAAH. HAAH.
Keep your nose out of other people's business!
SORRY TO INTERRUPT YOUR LITTLE CHAT.
!
You ...!

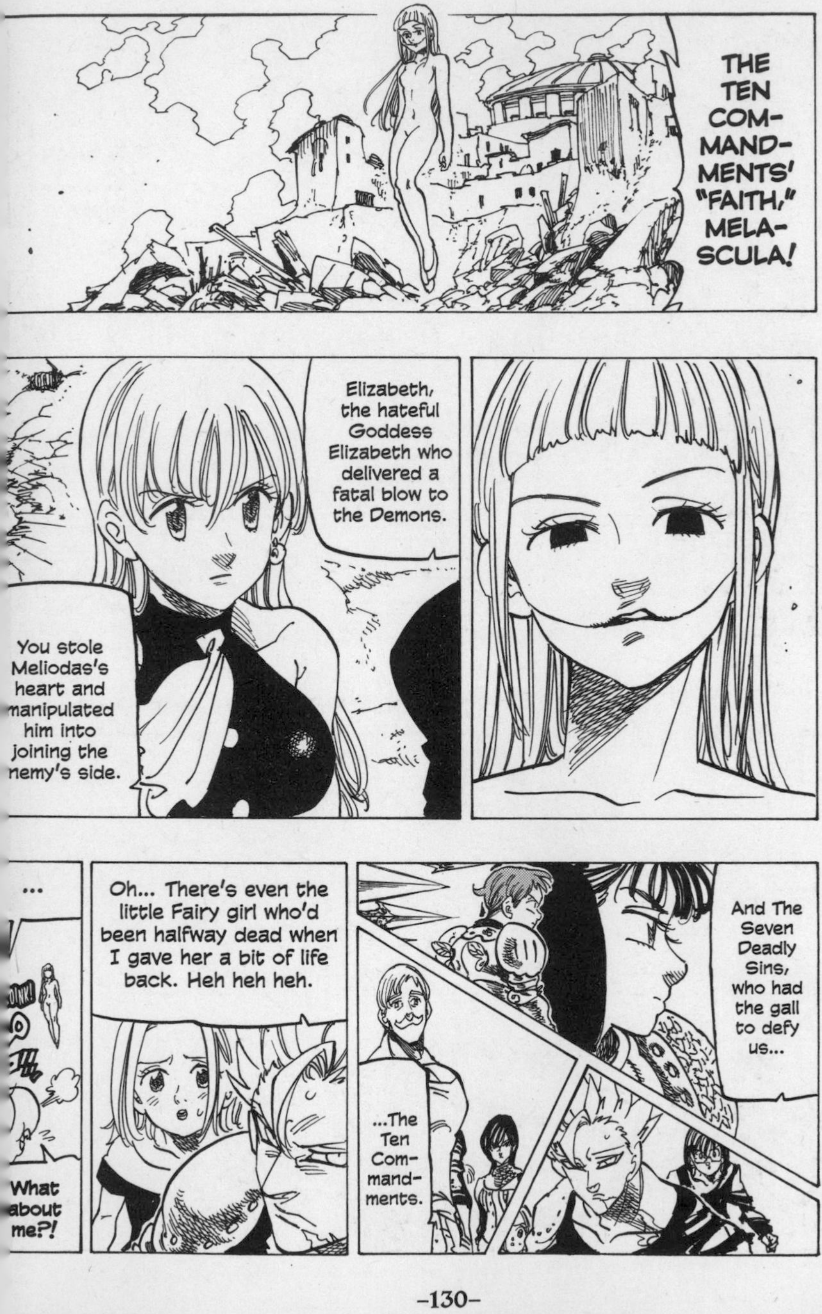

THE TEN COMMANDMENTS' "FAITH," MELASCULA!
Elizabeth, the hateful Goddess Elizabeth who delivered a fatal blow to the Demons.
You stole Meliodas's heart and nanipulated him into joining the nemy's side.
And The Seven Deadly Sins, who had the gall to defy us...
...The Ten Commandments.
Oh... There's even the little Fairy girl who'd been halfway dead when I gave her a bit of life back. Heh heh heh.
...
What about me?!

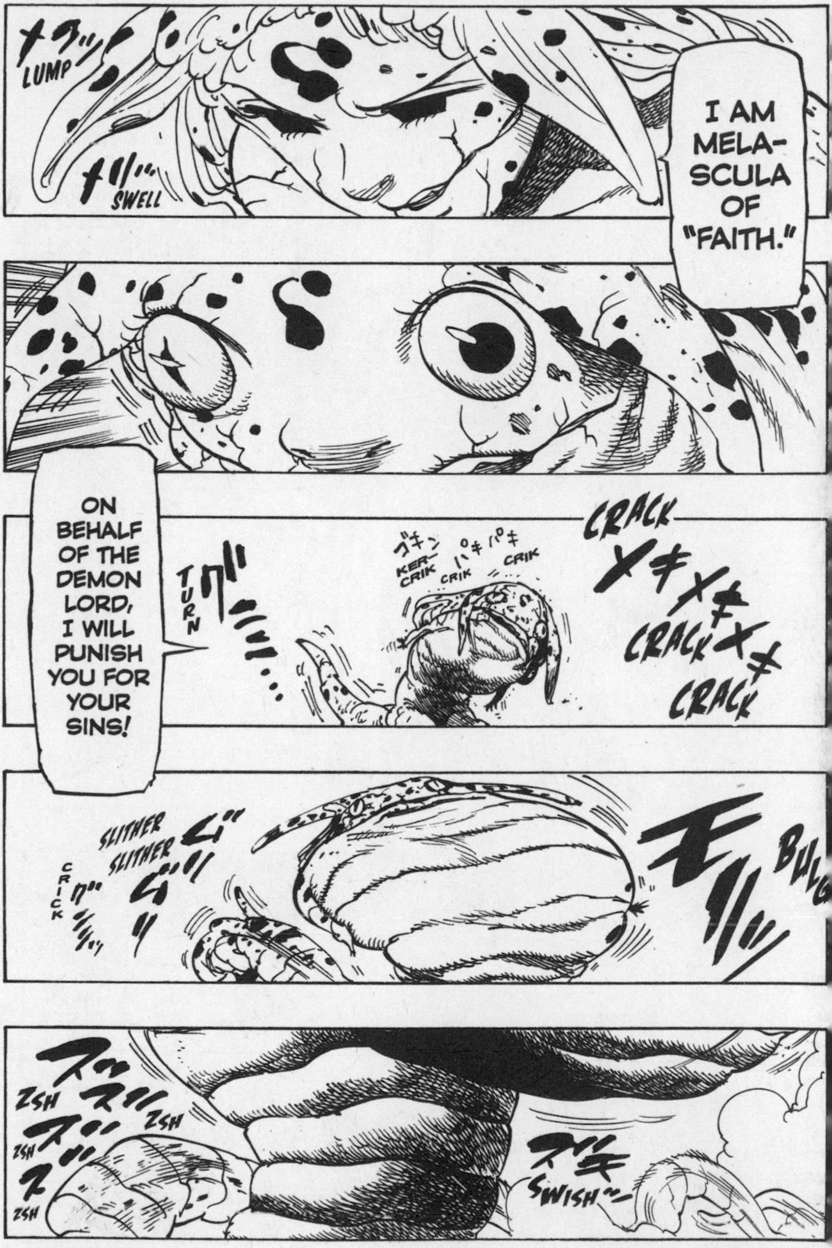

I AM MELA-SCULA OF "FAITH."
LUMP
SWELL
CRACK
CRACK
CRACK
KER-CRIK
CRIK
CRIK
TURN
ON BEHALF OF THE DEMON LORD, I WILL PUNISH YOU FOR YOUR SINS!
SLITHER
SLITHER
CRICK
SWISH
ZSH
ZSH
ZSH
ZSH

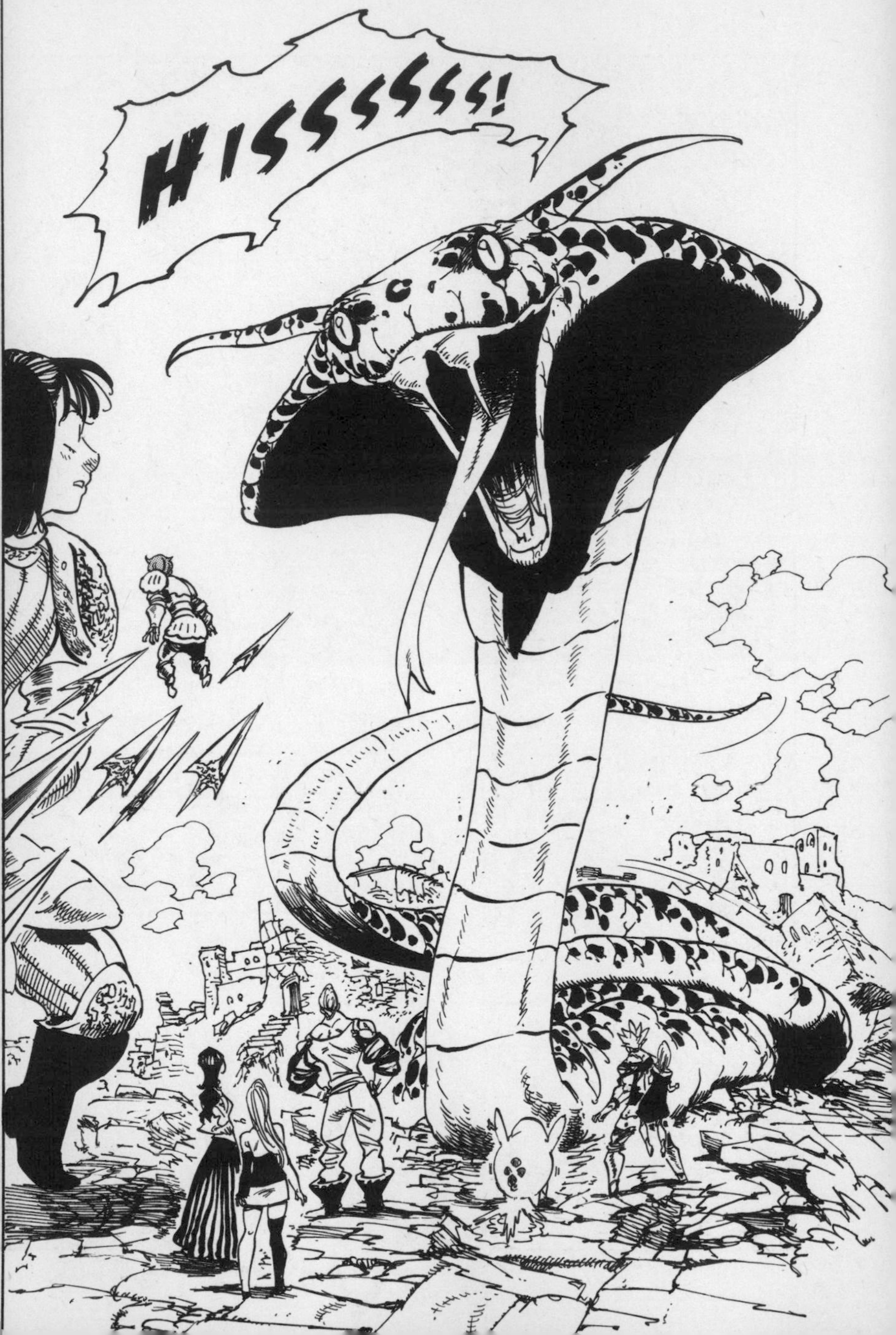
HISSSSSSS!

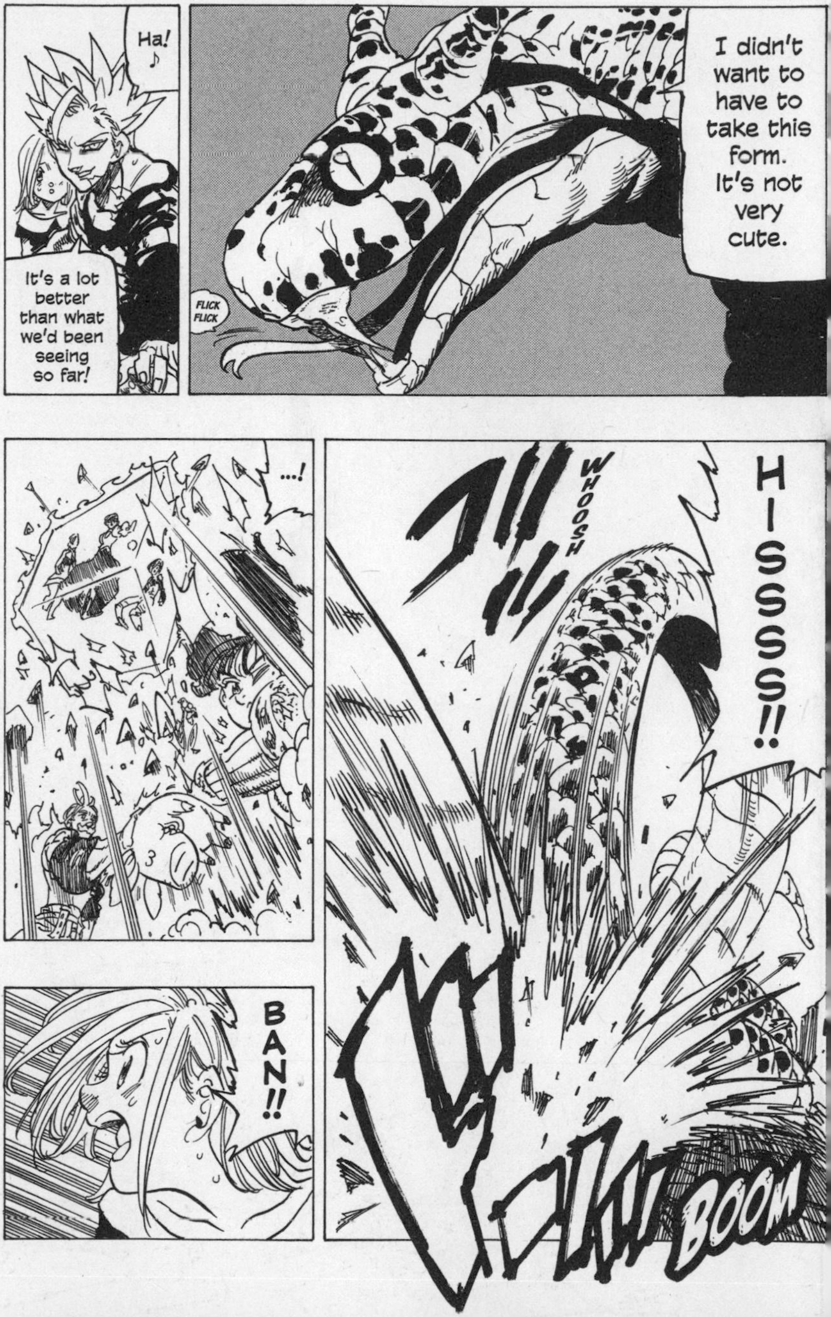
I didn't want to have to take this form. It's not very cute.
FLICK FLICK
Ha! ♪
It's a lot better than what we'd been seeing so far!
HISSSS!!
WHOOSH
BOOM
...!
BAN!!

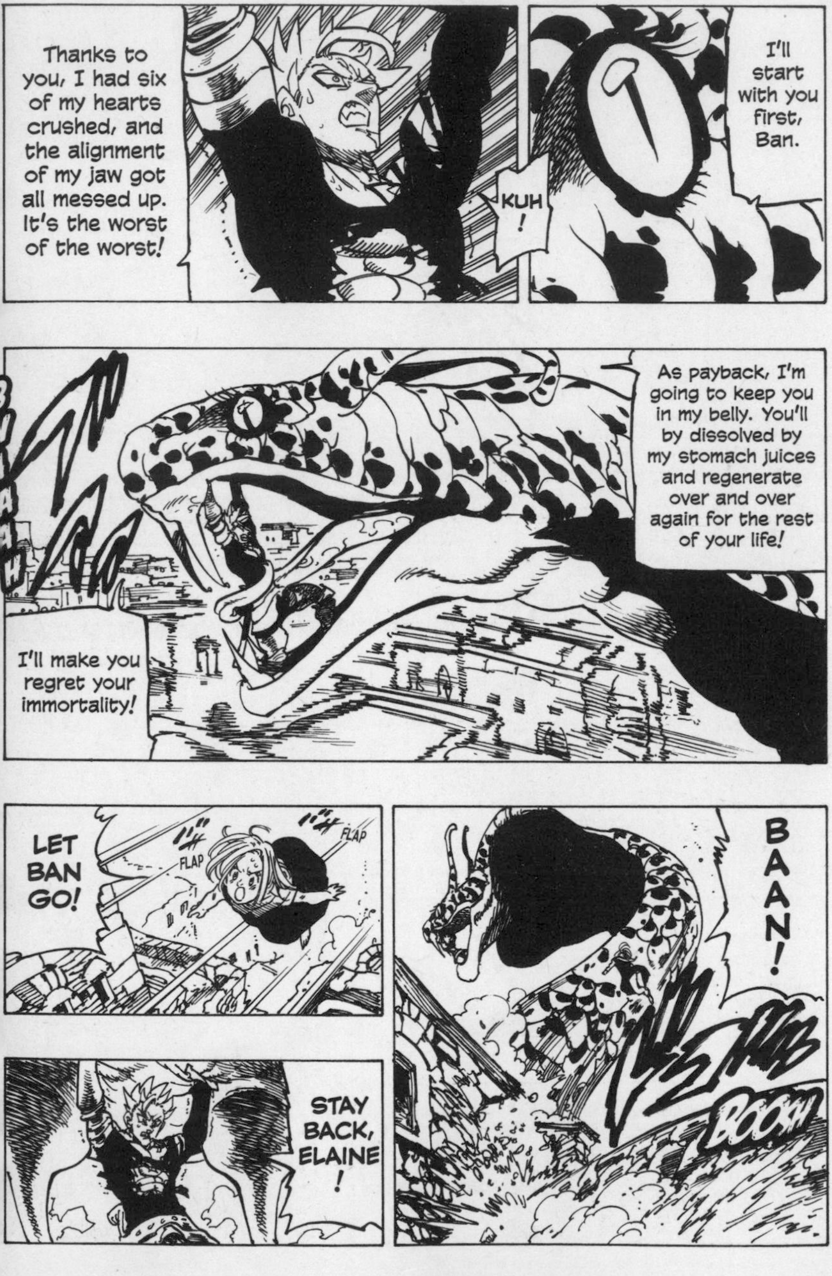
I'll start with you first, Ban.
KUH!
Thanks to you, I had six of my hearts crushed, and the alignment of my jaw got all messed up. It's the worst of the worst!
As payback, I'm going to keep you in my belly. You'll by dissolved by my stomach juices and regenerate over and over again for the rest of your life!
I'll make you regret your immortality!
BAAN!
LET BAN GO!
FLAP
FLAP
STAY BACK, ELAINE!

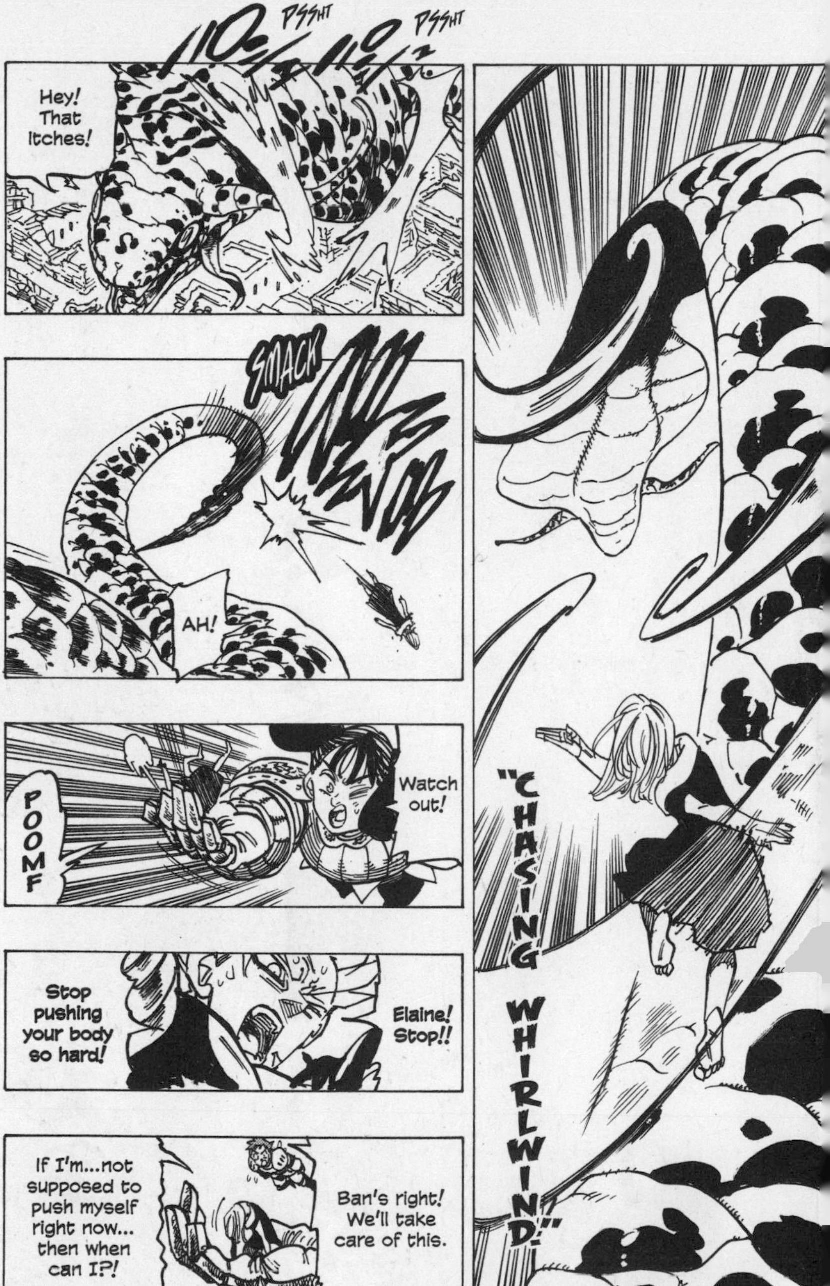
"CHASING WHIRLWIND."
PSSHT
PSSHT
Hey! That itches!
SMACK
AH!
Watch out!
POOMF
Elaine! Stop!!
Stop pushing your body so hard!
Ban's right! We'll take care of this.
If I'm...not supposed to push myself right now... then when can I?!

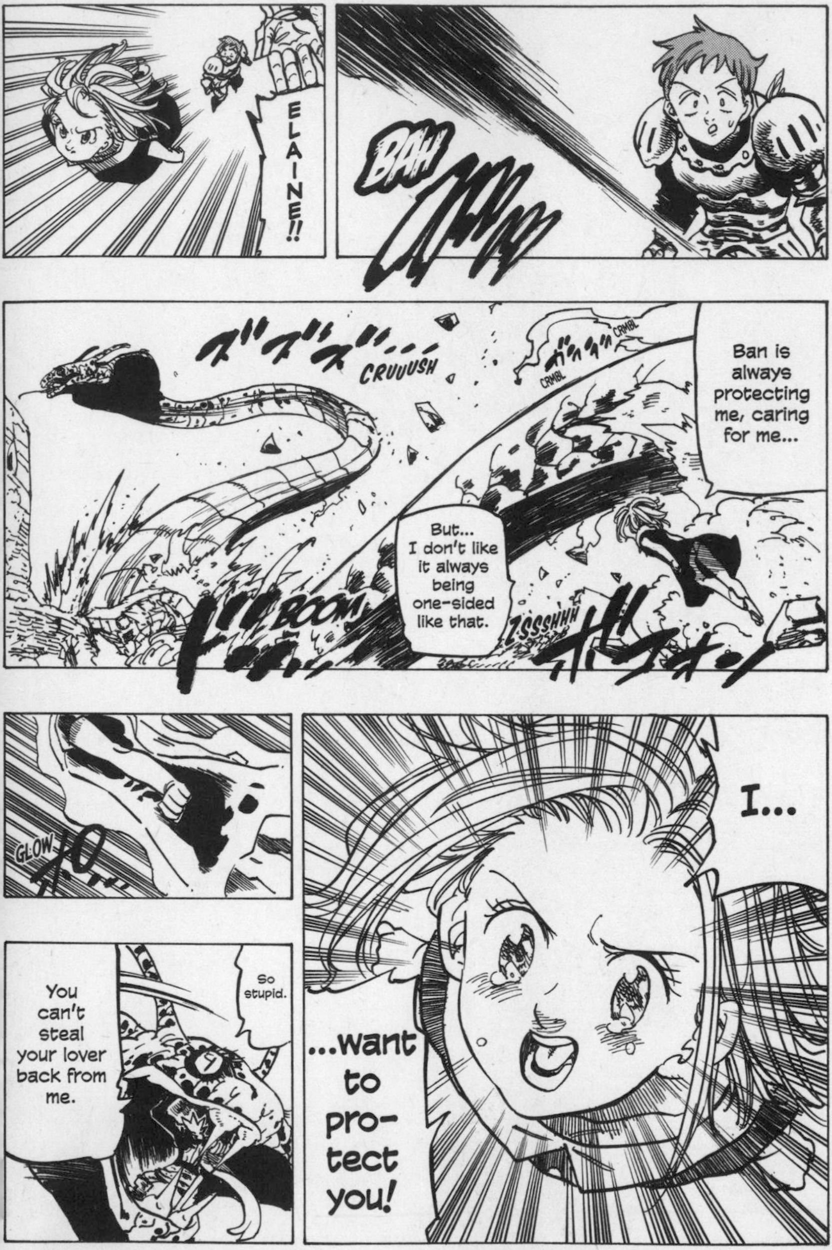
BAH
ELAINE!!
Ban is always protecting me, caring for me...
CRMBL
CRMBL
CRUUUSH
But... I don't like it always being one-sided like that.
ZSSSHHH
BOOM
I...
...want to protect you!
GLOW
So stupid.
You can't steal your lover back from me.

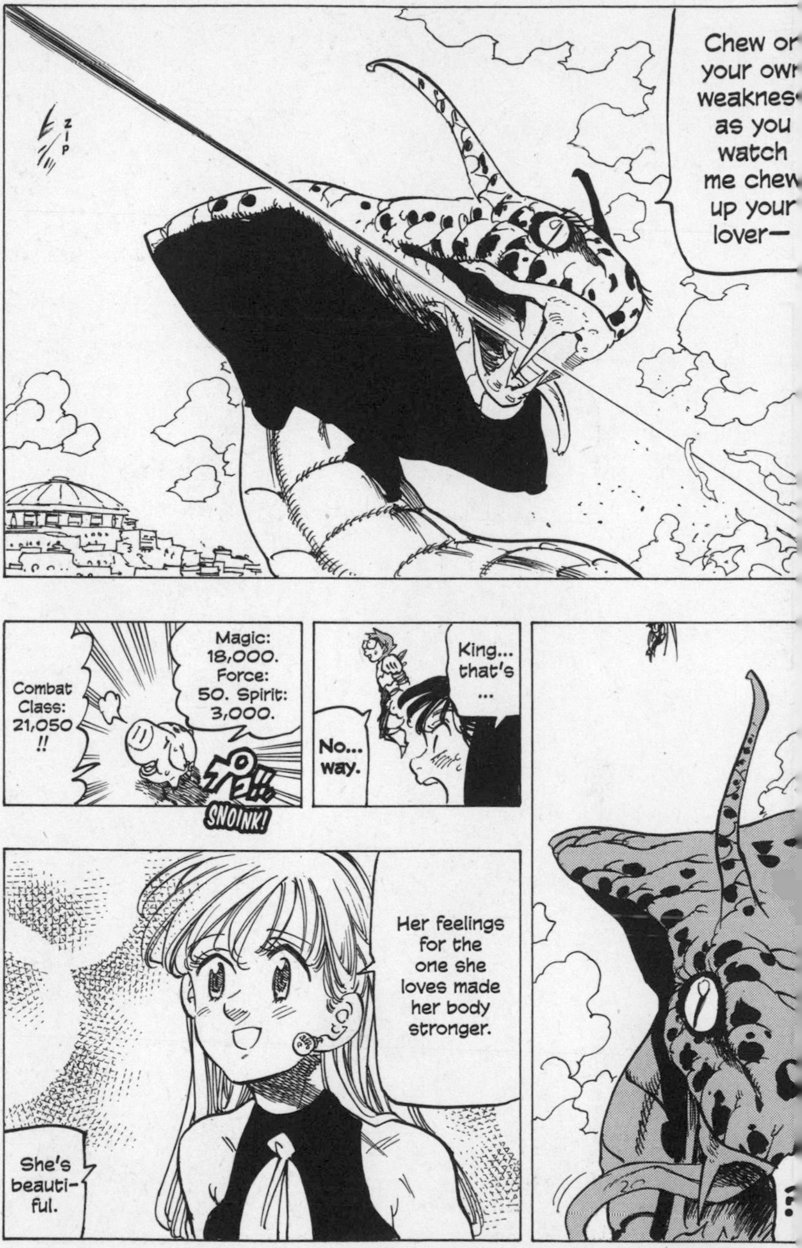
ZIP
Chew or your owr weaknes as you watch me chew up your lover—
King... that's ...
No... way.
Magic: 18,000. Force: 50. Spirit: 3,000.
Combat Class: 21,050 !!
SNOINK!
Her feelings for the one she loves made her body stronger.
She's beauti-ful.
!?

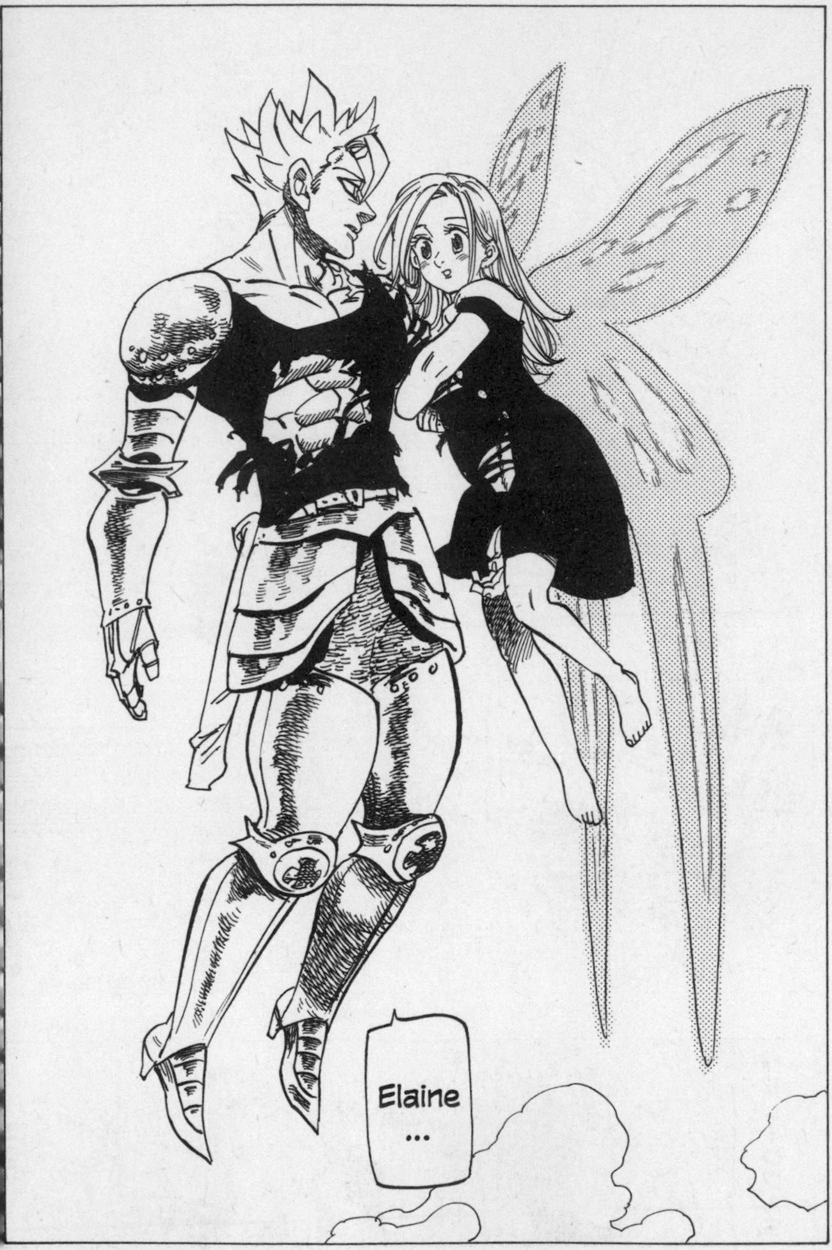
Elaine
...

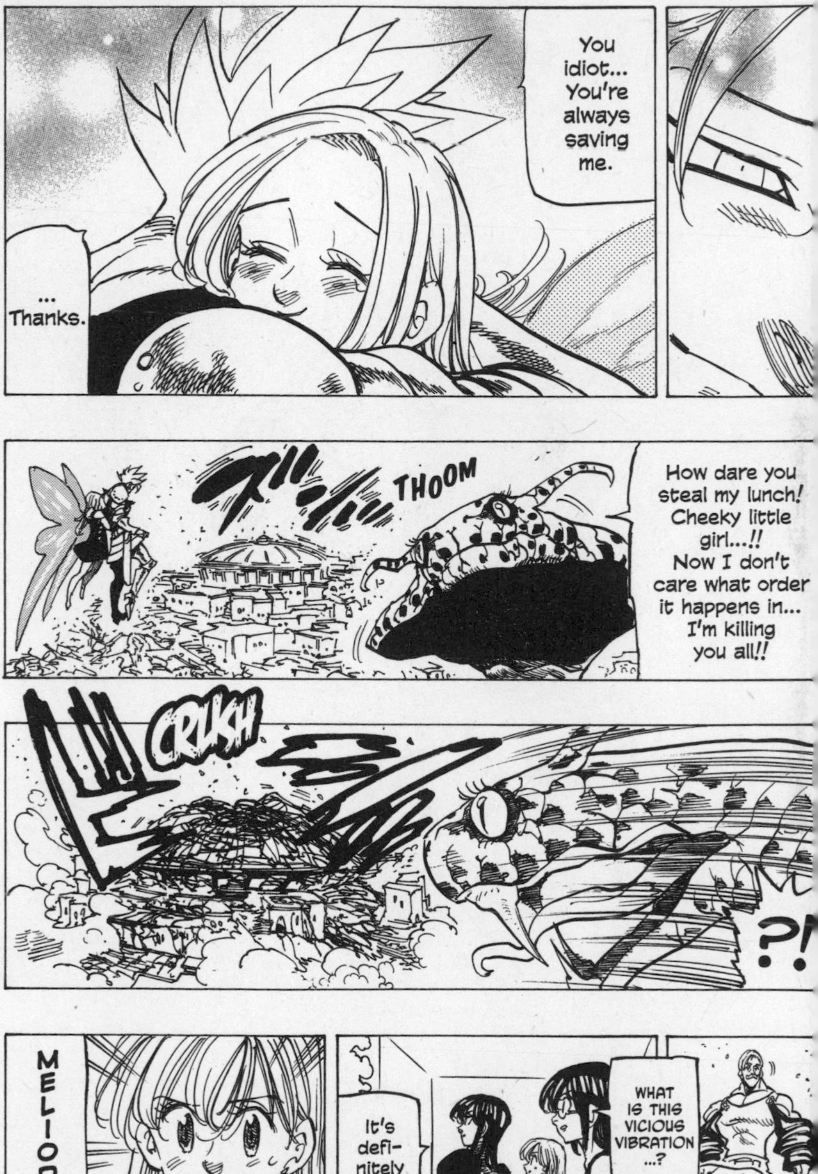
You idiot... You're always saving me.
... Thanks.
How dare you steal my lunch! Cheeky little girl...!! Now I don't care what order it happens in... I'm killing you all!!
THOOM
?!
CRUSH
WHAT IS THIS VICIOUS VIBRATION ...?
It's definitely from him.
MELIODAS.

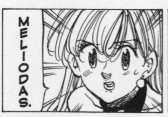

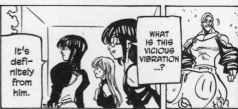

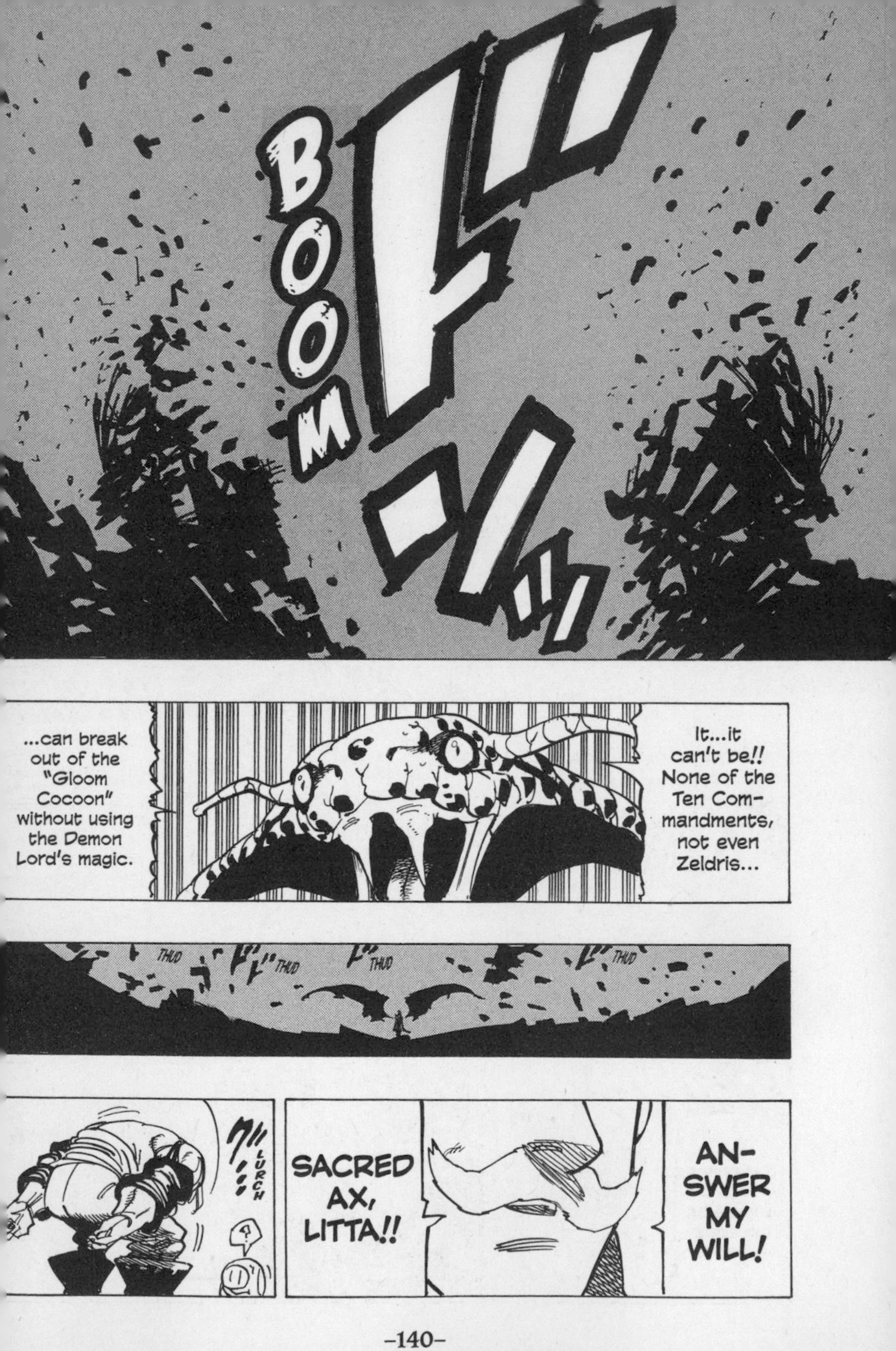
BOOOM
It...it can't be!! None of the Ten Commandments, not even Zeldris...
...can break out of the "Gloom Cocoon" without using the Demon Lord's magic.
THUD
THUD
THUD
THUD
ANSWER MY WILL!
SACRED AX, LITTA!!
LURCH

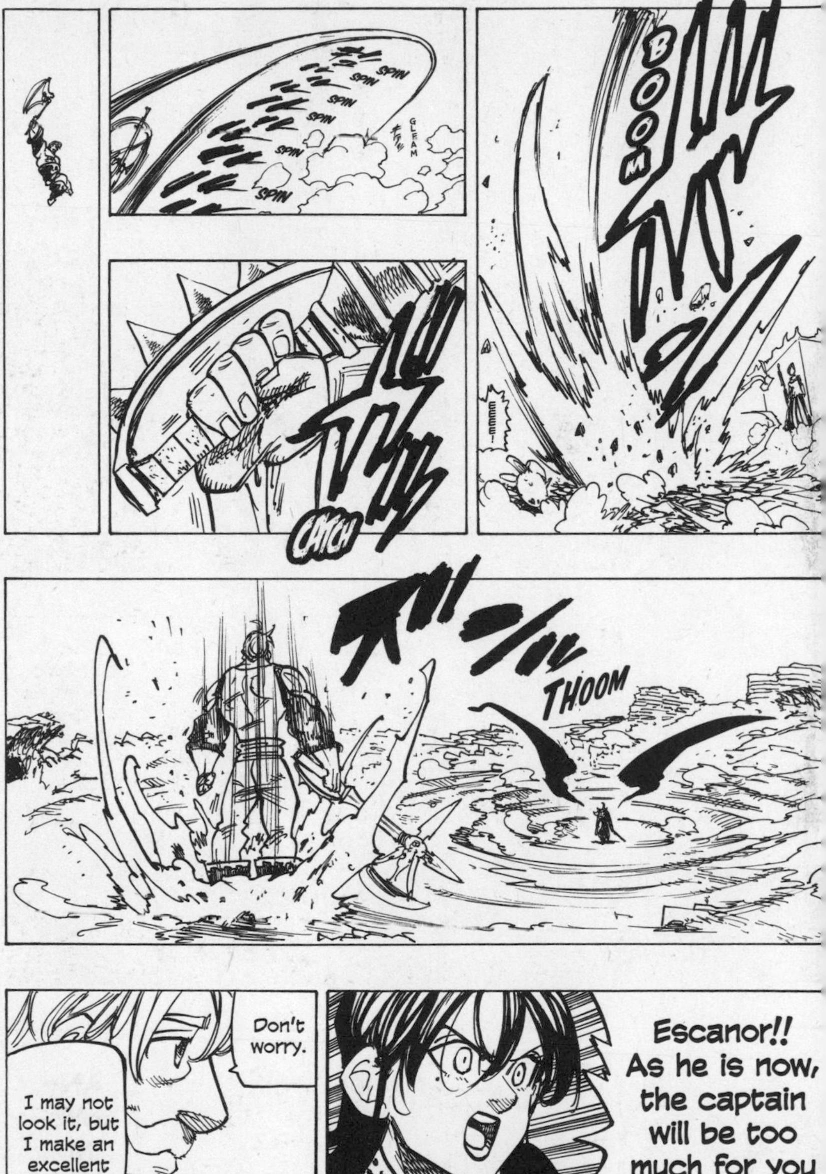

BOOOOM
EEEE!
SPIN
SPIN
SPIN
SPIN
SPIN
SPIN
GLEAM
CATCH
THOOM
Escanor!! As he is now, the captain will be too much for you to handle!
Don't worry.
I may not look it, but I make an excellent babysitter.

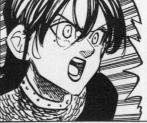

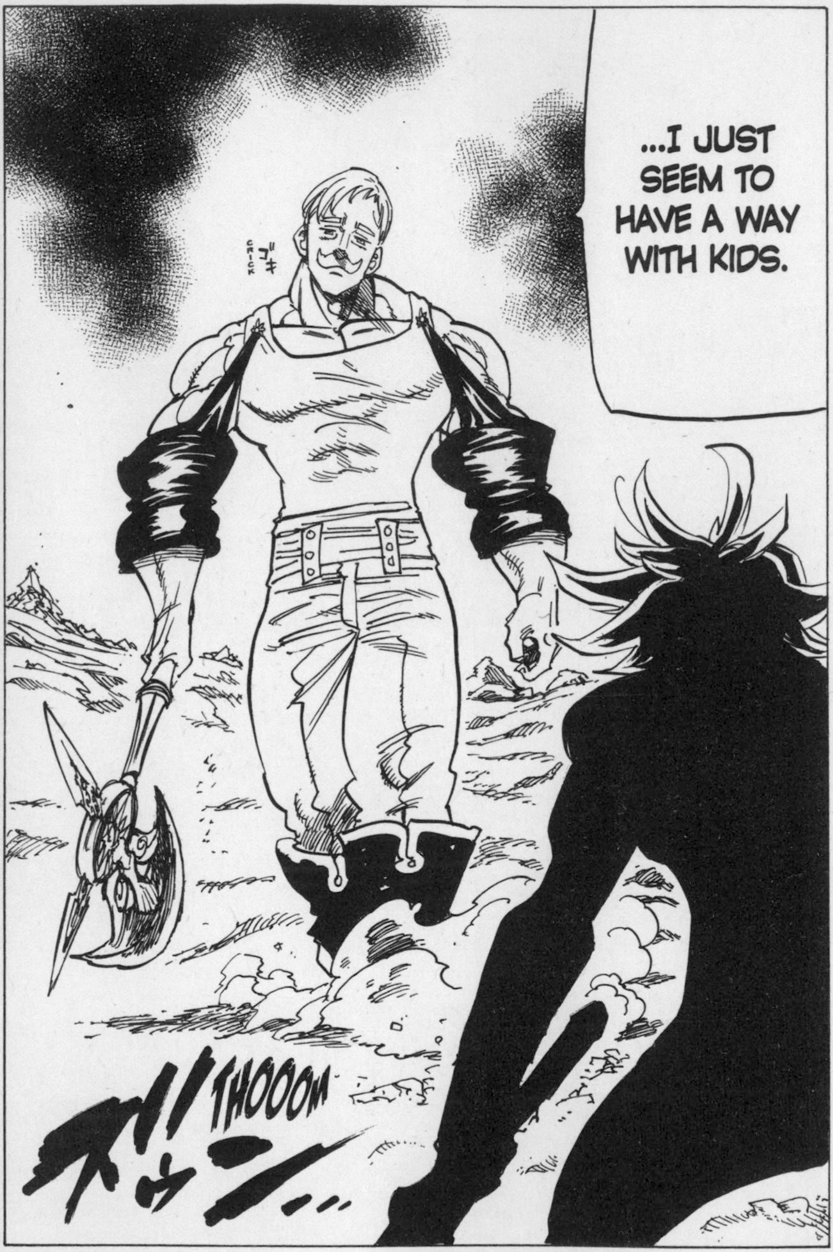
...I JUST SEEM TO HAVE A WAY WITH KIDS.
CRICK
THOOM

Chapter 230 - Melascula's Miscalculation

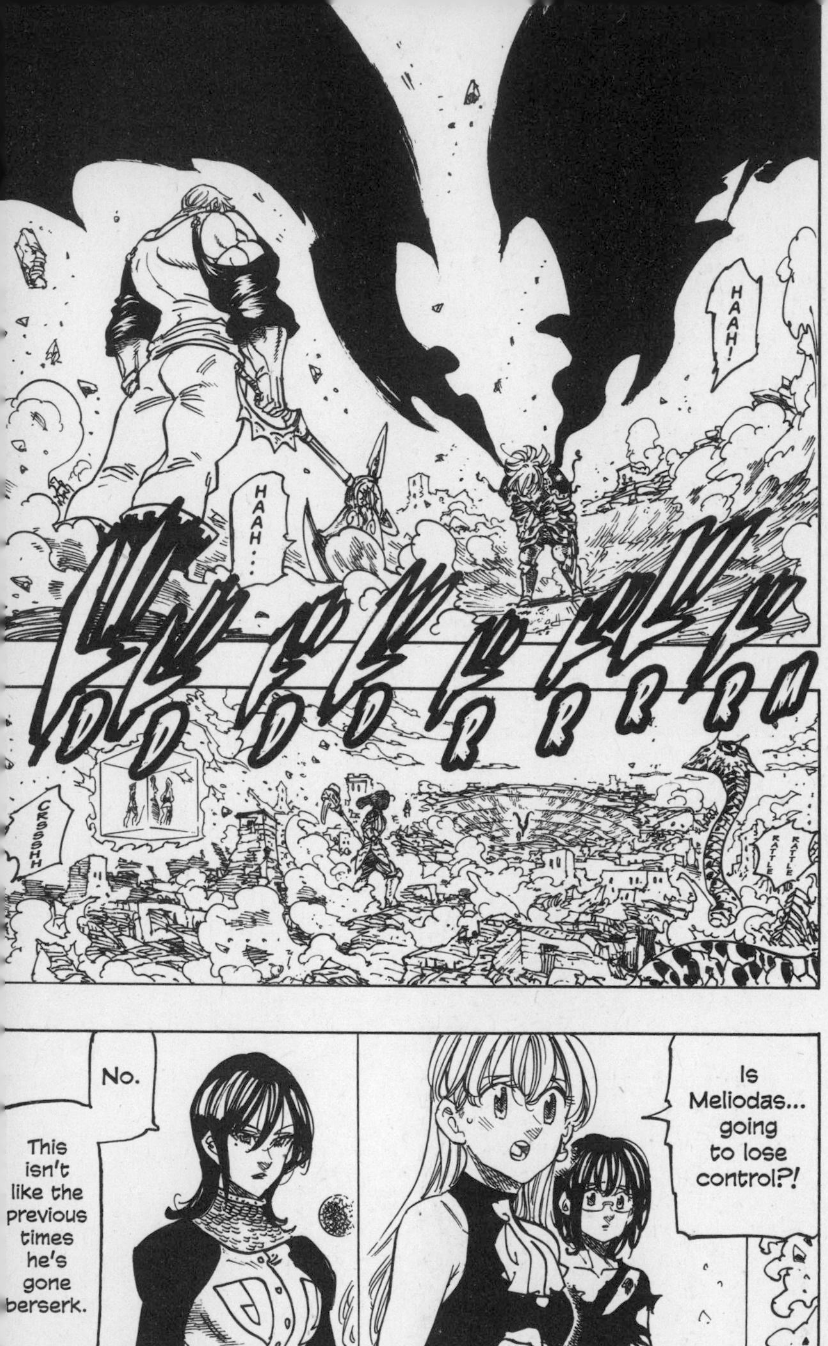
HAAH!
HAAH...
DDDDRRRRN
RATTLE RATTLE
CRSSSHH
Is Meliodas... going to lose control?!
No.
This isn't like the previous times he's gone berserk.

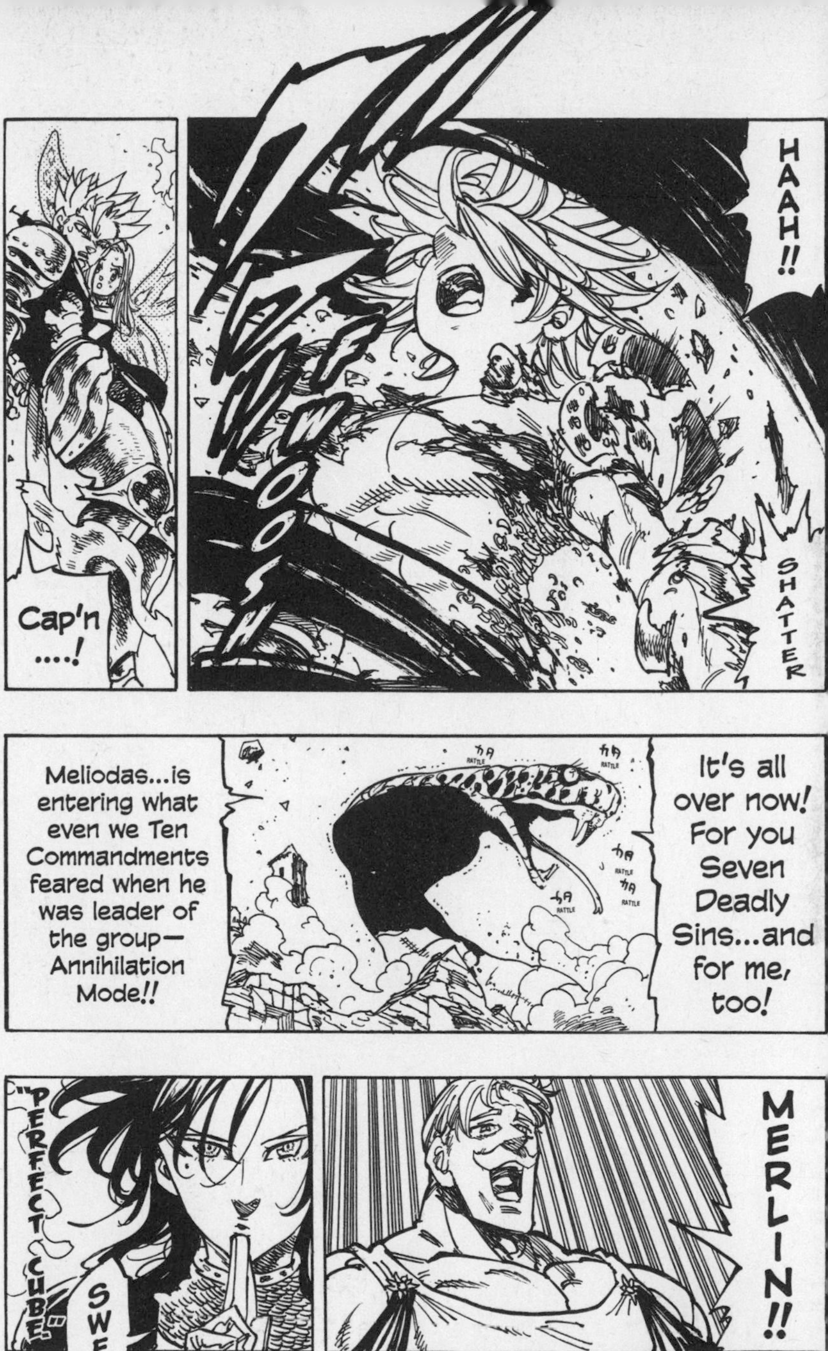
HAAH!!
SHATTER
Cap'n ....!
It's all over now! For you Seven Deadly Sins...and for me, too!
RATTLE
RATTLE
RATTLE
RATTLE
RATTLE
Meliodas...is entering what even we Ten Commandments feared when he was leader of the group—Annihilation Mode!!
MERLIN!!
SWF
"PERFECT CUBE."

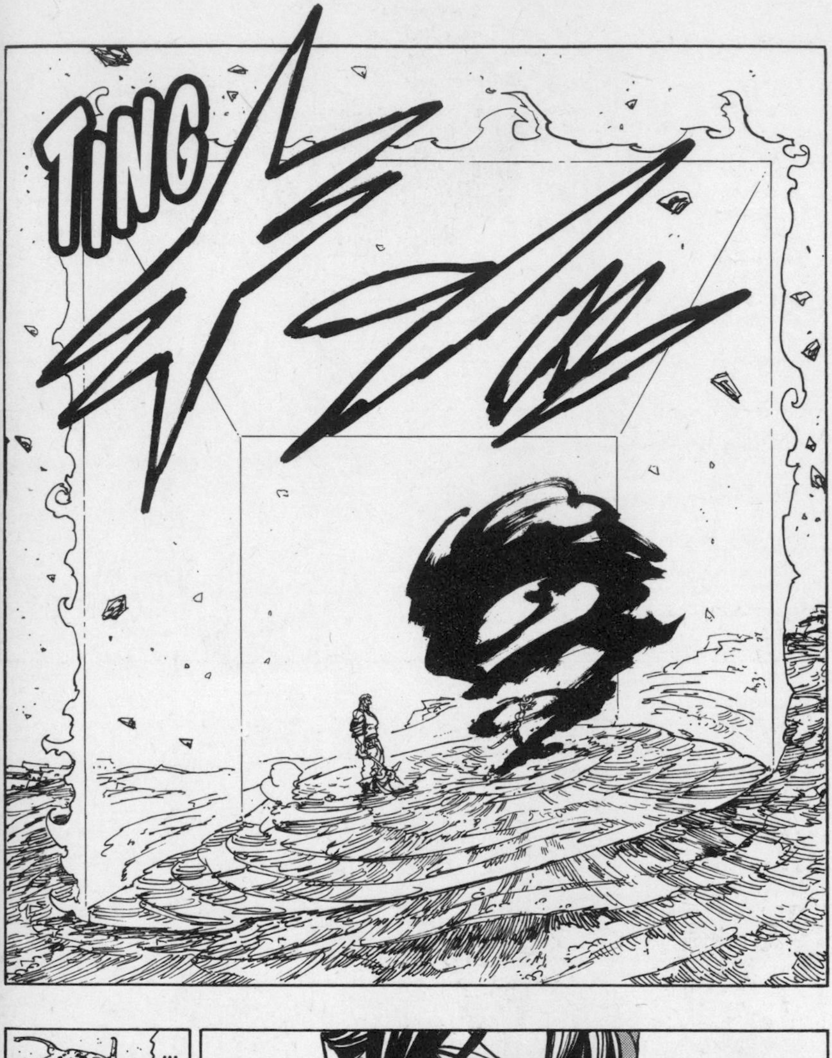
TING

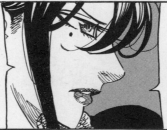

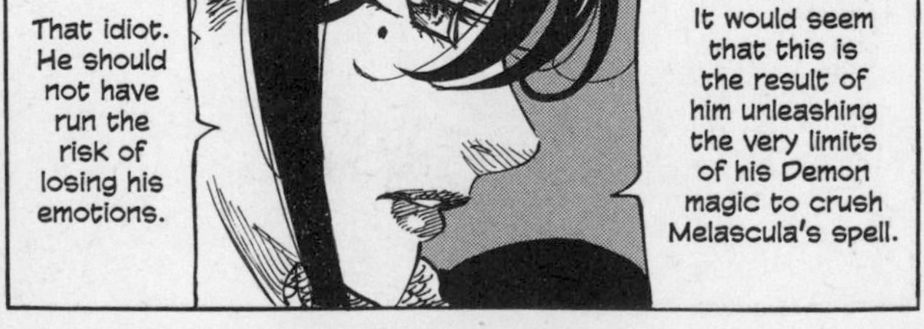
It would seem that this is the result of him unleashing the very limits of his Demon magic to crush Melascula's spell.
That idiot. He should not have run the risk of losing his emotions.

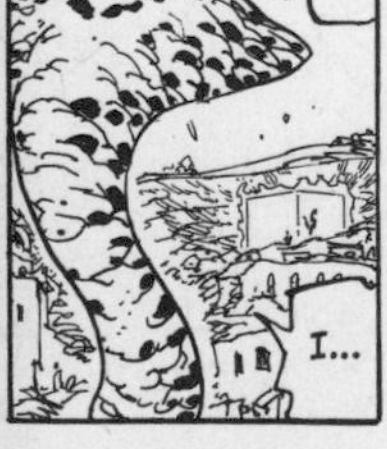
...
I...

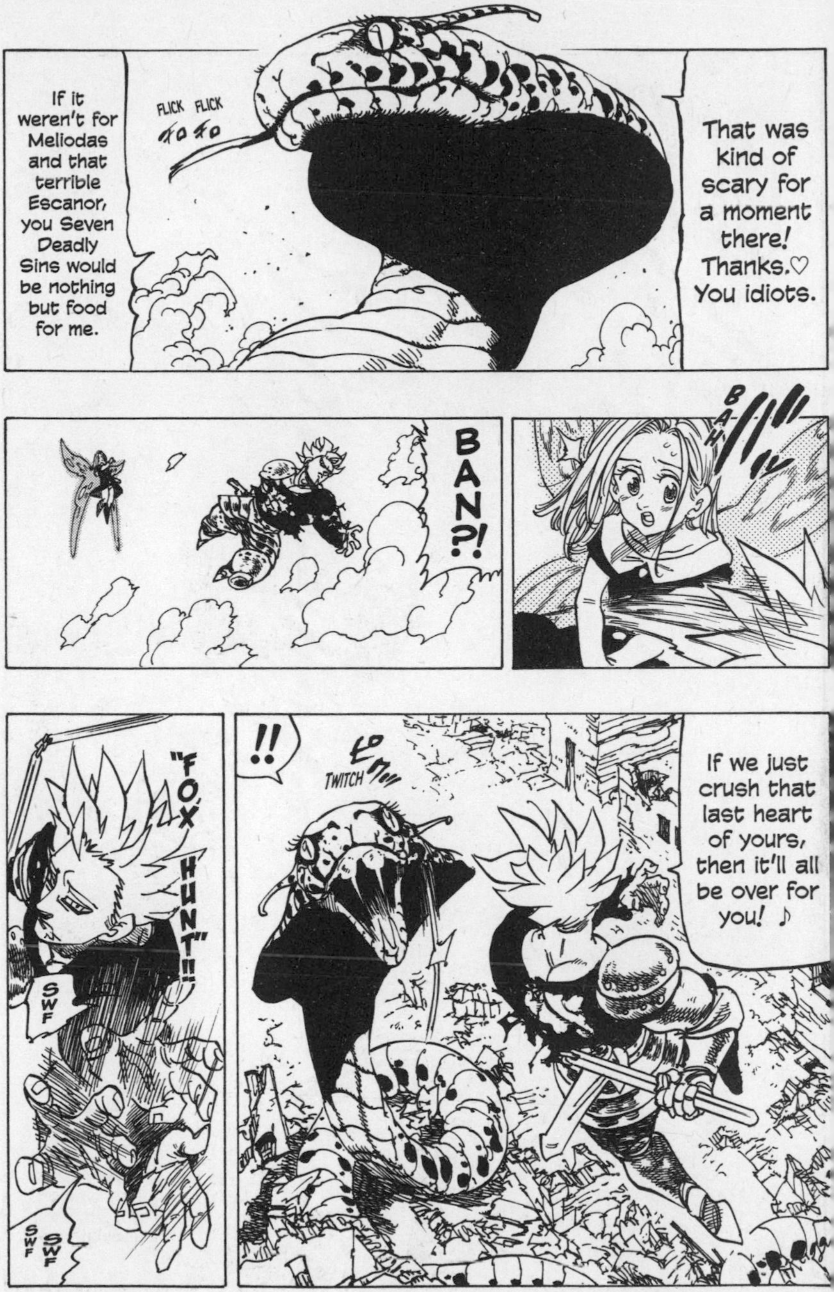

That was kind of scary for a moment there! Thanks.♡ You idiots.
FLICK FLICK
If it weren't for Meliodas and that terrible Escanor, you Seven Deadly Sins would be nothing but food for me.
BAH
BAN?!
If we just crush that last heart of yours, then it'll all be over for you! ♪
TWITCH
!!
"FOX HUNT"!!
SWF
SWF SWF

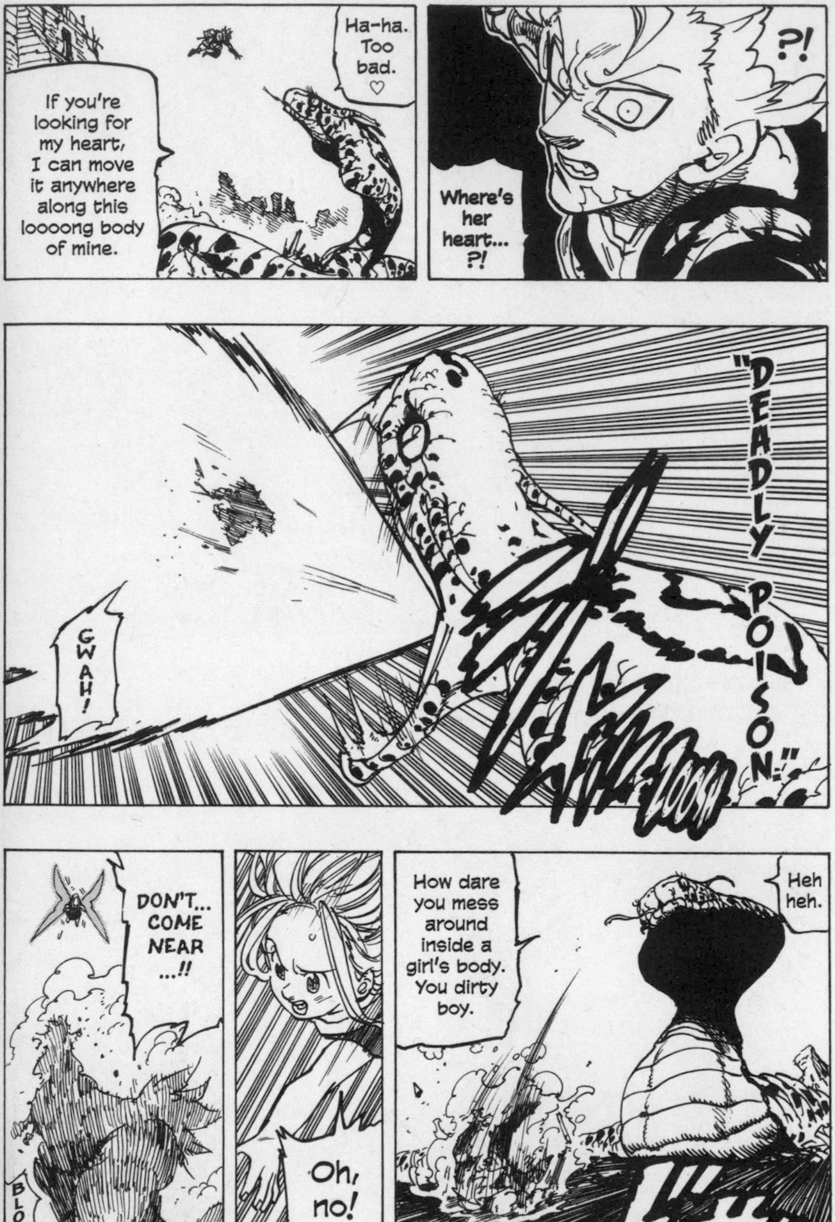
?!
Where's her heart... ?!
Ha-ha. Too bad. ♡
If you're looking for my heart, I can move it anywhere along this looooong body of mine.
"DEADLY POISON."
ZOOSH
GWAH!
Heh heh.
How dare you mess around inside a girl's body. You dirty boy.
THUD
Oh, no!
DON'T... COME NEAR ...!!
BLOP

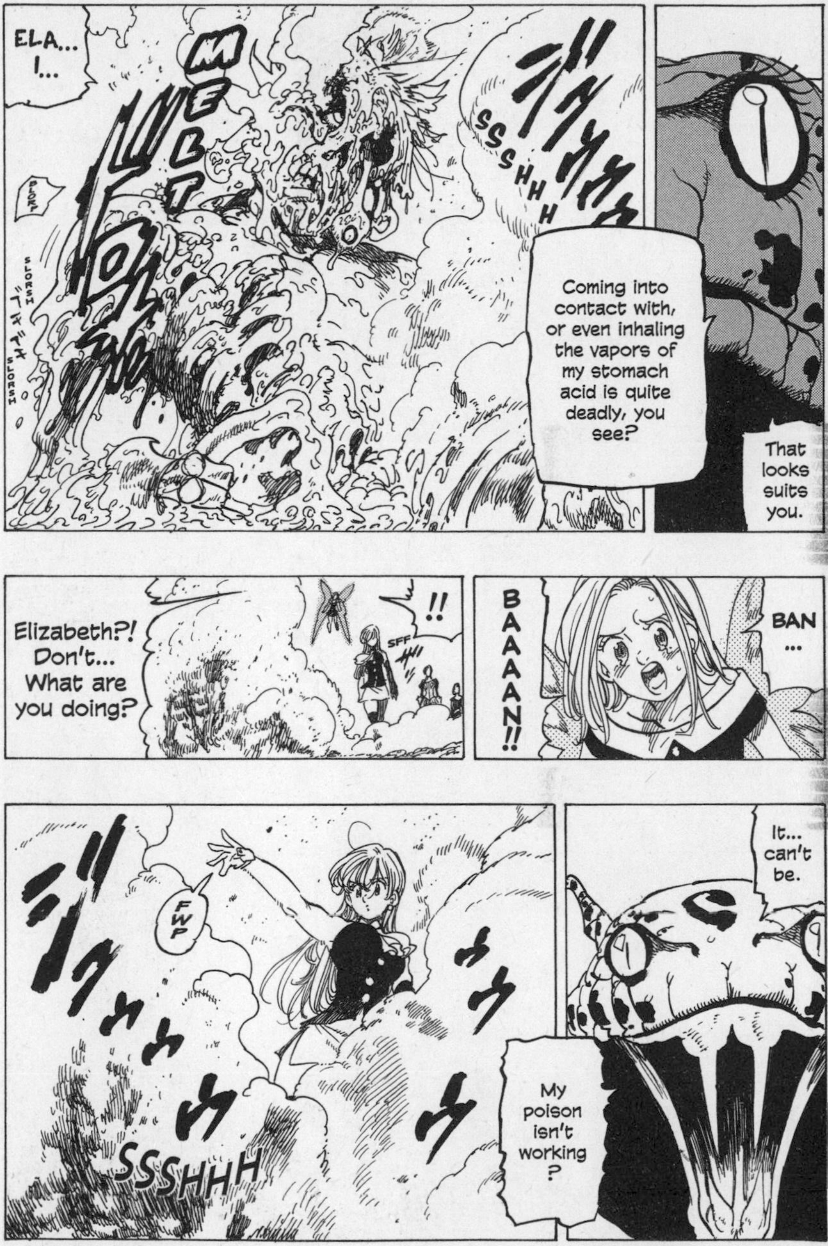
That looks suits you.
SSSHHH
Coming into contact with, or even inhaling the vapors of my stomach acid is quite deadly, you see?
MELT
ELA... I...
PLORP
SLORSH
SLORSH
BAN ...
BAAAAAN!!
!!
SFF
Elizabeth?! Don't... What are you doing?
It... can't be.
My poison isn't working?
FWP
SSSHHH

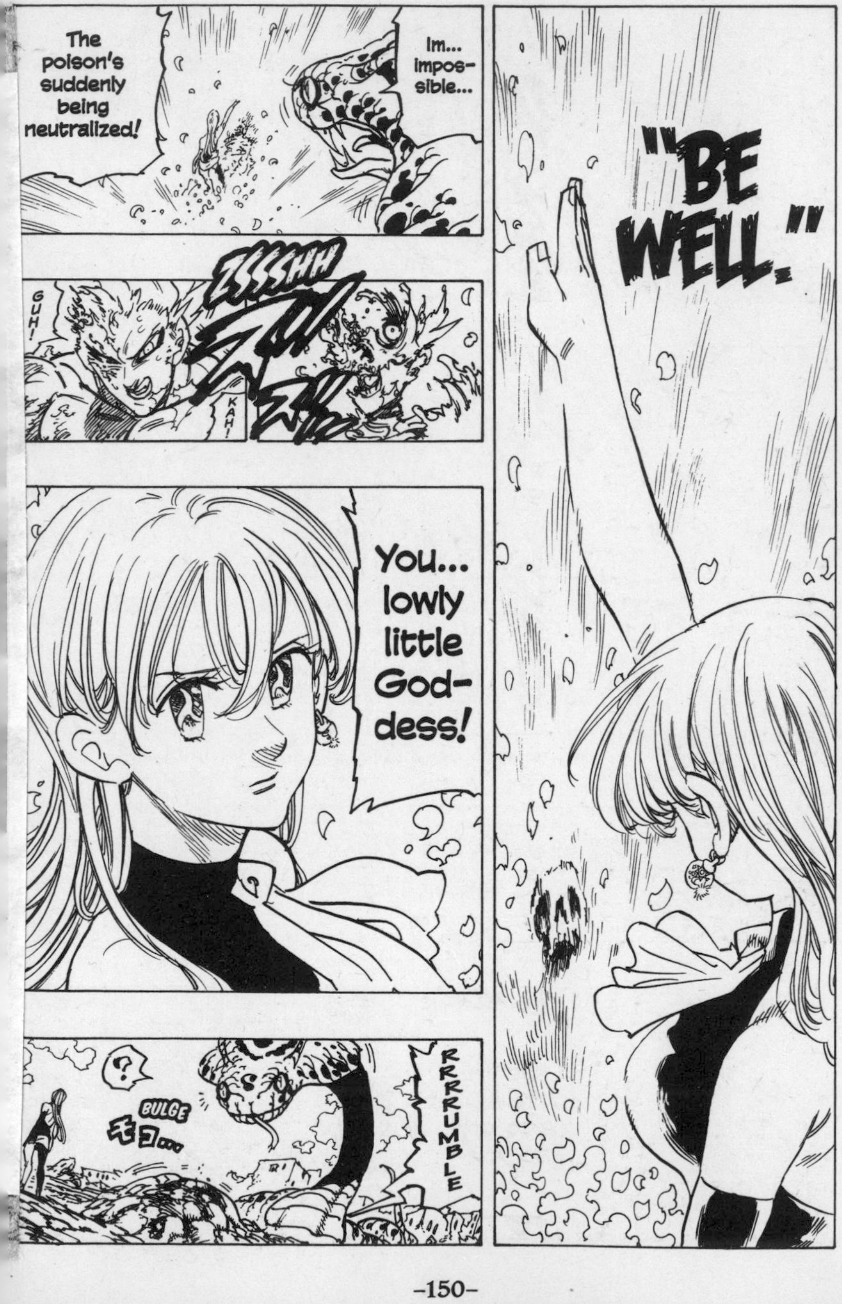
"BE WELL."
Im... impos-sible...
The poison's suddenly being neutralized!
ZSSSHH
KAH!
GUH!
You... lowly little God-dess!
RRRRUMBLE
?
BULGE
モコ…

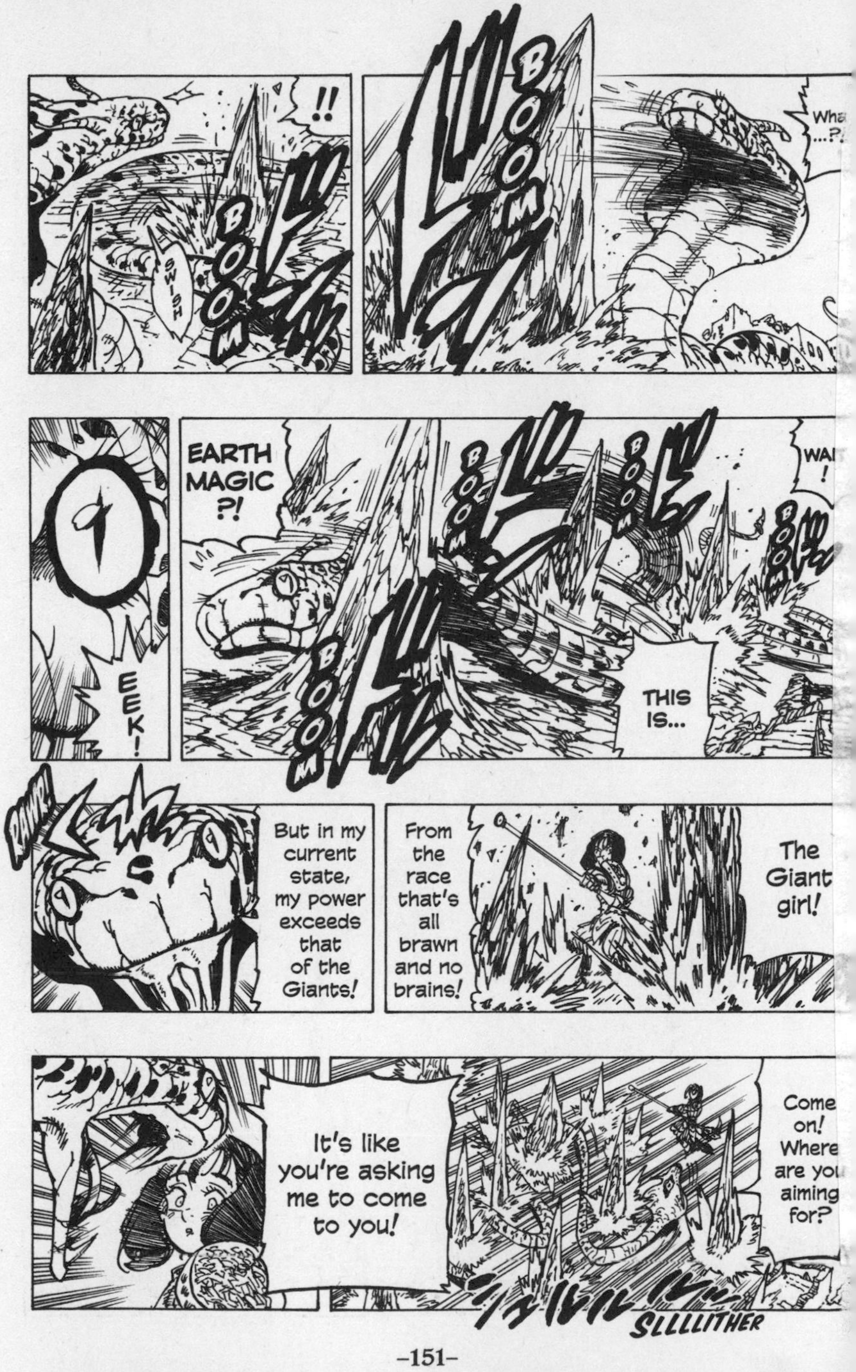
Wha
...?!
BOOOM
!!
BOOOM
SWISH
WAI
!
BOOOM
BOOOM
BOOOM
THIS IS...
BOOOM
EARTH MAGIC ?!
EEK!
The Giant girl!
From the race that's all brawn and no brains!
But in my current state, my power exceeds that of the Giants!
RAWR!
Come on! Where are you aiming for?
SLLLLITHER
It's like you're asking me to come to you!

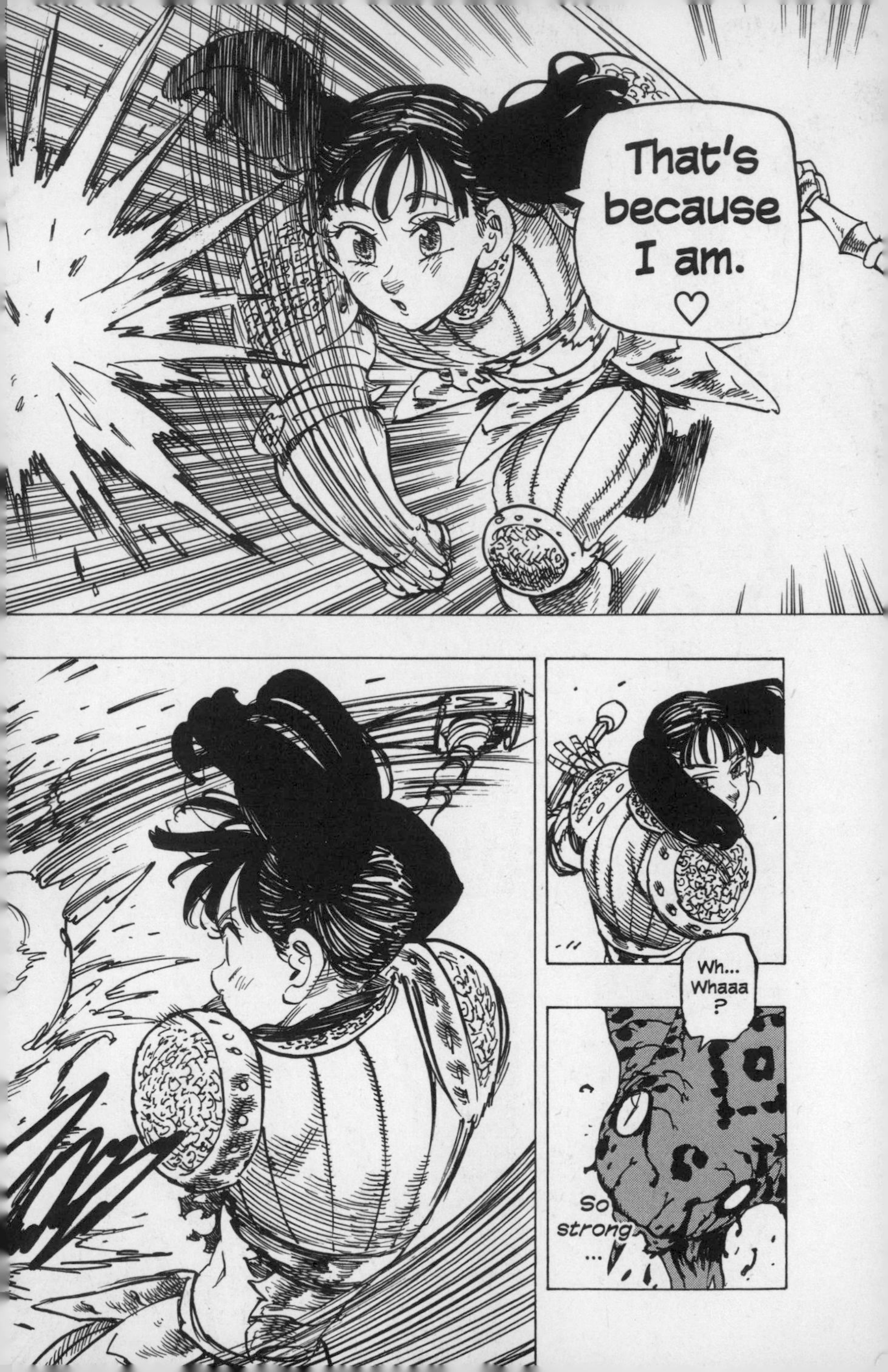
That's because I am. ♡
Wh... Whaaa?
So strong...

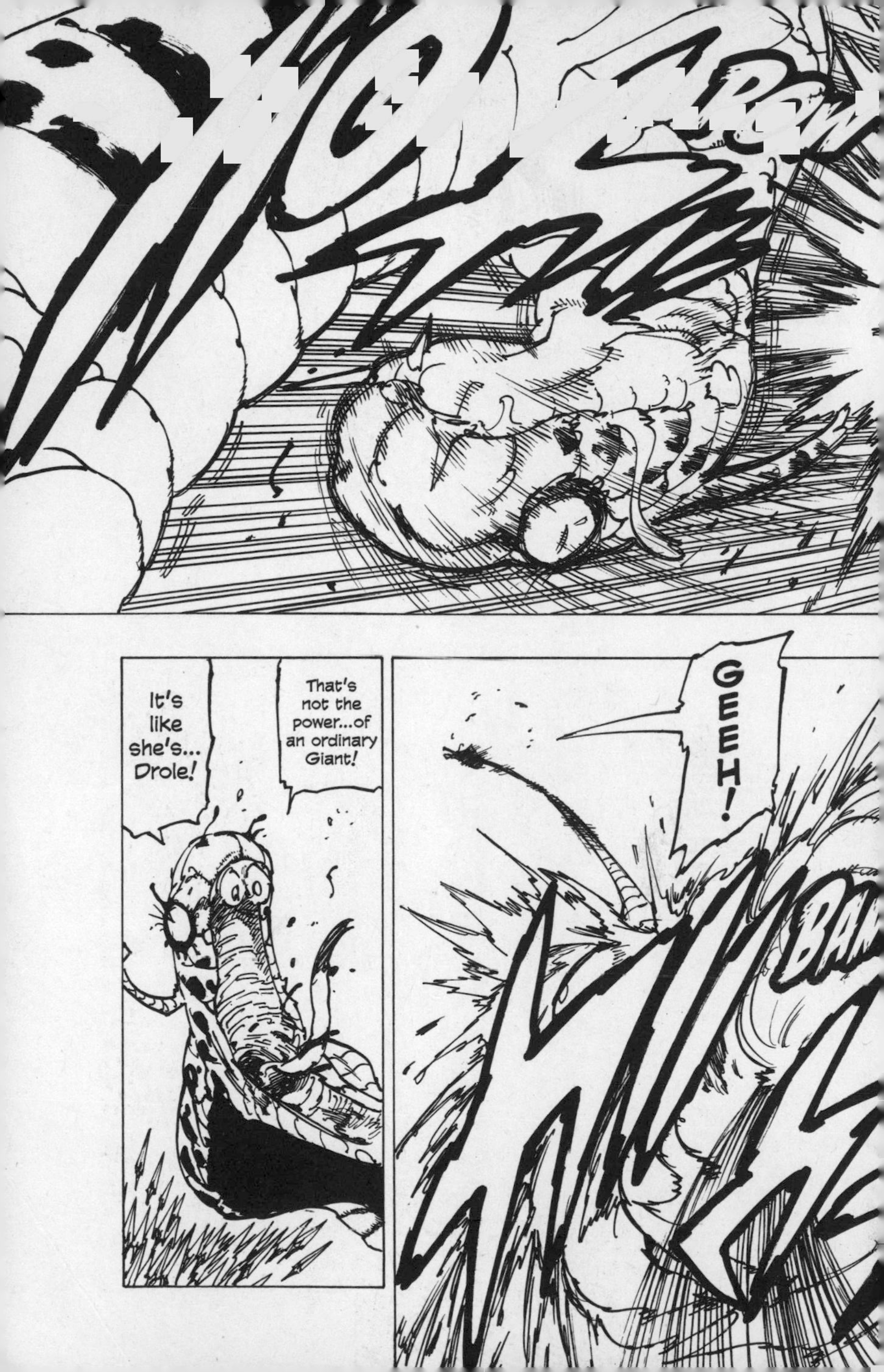
GEEH!
That's not the power...of an ordinary Giant!
It's like she's... Drole!

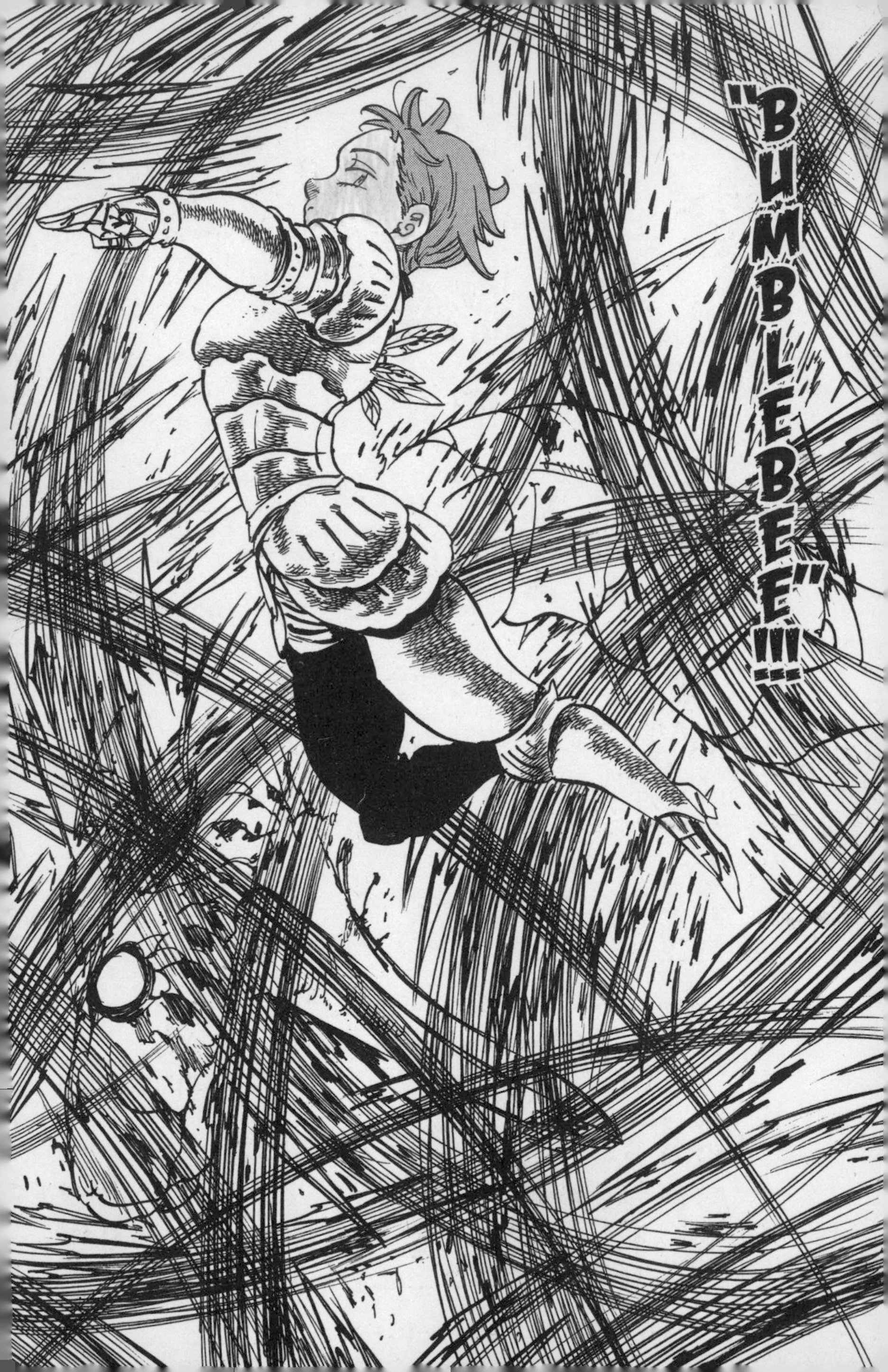
"BUMBLEBEE"!!!

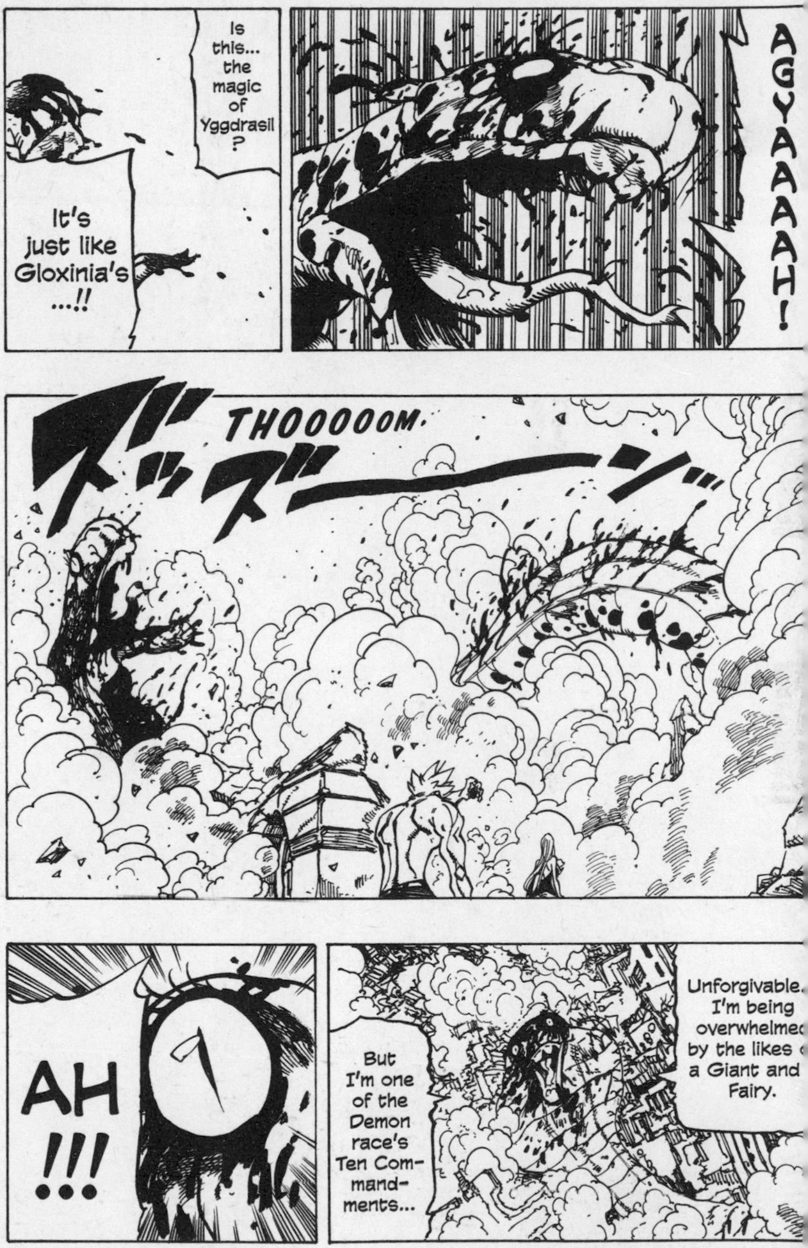
AGYAAAAH!
Is this... the magic of Yggdrasil?
It's just like Gloxinia's ...!!
ズッズーーン
THOOOOOM.
Unforgivable. I'm being overwhelme by the likes a Giant and Fairy.
But I'm one of the Demon race's Ten Commandments...
AH!!!

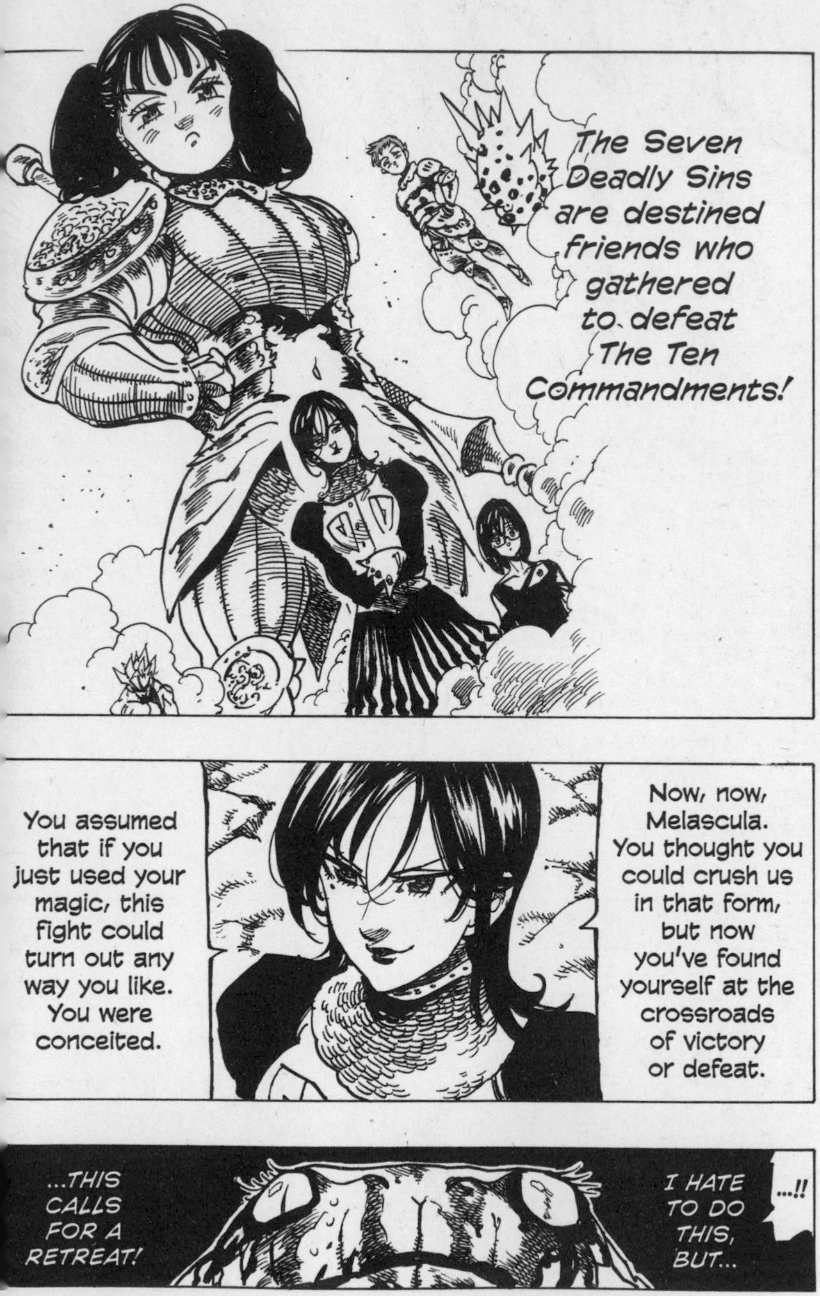
The Seven Deadly Sins are destined friends who gathered to defeat The Ten Commandments!
Now, now, Melascula. You thought you could crush us in that form, but now you've found yourself at the crossroads of victory or defeat.
You assumed that if you just used your magic, this fight could turn out any way you like. You were conceited.
...!!
I HATE TO DO THIS, BUT...
...THIS CALLS FOR A RETREAT!

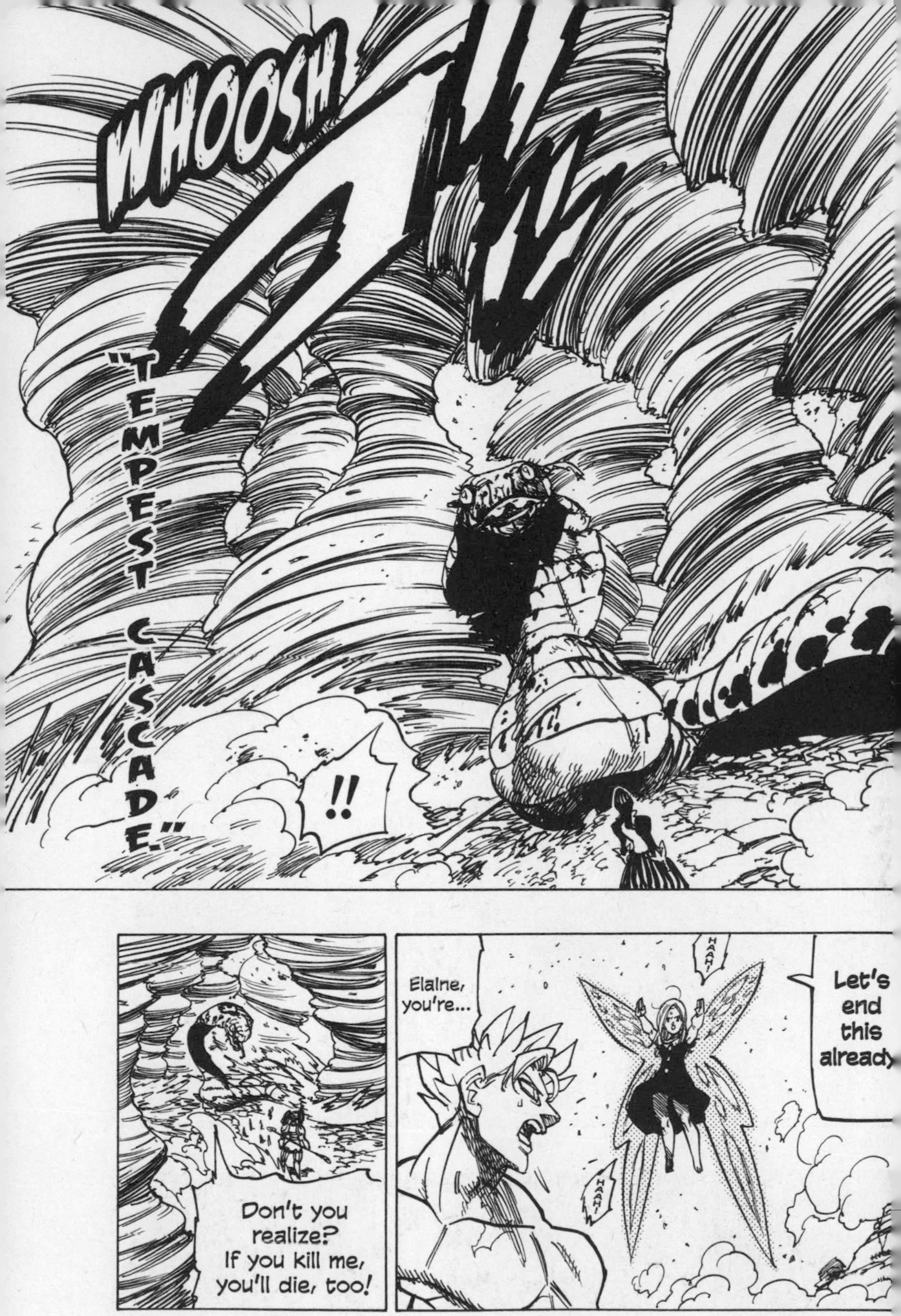
WHOOSH
"TEMPEST CASCADE."
!!
Let's end this already
HAAH!
Elaine, you're...
HAAH!
Don't you realize? If you kill me, you'll die, too!

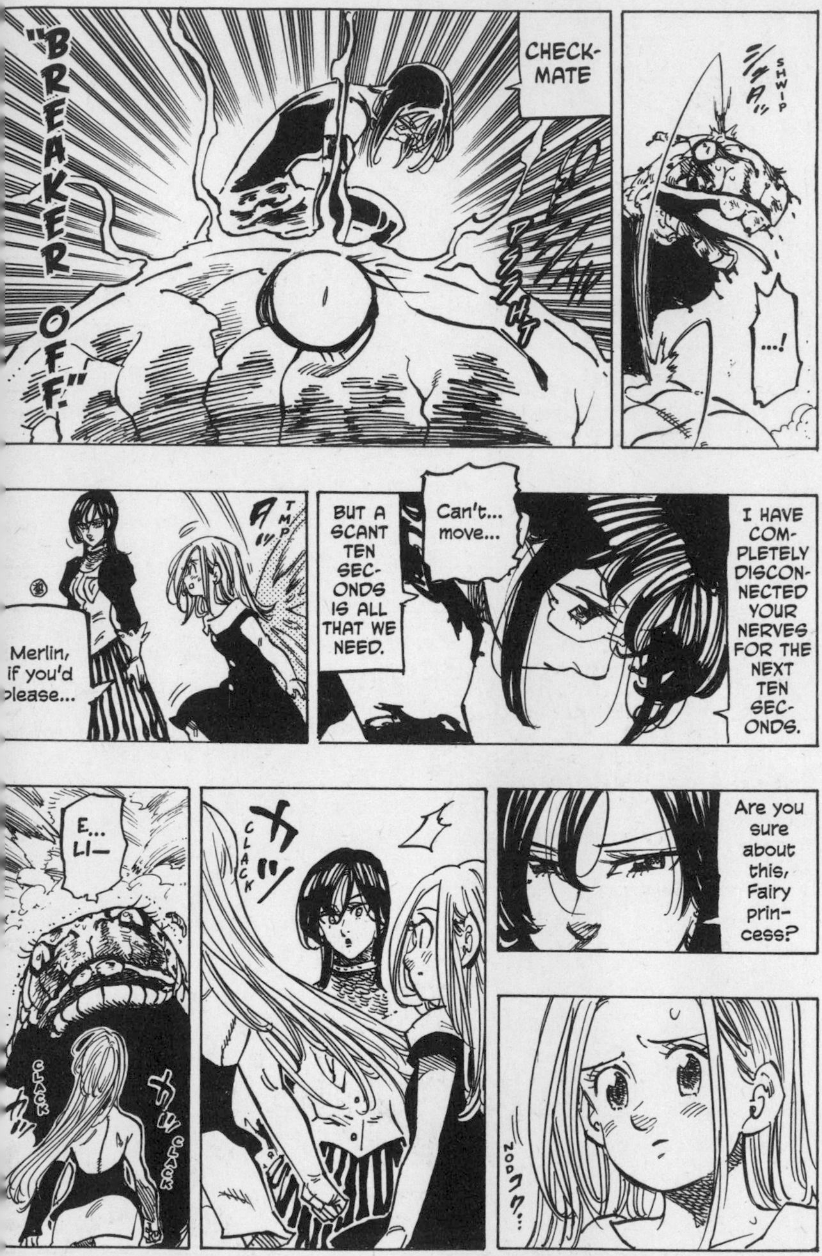
SHWIP
...!
CHECK-MATE
"BREAKER OFF."
I HAVE COMPLETELY DISCONNECTED YOUR NERVES FOR THE NEXT TEN SECONDS.
Can't... move...
BUT A SCANT TEN SECONDS IS ALL THAT WE NEED.
TMP
Merlin, if you'd please...
Are you sure about this, Fairy princess?
NOD
CLACK
E... LI—
CLACK
CLACK

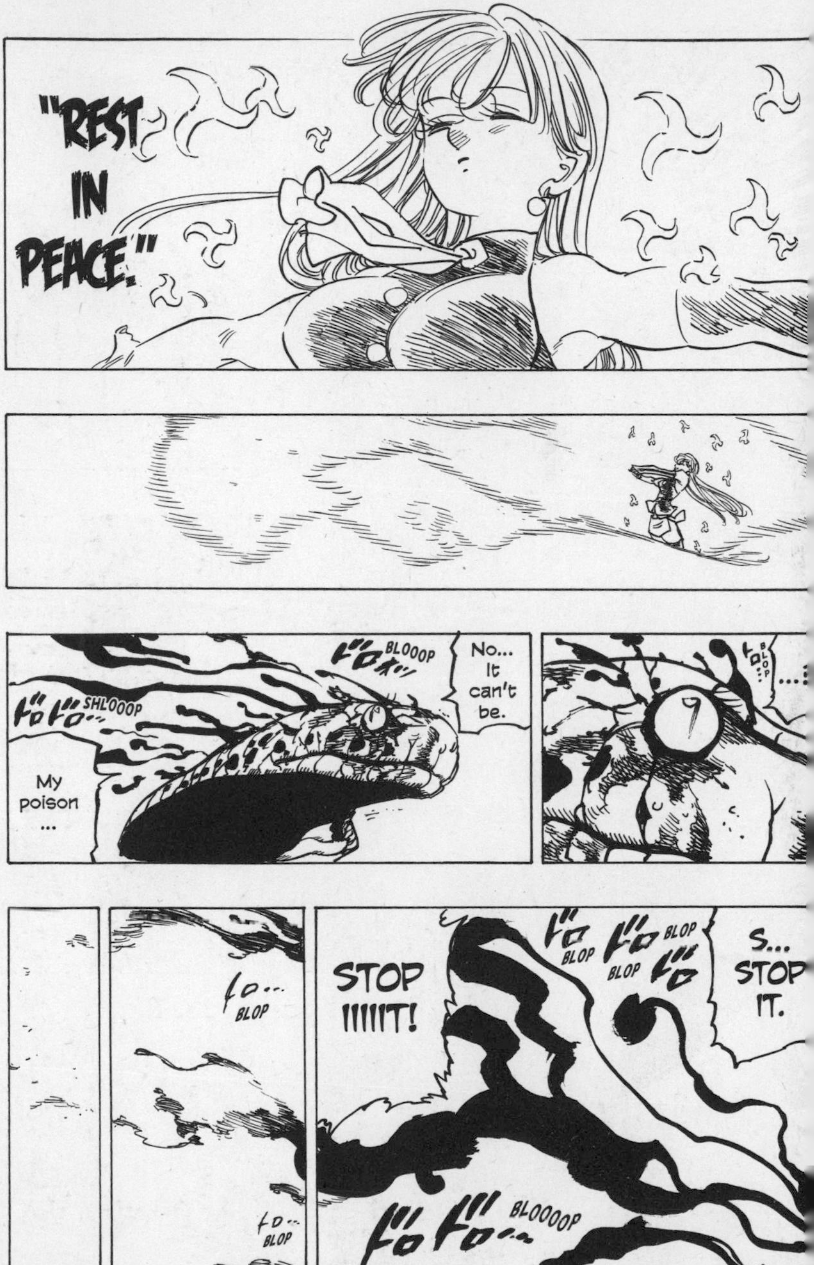

"REST IN PEACE."
BLOP
...!
BLOOOP
No... It can't be.
SHLOOOP
My poison ...
S... STOP IT.
BLOP
BLOP
STOP IIIIIT!
BLOOOOP
BLOP
BLOP

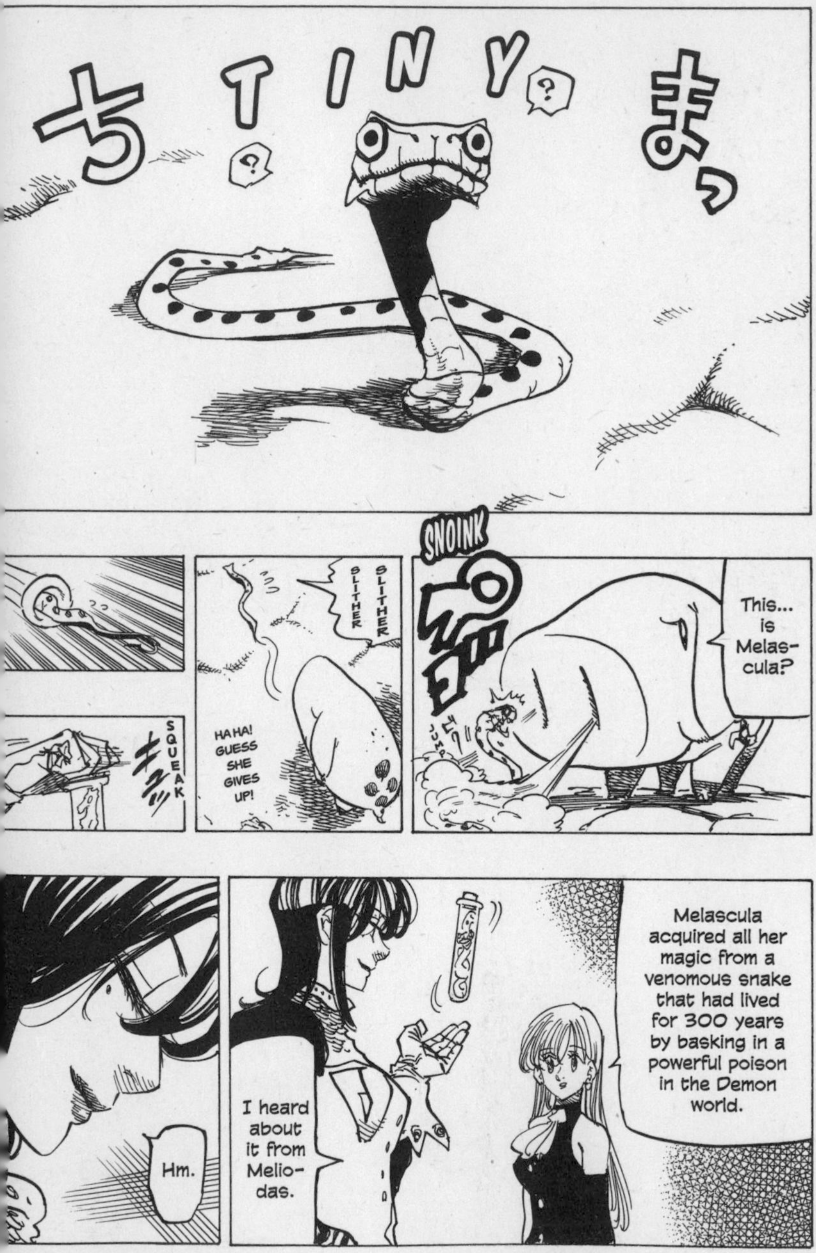

ち TINY まっ
?
?
SNOINK
This... is Melascula?
JUMP
SLITHER SLITHER
HA HA! GUESS SHE GIVES UP!
SQUEAK
Melascula acquired all her magic from a venomous snake that had lived for 300 years by basking in a powerful poison in the Demon world.
I heard about it from Melio-das.
Hm.

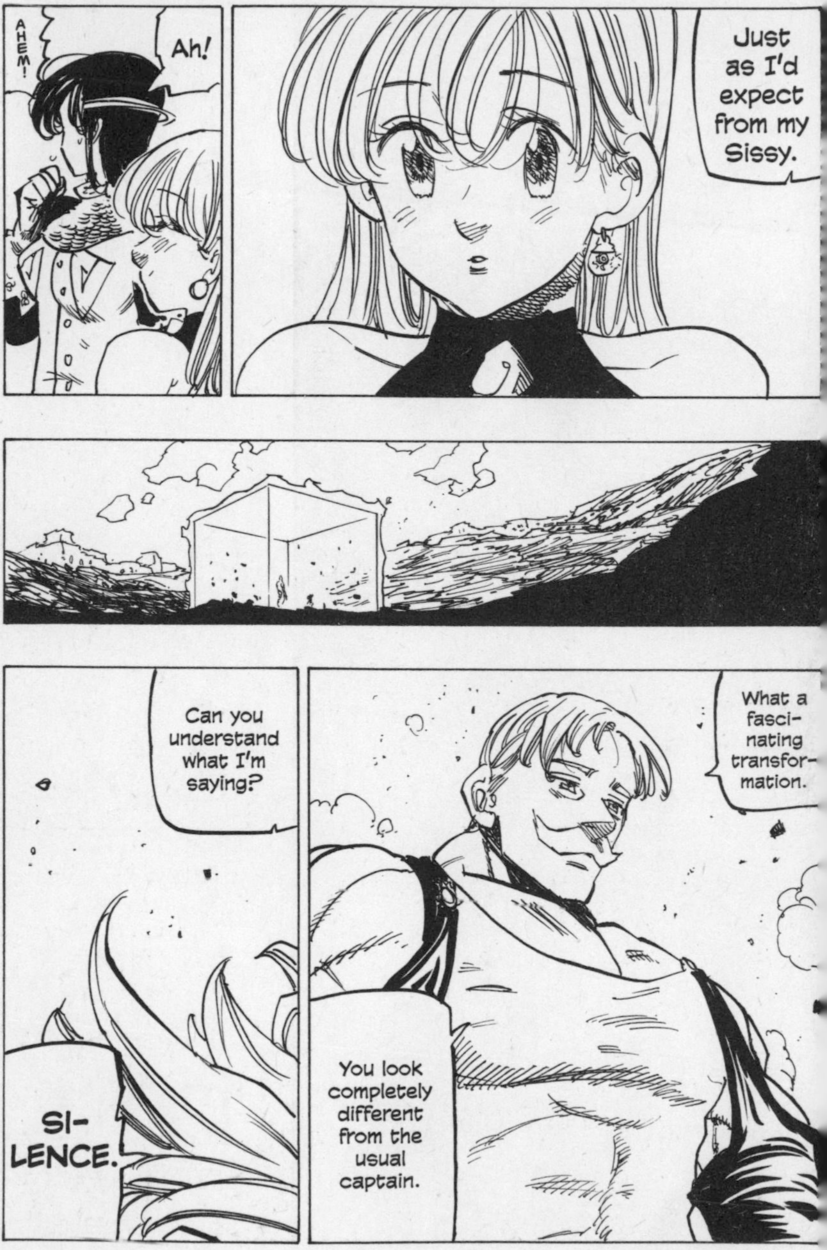
Just as I'd expect from my Sissy.
Ah!
AHEM!
What a fascinating transformation.
You look completely different from the usual captain.
Can you understand what I'm saying?
SI-LENCE.

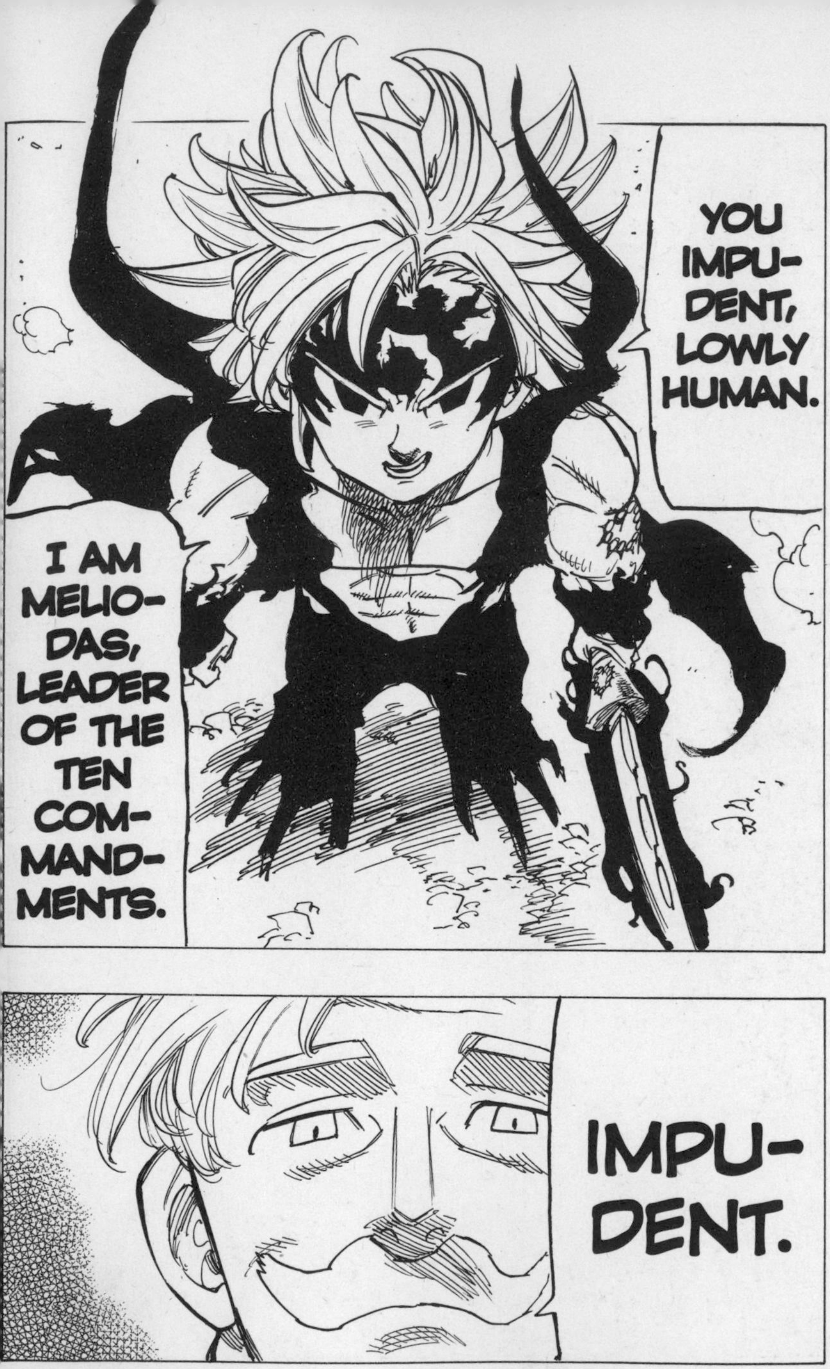
YOU IMPU-
DENT,
LOWLY
HUMAN.
I AM MELIO-
DAS,
LEADER
OF THE
TEN
COM-
MAND-
MENTS.
IMPU-
DENT.

Front Page Illustration Request Corner!! [1] / “What if The Deadly Sins were in sports clubs?”

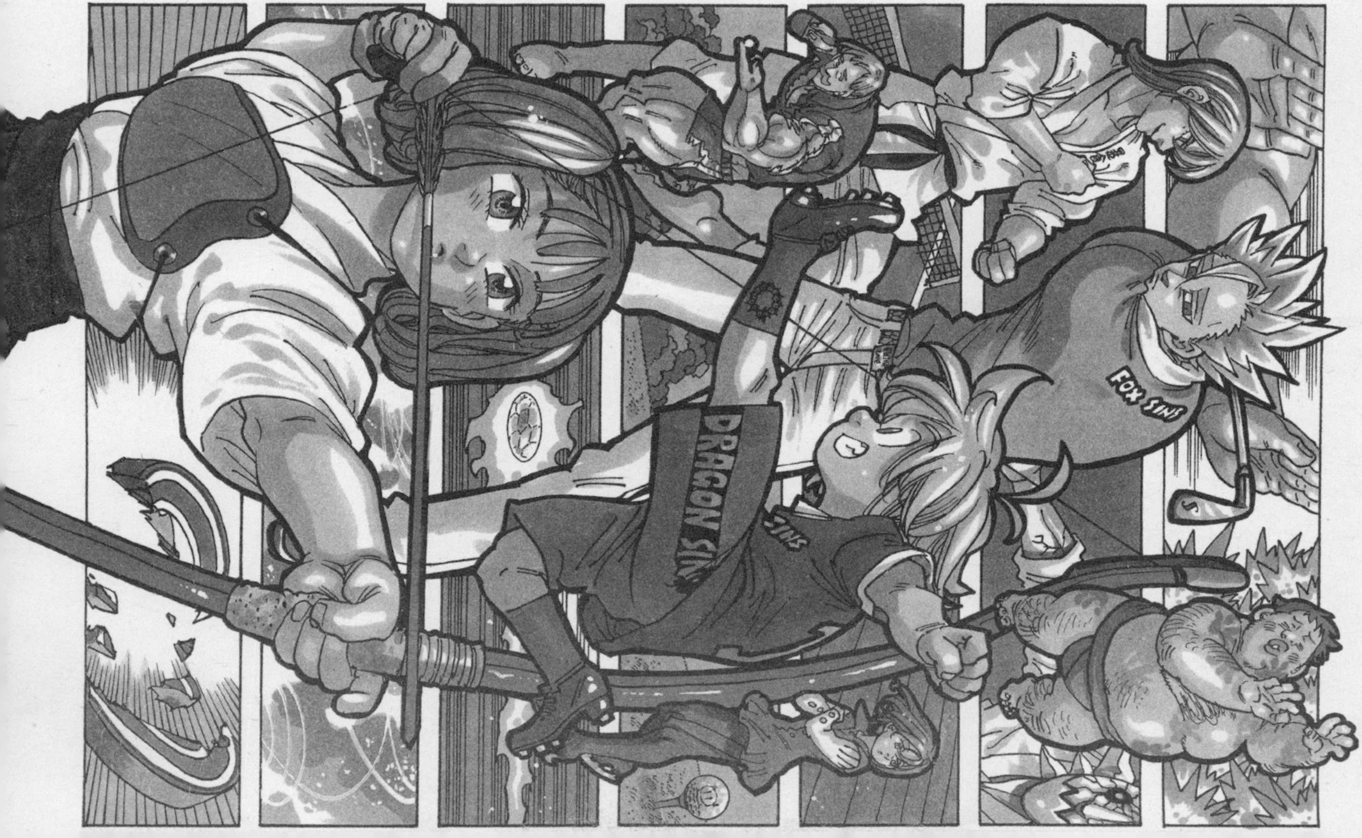
FOX SINS
DRAGON SINS

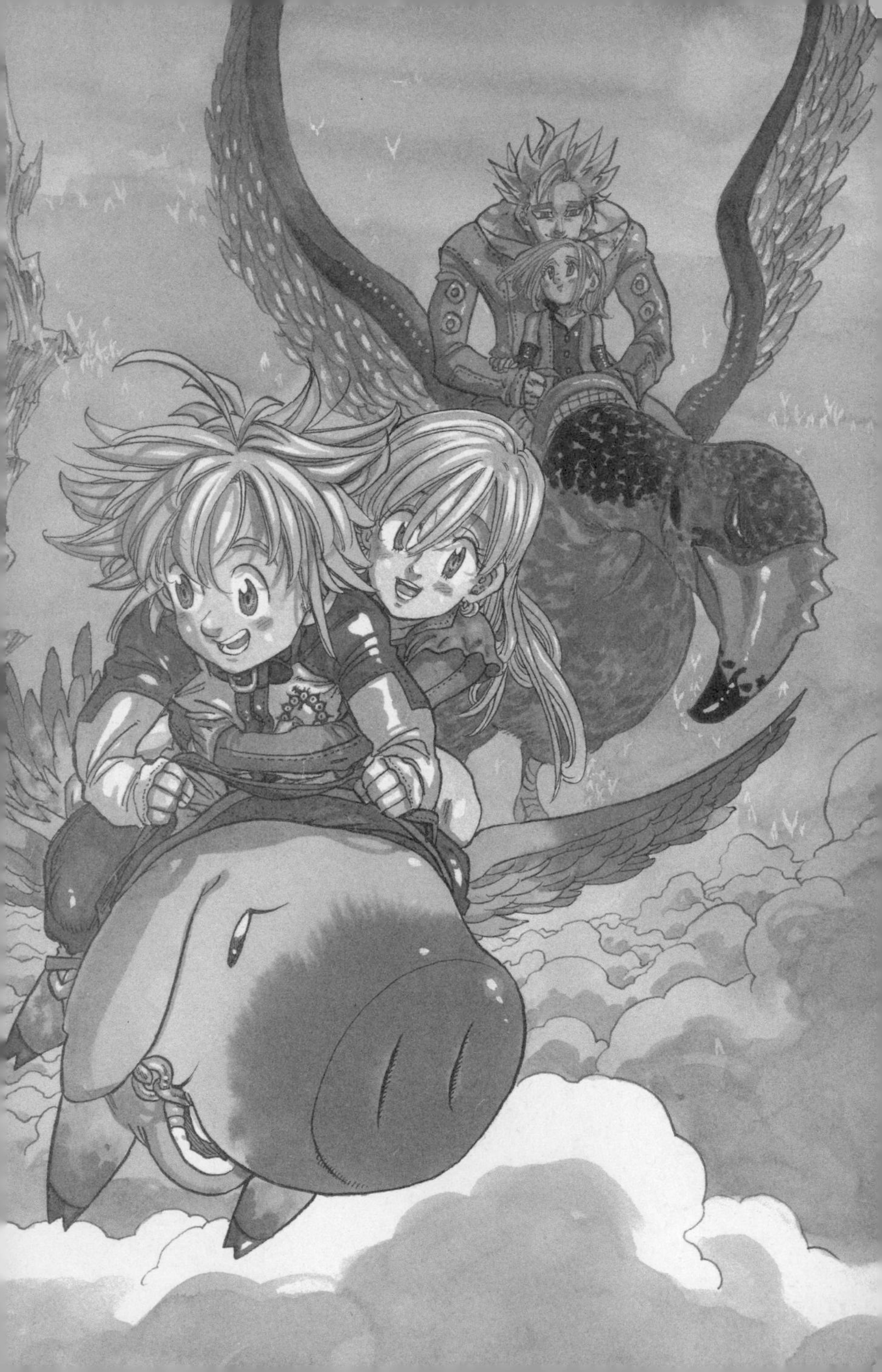

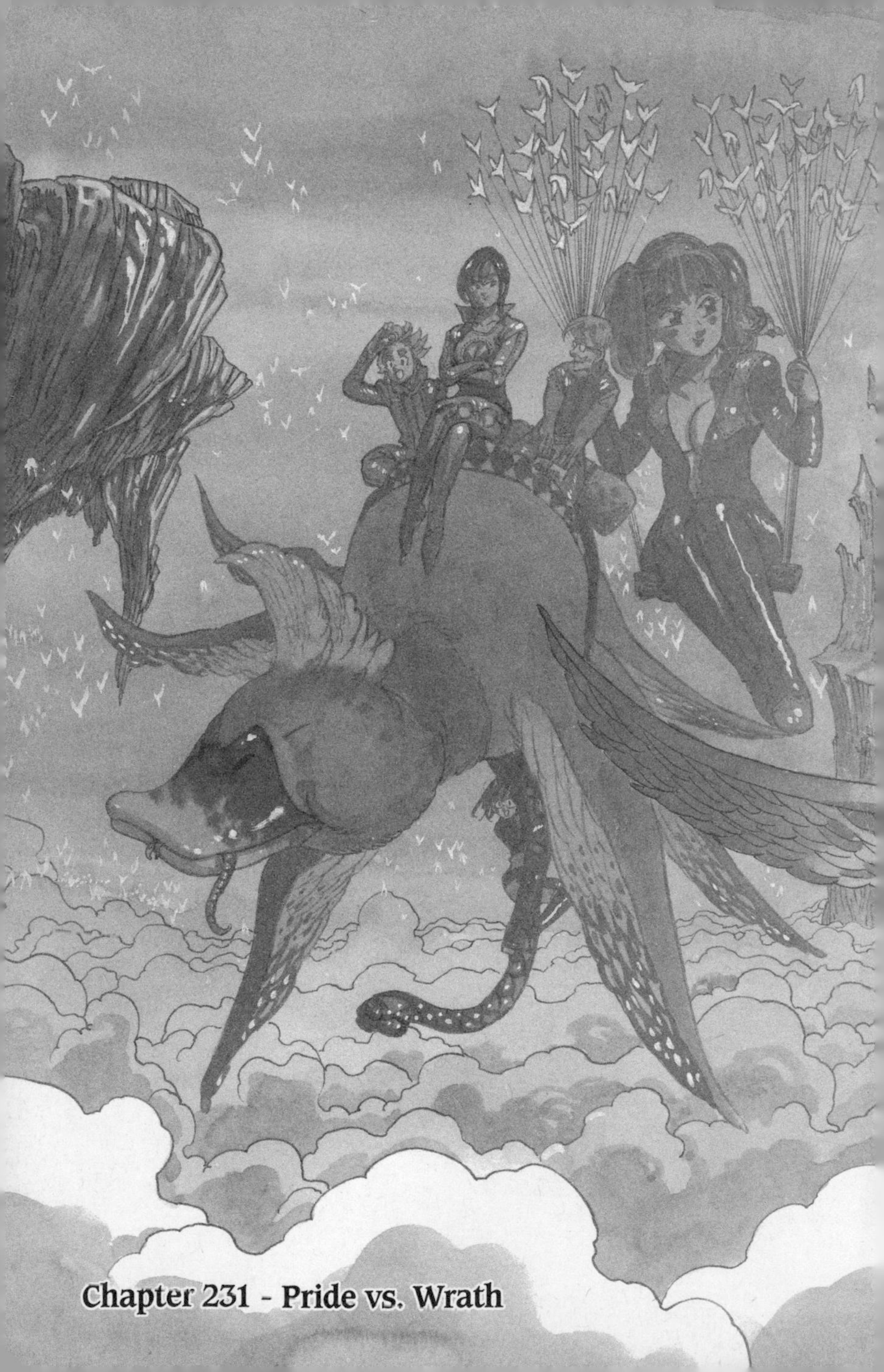

Chapter 231 - Pride vs. Wrath

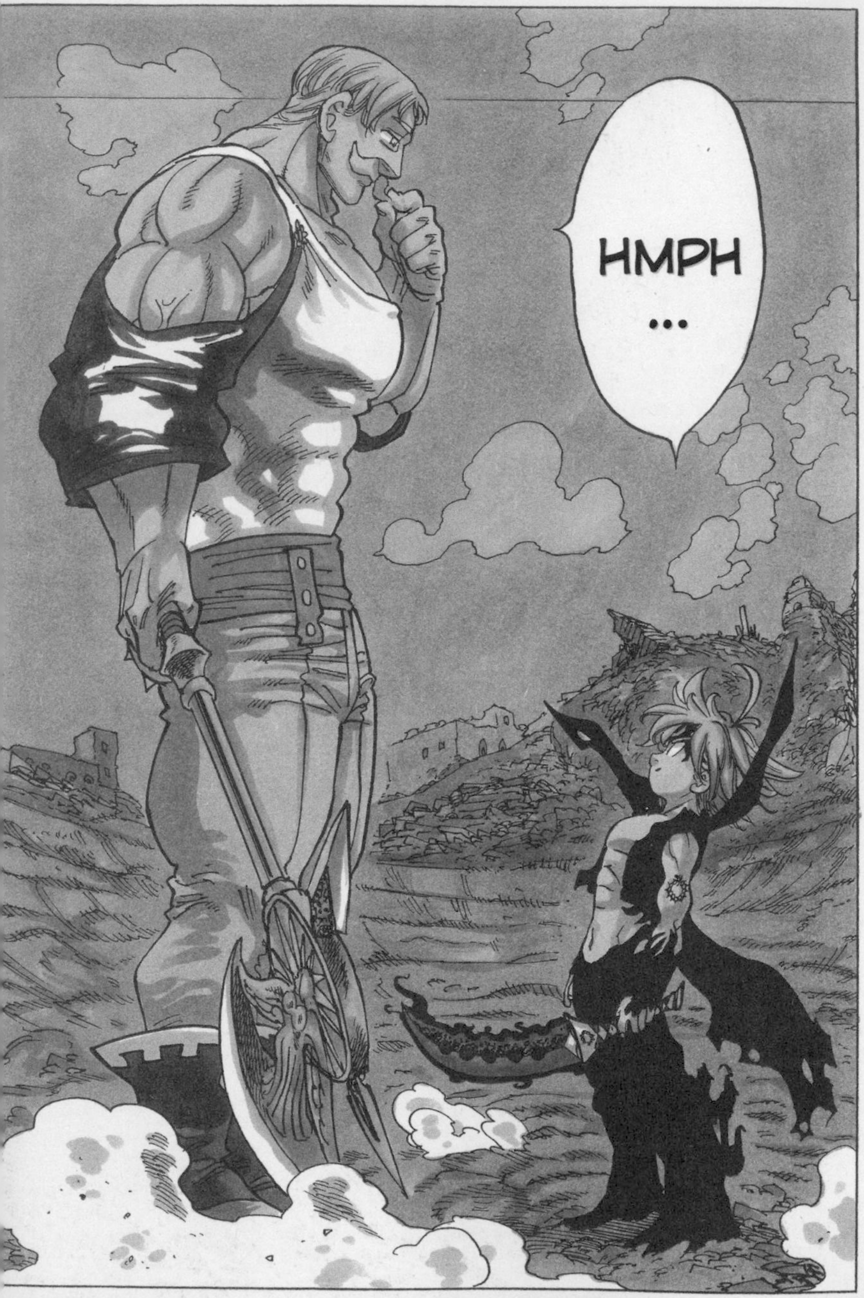
HMPH
...

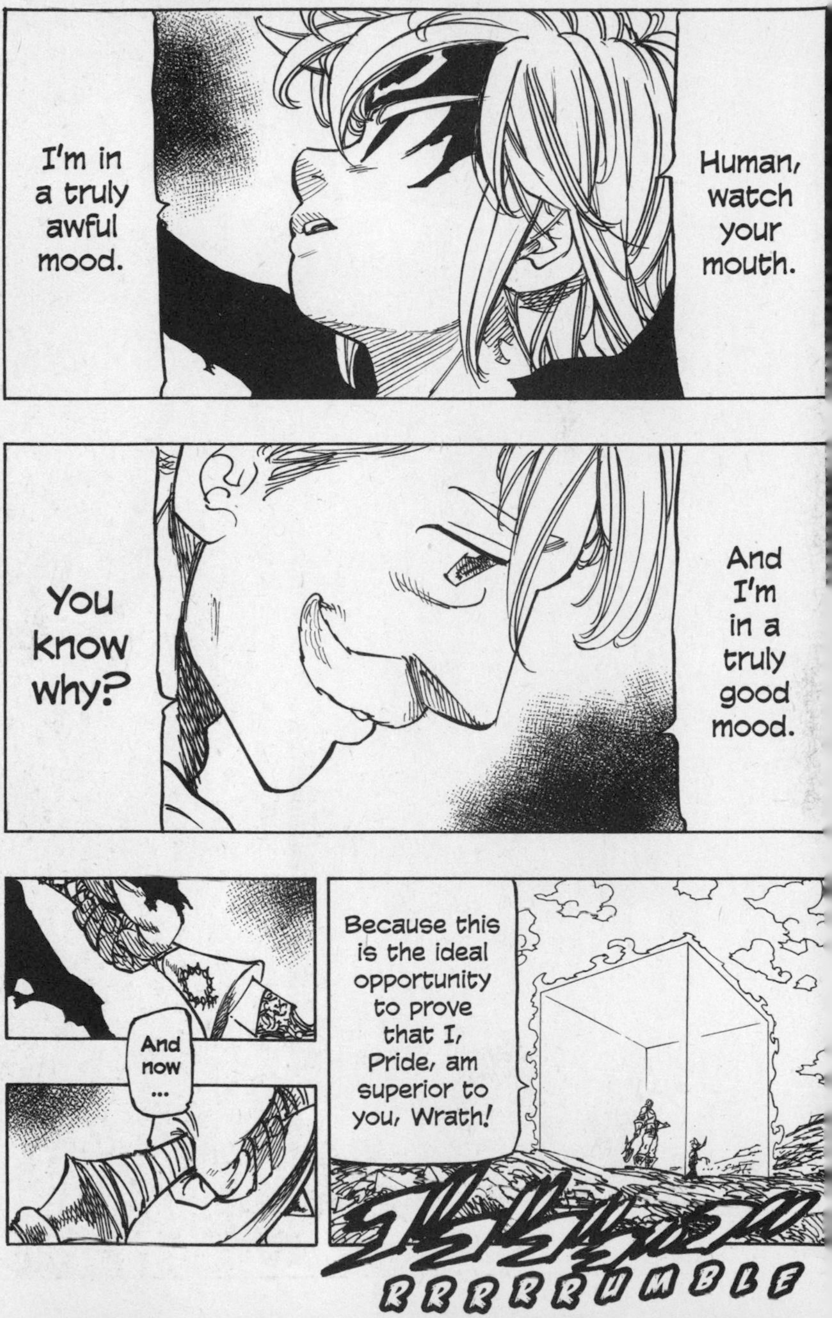
Human, watch your mouth.
I'm in a truly awful mood.
And I'm in a truly good mood.
You know why?
Because this is the ideal opportunity to prove that I, Pride, am superior to you, Wrath!
And now ...
RRRRRUMBLE

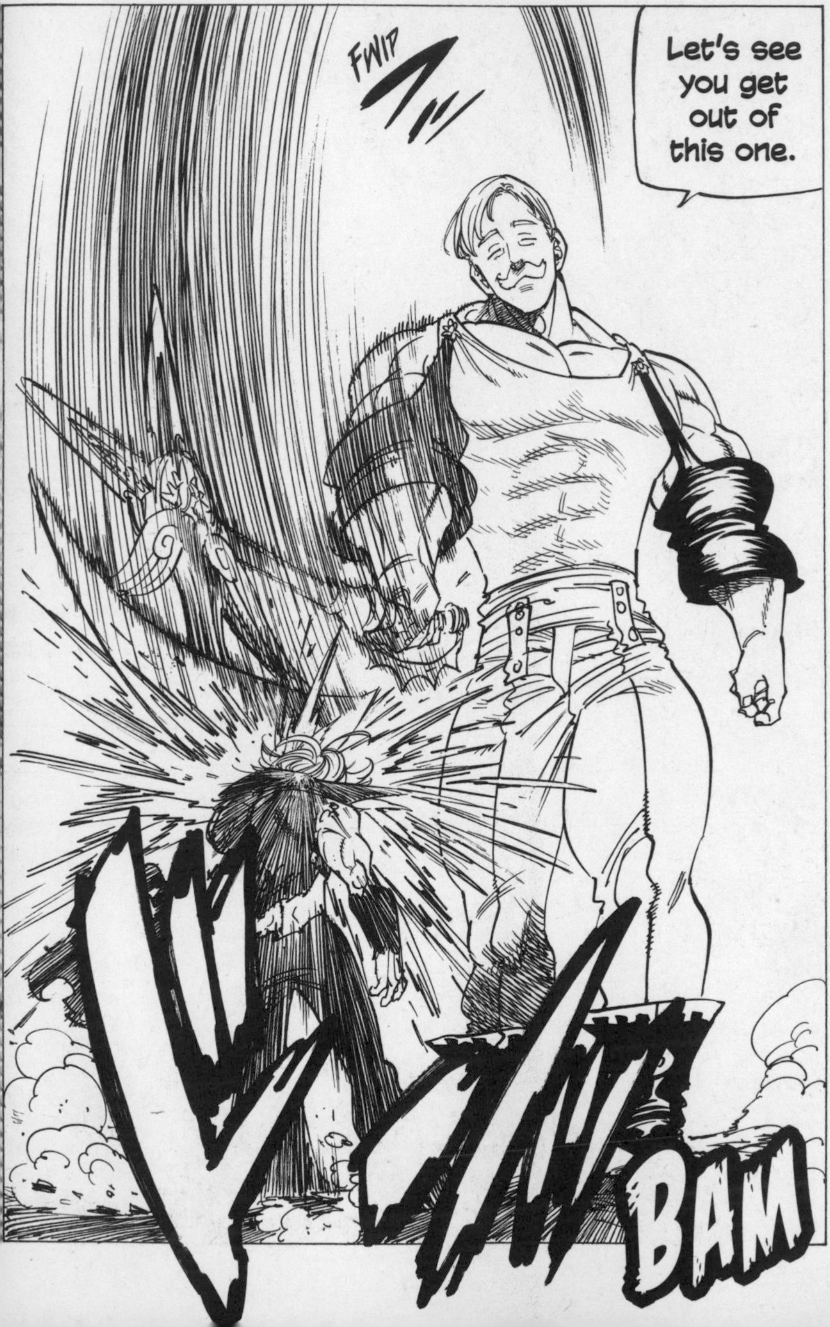
Let's see you get out of this one.
FWIP
BAM

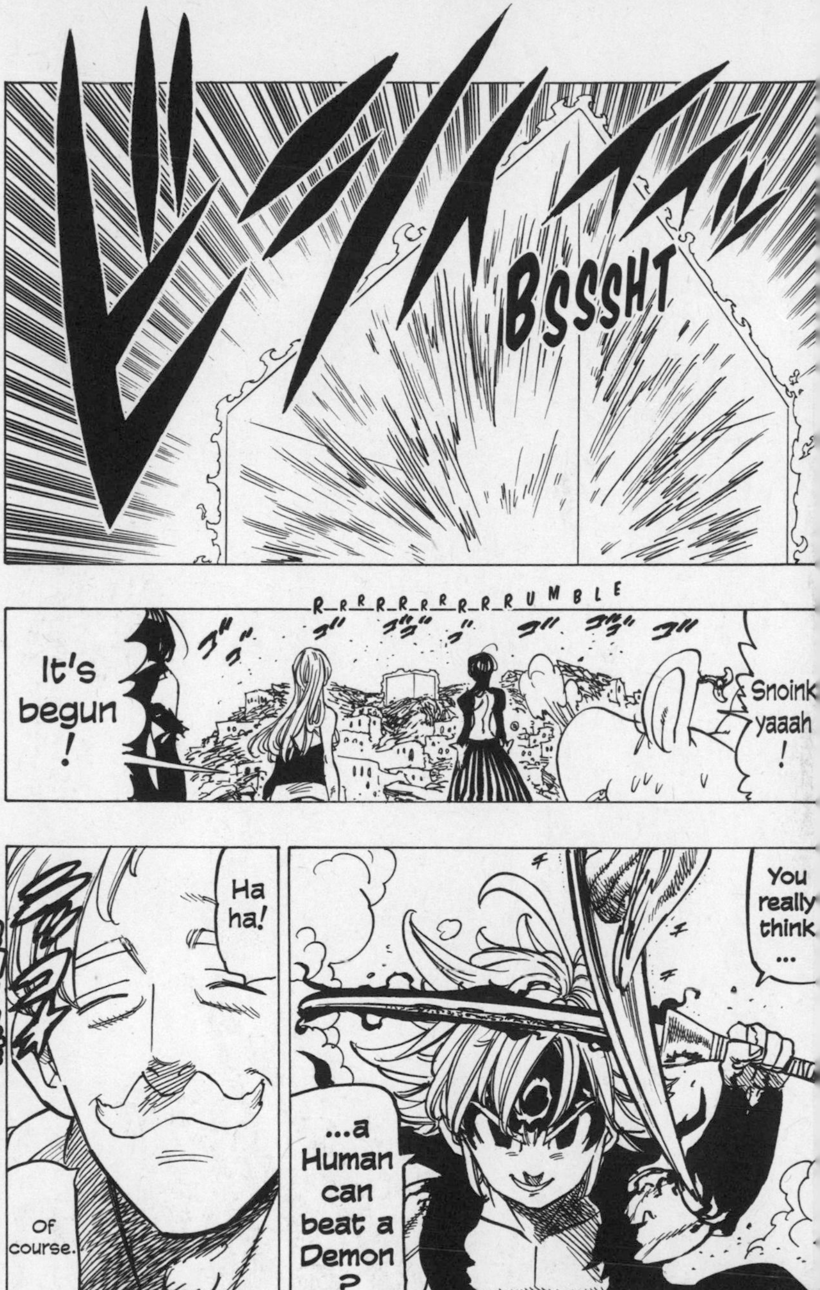
BSSSHT
RRRRRRRRRRUMBLE
Snoink yaaah!
It's begun!
You really think...
...a Human can beat a Demon?
Ha ha!
SMILE
Of course.

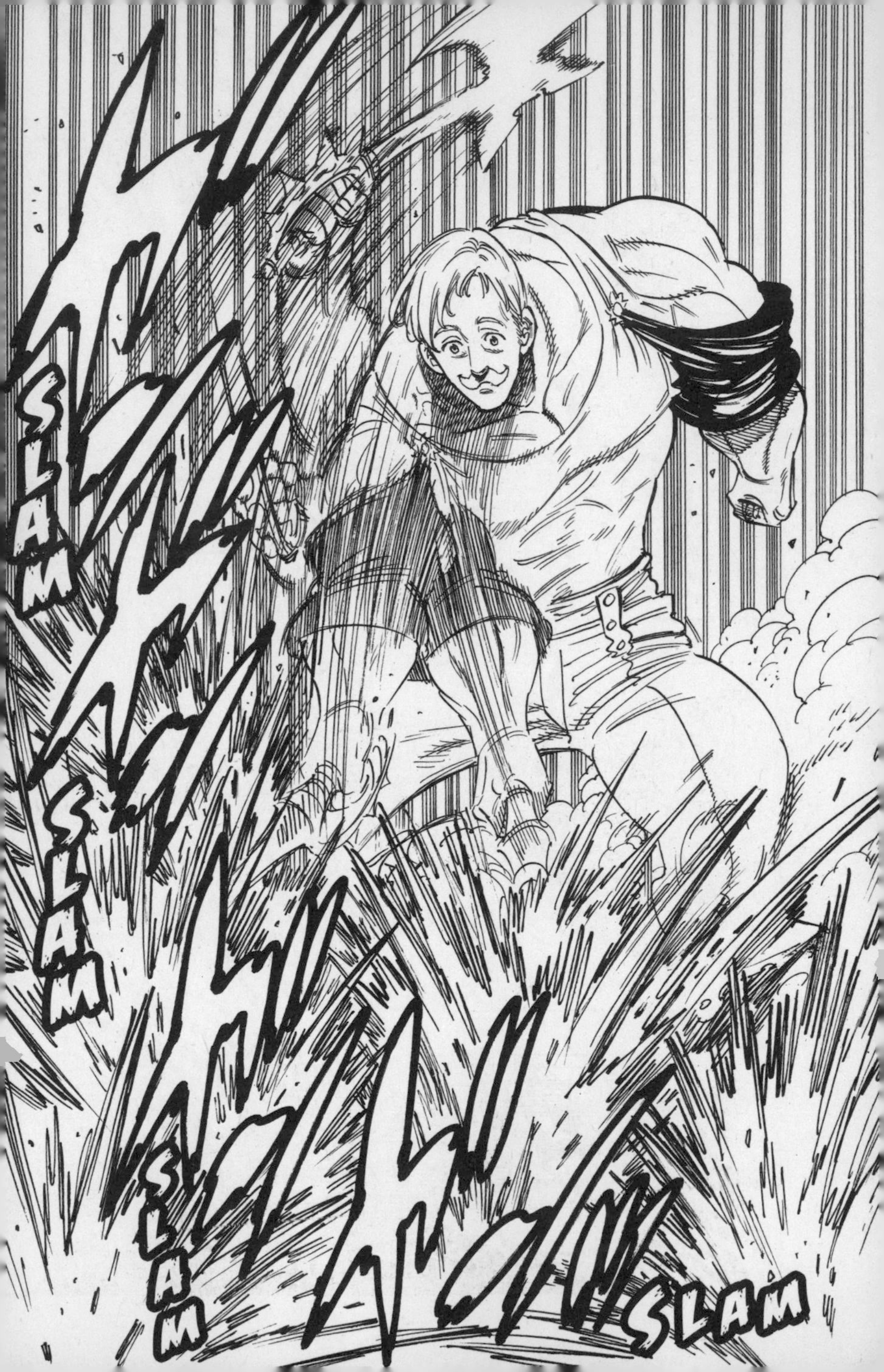
SLAM
SLAM
SLAM
SLAM
SLAM

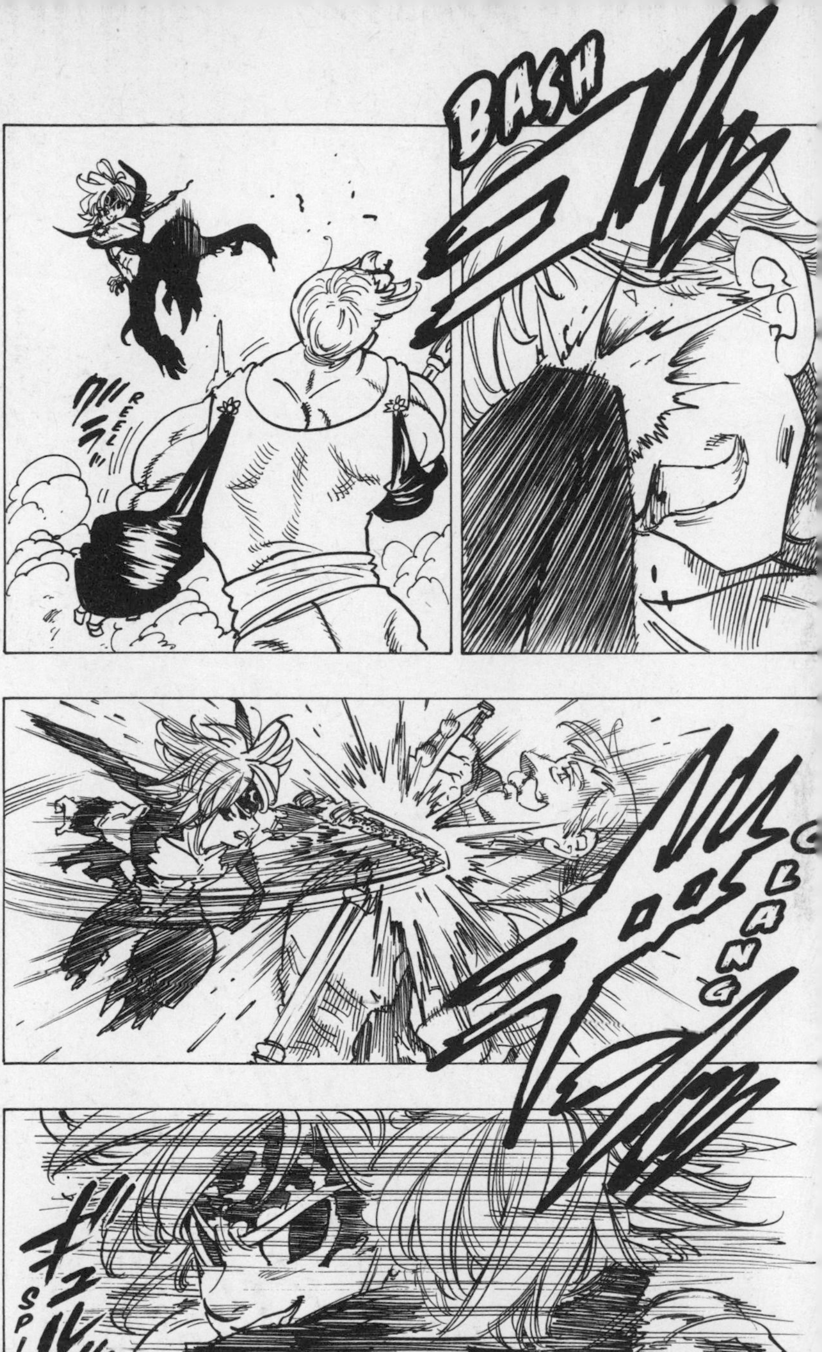
BASH
REEL
CLANG
SPIN

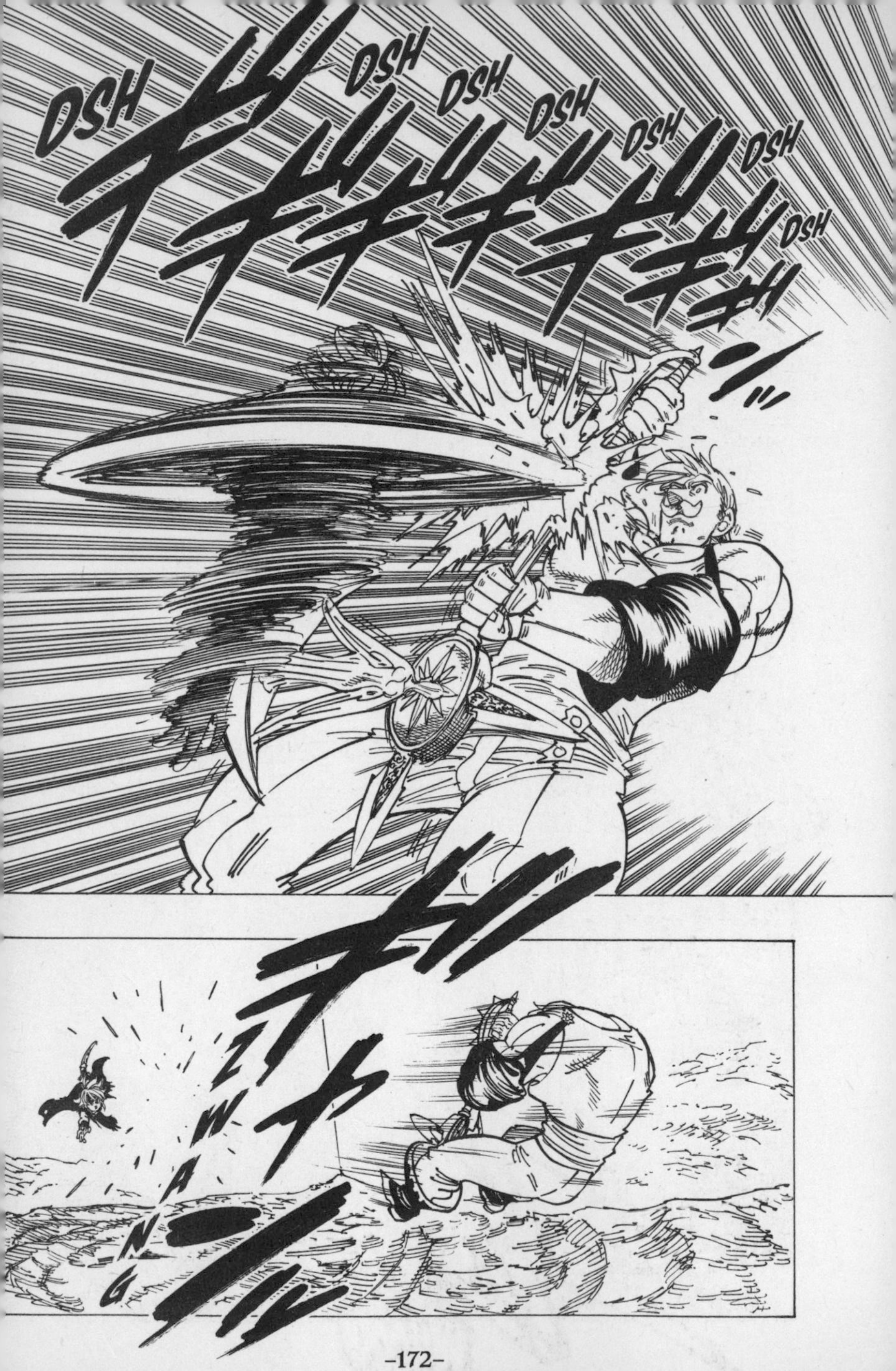
DSH
DSH
DSH
DSH
DSH
DSH
DSH
ZWANG

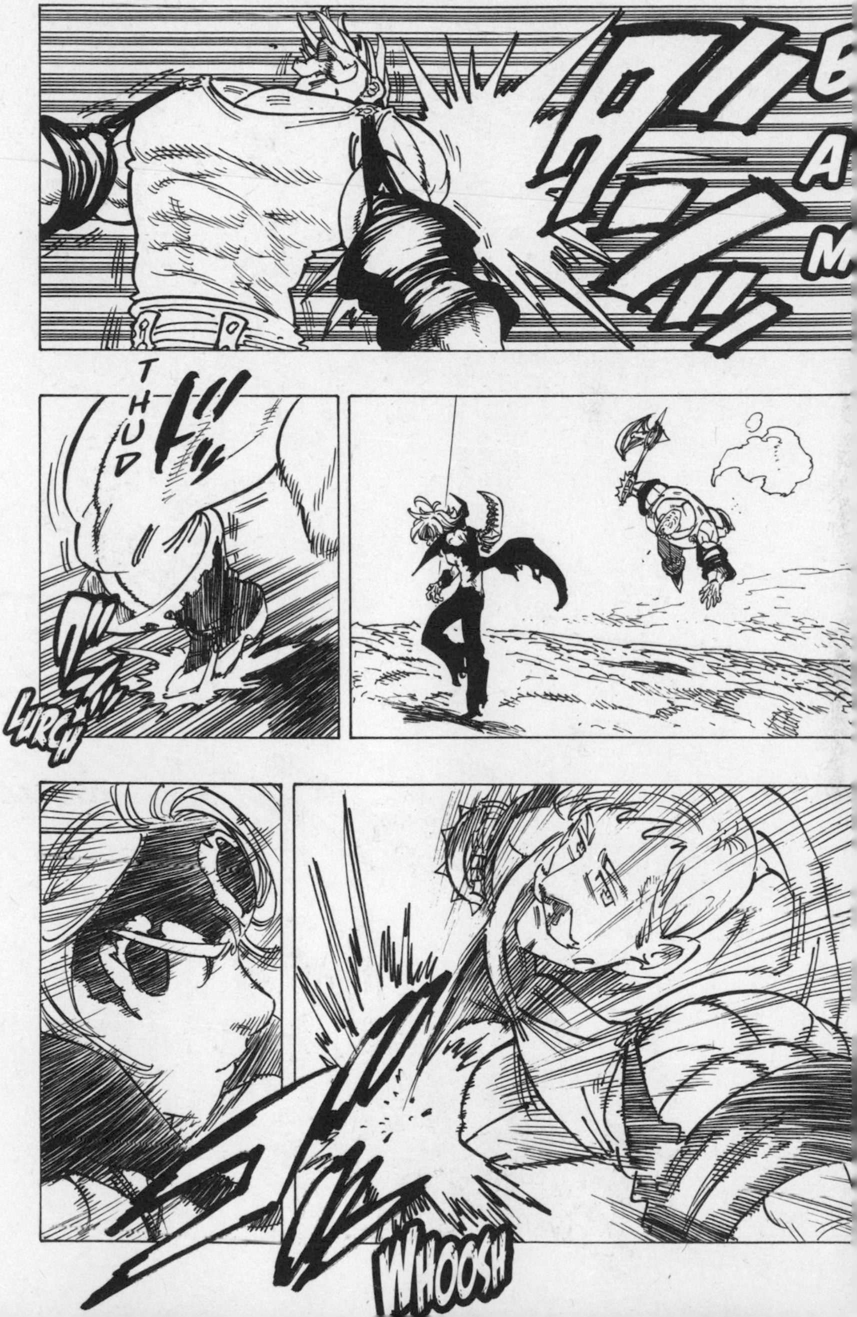
BAM
THUD
LURCH
WHOOSH

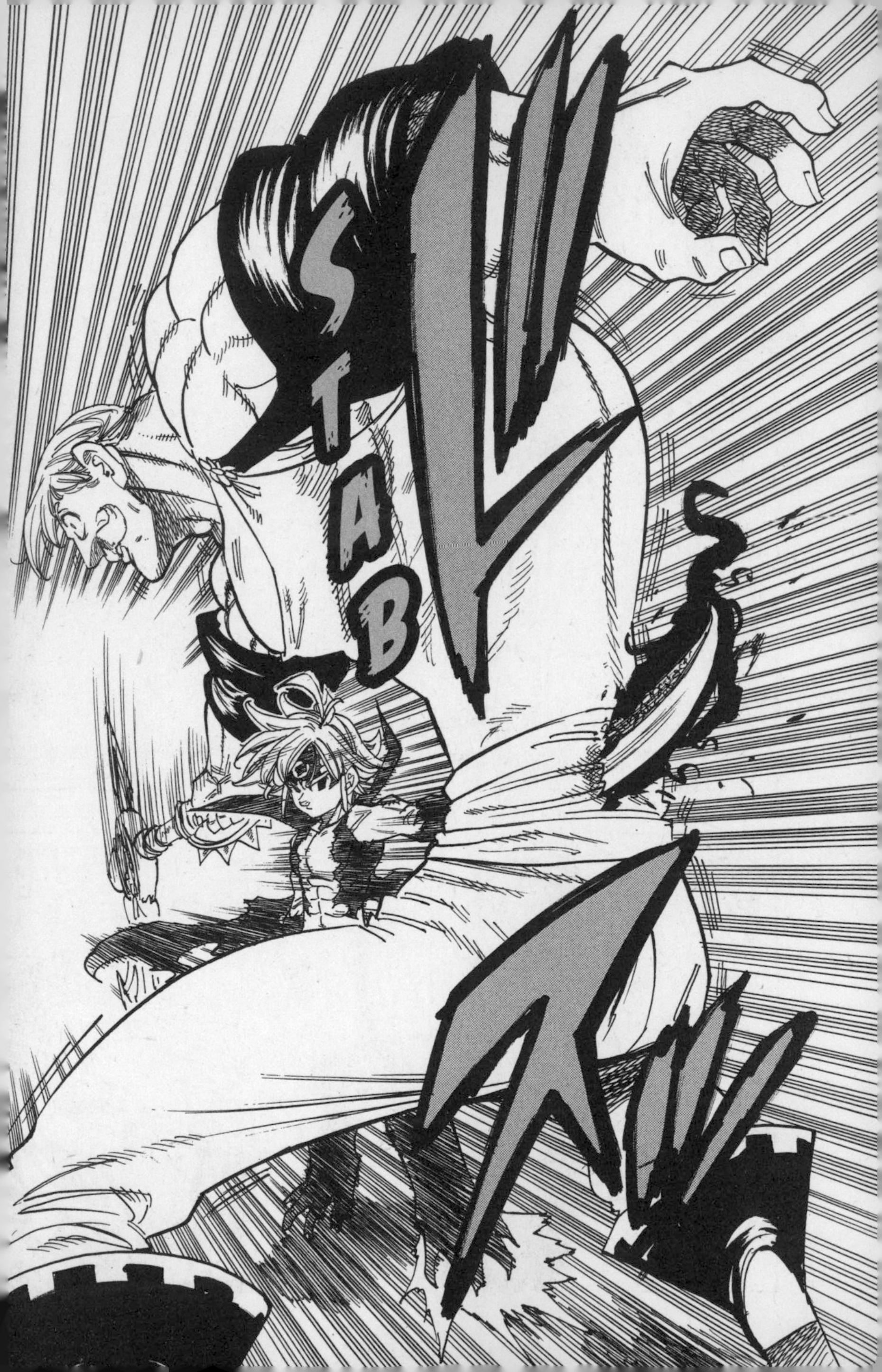
STAB

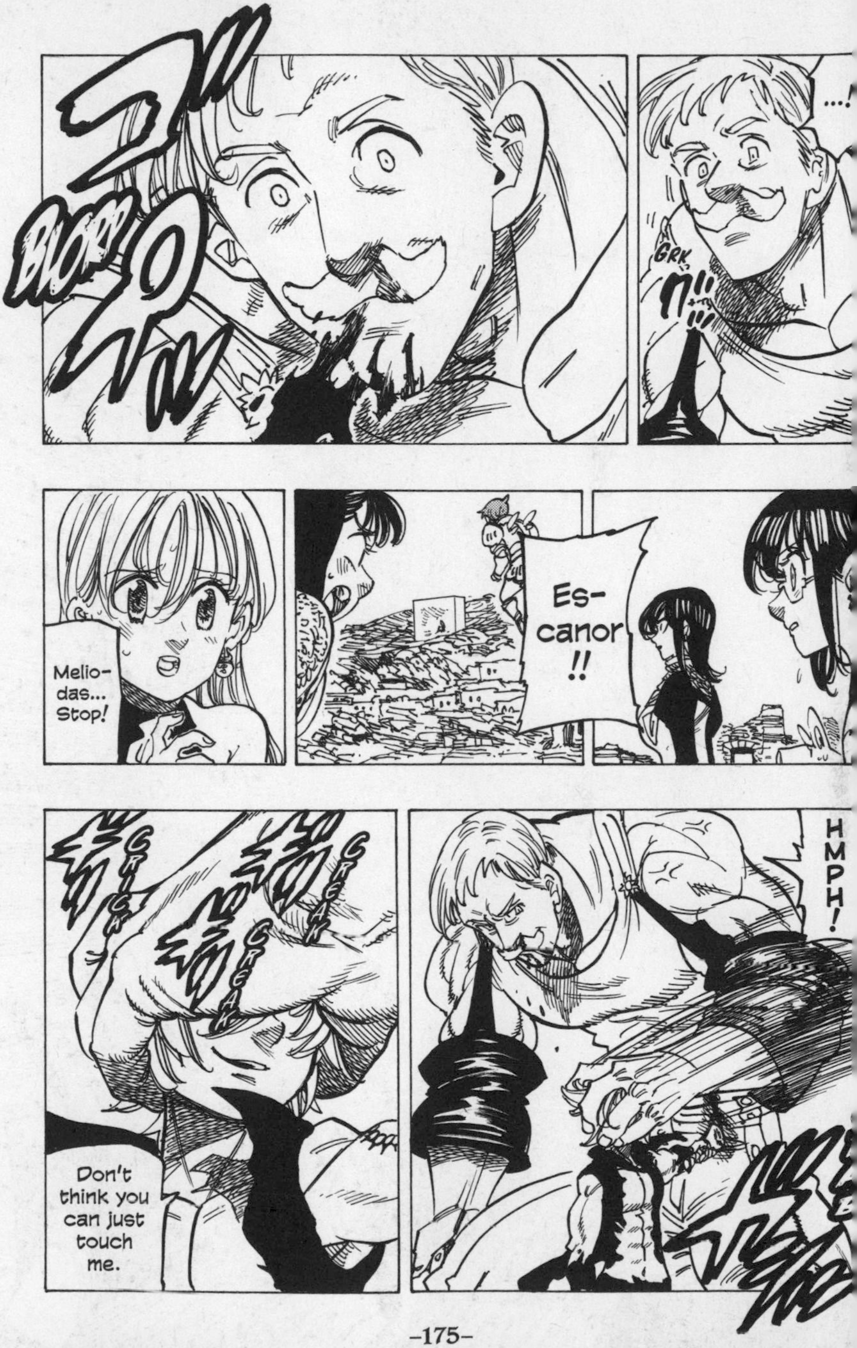

...!
GRK
BLORP
Es-canor!!
Melio-das... Stop!
HMPH!
CREAK
CREAK
CREAK
Don't think you can just touch me.

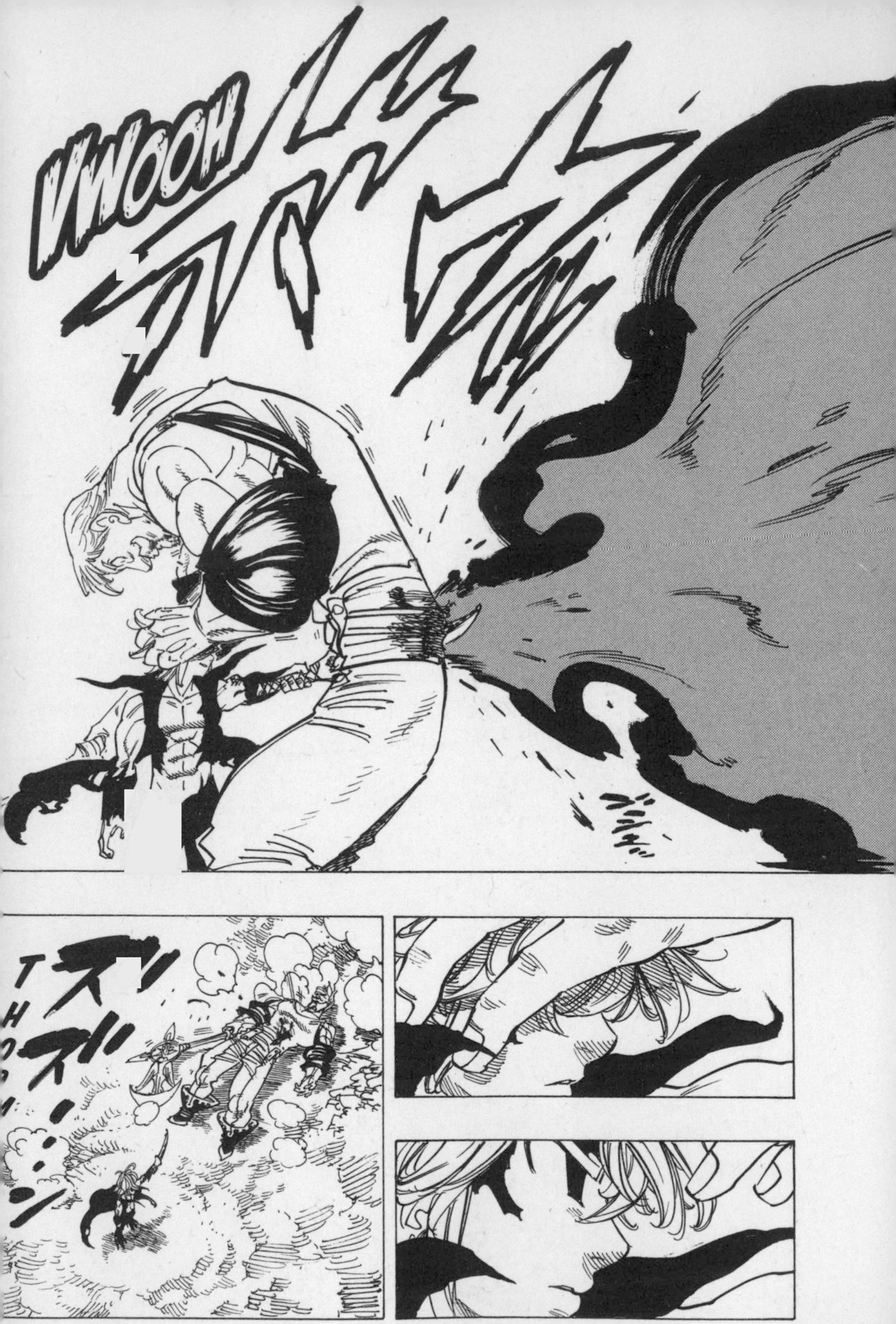
VWOOH
THOOM

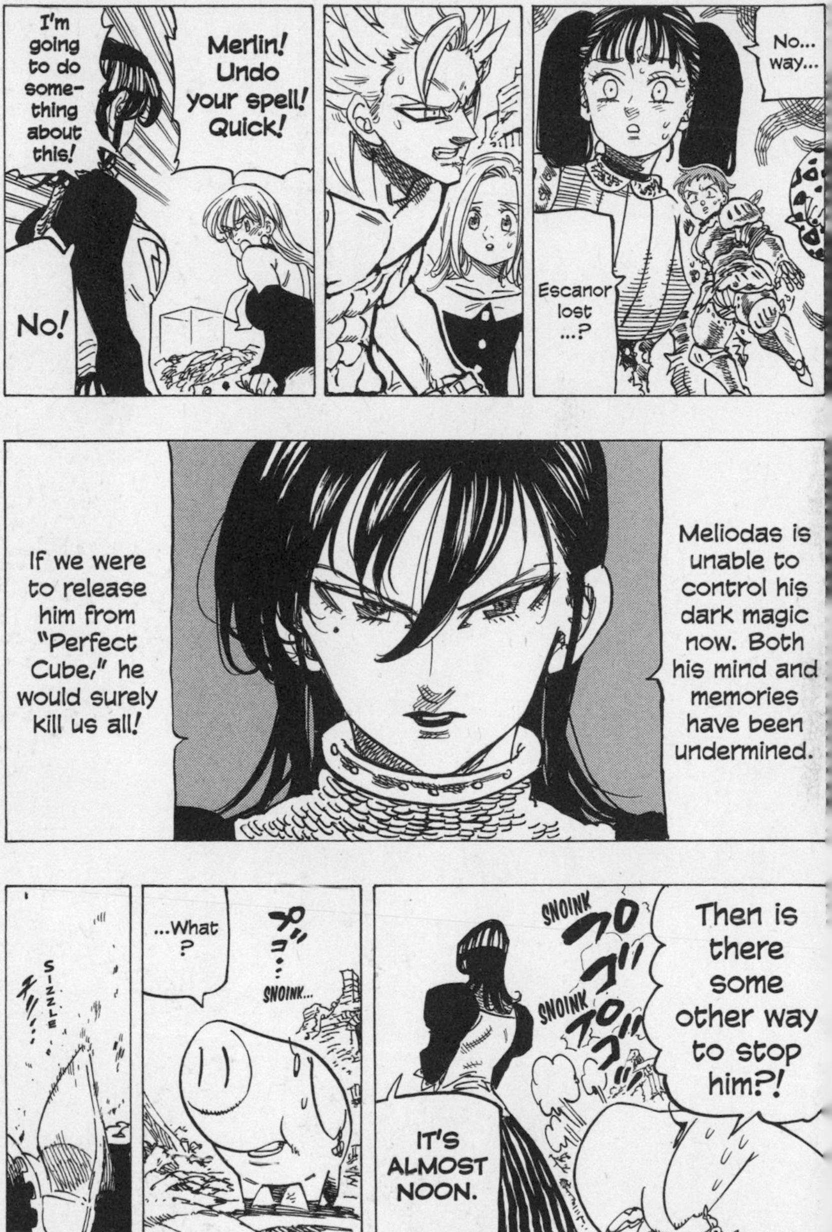
No... way...
Escanor lost ...?
Merlin! Undo your spell! Quick!
I'm going to do some-thing about this!
No!
Meliodas is unable to control his dark magic now. Both his mind and memories have been undermined.
If we were to release him from "Perfect Cube," he would surely kill us all!
Then is there some other way to stop him?!
SNOINK
SNOINK
IT'S ALMOST NOON.
SNOINK...
...What?
SIZZLE

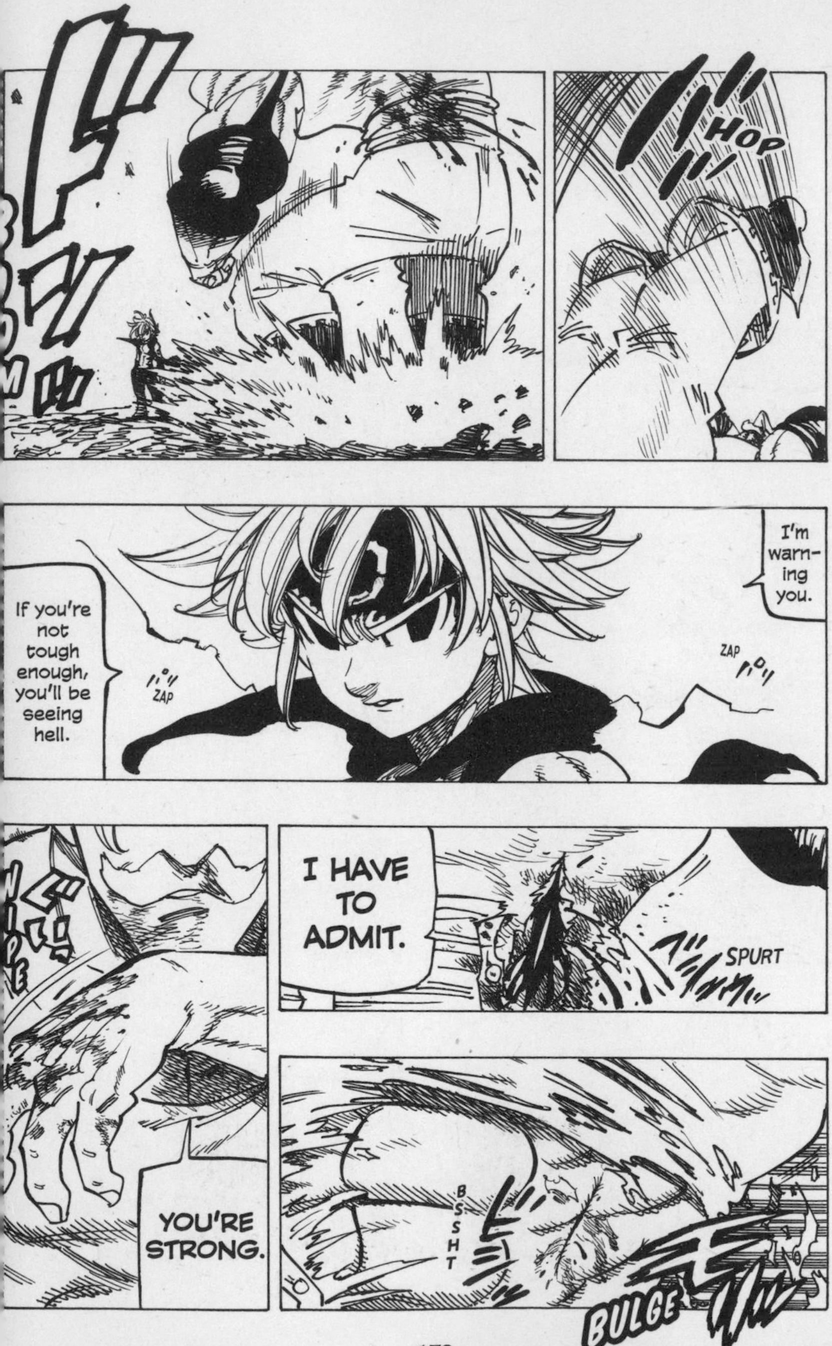
HOP
I'm warning you.
ZAP
If you're not tough enough, you'll be seeing hell.
ZAP
I HAVE TO ADMIT.
SPURT
BSSHT
BULGE
WIPE
YOU'RE STRONG.

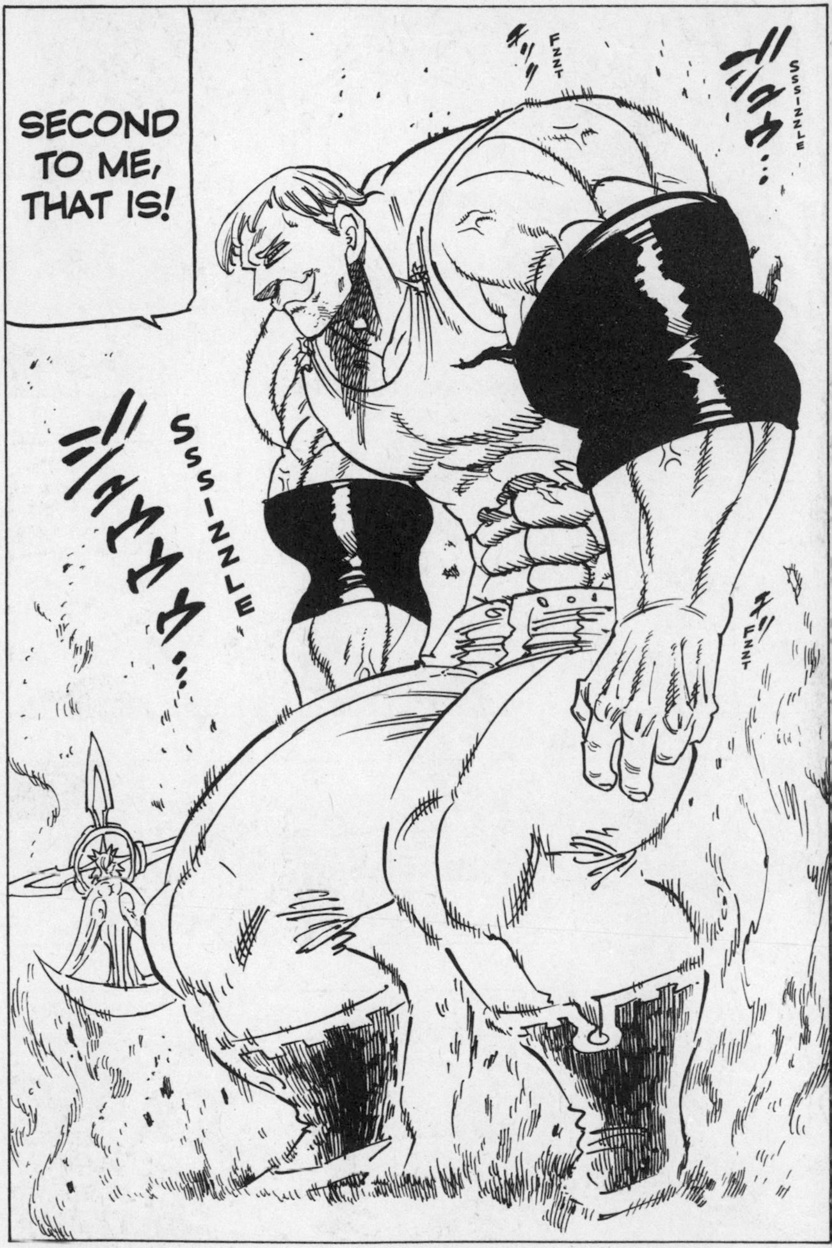
SSSIZZLE
FZZT
SECOND TO ME, THAT IS!
FZZT
SSSIZZLE

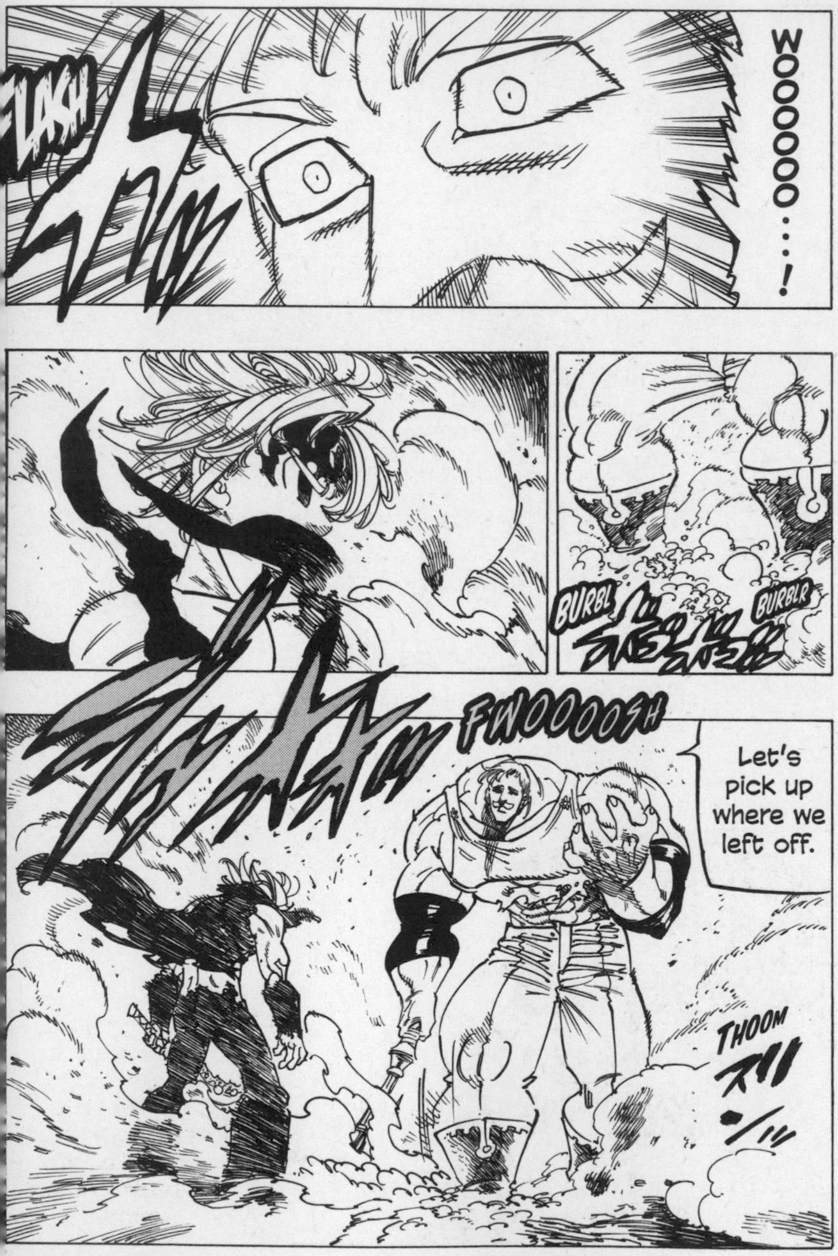
WOOOOOOO...!
LASH
BURBLR
BURBL
Let's pick up where we left off.
FWOOOOSH
THOOM

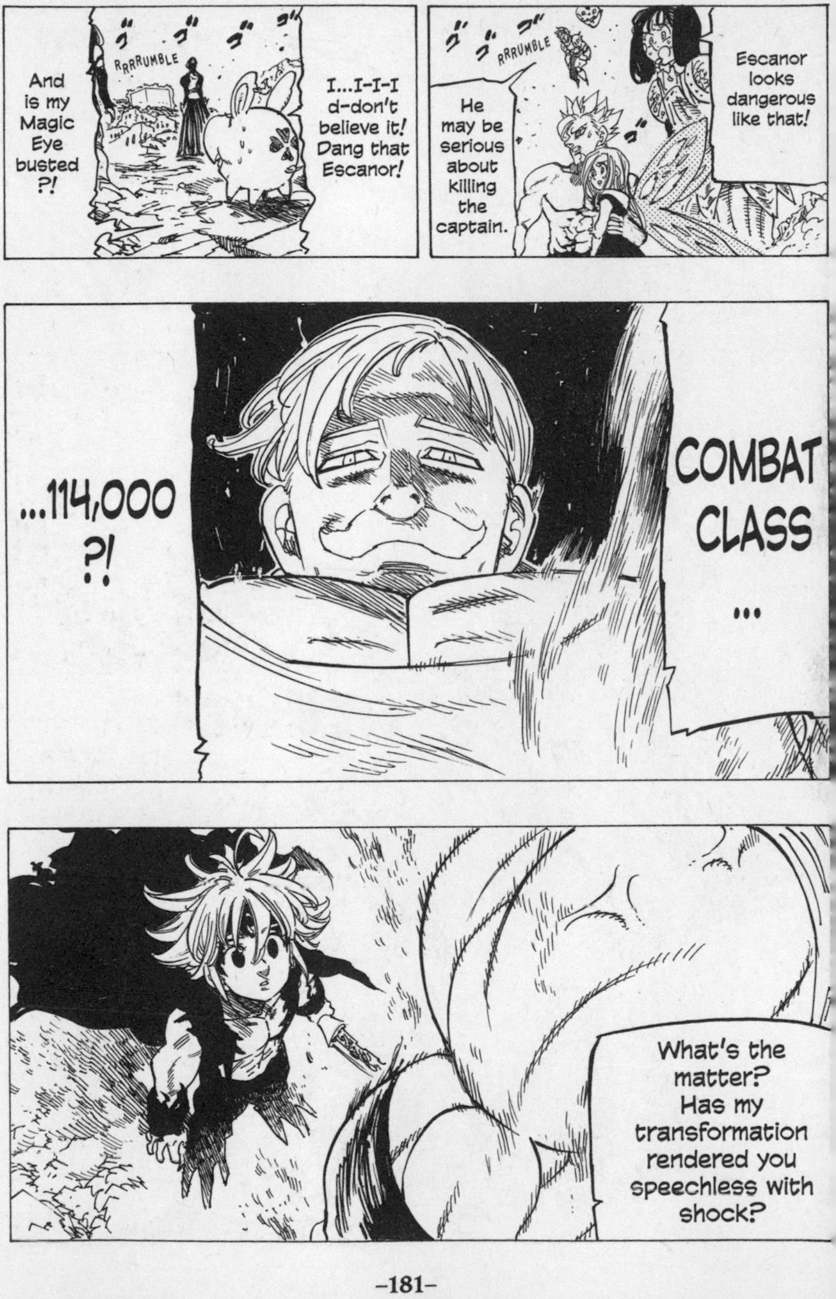
RRRUMBLE
Escanor looks dangerous like that!
He may be serious about killing the captain.
RRRUMBLE
I...I-I-I d-don't believe it! Dang that Escanor!
And is my Magic Eye busted?!
COMBAT CLASS ...
...114,000 ?!
What's the matter? Has my transformation rendered you speechless with shock?

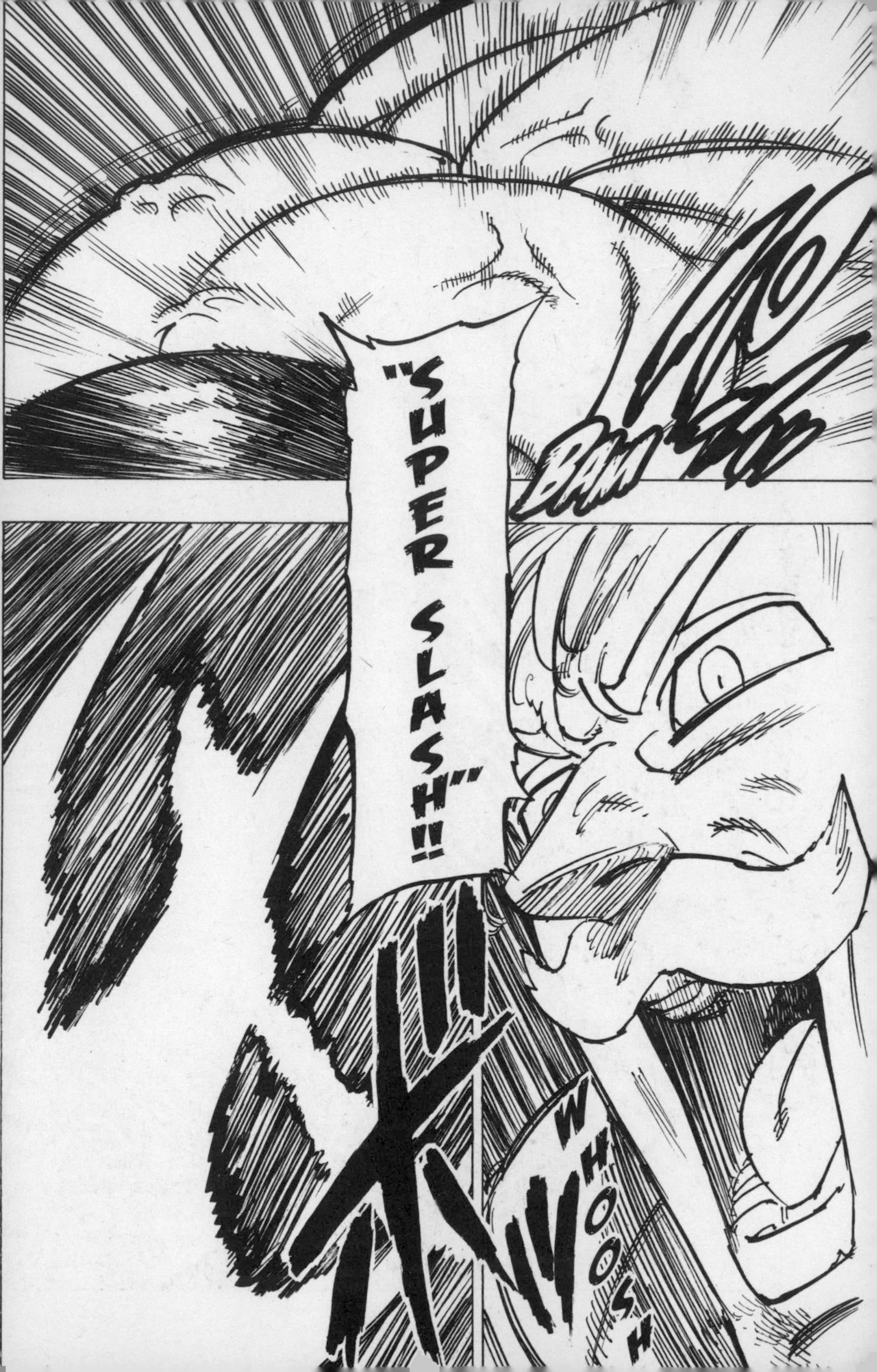
"SUPER SLASH"!!
WHOOSH

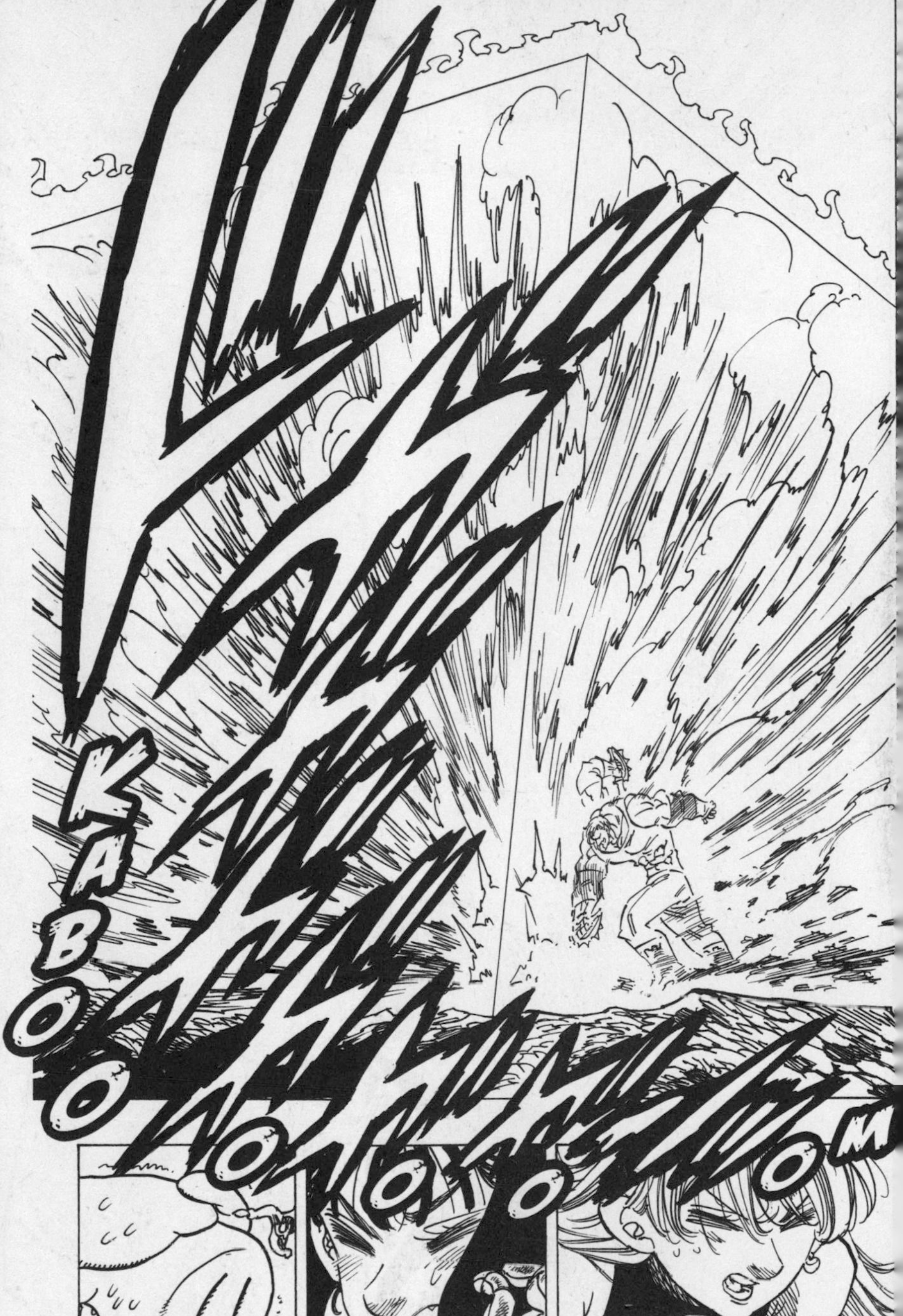
KABOOOOOOM

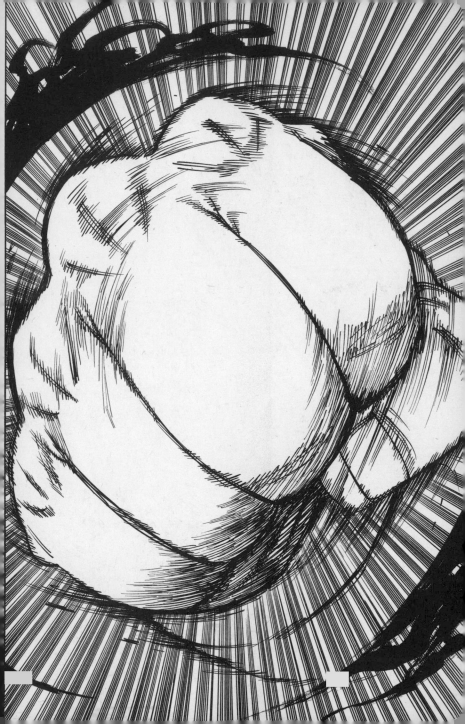

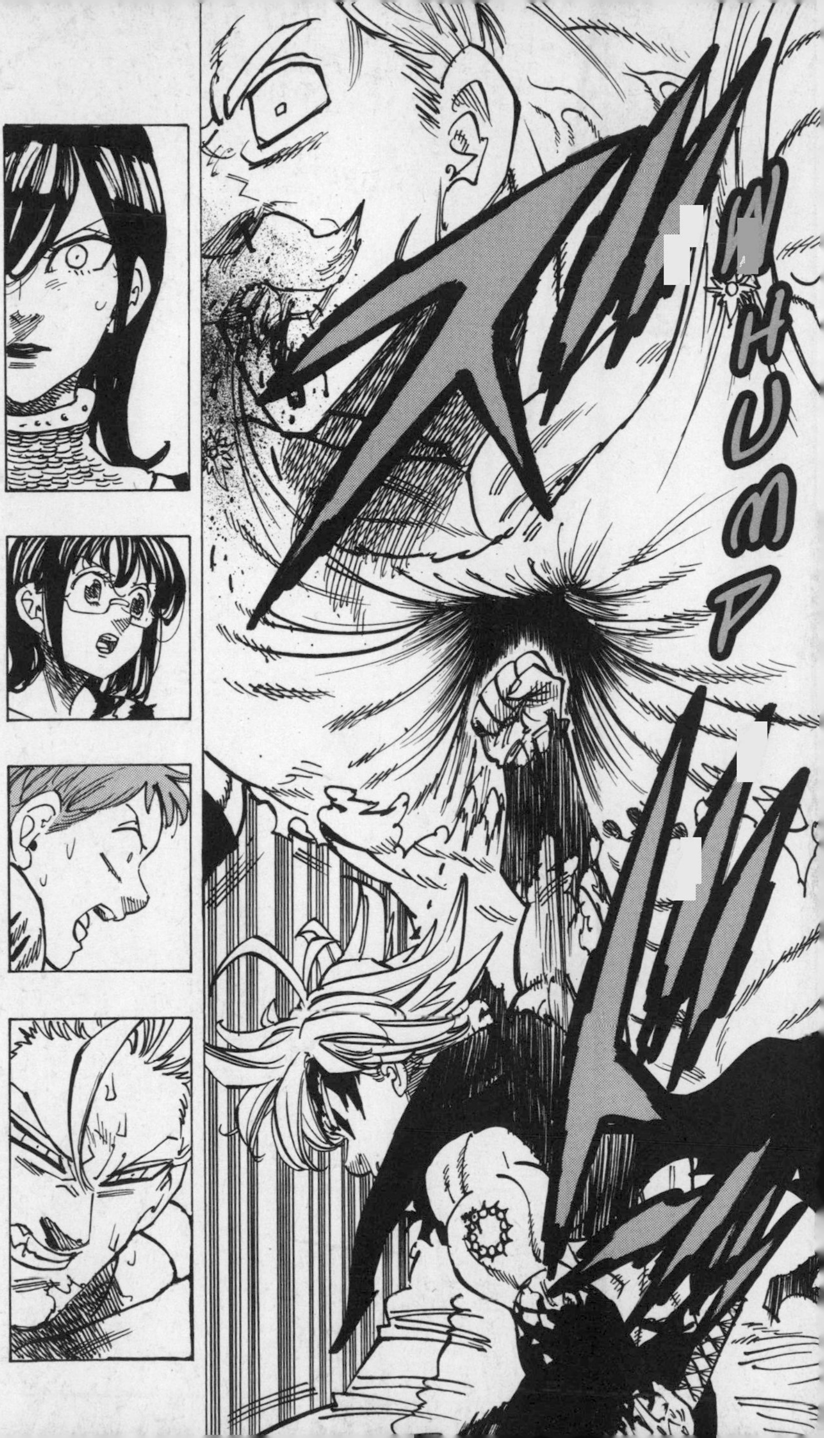
WHUMP

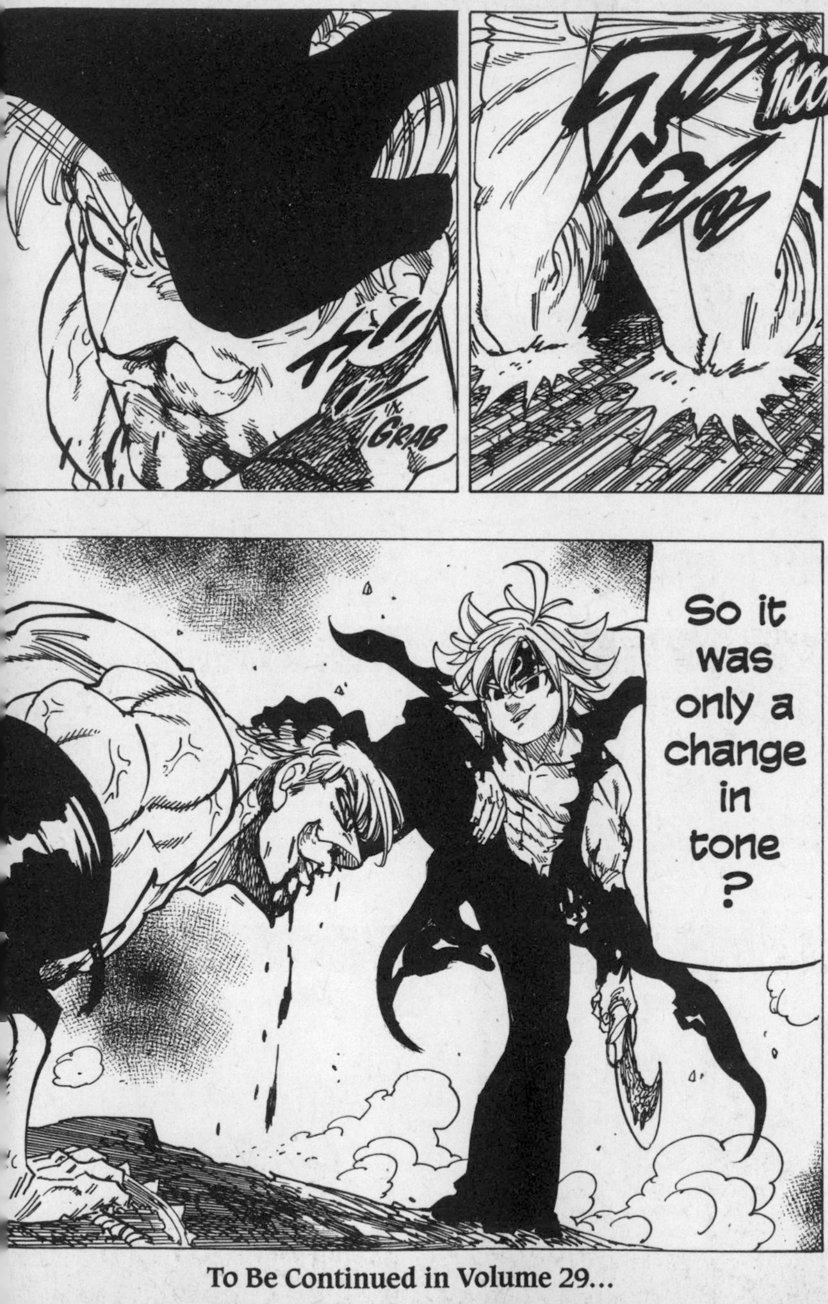
THOOM
GRAB
So it was only a change in tone?

To Be Continued in Volume 29...

Bonus Story - Ruler of the Altar (7)

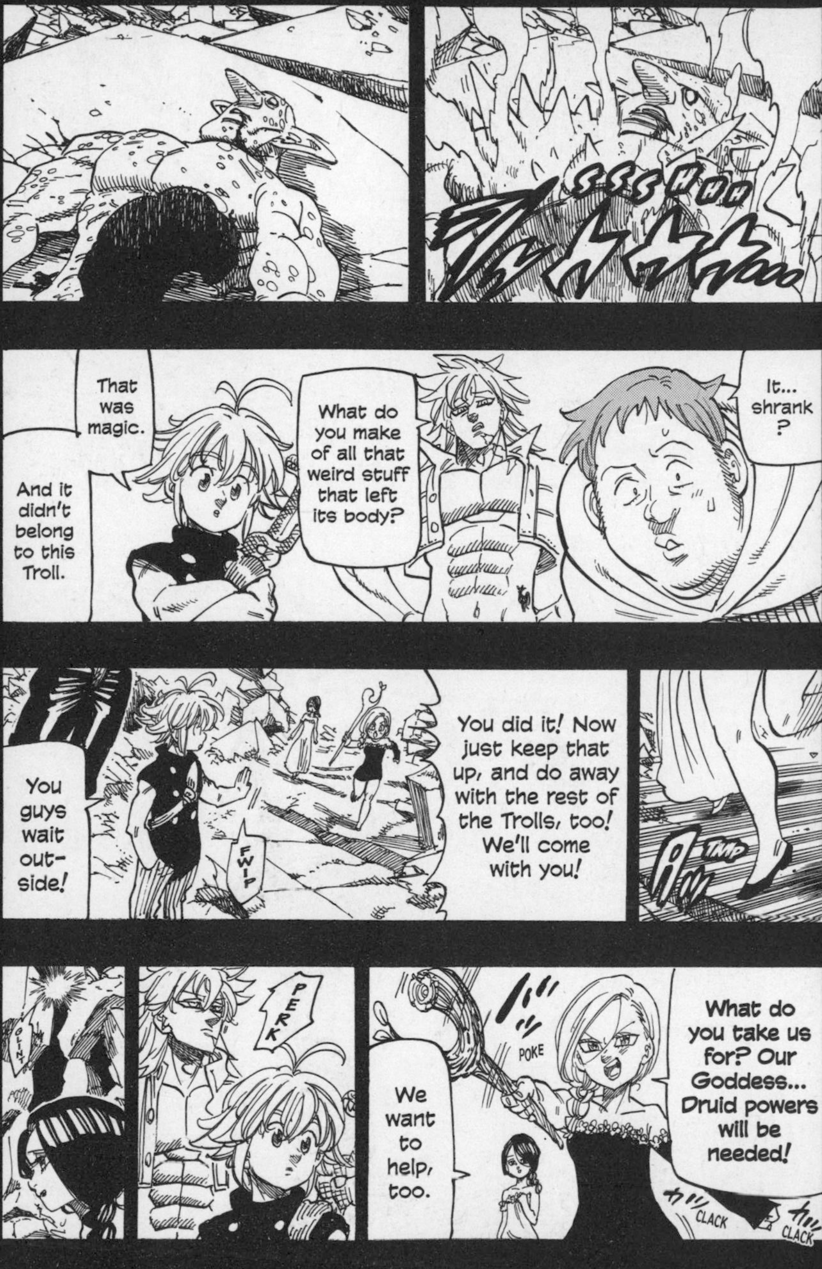

It... shrank?
What do you make of all that weird stuff that left its body?
That was magic.
And it didn't belong to this Troll.
TMP
You did it! Now just keep that up, and do away with the rest of the Trolls, too! We'll come with you!
FWIP
You guys wait outside!
What do you take us for? Our Goddess... Druid powers will be needed!
CLACK
CLACK
POKE
We want to help, too.
PERK
GLINT

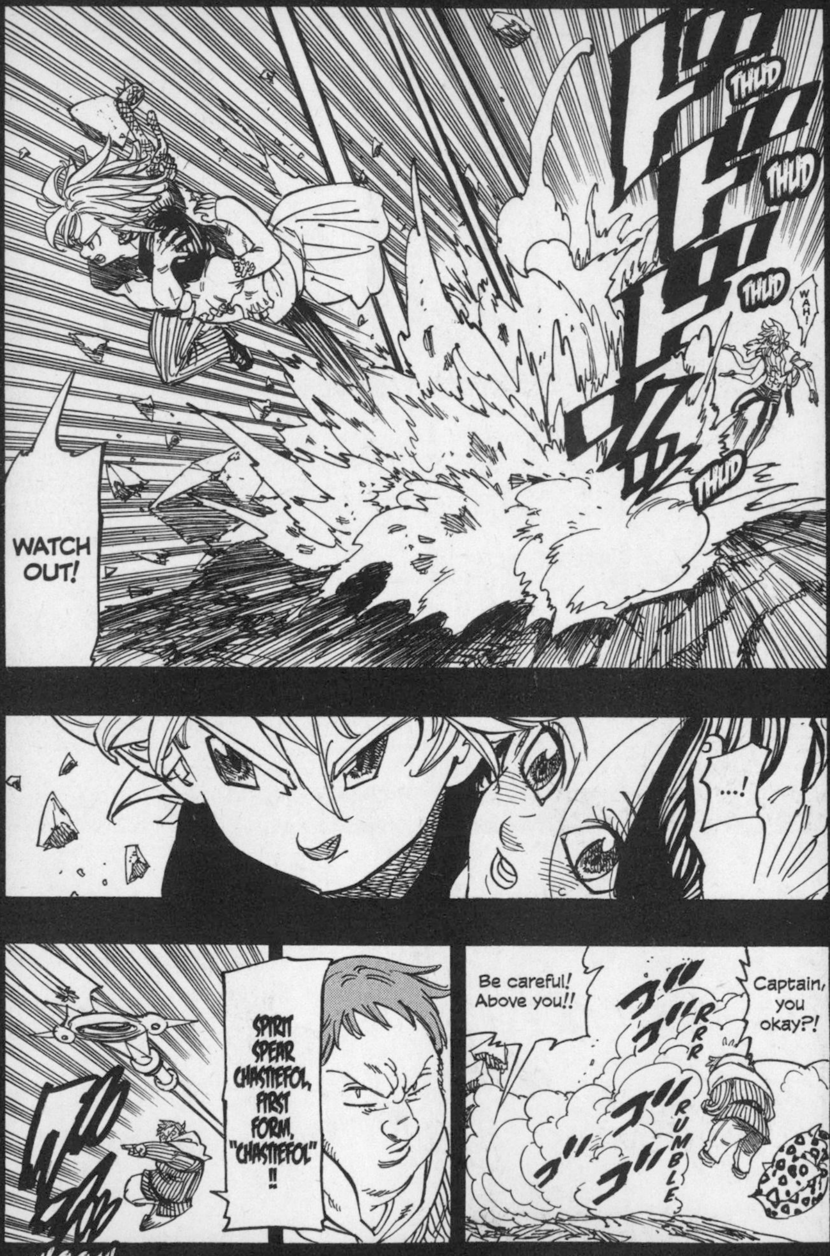
THUD
THUD
THUD
THUD
WAH!
WATCH OUT!
...!
Captain, you okay?!
Be careful! Above you!!
RRR
RUMBLE
SPIRIT SPEAR CHASTIEFOL, FIRST FORM, "CHASTIEFOL" !!
SWOOSH

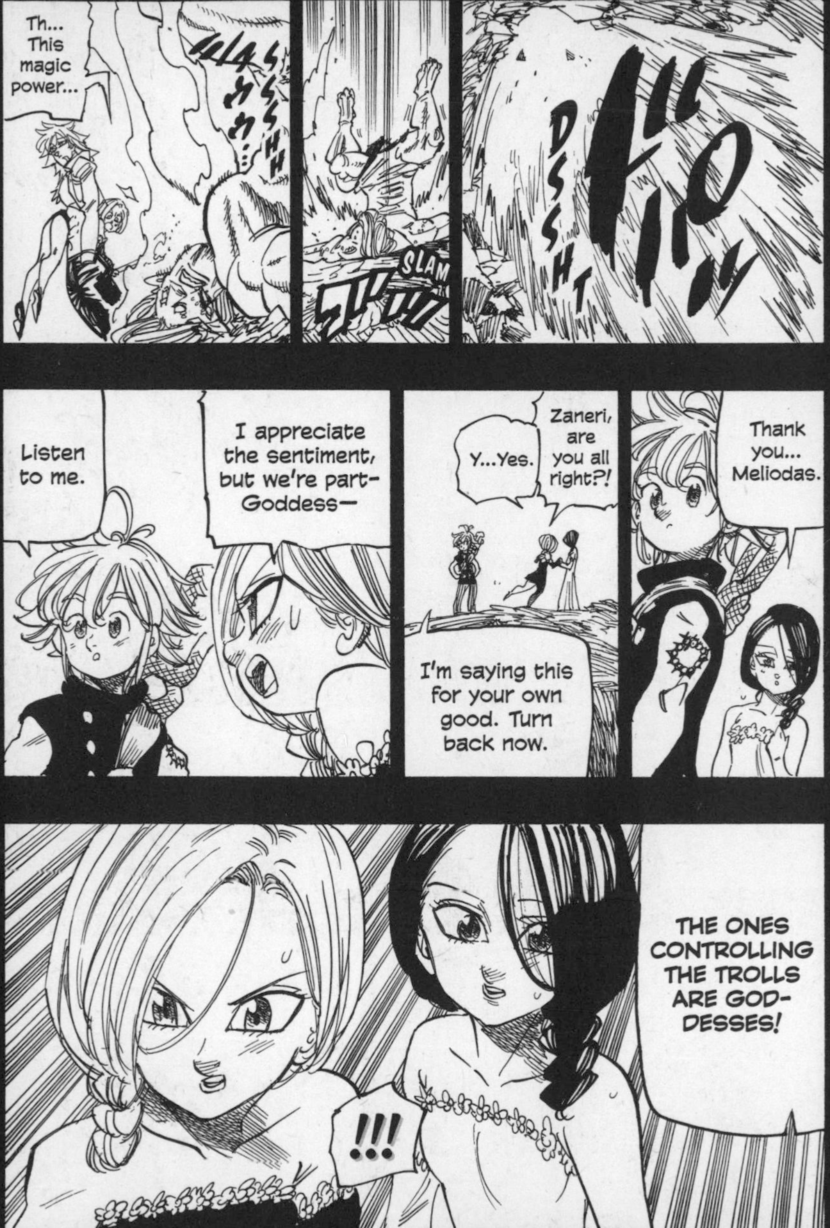
DSSHT
SLAM
SSSHH
Th... This magic power...
Thank you... Meliodas.
Zaneri, are you all right?!
Y...Yes.
I'm saying this for your own good. Turn back now.
I appreciate the sentiment, but we're part-Goddess—
Listen to me.
THE ONES CONTROLLING THE TROLLS ARE GOD-DESSES!
!!!

To Be Continued...

A new series from the creator of *Soul Eater*, the megahit manga and anime seen on Toonami!

"Fun and lively... a great start!"
-Adventures in Poor Taste

FIRE FORCE

By Atsushi Ohkubo

The city of Tokyo is plagued by a deadly phenomenon: spontaneous human combustion! Luckily, a special team is there to quench the inferno: The Fire Force! The fire soldiers at Special Fire Cathedral 8 are about to get a unique addition. Enter Shinra, a boy who possesses the power to run at the speed of a rocket, leaving behind the famous "devil's footprints" (and destroying his shoes in the process). Can Shinra and his colleagues discover the source of this strange epidemic before the city burns to ashes?

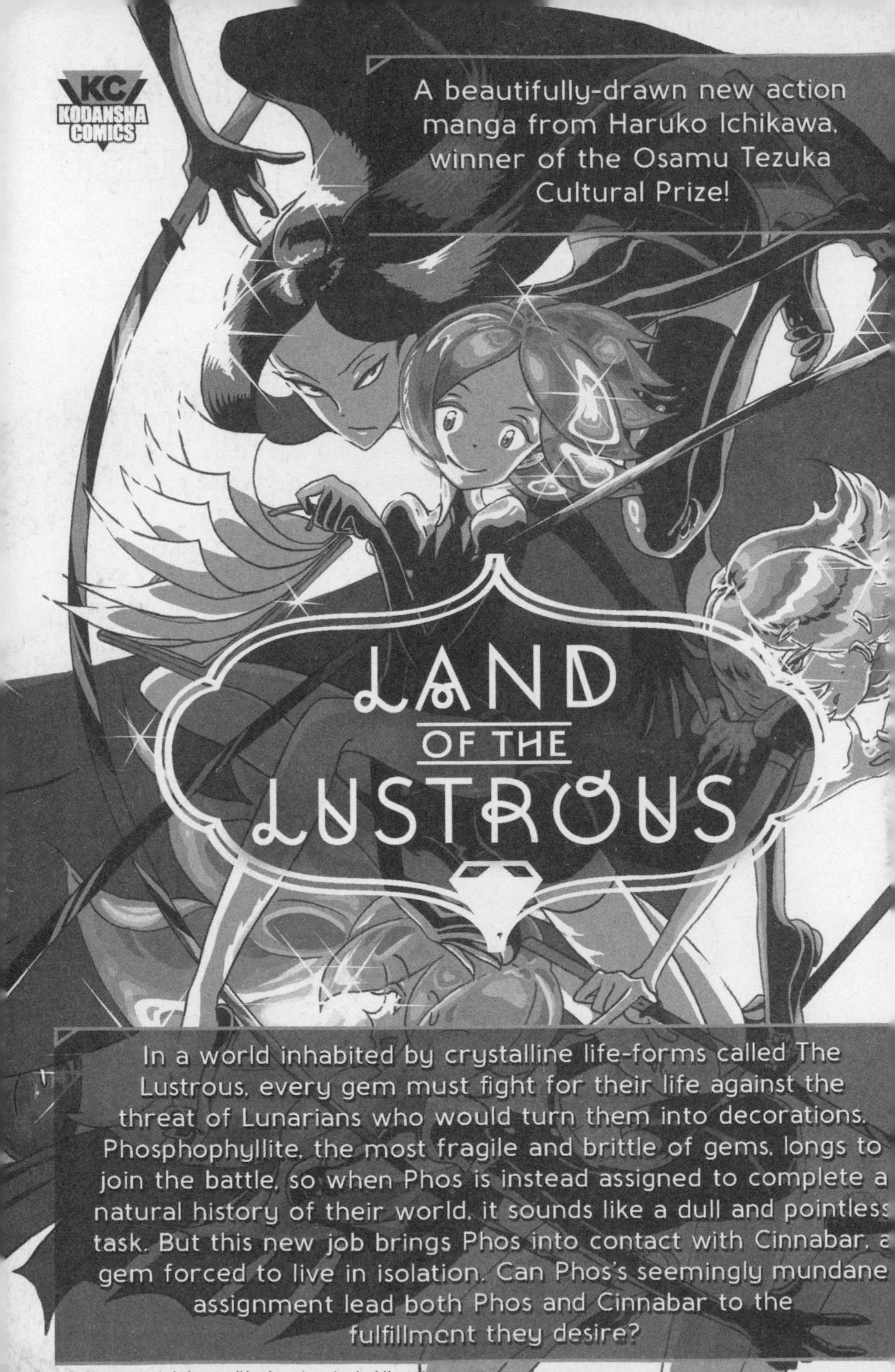
KC KODANSHA COMICS
A beautifully-drawn new action manga from Haruko Ichikawa, winner of the Osamu Tezuka Cultural Prize!
LAND OF THE LUSTROUS
In a world inhabited by crystalline life-forms called The Lustrous, every gem must fight for their life against the threat of Lunarians who would turn them into decorations. Phosphophyllite, the most fragile and brittle of gems, longs to join the battle, so when Phos is instead assigned to complete a natural history of their world, it sounds like a dull and pointless task. But this new job brings Phos into contact with Cinnabar, a gem forced to live in isolation. Can Phos's seemingly mundane assignment lead both Phos and Cinnabar to the fulfillment they desire?

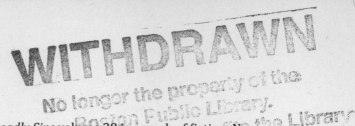

The Seven Deadly Sins volume 28 is a work of fiction. Names, characters, places, and incidents are the products of the author's imagination or are used fictitiously. Any resemblance to actual events, locales, or persons, living or dead, is entirely coincidental.

A Kodansha Comics Trade Paperback Original.

Published in the United States by Kodansha Comics, an imprint of Kodansha USA Publishing, LLC, New York.

Publication rights for this English edition arranged through Kodansha Ltd., Tokyo.

First published in Japan in 2017 by Kodansha Ltd., Tokyo.

ISBN 978-1-63236-681-8

Printed in the United States of America.

www.kodanshacomics.com

9 8 7 6 5 4 3 2 1

Translation: Christine Dashiell
Lettering: James Dashiell
Editing: Lauren Scanlan
Kodansha Comics edition cover design: Phil Balsman